DELIVERING HUMAN SERVICES

HARPER SERIES IN SOCIAL WORK
WERNER W. BOEHM
Series Editor

Editor's Foreword

This text is included in the Harper series on social work textbooks because it takes cognizance of recent developments in the field. One is the emergence of educational programs on the community college level. These programs, while containing a social work core and in a sense stemming from social work, aim to create personnel in a wide range of activities, subsumed under the area of human services. The emergence of this new category of personnel, the human services workers, is another development to which the book addresses itself. Human service agencies in most states of the union include, as the authors suggest, public welfare, vocational rehabilitation, mental health, mental retardation, youth and adult correction, drug abuse, and aging. A third development is the need, on the baccalaureate level, to provide material for enriching and specifying learning experience in the practicum component of undergraduate instruction of social welfare.

A characteristic of this text is its flexibility. It features a programmed approach and thereby engages the learner in self-instruction. Thus it can serve primarily but not exclusively as a staff development tool in a great variety of human service agencies for a great variety of personnel who may be at different levels of competency and sophistication.

We believe that the authors, through this text, perform a pioneering task by codifying practice wisdom, and contributing, thereby, to the emerging literature on training personnel for the human services.

Werner W. Boehm

DELIVERING HUMAN SERVICES

AN INTRODUCTORY PROGRAMMED TEXT

MICHAEL J. AUSTIN
University of Washington

ALEXIS H. SKELDING
Florida Department of Health and Rehabilitative Services

PHILIP L. SMITH
University of South Florida

HV
11
.A97
WEST

A15050 039464

HARPER & ROW, PUBLISHERS
New York   Hagerstown   San Francisco   London

'ASU WEST LIBRARY

Sponsoring Editor: Dale Tharp
Project Editor: Pamela Landau
Designer: T. R. Funderburk
Production Supervisor: Stefania J. Taflinska
Compositor: Maryland Linotype Co., Inc.
Printer and Binder: The Murray Printing Company
Art Studio: Vantage Art, Inc.

Delivering Human Services
An Introductory Programmed Text

Copyright © 1977 by Harper & Row, Publishers, Inc.

All rights reserved. Printed in the United States of America. No part of this book may be used or reproduced in any manner whatsoever without written permission except in the case of brief quotations embodied in critical articles and reviews. For information address Harper & Row, Publishers, Inc., 10 East 53rd Street, New York, N.Y. 10022.

Library of Congress Cataloging in Publication Data

Austin, Michael J
    Delivering human services.
    1.   Social work education—Programmed instruc-
tion.   I.   Skelding, Alexis H., joint author.
II.   Smith, Philip L., joint author.   III.   Title.
HV11.A97   361′.06′77   77-7630
ISBN 0-06-040396-9

CONTENTS

PREFACE

This introductory text is based upon the pioneering research of the Southern Regional Education Board, which led to the identification of the primary functions performed by human service workers. This text represents the first effort to operationalize this research in the form of a self-instructional training text for beginning human service workers. The programmed instruction format allows for the use of the text in both agency in-service training programs as well as college human service education programs.

The book is divided into four units. The first unit includes a discussion of human service work and identifies the unique characteristics of the consumer, the organization, the human service worker, and the nature of human service work. The second unit describes the process of getting services to people in need, with emphasis on the roles of brokering, consumer advocating, and mobilizing. These three roles are rarely described in human service texts. The third unit focuses on ways of helping consumers to function more effectively and includes a discussion of counseling, rehabilitating, and consulting. While these are traditional roles assumed by human service workers, special attention has been given to the development of a supportive helping relationship. The last unit includes a discussion of managing work to deliver effective and efficient services. Emphasis is placed on the management of data in the form of information collecting and processing. The worker's use of supervision is also reviewed. The information in the last unit identifies the importance of data for both the agency and the worker, a perspective rarely found in human service texts.

This text can be used in many different areas of human service training, especially as a resource for in-service training. Rapidly expanding human service programs in over 75 percent of the states in this country have recently been reorganized by state legislatures to create large umbrella human service agencies which include public welfare, vocational rehabilitation, mental health, mental retardation, youth corrections, adult corrections, drug abuse, aging, and others. Since agency training programs include special learning experiences for their staff around specific worker and/or agency problems, this programmed text allows trainers to utilize each unit for entry level staff in a wide variety of human service programs. The programmed format of this text also lends itself to computer assisted instruction in that the entire text could be programmed on the computer for workers to use on terminals in the agency.

The text can also be a resource for students in the hundreds of community colleges across the country which have developed education programs in human service technology, mental health technology, law enforcement and corrections, health care technology, and child care. Recent findings by the Center for Human Services Research at the Johns Hopkins University School of Medicine indicate both a rapid expansion of mental health technology programs (7,000 graduates as of June 1973 and 20,000 expected by 1976) and a high success rate regarding the performance of such community college graduates.

Another major area includes the over three hundred undergraduate university programs in social work and social welfare. Many of these programs include field placements in human service agencies where student practicum experiences could be supplemented by this text, which has a strong agency orientation. Each chapter lends itself to potentially rich learning discussions between a student and the agency supervisor. If so used, this text could be one of the first practical field-instruction texts for the human services.

In comparison with current texts in the human service field, this book differs in the following ways: (1) it is more comprehensive in its approach to the functions of a human service worker; (2) it does not overemphasize the counseling function but places it in the context of other worker functions; (3) it is more practical in its emphasis on skill development; (4) it is one of the few texts that thoroughly engages the learner in a self-instructional process. The approach taken in this text is to provide partial bodies of knowledge and practical techniques to be acquired by a learner. In addition, many examples are used to illustrate the material.

It is important to note that the answers used in each chapter were designed as preferred responses. This means that both the learner and instructor should find numerous areas of disagreement with the text based on their prior experience. This disagreement should lead to fruitful discussions. Delivering human services is an area in which scientific evidence is still lacking to support the correctness of all the methods of intervening to help consumers in need. This text represents our effort to compile and illustrate the best *practice wisdom* available for the newcomer to human services. Much work remains to be done to reach consensus on the most appropriate techniques for delivering human services.

ACKNOWLEDGMENTS

Acknowledgments must first be expressed in the form of thanks to the numerous students and agency workers who used and commented on the earlier drafts of this book. Special thanks goes to Dr. Jon Prothero for his assistance as an instructional programmer and to Arthur Slater and Richard Coane for their assistance in providing the background information in several areas.

The development of this text would not have been possible without the encouragement and support of Ms. Eulene Hawkins, staff development specialist in the Atlanta Regional Office of the Social and Rehabilitation Service of the U.S. Department of Health Education and Welfare, and Mrs. Ruth Light Stanley, staff development consultant of the Division of Family Services in the Florida Department of Health and Rehabilitative Services. The constant support of Secretary O. J. Keller and Deputy Secretary Emmett Roberts in the Florida Department of Health and Rehabilitative Services was also greatly appreciated. The development of this text was supported by a grant from the Florida Division of Family Services, #2490–600.

And last but definitely not least, we want to thank Sharon Lewis, Beverly Harness, and Mary Harvey for their patience and thoroughness in the typing of numerous drafts and revisions of this text.

Mike, Lexi, and Phil

INSTRUCTIONS TO THE USER

FRAME i

You are about to be introduced to a book that is quite different from the traditional books with which you are familiar. This is not a textbook, but an *instructional program*. It may be used as a self-instructional text or in a class in which there is a teacher and in which you may be referred to other written materials, films, slides, or other instructional aids and activities. If you follow the instructions in this program, you should find it a very rewarding learning experience.

Each lesson in this book is made up of two parts and should be read and followed as directed. Each begins with a listing of objectives which specify exactly what you are expected to be able to do at the conclusion of the lesson. The programmed lesson which follows the learning objectives presents content related to the objectives and requires you to respond to questions related to this content. You will be given immediate feedback on each question when you turn to the answer which corresponds with the item of your choice. This technique, called the *scrambled text* may bother you at first, *but if you follow the directions given,* you will find that reading this portion is interesting and challenging. In addition, at the end of each chapter, review questions are presented so that you may find out if you have a good grasp of the material that has been presented.

Now read the directions in Frame ii

FRAME ii

DIRECTIONS

This instructional program contains the same kind of material you would expect to find in an ordinary textbook. The material, however, has been broken down into different frames labeled with a number (1, 2, 3, 4, etc.). A frame may contain content material, a question, or an answer. From every frame you will be referred to another frame (for example, turn to Answer 3 or turn to Frame 1). The answer frames are located at the end of each lesson, so follow the directions carefully to avoid unnecessary page turning.

You have now completed Frame ii (see frame number in the upper right-hand margin of this page).

Now go on to Frame iii

FRAME iii

Many items throughout this program will ask you to make some form of response. In most cases, such responses will require that you choose one of several given alternatives. In a few cases, you will be asked to construct a word, phrase, sentence, or short description.

Be sure to follow directions, and when asked to write a response, do so in the spaces provided. After you have selected your response, turn to the answer number indicated, which is found at the end of the lesson. This answer will tell you whether or not your response choice was correct. A correct response will send you on to the next frame. An incorrect response will give you the information you need to answer the question correctly. The important thing to remember is to follow the directions and *write down* your answers. This will lead to the most effective learning.

Since this program is designed to help you learn through the presentation of a wide variety of material, do not spend time attempting to write perfect answers. In those few cases where it is required, answer each question as best you can and move on.

Go on now to Frame iv below

FRAME iv

If you apply yourself to this material you will
A. be unable to answer most questions.

Turn to Answer i

B. be able to answer most questions.

Turn to Answer ii

ANSWER i

If you selected this answer, then you either have not read the material carefully or you have little confidence in your own abilities since you have said that you will be unable to answer most questions if you apply yourself to the material presented in this program.

Whatever the case, this is an incorrect answer and you should return to Frame iv to answer the question correctly. (If, during the program, you should choose the wrong answer to a question, you will often be given further information to clarify any misunderstanding or be told to review the material you may have missed).

ANSWER ii

Yes, you have answered Frame iv correctly if you turned to this frame. You will be able to answer most questions if you apply yourself to the material presented in this program.

Go right on to Frame v below.

FRAME v

You should be able to finish each programmed lesson during one study session. However, if you find that you must take breaks during a lesson, try to make them short. It is recommended for most effective learning that you do not wait more than one day between study sessions for any single programmed lesson.

When you are ready to begin this program, turn to the next page. Happy studying!

GUIDE FOR THE USER

The purpose of this guide is to provide information which will help prospective instructors and learners make the most appropriate and effective application of this programmed text. The guide will also be useful as a source of information for determining the appropriateness of the text in various human service situations. The following information is provided to accomplish these purposes: (1) assumptions and content summary, (2) definition of the target population, (3) results of field evaluations, (4) limitations and (5) suggestions for application.

1. Assumptions and Content Summary

Traditional approaches to staff development and training in the human services have emphasized the uniqueness of each human service setting in terms of knowledge, skills, and values, rather than the commonality of knowledge, skills, and values upon which all human service practice is based. With the current trend toward comprehensive and unified delivery of human services and the corresponding need for workers who can function in a variety of human service settings, the traditional *setting specific* approach to training is no longer sufficient. A new training model is needed to meet worker demands for career mobility and to provide organizations with flexible sources of manpower.

This text was developed in an effort to identify a generic framework of human service knowledge and skills required for beginning competence in delivering human services. As with any curriculum design process, the text rests on a set of basic assumptions regarding the training content, the learner, and the training method. We have assumed that there is a body of knowledge and theoretical concepts upon which human service practice is based. Training content should include a range of skills required for successful entry level work in the human services. Services can be improved when entry level staff acquire an integrated and generic body of human service knowledge and skills.

This text is also directed to the entry level worker as an adult learner (andragogy) whose training needs will be met most efficiently through programs based on the andragogical process. Since the traditional training methods have been based on a pedagogical approach to learning, the tendency has been to transmit knowledge and skills primarily through a directive, didactic relationship, where the learner is passive. However, when the learner is an adult, these traditional methods for training are no longer viable.

Our final set of assumptions concern the training method. Basically we have assumed that entry level training will be most effective when—

1. the learner is given the opportunity to learn by doing and by practicing;
2. the goal of the method is the acquisition of problem solving skills (i.e., learning must be problem centered);
3. the method provides the learner with constant knowledge of his progress; and
4. the method provides a measure by which results can be evaluated through objective and observable criteria.

Therefore, the individualized training technique of programmed and adjunct auto-instruction was selected as the method which would meet both the special needs of the learner and the staffing needs of the human service organization.

We have accepted the importance of identifying and describing the skill development areas and the corresponding principles of practice which can serve as guidelines for operationalizing these skills. The objectives of the text are (1) that after completing the text, the learner should have acquired a beginning understanding of the basic skills required of entry level personnel performing as human service technicians and (2) that the learner should be capable of successfully applying the basic vocabulary and practice principles to real-life agency situations.

Human services, broadly applied, include public welfare, mental health, corrections, mental retardation, vocational rehabilitation, services to the elderly, pupil personnel, public health, employment services, services to delinquent youth, hospital and health care, social security, and related programs. We refer to the client, patient, inmate, student, or resident who receives these services as the *consumer*. This term reflects a new approach to serving people by using a less stigmatized label in order to emphasize that we are all human and only differ according to special needs.

Four primary areas requiring specialized skills are the framework for this training text: (1) working in the human services, (2) getting services to people in need, (3) helping consumers function more effectively, and (4) managing work to deliver effective and efficient services. The first area is an orientation to the world of human service work, while the remaining three are the general goals from which service roles and activities are derived.

These four areas correspond to the four units of the text. The first unit describes the world of human service work from the perspective of the systems approach and aims at an understanding of the consumer and the service systems which are designed to meet the consumer's needs. It also analyzes work in the human services from the perspective of the worker, including the influences of the organization, interpersonal relationships, values, and roles.

The next three units define the major roles assumed by the worker in accomplishing the goals of human service work, with each unit describing the range of skills needed to meet the three general goals. Unit 2 defines the roles performed in getting services to people in need and includes linking the consumer with appropriate community resources, advocating on behalf of the consumer when services are unjustly denied, and developing new consumer services where none exist. The roles of brokering, consumer advocating, and mobilizing are emphasized in the three chapters in this unit.

Unit 3 addresses helping consumers function more effectively, and emphasis is placed on helping consumers modify or change their behavior, either through short-term helping and coaching or long-term treatment in a controlled environment, such as a mental hospital. While all human service work involves relationships with other workers, the activities performed in helping consumers function more effectively also illustrate the necessity of developing abilities in asking for help from other workers and giving help to other workers. Consequently the roles of counseling, rehabilitating, and consulting are the focal points for three chapters in this unit.

Unit 4 defines the roles performed in managing work to deliver effective and efficient services, including activities such as observing, communicating, interviewing, recording, reporting, and supervising, which must be performed to maintain the organization and control the quality of work performed. The three chapters in Unit 4 are concerned with information collecting, information managing, and supervising.

Taken together, these units represent our beginning effort to define the baseline information needed for developing entry level competence in delivering human services. This is the first step needed to bridge the gap which exists in our knowledge regarding entry level competence. Relating training to the skills required at the entry level can also serve as the foundation for developing the more specific knowledge and skills for special program areas in the various human service settings. While this program does not guarantee the delivery of effective services, it does expose the entry level worker to the minimum knowledge and skill areas needed.

2. Definition of the Target Population

The text was designed primarily for entry level workers, or those persons entering or planning to enter human service employment for the first time, and for paraprofessionals, or those persons already employed in entry level human service jobs. Entry level positions generally entail direct client contact and require up to two years of college training; however, we would also include in this category positions accepting persons with baccalaureate degrees in fields unrelated to the human services.

To specify the general characteristics of this population, the authors reviewed studies made between 1966 and 1975 and conducted a descriptive survey of paraprofessionals in a human service program in Florida. Since these studies varied considerably in terms of job definitions and work responsibilities, it was impossible to draw any precise conclusions. Accurate generalizations can be made, however, regarding demographic characteristics, and these were used in our assumptions regarding the training content, the learner, and the training method. They are reported here to assist potential users in deciding whether this program is appropriate for their particular situation.

It is clear that the population of potential trainees is predominantly female, although the number of males is gradually increasing. Racial or ethnic minority groups comprise a substantial portion of the population. However, our broad definition of entry level suggests that the population is almost equally divided between whites and other racial or ethnic minority groups. Ages range from 18 to 65 years, but most cluster between the ages of 21 and 30 years and 40 to 60 years. Finally, demographic patterns of relatively low socioeconomic status and limited educational opportunities are evident.

These characteristics are not viewed as constrictive parameters in using this text, but rather as special characteristics which were recognized in constructing the program. To emphasize the generalizeability of the text, the target population was further defined in terms of education and employment, including the following:

1. **Community colleges.** Many community colleges offer technical programs in human services such as day-care, mental health, criminal justice, police science, counseling, social welfare, and mental retardation. An introduction to the range of skills required for effective delivery of human services is important in these specialized programs, and this text can expand students' knowledge of the total human service industry and their awareness of the skills needed.
2. **Staff development programs in human service organizations.** Organizations interested in orienting new entry level workers and developing the skills of workers already employed in entry level jobs will find this comprehensive introduction to the human service industry useful for a wide range of workers, including those with less than a high school education and those with baccalaureate degrees unrelated to the human services.
3. **College and university human service programs.** For professional programs in social work, counseling, criminology, special education, nursing, and rehabilitation, the text is useful as a foundation of knowledge for students and also as an agenda for supervisors responsible for teaching the skills needed in student internship or field placement programs.
4. **Volunteer organizations.** Volunteer groups working in various human service settings may find the text helpful in clarifying their understanding of the skills needed for human service work and in expanding their own volunteer activities.
5. **High schools and vocational training schools.** Students may find the text useful as a source for examining their interest in a human service career. Continuing education programs offered in the community and in institutions such as prisons can also use the text as an introductory source for persons planning careers in the human services.

While the target population encompasses a wide range of persons with varied personal characteristics and life experiences, the common characteristic shared by all the prospective learners is their status as an adult, despite the fact that some may have limited formal educational training.

3. Results of Field Evaluations

Field evaluations were conducted in order to assess the effectiveness of the text from two perspectives. First, human service educators and practitioners and experts in instructional design were asked to review both the content and the design in order to assess the appropriateness of the text in various human service settings. Second, measures of the actual effects of the program were obtained from preprogram to immediate postprogram tests of two groups of target population learners. The results of these field evaluations were as follows.

Concerning the content, portions of the text were reviewed by faculty members in programs related to human services and instructional design at Florida State University, Hunter College, the University of Georgia, Morgan State College, Sante Fe Community College, and St. Petersburg Community College. In addition, practitioners in the Florida Department of Health and Rehabilitative Services provided feedback from an agency perspective.

College and university educators generally thought the program would be most useful for undergraduate students beginning their study of the human services, and especially helpful for students involved in field placement and internship activities. There was some concern regarding the presentation of complex concepts and skills at the entry level, the depth of coverage, and the method of programmed instruction. These concerns are addressed in the next section of this guide. All the reviewers indicated that the text would be a resource with considerable potential in the special areas of their programs.

Community college faculty were extremely positive and indicated that the text would have a wide range of immediate applications in many facets of their programs. They were particularly impressed with the broad definition of human services and felt that the community college student needed such a broad perspective as a foundation for effective work and further specialized studies. This group expressed some concern regarding the presentation of interpersonal skills in a programmed format, but were otherwise generally positive regarding both the method of programmed instruction and the content.

Practitioners, particularly those responsible for orientation and in-service training for entry level workers, considered the program to be a valuable resource for training. Since these practitioners were primarily workers in a comprehensive human service agency which includes programs in health, mental health, corrections, retardation, public welfare, and aging, the generic definition of human service knowledge and skills was particularly suited to their organization. This group was less concerned with the presentation of complex concepts and interpersonal skills, since they viewed the program as providing one component of a staff development program to be supplemented with role-playing activities, group discussions, and lectures.

While we considered these responses to be positive, they were also simply criteria that were *believed* to be predictive of program effectiveness. Therefore the series of field evaluations were concerned with evidence of the gains indicated by preprogram and immediate postprogram tests. Two separate field evaluations were conducted, one in a community college and one in a human service agency. Forty students in the second year of a program for human service technicians (leading to an associate of science degree) completed the text as part of a course requirement. Fifteen entry level workers, paraprofessionals and volunteers, in various programs of the Florida Department of Health and Rehabilitative Services completed the text as part of a nine-week in-service training program. The ages in these groups ranged from 18 through 60 years; levels of education ranged from eighth grade through the third year of a baccalaureate proram; the population was predominantly female; and racial or ethnic minority groups comprised approximately one-third of the participants.

Since the community college students were in the second year of their studies, many were already familiar with portions of the program as evidenced by their high preprogram test scores. Generally speaking, however, the data indicated substantial gains from preprogram to immediate postprogram tests. Similar results were also obtained with the workers and volunteers in the agency in-service training program. The time required to complete a chapter in the text ranged from thirty minutes to two hours. Given the diverse groups participating in the field evaluations and the varying lengths and degrees of complexity of the chapters, this range was anticipated by the authors and considered reasonable.

Student and worker responses to the content of the text were overwhelmingly positive. The material in Units 2 and 4 was judged to be the most helpful and also the most frequent source of new concepts and issues. Participants with the least amount of formal educational training (high school or less) commented that the text was the first they had been able to read and understand, and found the exercises and answer frames particularly useful ways of learning. Participants with more formal training (associate and baccalaureate) found the language and material "too easy" in some cases; however, they were surprised to discover that there were a number of concepts and issues which were both new and useful in terms of their current or future jobs.

Most of the students and workers participating in these evaluations were unfamiliar with the method of programmed instruction and responded to the method in a number of interesting ways. At first they were intrigued with the novel effect of self-instructional material. One commented, for example, "this book talks to me—it's fun to read." They experienced some information overload, feeling they were being asked to absorb more information than they could handle. They soon passed from this response to a feeling of confidence derived from mastering a wide range of information, and they began to show an interest in pursuing additional areas of study and in adapting the content to their personal work experiences. As a result of their success with and exposure to such a wide range of information, they began to realize the tremendous responsibilities and personal value conflicts inherent in human service work, and thus found the organizational framework of the text a useful schema for furthering their understanding of delivering effective human services.

We considered the results of these evaluations important indicators of the effectiveness of the program. However, in the absence of a framework of rigorous experimentation and statistical hypothesis testing, these results should be interpreted as descriptive generalizations of the program's effectiveness.

4. Limitations

Since this text is a comprehensive overview of the basic knowledge and skill areas required for beginning competence in delivering human services, there is a potential danger for the user to set unrealistic expectations regarding the ultimate effects of the program. The successful completion of this text will *not* produce a trained therapist, a skilled counselor, a professional community organizer, a certified behavior modification specialist, or a competent supervisor. As we stated earlier in this guide, successful completion of the text should produce a beginning understanding of the basic skills required for performing as entry level human service technicians and a beginning capability of successfully applying the basic vocabulary and practice principles to real-life agency situations. Similarly, it is important to realize that the trade-off involved in such a comprehensive approach is the necessity of sacrificing the depth perspective, which is also necessary for competent practice. This text simply defines the components necessary for beginning practice. Each component requires further elaboration in terms of in-depth training, additional course work, outside reading, instructor clarification, and actual agency practice. The text talks about how to deliver human services, but as in all occupations, talk must be translated into action. Therefore the ideas in this text need to be implemented and tested by each learner under agency or educational supervision through on-the-job training or practicum experiences.

Another area of concern is the how-to aspect of the text. Our statements of practice principles are in no way intended to serve as rules to be followed in delivering human services. We do believe, however, that it is possible to learn from experience and to translate the practice wisdom derived from this experience into principles which can guide new workers entering human service agencies. Thus it may be necessary to remind the learner periodically of the significant gap between the seemingly simple issues and principles described in the text and the actual complexity involved in working with consumers who have a variety of human problems and individual differences in age, sex, personality, and life experiences. We have no rules for developing rehabilitation plans with neat solutions to particular consumer problems.

Obviously our definition of beginning competence is only part of the full spectrum of knowledge, skills, and values required for effective entry level performance. The text does not include the knowledge needed about the social environment or the behavioral science concepts found in abnormal psychology, adolescent psychology, family sociology, sociology of deviance, cultural anthropology, child development, and gerontology. Reference to the organizational and societal constraints prevalent throughout the human services points to the need for beginning workers to have a thorough understanding of the social science concepts of health and welfare economics; of the political science concepts of federal, state, and local government; of the sociology of complex organizations; and of the sociology of group and community behavior. The suggestions for further study and references found at the end of each chapter hopefully provide some assistance for continuing study in these and other areas.

In addition to the social and behavioral sciences, the entry level worker also needs to acquire a thorough understanding of the values and attitudes necessary for effective service delivery. While we alert the user to some of these issues, the instructor will need to expand the concepts of consumer confidentiality and self-determination as they are applied in discussion sessions and on-the-job experiences. The issues of racism and sexism require that the learner be alerted to the fact that sometimes human service organizations claim to serve the needs of consumers when in actual practice they operate as repressive, racist institutions. While the knowledge and skills required to handle all these areas are beyond the scope of this text, they are recognized as necessary educational components for the development of competent entry level personnel.

A final note of caution concerns the method of programmed instruction. The text is based on the concept of adjunct autoinstruction, which means it is a self-contained text and includes questions and exercises to help learners assess their mastery of the content. While one of the strengths of this approach is separating and analyzing the component parts of the areas of human service skills, a corresponding limitation is the temptation to assume that an understanding of the components leads directly to a mastery of the skills. In the final analysis, skills are developed only through a combination of knowing and doing. It is important to recognize that this text emphasizes the knowing, while discussions, role playing, and on-the-job experiences will emphasize the doing.

5. Suggestions for Application

A variety of procedures can be used for structuring and presenting the content of this text. For example, it can be used as part of an intensive one-week workshop for agency personnel or as part of a semester or quarter course focusing on working with individuals and families in need of human services. The four units can be used separately in several courses or in a different sequence.

Several recommendations ought to be considered in any application. Through self-instruction the learner is encouraged to test his or her understanding of the content in frames which either reinforce learning or require the learner to apply the content to a real life situation. We view the instructor as playing a crucial role in this testing process. The answers indicated as the correct responses represent the preferred answers and are therefore not necessarily the only answers. Since delivering human services is both an art and a science, there are few situations in reality where there is only one correct action. Our selection of the preferred answers is based on the current state of our knowledge and available practice wisdom. Instructors and learners should be encouraged to argue and present alternative interpretations based on new knowledge, prior experiences, or special situations. If our preferred responses serve as focal points for discussion and debate, we shall have accomplished one of our major objectives which was to stimulate further thinking about the concepts, skills, and practice principles needed for effective performance of entry level human service work.

Another recommendation concerns the methods employed to evaluate the learners' mastery of the material. The tests included at the end of each chapter are nonstandardized multiple-choice tests, specially constructed for this program. While we are concerned about the limitations of such tests, we consider them to be adequate for the self-instructional purpose of reinforcing knowledge acquisition. We therefore strongly encourage instructors and learners to develop their own testing instruments (which should not be limited to the multiple-choice format), and in so doing, to emphasize the application of the text material to real-life agency situations.

Group discussions regarding the actual concepts and practice principles, as well as discussions of topics which are related but not included in the chapters, are considered important supplements to the program. For example, discussions regarding values, attitudes, racism, and sexism can lead to insights regarding ways of seeking change within an organization. Similarly, while we have taken a systems perspective to understanding consumers and human service agencies, it will be important to balance our perspective through group discussion by giving equal time to the humanistic or behavioral perspective.

We also strongly encourage instructors to utilize the experience of professional workers involved in human service organizations by including them in discussion sessions and role-playing activities. For example, discussion of the role of consumer advocating can be greatly enhanced by involving civil rights or consumer rights attorneys. Psychologists and social workers experienced and trained in the use of various counseling and rehabilitating techniques can add considerably to classroom discussions and also serve as role models to be observed through one-way mirrors or other devices as they apply the techniques discussed in helping consumers function more effectively. Learners might also observe a token economy operating in a mental retardation setting as one way of fully grasping some of the concepts of behavior modification. Additional examples are observing a case conference in either an institutional or a community setting, and examining consumer recording forms used by different human service agencies as a means of learning about the range and form of information required by different agencies.

Understanding the role of brokering can be enhanced through reenacting the telephone situations commonly experienced by the information and referral units of human service agencies or the efforts of human service workers in institutions (such as mental hospitals and retardation training schools) to link consumers with other institutional resources (such as occupational therapy programs and recreational programs). To illustrate the role of consulting, the instructor could employ role-playing by inviting another instructor into the classroom situation to engage in the consultation process, providing the learners with an opportunity to observe, participate in, and critique the process.

In conclusion, the authors solicit your comments and reactions to our approach to defining a baseline of human service knowledge and skills, and we welcome suggestions from both instructors and learners for improving this program.

UNIT ONE:
WORKING IN THE
HUMAN SERVICES

INTRODUCTION

In beginning the study of delivering human services, it seems logical to define the system in which services are delivered and the issues confronting the workers in this system. This will provide you with a broad framework and perspective for viewing work situations. It will also make it easier for you to learn the skills which are necessary for effective human service work.

You will notice that the first lesson in this unit is about human service consumers. This lesson is first because it reflects the primary target of all human service work: providing consumers with the best possible services. Far too often, workers, students, lawmakers, and others overlook this important fact. We tend to emphasize skills, procedures, treatment techniques, and a range of activities and issues both in our training and in our work situations. But our foremost concern should always be the consumer and how we can understand and help him or her to the best of our ability.

In this unit, you will be learning about the components of human service systems and the important factors which affect your ability to function in a human service agency. The goal of this unit is to provide you with a framework for effectively delivering human services. As you work through the chapters in this unit, remember that ultimately the target of all of your efforts is the consumer of human services.

**Turn to the next page
to begin Chapter I**

CHAPTER I:
AN OVERVIEW OF
THE HUMAN SERVICES

INTRODUCTION

If we could assume that all people had the ability to meet their own needs adequately, there would be no reason for the existence of most of our human service organizations. Obviously there are many individuals and groups in our society confronted with a host of problems they are unable to solve, and we have therefore found it necessary to create a system of human services to deal with social and human problems. Within this broad framework of human services, organizations have been given substantial responsibilities for (1) preventing or lowering the incidences of certain problems, (2) reducing the duration of certain problems, and (3) rehabilitating persons who have experienced certain problems in living.[1]

Prisons, mental hospitals, health departments, welfare departments, vocational rehabilitation services, homes for delinquents, and services to the retarded all are organizations established to help people deal more effectively with their personal environment so they can accomplish their life tasks and realize their aspirations.[2] In this chapter, you will be learning about the people who receive human services and the system through which these services are delivered. The overall objective of this chapter is to provide you with a comprehensive understanding of the human services.

**Turn to the next page
to begin Lesson 1**

---

[1] Harold W. Demone, Jr. and Dwight Harshbarger, "The Planning and Administration of Human Services," in Herbert C. Schulberg, Frank Baker, and Sheldon R. Roen, *Developments in Human Services*, vol. 1 (New York: Behavioral Publications, 1973), p. 144.

[2] Allen Pincus and Anne Minahan, *Social Work Practice: Model and Method* (Itasca, Ill.: F. E. Peacock Publishers, Inc., 1973), p. 9.

LESSON 1:
HUMAN SERVICE CONSUMERS

Who are the people who receive human services? How can you begin to understand their needs and problems in order to provide them with the best services? These questions are of concern to every human service worker. The goal of this lesson and the enabling activities that will help you reach this goal are presented below:

GOAL

Given a description of a consumer needing services, you will be able to identify (1) his/her various problem areas, (2) his/her levels of functioning, and (3) the obstacles to his/her effective functioning.

ENABLING ACTIVITIES

After completing this lesson, you will have done the following:

1. Identified ten possible problem areas that should be considered in assessing a consumer's situation
2. Reviewed a consumer's level of functioning in each problem area
3. Identified the obstacles associated with each problem area
4. Examined some of the characteristics that may influence the behavior of human service consumers

Turn to Frame 1

A *consumer* is someone who uses or receives a commodity or service. Human service consumers are people who use or receive human services—clients, patients, residents, inmates, students. We are using the term *consumer* to represent a new way of thinking about people who need help. It is not merely a change in title but represents a fundamental shift away from viewing some people as second-class citizens. Because people who need help are human beings like all of us, we have used the term *consumer* throughout the text.

Since there are many problems which confront human service consumers, it is important to learn about the range of problems and to organize this information so that a plan can be developed to meet the needs of consumers. This process involves assessing the situation by gaining a clear understanding of the consumer's problem and the areas that need your intervention. This is not a simple process and requires that you examine at least three basic areas in relation to each consumer:[1]

1. The problem area
2. The consumer's level of functioning
3. The nature of the obstacles to effective functioning

For example, an emotionally upset consumer may be bothered by the fact that the welfare check has not arrived or upset over the loss of a family member. These are two very different problems. In addition, problems may be momentary crises or long-standing problems which affect the consumer's level of functioning. Level of functioning is a result of the impact of problems on consumers. Are they so immobilized or paralyzed by their problems that they can not continue their jobs or rear their children, or are they only momentarily blocked from carrying out their normal duties? In assessing the obstacles to functioning, you might find that a call to the welfare department will resolve the problem of the missing check, whereas several supportive counseling sessions may be necessary to overcome the grief of a lost family member. In the first case you may be dealing with rigid rules and regulations while in the second case you might be dealing with the consumer's environment and/or personal deficiencies. As you can see, the assessment process is not simple.

A discussion of problem areas, levels of functioning, and obstacles to functioning will provide you with a framework for identifying the consumer's problem and for preparing a plan to provide services to a consumer. The rest of this lesson discusses how this is accomplished.

Proceed to Frame 2

FRAME 2

THE PROBLEM AREA

As human beings, we function in many different areas, including the physical, emotional, financial, and spiritual. Usually, human service consumers are having difficulty in one or more of these areas. Therefore, identifying the area of the consumer's problem will help you direct your efforts to correct the problem. The ten basic areas to consider are:

1. **Physical functioning.** Is the consumer's service need related to chronic (long term) or acute (brief and severe) illness or disease, to physical deterioration or disability, or to a lack of needed medical care?
2. **Emotional functioning.** Is mental illness or an emotional disorder a problem area for the consumer? Is the problem related to getting along with peers or other important people in his or her environment?
3. **Education and employment.** Is the problem related to a significant lack

(Frame 2 continued)

[1] See Robert J. Teare and Harold L. McPheeters, *Manpower Utilization in Social Welfare* (Atlanta: Southern Regional Education Board, 1970), pp. 11–17.

of education, to the ability to secure and retain employment, or to poor or dangerous working conditions?

4. **Financial functioning.** Is the problem related to an inability to earn an income or maintain an income or to an inability to adequately manage available funds?

5. **Transportation.** Does a lack of reliable and inexpensive transportation play a part in the consumer's problem? Is he able to utilize normal modes of transportation, or are there special needs?

6. **Family functioning.** Does the problem have to do with family relationships such as husband-wife, parent-child, brother-sister, and extended-family involvements?

7. **Housing.** What is the consumer's shelter situation? Is this a problem area? Is it adequate or inadequate in terms of its facilities, its condition, and the number of people living in it? Is it public or private, owned or rented, expensive, etc.?

8. **Safety and security.** To what extent is the consumer's physical environment a problem? Can he feel safe where he lives or works? Does he have adequate police and fire protection? Does he have access to other necessary services such as legal advice and health care?

9. **Spiritual and aesthetic functioning.** Has the consumer made an acceptable adjustment to life and the world around him? Is there a problem in relationship to the consumer's lack of contentment and accomplishment in life? Does he feel he has nothing to live for?

10. **Leisure and recreation.** Does the consumer have an opportunity to relax and enjoy recreational activities either individually or in a group? Is the lack of such opportunities a problem for the consumer?

Turn to Frame 3

FRAME 3

Listed below are some common problems that a consumer might bring to you for help. Indicate the appropriate problem area after the given explanation of the problem.

1. I don't have any way to take my children to the health clinic each week for their appointment.

   _____

2. I have to keep my children indoors all the time because the neighborhood we live in is so rough. I'm afraid to let them play outside.

   _____

3. I am so old and weak that I am afraid to die, and yet I really have nothing to live for.

   _____

4. I just don't get along with my parents. They don't understand me, and if things don't get better, I am going to run away from home.

   _____

Turn to Answer 1

FRAME 4

In your own words, explain what consumer problems might occur in the following areas of functioning.

1. Physical functioning:

2. Financial functioning:

3. Housing:

4. Education and employment:

Turn to Answer 2

FRAME 5

LEVELS OF FUNCTIONING

The second area to consider involves determining how the consumer is functioning with regard to each problem area. The levels of functioning range from well being, at the highest level, to disability at the lowest. The entire range is difficult to describe except in broad categories such as:

$$1 \quad\quad 2 \quad\quad 3 \quad\quad 4 \quad\quad 5$$
well-being → stress → problem → crisis → disability

Stages 2 and 3 are the points at which intervention would be most effective, but workers are seldom able to become involved at this early stage. Disability, however, is a state you probably see often. A working definition of each stage should help you locate any given client on the continuum:

1. **Well-being:** This is a high level of functional health. The consumer is getting along well in all vital areas of functioning. Intervention of any kind at this stage is unlikely.
2. **Stress:** No problems of functioning have developed at this point, but the risk has increased considerably. Ideal intervention at this point, if assistance were requested, would be in the form of some sort of support to prevent problems from occurring.
3. **Problems:** At this stage problems have begun to occur but they remain within the ability of the consumer to deal with. Any intervention at this point is focused on preventing the consumer from reaching a point of crisis.
4. **Crisis:** The crisis stage indicates that the problems are beyond the ability of the consumer to deal with. This is the point at which most service agencies become involved. Continued crisis level functioning may lead to disability. Intensive services of the needed type should be employed at this stage.

(Frame 5 continued)

5. **Disability**: At this stage considerable damage has occurred. Problems will be chronic or permanent. The usual services are remedial, that is, aimed at attempting to help the consumer adapt to the situation or learn compensating methods of functioning.

Whereas most human services relate to helping consumers solve problems related to their level of functioning, increased attention is now being given to preventing problems before they arise (e.g., more playgrounds and youth activities to prevent delinquency or more home health services to prevent social and physical deterioration and to keep the elderly out of costly institutions).

Turn to Frame 6

FRAME 6

The five levels of functioning are well-being, stress, problems, crisis, and disability. Fill in the blanks below with the appropriate level of functioning.

The highest level of functioning is _____ and the lowest level of functioning is _____.

Turn to Answer 3

FRAME 7

OBSTACLES TO FUNCTIONING

The third area to consider in understanding the needs and problems of human service consumers involves the identification of obstacles which prevent them from effective functioning. Obstacles may come from one or more basic sources and are important to identify so that appropriate services can be planned with a consumer. There are four general categories of obstacles to functioning.

1. **Personal deficiencies.** Deficiencies may relate to physical handicaps, whether from birth or from accidents, as well as psychological handicaps, either from early childhood or more recent experiences. Obstacles to functioning in this area include mental retardation; learning disabilities; physical limitations, such as blindness, deafness, and physical defects; and emotional problems relating to deficiencies in the opportunities for personal growth.
2. **Environmental deficiencies.** There is a range of consequences that can result from certain deficiencies in the environment which are usually beyond the control of individual consumers. Poor housing with inoperative sanitary facilities, torn or missing screens that don't keep out flies, mosquitoes, rats, poor garbage collection, and many other environmental defects can have consequences that can negatively influence an individual's entire life. Similarly, an institution such as a prison or a mental hospital may create dependency and thereby may become an environment which does not contribute to consumer rehabilitation. Other environmental defects include racist and/or sexist attitudes of significant people in the consumer's environment.
3. **Rigid laws and regulations**: Regulations and laws sometimes play a part in keeping an individual from obtaining a certain job or type of employment. Restrictive policies and practices based on race, creed or color often serve to restrict access to jobs, education, and housing. Restrictive policies and procedures may even prevent an individual from obtaining needed agency services.

4. Catastrophies: Unexpected devastating events are potential obstacles for everyone. These events include sudden death, illness, or disability. Automobile accidents and home accidents may also be the source. Natural disasters such as storms, earthquakes, and fire are well known. Most of these catastrophies are subject to little control and may require extensive remedial treatment and maintenance, especially at the individual level.

Turn to Frame 8

FRAME 8

For the following statements write in the letter of the obstacle that best completes the sentence. Statement 1 is an example.

OBSTACLES
P = personal deficiency
E = environmental deficiency
R = rigid laws and regulations
C = catastrophe

1. Mental retardation is an example of _P_.

2. A company policy not to hire Chinese taxi drivers is an instance of __.

3. Being struck by lightning and left paralyzed is __.

4. Blindness is __.

5. A child who cannot pay attention in class because he is hungry is probably suffering from __.

6. Being kept awake all night by insects and rats in your home is a case of __.

7. Having a realtor refuse to sell you a house in an all white suburb because you are black is a result of __.

8. Having the head of the household die unexpectedly is __.

Turn to Answer 4

FRAME 9

Practice Exercise

The preceding material has outlined a method for organizing consumer information about problem areas, levels of functioning, and the obstacles that prevent the consumer from functioning independently. It is possible to use these three perspectives to organize information about the current status of a consumer. The following example is designed to give you an opportunity to see how consumer problems can be analyzed.

As a social service worker in a neighborhood service center you have been visiting residents at their homes to discuss their need for services. Today you met Mr. Davis who is 73 years old, retired, and living alone in a small efficiency apartment on a monthly social security benefit of $90. The neighborhood is slowly deteriorating

(Frame 9 continued)

and to get to stores, doctors, or recreation he must walk through an
area that is considered unsafe, especially after 5:00 P.M. The local
bus system does not have a stop closer to him and a taxi is too
expensive. Mr. Davis enjoys good health for his age and has Medicare
coverage. In the course of your conversation with him he states that
he would like very much to find a place to live that would be closer to
a recreation center for people in his age group and also closer to shopping.
He feels he cannot pay more rent than the $35 he is paying now.

It is important to remember that through work experience in a human service
agency you should be able to increase your skills in making judgments about the
range and type of consumer problems. In essence, practical experience is needed
in order to use this approach effectively in organizing consumer information.

The following chart will help you see how the potential problem areas of functioning, levels of functioning, and obstacles to functioning might be identified for
Mr. Davis.

Turn to the chart

	Levels of Functioning					
Areas of Functioning	Well Being (1)	Stress (2)	Problems (3)	Crisis (4)	Disability (5)	Obstacles to Functioning (Personal, Environmental, Rigid Laws, Catastrophes)
Physical	X					
Emotional		X				There appears to be an environmental deficiency related to the deteriorating neighborhood, distance from shopping, etc., that is causing him stress.
Education & employment	X					
Financial			X			Due to a personal deficiency, age, he is not employed and probably could not get a job. His low social security benefits may make him eligible for public assistance.
Transportation			X			One of the obstacles in this area is simply a lack of inexpensive transportation. He is physically capable of walking, but this may be unsafe. This is an environmental deficiency.
Family	X					
Housing		X				The obstacle here is the nature of the neighborhood slowly running down. A more convenient location would be much better. This is an environmental deficiency.
Safety & security			X			He definitely feels, with apparent good reason, that he is not safe walking along the streets. This reality serves to restrict his activities. This is an environmental deficiency.

LEVELS OF FUNCTIONING	WELL BEING	STRESS	PROBLEMS	CRISIS	DISABILITY	
Spiritual & aesthetic	X					
Leisure & recreation		X				One of his primary concerns is to be situated more conveniently, near friends and recreation. The obstacles here are environmental—the type of neighborhood he lives in and the area he must walk through to get to stores and recreation.

Turn to Frame 10

FRAME 10

Practice Exercise 2

Are you ready to try one on your own now? Good. Here's the situation:

> Mrs. Collins is 34 years old and supports herself and three children (16, 14, 12) on an AFDC grant of $270 a month. She seems to be doing a commendable job as a money manager. The two older children have part-time jobs through the work study program.
>
> You are a public health nurse and have just been told by your supervisor that x-rays of Mrs. Collins' abdomen confirm the presence of a large tumor which needs to be removed immediately. There is some chance that it is cancerous but the doctor thinks this unlikely. The supervisor has talked to Mrs. Collins about making preparations to have the operation. Mrs. Collins was very upset but agreed to come in for further medical examination. Since that time she has failed to show up for two appointments, explaining that she is "very busy." The supervisor wants you to arrange a home visit with Mrs. Collins and help resolve the problem. After some trouble and delays you finally see her at home. She is obviously scared and gives three reasons why she can't consider having an operation now:
>
> —There is no one to take care of her children while she is in the hospital.
> —She doesn't have anyone to help her at home after she leaves the hospital.
> —If she dies, her children will be orphans.

Turn to the next page and complete the form there. Leave blank those areas of functioning for which the example does not give information.

Go on to the chart on next page

	LEVELS OF FUNCTIONING					
AREAS OF FUNCTIONING	WELL BEING (1)	STRESS (2)	PROBLEMS (3)	CRISIS (4)	DISABILITY (5)	OBSTACLES TO FUNCTIONING (PERSONAL, ENVIRONMENTAL, RIGID LAWS, CATASTROPHIES)
Physical						
Emotional						
Education & employment						
Financial						
Transportation*	X					*
Family*	X					*
Housing*	X					*
Safety & security*	X					*
Spiritual & aesthetic*	X					*
Leisure & recreation*	X					*

* Since this is a crisis situation, the focus is on the major problem. No information was received that any of these areas were causing problems.

Turn to Answer 5

FRAME 11

TOWARD A BETTER UNDERSTANDING OF CONSUMERS

In this lesson you looked at various areas of functioning where a consumer might be experiencing problems. You also looked at different levels of functioning and obstacles to effective functioning. All of this should improve your understanding of the consumers you serve and how to help them. It is also important to recognize the many different characteristics of all human beings, whether they are consumers, human service workers, or people you meet on the street. Being aware of whether a person is male or female, black, white, or another racial origin, young or old, or from an urban or a rural area will help you understand people in general and especially the consumers you serve.

It is important for you to remember that these characteristics do not necessarily determine whether a person becomes a consumer of human services (e.g., the majority of welfare recipients are white, not black, which is contrary to popular opinion).[1] For example, if you are working with a consumer who is a member

[1] U.S. Department of Health, Education and Welfare, *Welfare Myths vs. Facts.* (Washington, D.C.: Superintendent of Documents, 1971.)

of a racial minority, you should be aware of the frustration caused by discrimination and the resulting lack of trust and confidence that may occur because of it. Elderly consumers may not display the same vigor that you may see in the young, and they may also be physically incapable of participating in certain kinds of services. Sex discrimination in employment may be a factor in working with female consumers in job training programs. A person from a small rural community may have a very difficult time adjusting to the rapid pace of the big city, and his or her cultural values may be significantly different. Being aware of these characteristics, their consequences, and how they affect people will lead to a better understanding of the consumers you serve.

Congratulations! You have now completed Lesson 1. You may want to review this lesson briefly before continuing to the next. Keep up the good work!

ANSWERS TO LESSON 1

ANSWER 1

Your list of problem areas should look like this:

1. transportation
2. safety and security
3. spiritual and aesthetic functioning
4. family functioning

Go on to Frame 4.

ANSWER 2

The definitions should have mentioned most of the following:

1. Physical functioning: problems related to chronic or acute illness or disease, physical deterioration, disability or lack of medical care.
2. Financial functioning: problems related to the inability to earn an adequate income and/or manage available income.
3. Housing: problems related to adequate housing; condition of housing, space, cooking, sanitary, living, and sleeping facilities.
4. Education and employment: problems related to a lack of education and job skills, the ability to find and keep a job, and poor or dangerous working conditions.

Go on to Frame 5.

ANSWER 3

The correct words in each space complete the sentence as follows:

The highest level of functioning is well-being and the lowest level of functioning is disability.

Go on to Frame 7.

ANSWER 4

If you correctly matched every statement with the obstacle, it will look like this:

1. P.   5. E
2. R   6. E
3. C   7. R
4. P   8. C

How did you do? If you missed more than one or two you might do well to go back and review Frame 7 before going on. Otherwise, go on to Frame 9.

ANSWER 5

Areas of Functioning	Levels of Functioning					Obstacles to Functioning
	(1)	(2)	(3)	(4)	(5)	
Physical				X		Mrs. Collins has a personal deficiency, a large tumor, that is in need of immediate medical treatment.
Emotional				X		Her emotional state is near panic and she is refusing to face her situation realistically. This is also a personal deficiency.
Education & employment			X			Since she is receiving public assistance it is highly probable that she is either unemployed or is able to earn only low wages. This is probably an environmental deficiency.
Financial		X				Although she manages her income well, it is a very limited amount that she is apparently unable to increase through employment. Rigid laws fix public assistance grants at unrealistically low levels.
Transportation*	X					
Family*	X					
Housing*	X					
Safety & security*	X					
Spiritual & aesthetic*	X					
Leisure*	X					

* Since this is a crisis situation, the focus is on the major problem. No information has come out that any of the remaining areas was causing problems.

Turn to Frame 11

LESSON 2:
HUMAN SERVICE SYSTEMS

Understanding how human service systems are organized and operated will make it easier for workers to function in their effort to achieve the agency's service objectives. While the human service system includes both public and private agencies, there are many problems in linking the agencies together to enable consumers to meet their needs. This lesson covers the general characteristics of both the system and the consumer, and shows you some ways this knowledge can be helpful. The goal of the lesson and the enabling activities that will help you achieve this goal are presented below.

GOAL

To be able to define what a system is, how it operates, and to apply that definition to agency and community groups.

ENABLING ACTIVITIES

After completing this lesson, you will have done the following:

1. Reviewed the definition of a system and the system process
2. Compared two different types of human service organizations to the definition
3. Considered consumer community groups as systems
4. Identified eight ways that understanding agencies and consumers as systems can help you in your work

**Turn to Frame 1
to begin this lesson**

FRAME 1

When we describe human service agencies, we usually envision large, complex organizations which include a number of related and coordinated parts. Welfare departments, mental hospitals, and prisons are all examples of complex organiza-
(Frame 1 continued)

tions. These organizations operate with rules and procedures that are sometimes difficult to understand. One approach to gaining an understanding of an organization is to first analyze its components systematically and then identify the relationship of one organization to another organization. This approach is known as systems analysis and has received a great deal of attention in recent years. Since many of our human service agencies are changing constantly, workers need to acquire an understanding of all the parts of a human service system, even though the relationship between the parts may change. Workers can also play important roles in helping agencies change as they attempt to improve services, and this role requires knowledge of the human service system.

In a much less formal and structured manner, the systems approach can be applied to the groups of people we serve. Consumers request and use services as the need arises and as the service is made available. We also discuss the community of consumers as a system and look at the interaction of the consumer system with the agency system. Throughout the pages of this lesson we describe an approach to understanding a human service agency as a system acting in a particular and predictable way.

Turn to Frame 2

FRAME 2

WHAT IS A SYSTEM?

There is a growing body of knowledge called systems theory based on studies which describe the operation of organizations and groups. We need to define the term *system* to improve our understanding of how it is used in the human services.

A system is a set of components interacting with each other. It has a mechanism which filters the kind and rate of flow of the inputs and outputs to and from the system.

The essential parts of this definition have to be clearly understood:

1. **A set of components.** If we consider an automobile to be a system, then the various smaller parts of which it is made up would be the components. A few components are the tires, the battery, the steering wheel, and the brakes. Some of these are related to subsystems such as the electrical system and the fuel system. A human being is also a system that we understand as being made up of a number of individual parts (arms, legs, etc.) and smaller systems such as the circulatory system, digestive system, respiratory system, and nervous system.
2. **Interaction with each other.** Unless all the parts of a car work together, the entire car may not operate properly, and we shall end up taking a taxi. A disorder in a person's circulatory system (a heart attack for instance) may threaten his survival. Even a stomachache may affect other systems, make normal functioning difficult, and affect the way a person feels and acts.
3. **Boundary mechanism filters kind and rate of flow of inputs and outputs.** An automobile is designed to accept only a limited range of inputs through mechanisms such as the starter (ignition), the gas tank, and mechanisms such as the gear shift, accelerator, steering wheel, and brakes. These mechanisms are all at the boundary or surface of the automobile and not under the hood. The automobile produces transportation as an output. In a similar manner, a human being accepts a wide variety of inputs, such as heat, cold, and communication, through such mechanisms as skin, eyes,

and ears. Sometimes people do not seem to hear or accept things that are communicated to them. This may reflect a defect in the mechanism (deafness) or it may reflect an unwillingness to accept that particular input. People produce a wide variety of outputs, some of which are observable and called behavior. Some we cannot see, such as mental processes and nervous system reactions.

A human service system also consists of various components, interactions, boundary mechanisms, inputs, and outputs. Components of a human service system include (1) public agenices such as health departments, prisons, and mental hospitals; (2) private agencies such as the Salvation Army, YWCA, Boy Scouts, and family services agencies; and (3) voluntary associations like the Big Brothers, Junior League, and Lions Club. All these public and private agencies and voluntary associations are components of a human service system. They interact with one another to provide services and resources to meet the human needs of people. Each has its own boundary mechanisms which filter the inputs such as eligibility requirements for services, criteria for membership, and procedures for discharge. The primary input of the human service system is the consumer. Added to this input are the money, manpower, and materials which are combined to produce a service. The output is also the consumer who has hopefully been rehabilitated, treated, reformed, trained or supported.

Turn to Frame 3

FRAME 3

Match the following aspects of a human service system to the examples listed.

___ Components   1. Admissions procedures
___ Boundary mechanisms 2. Welfare department, hospital, and YMCA
___ Inputs   3. Rehabilitated consumers
___ Outputs   4. Consumers in need of help

Turn to Answer 1

FRAME 4

The System Process

The process of any system looks like this:

$$\rightarrow \text{input} \quad \rightarrow \text{processing} \quad \rightarrow \text{output} \quad \rightarrow \text{feedback}$$

Or, in action terms, like this:

$$\rightarrow \text{request for services} \quad \rightarrow \text{service planning \& organization} \quad \rightarrow \text{service action} \quad \rightarrow \text{feedback}$$

When a request for service is received by an agency, one of two actions is taken: the request is accepted if the service is available or is rejected if the service is not available or the applicant is not eligible. In the case of rejection, the consumer may be referred to another agency.

(Frame 4 continued)

Once an input is accepted there is a certain amount of internal processing that takes place—assembly of a case record, information collecting, and development of a plan to provide services. For consumers, the most important part of the process is the service they receive. This is also of considerable importance to the agency; so important in fact that most agencies make continuous checks on the quality of the services consumers receive as part of an ongoing process of making needed changes and improvements. This is called feedback and without it a system could not function properly. The consumer also provides feedback in the form of a request for additional services or complaints about existing services. Feedback represents a process of giving information such as complaints or compliments back to the provider, namely, the worker or the agency.

Continue with Frame 5

FRAME 5

Check the correct response to the following statement.
A request for service represents part of the

__ A. input phase.

__ B. output phase.

__ C. feedback phase.

Turn to Answer 2

FRAME 6

Check the correct response to the following statement.
Getting information on how well the agency is meeting consumer needs is called

__ A. action work.

Turn to Answer 3

__ B. processing.

Turn to Answer 4

__ C. feedback.

Turn to Answer 5

FRAME 7

HUMAN SERVICES AND THE CONSUMER

We live in a complex society where providing human services is also complex. While we have mentioned private agencies and voluntary associations, let's focus primarily on the public sector and look at the various levels of organizations that provide services and at the community groups that consume them. As you can see in Figure 1, we have described in simplified form each of the three levels of public human services at the federal, state, and local levels. In terms of systems, the highest level of involvement is the federal Department of Health, Education and Welfare (HEW), which is primarily concerned with policy making and the funding of programs on a national basis. The consumer group served by HEW is nearly the entire population of the United States.

The state is the next major level of concern. In many states there are independent agencies, such as health departments and welfare departments, and each provides a specific range of services. In recent years, many states have organized

Figure 1 SERVICE AND COMMUNITY SYSTEMS

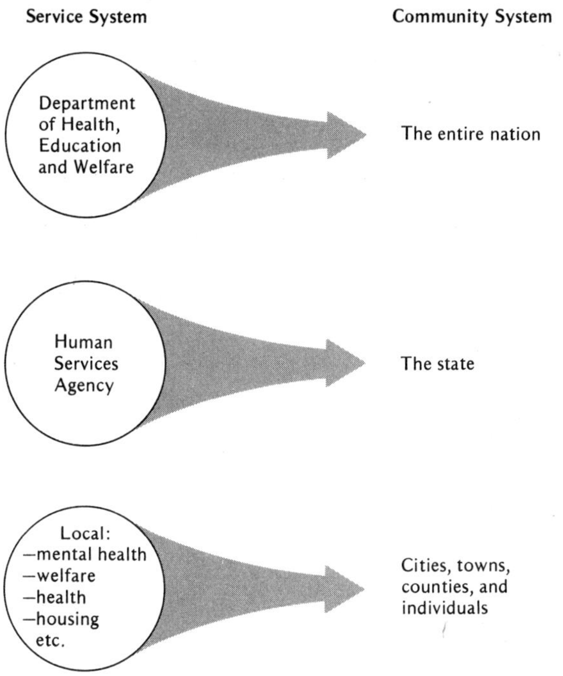

Service System   Community System

Department
of Health,
Education   The entire nation
and Welfare

Human
Services   The state
Agency

Local:
—mental health
—welfare   Cities, towns,
—health   counties, and
—housing   individuals
etc.

these agencies into one large agency in order to provide more efficient and effective services. These large agencies are called umbrella agencies. The Florida Department of Health and Rehabilitative Services is one such agency, and it administers a broad range of state and federally financed human services including health, welfare, mental health, mental retardation, youth services, vocational rehabilitation, aging, and drug abuse. The community served by such an organization is the entire state of Florida.

The level with which most workers have the greatest familiarity is the local community level. This is where policy and program are translated into specific services for individuals. There is usually a wide range of services available to consumers with special needs. Some examples of community services and consumers are the following:

LOCAL HUMAN SERVICES

Mental health centers and hospitals
Public health department
Public welfare
Retardation centers and hospitals
Youth services institutions and programs
Vocational rehabilitation
Prisons, halfway houses, community correctional centers

COMMUNITY CONSUMERS SERVED

Emotionally disturbed persons
Physically ill persons
Financially dependent persons
Mentally retarded persons
Delinquent minors
Physically and emotionally disabled
Convicted offenders

This is not a complete listing of the public community human service agencies but is intended to be generally representative. There are also some other human service agencies operating at the local level that you should be familiar with in planning services for consumers:

Other local public agencies. These are generally supported by local public funds, sometimes matched with state and federal funds. Public housing authorities fall in this category, as do some urban renewal programs.

(Frame 7 continued)

Private social service agencies. These usually exist for a specific purpose. For example, a children's home society primarily handles child care and adoptions.
Church affiliated social services. Every major denomination offers some services to people. Catholic Charities, Jewish Family Service, and the Salvation Army are typical.

Go on to Frame 8

FRAME 8

Local Human Service Organizations

Let's take a closer look at the kinds of human services that consumers find at the local level and then examine the consumer and community groups that utilize these services. There are generally two ways of organizing to provide human services—the comprehensive service center and the traditional separate agency. The comprehensive service center (CSC) brings together a wide array of human services in one location where the consumer can go for assistance. Staff from agencies which have been separate and disconnected from one another work together to provide such services as public welfare, vocational rehabilitation, youth services, public health, and mental health.

The more traditional pattern of service includes independent, separate agencies at the local level maintaining separate offices and procedures for delivering services where the health department is in one place, welfare in another, and vocational rehabilitation is somewhere else. Usually little effort is made to locate these offices in a central area convenient for consumers. Each one of the agencies functions as a system virtually independent of the others, and, as a result, coordination between them is often poor. Consumers often find themselves using considerable time and money going from one office to another and repeating the application and interview procedure in efforts to find the services they need.

We have just discussed some different types of systems. The table that follows compares the two approaches to service delivery in terms of the definition of a system. Please review it carefully.

Go on to study the table

Table 1

	COMPREHENSIVE SERVICE CENTER	SEPARATE LOCAL AGENCIES
A set of components	The various agencies, and the services offered by them, are housed in the Center. These would include most of the public social services such as public welfare, youth services, health, vocational rehabilitation, and perhaps some of the locally financed social services such as public housing and legal aid.	The programs and services offered by a particular agency would be directed toward a certain set of social needs and consumers.
Interaction with each other	Generally there is a person in charge of coordinating the different service agencies represented, however, it is up to the various agencies to accept a consumer for service and to plan and deliver the needed services. Some mutual concerns of all the agencies are information exchange, service planning, record	Within the office or offices of the local agency are many workers attached to different programs and with specific responsibilities. There are several administrative levels as well. There is considerable interaction between them as each attempts to do a particular part of a much larger total operation.

Table 1 (Continued)

	COMPREHENSIVE SERVICE CENTER	SEPARATE LOCAL AGENCIES
	keeping and handling, traffic flow, hours of operation, and referral procedures. Each influences the others by having particular needs and objectives.	
A boundary with the ability to filter the kind and rate of flow of inputs and outputs	The CSC has a boundary defined by the range of services provided by the center. This range will almost certainly be larger than the services offered by any single agency and usually includes the major human services available. Some of the agencies will have legally defined eligibility requirements. The inputs include the requests for services received, and the outputs include the services given.	Agencies have certain requirements that an applicant must meet in order to qualify for services (e.g., for financial assistance, income must be under a certain amount). Other services are only for those with certain types and severity of physical or mental disorders. Inputs include the requests for services received and outputs include the agency responses to those requests.

Turn to Frame 9

FRAME 9

The Consumer as a System

The object (i.e., the input and output) of all service systems is the consumer. Individually, a consumer represents a biological system. The consumer is also part of a larger community system. A family is a well-known system with parents, children, grandparents as components. Organizations that include consumers are also systems, such as inmate associations, associations for retarded persons, and welfare rights organizations. Other groups of consumers include church congregations, civic and fraternal groups, social and recreational groups, kinship and friendship groups. Society is made up of a vast number of different kinds of groups. Every group has components, boundary mechanisms, inputs, and outputs. Every group exerts influence on its members and the outside world in an attempt to achieve its goals.

Continue with Frame 10

FRAME 10

The following exercise requires you to apply the definition of a system to the family. Beneath each of the parts of the definition, you should indicate which aspect of the family it refers to.

DEFINITION

1. Identify the set of components in the family system.

2. Explain how these components interact with each other.

3. Identify a boundary mechanism which filters the kind and rate of flow of inputs and outputs to and from the family system.

Turn to Answer 6

INTERACTIONS BETWEEN SYSTEMS

You are familiar with the range and variety of interactions that take place between people. There are a number of related interactions that also take place between systems. The interaction between human service and consumer systems is extremely important because of the need each has to communicate clearly and successfully with the other. This communication is integral to the basic processes of systems. While it is obvious that the two systems depend on each other, it is equally obvious that there may be conflict between them. A system exercises control over a certain set of functions. For example, a human service agency controls the expenditure of local, state, and federal funds allocated for services. Consumer organizations may seek to influence the operations of an organization. This may generate conflict, since the sharing of decision making in agency programs may threaten those in control of the agency. Whether the conflict is constructive or destructive depends on agency responses to the consumer actions and on whether the two systems are able to reach an acceptable accommodation. While consumers have won some significant victories in recent years, the service systems continue to exercise strong control over the services available. Recent efforts to develop citizen advisory committees as part of human service agencies indicate the beginning recognition of the importance of consumer involvement in the operation of human service agencies.

Turn to Frame 12

Read each of the following statements and decide whether it is true or false. Write T or F in the space before the statement.

___ A. Consumer involvement in trying to change an agency in a certain direction may create conflict.

___ B. Communication is unnecessary in most systems.

___ C. System conflict can be either constructive or destructive.

___ D. Consumers now control most human service systems.

Turn to Answer 7

SUMMARY

This discussion about systems was intended to help you understand the overall context of your work with consumers. You are not alone in trying to meet the human service needs of consumers. Your work relates to the work of others, as your agency is linked to other agencies in a network of human services. A major benefit of the systems approach is having a framework that enables you to understand all the situations and people involved in the provision of particular services. Having some way of understanding organizations and consumers will make it easier to achieve the desired objectives of your agency. The following summary should help you itemize some of the specific benefits which may be gained from an understanding of systems:[1]

1. The systems framework will make it easier to identify the problems that you can expect to face and to anticipate the kinds of tasks that will be necessary to solve these problems. We shall describe these tasks in subsequent chapters.
2. It will help you to realize that the person or group seeking help is not always the major target, that the problem may be in a different system (e.g., environmental deficiencies).
3. The systems perspective makes it clear that only after the major factors affecting a consumer (e.g., problem area, level of functioning, and obstacle to functioning) have been identified can you determine what kind of service plan is most appropriate. The systems perspective is a planning tool.
4. You will be able to recognize that the performance of your tasks requires relationships not only with consumers but with people who are not consumers.
5. You will be able to understand the importance of viewing agencies as social systems and of understanding the potential impact of new activities that will change or modify an organizational system.
6. Understanding your agency as a system and how systems can be dealt with will help you understand that your own agency may need changing in order to help clients.
7. Understanding the system helps identify the various points where service coordination is needed as well as the areas requiring evaluation of service effectiveness.

Go on to Frame 14

FRAME 14

Place a check in front of the correct statements.

A human service worker's understanding of service agencies and consumers will lead to which of the following?

___ 1. In the course of providing services, the worker must deal with people other than the consumer.

___ 2. The worker may find that changes are needed in the agency.

___ 3. The worker will be able to anticipate problems in service delivery and how to solve them.

___ 4. Helping a consumer may require changes in some other system.

___ 5. The worker will be able to understand how to approach making changes in the agency.

Turn to Answer 8

---

[1] Allen Pincus and Anne Minahan, *Social Work Practice: Model and Method* (Itasca, Ill.: F. E. Peacock Publishers, Inc., 1973), pp. 64–68.

ANSWERS TO LESSON 2

Your answer should look like this:

<u>2</u> components

<u>1</u> boundary mechanisms

<u>4</u> inputs

<u>3</u> outputs

If your answer was not right, then you should go back and review the definition of a system in Frame 2.
Go on to Frame 4.

You should have checked A, input phase.
If you got it correct, you are on your way to understanding how a system works. If you missed it, go back to Frame 4 and carefully review the system process.
Go on to Frame 6.

Sorry—the term "action work" is not even mentioned in Frame 4. Go back to Frame 6 and try again.

Not quite right. Processing is an internal system process. It is the step between input and output. Go back to Frame 6 and try again.

ANSWER 5

Very good. *Feedback* is the way agencies determine how well they are doing in providing services.

Go on to Frame 7.

ANSWER 6

Your answer should look something like this:

1. A set of components: the people in the family such as the mother, the father, children and any other close relatives living there.
2. Interacting with each other: each family member *talks to* and has relationships with the others. Parents *teach* children how to behave and *advise* them on choices to be made.
3. A boundary mechanism which filters both the kind and rate of flow inputs: a family is usually made up of people with very *close bond* with one another. Strangers or outsiders cannot easily step in and function as part of the family because they do not have that degree of closeness of relationship. They do not "belong." Families have certain *beliefs*, *values* and *habits* and they usually work hard to maintain these. They communicate the family's feelings and beliefs to others that they come into contact with and produce offspring molded by the family.

Go on to Frame 11.

ANSWER 7

Compare your answers with the following:

A. True: Consumer involvement in trying to change an agency in a certain direction may generate conflict.
B. False: Communication is necessary in most systems.
C. True: System conflict can be either constructive or destructive.
D. False: Consumers do not control most human service systems.

Go on to Frame 13.

ANSWER 8

If you have successfully learned the material in this lesson, all of the statements should have a check mark in front of them.

You have now completed Chapter I. Go on to the summary and review questions.

SUMMARY

This chapter was designed to provide a basic understanding of the human services. Specific attention was given to the consumers of human services and to the importance of understanding their needs and problems. A method for organizing the wide range of consumer information was presented as a means of identifying problems and preparing service plans. This method basically involved examining (1) the consumer's problem area, (2) the consumer's level of functioning, and (3) the nature of the obstacles to effective functioning. Attention was also given to the importance of recognizing the different characteristics of consumers.

We also discussed the general features of human service systems and identified some of the ways this knowledge might be useful to your work. The chapter provided a definition of a system and this was then applied to the structures of human service systems at the national, state, and local levels. At the local level we compared two common patterns of organization—comprehensive service centers and separate local agencies. The consumer was described in terms of the systems framework, and the concept of system interaction was discussed. Finally, some of the benefits derived from understanding systems theory were presented.

SUGGESTIONS FOR FURTHER STUDY

The concept of human services is very new in the helping services, and, as a result, there are a limited number of sources available for further study. However, this concept is becoming increasingly important and useful as attempts are made to consolidate and improve the delivery of human services. Some useful approaches can be found in the literature on human service organizations, which addresses the problems of defining and studying this special kind of organization. While some of it is very technical, it should be useful in gaining a broad overview of the field.

Additional study will also be needed to understand and work with consumers. There are many sources on consumer problems and characteristics in areas such as retardation, mental illness, juvenile delinquency, poverty, aging, and physical illness.

Our discussion of systems was, at best, a preliminary introduction to an interesting and challenging field. Additional references on systems theory are included in the bibliography which follows. As Brill notes, human service workers should reflect on three questions: (1) What are the boundaries of the system or systems with which they are dealing? (2) What are the patterns and channels of communication both within the individual system under consideration (e.g., family, neighborhood, agency and among the related external systems (e.g., network of agencies, network of family relations)? (3) What are the explicit and implicit rules that govern the relationships among the parts, both internally and externally, particularly with respect to input (openness to new ideas and materials), processing (working with these materials), and output (results of this work and feedback)?[2]

While we have emphasized the role of the consumer and the agency in our discussion of systems concepts, it is also important to use these concepts in analyzing the process by which you help consumers. Meyer has addressed this perspective in the following way.

> In a systems framework, where concepts of input and output and reciprocity take on meaning, we can cease our unending search for cause and effect. We find in the notion of equifinality (i.e., systems are open and not necessarily static) that there is more than one way to achieve an outcome in a case because each action taken will rebound upon another which will set in motion yet other movements for change. . . . The case might be defined as a person, a family, a hospital ward, a housing complex, a particular neighborhood, a school population, a group with particular problems and needs, or a community with common concerns. . . . The case then, might be defined geographically, functionally, or according to problem or interest groupings. . . . The systemic framework does not make individual assessments in a case unnecessary, on the contrary, it provides a conceptual structure that insures a true transactional understanding of the person-in-situation.

---

[2] Naomi I. Brill, *Working With People: The Helping Process* (Philadelphia: Lippincott, 1973), p. 66.

Its most salutary feature is that it provides for multifaceted interventions, determined by the needs of the case and made possible by the opportunity to utilize the available manpower from all levels of education, experience and expertise.[3]

These additional perspectives should serve as the basis of further reading and discussion.

SUGGESTIONS FOR FURTHER READING

Anderson, Ralph E., and Carter, Ira E. *Human Behavior in the Social Environment.* Chicago: Aldine, 1974.

Berrien, F. Kenneth. *General and Social Systems.* New Brunswick, N.J.: Rutgers University Press, 1968.

Bloedorn, Jack C.; Maclatchie, Elizabeth B.; Friedlander, William; and Wedemeyer, J. M. *Designing Social Service Systems.* American Public Welfare Association, Chicago, 1970.

Brill, Naomi I. *Working With People: The Helping Process.* Philadelphia: Lippincott, 1973.

Federico, Ronald. *The Social Welfare Institution.* Lexington, Mass.: Heath, 1973.

Goffman, Erving. *Asylums.* Garden City, N.Y.: Doubleday (Anchor Books), 1961.

Hasenfeld, Yeheskel, and English, Richard, eds. *Human Service Organizations.* University of Michigan Press, 1974.

Hearn, Gordon. *The General System Approach.* Council on Social Work Education, New York, 1967.

Irelan, Lola M., ed. *Low Income Life Styles.* U.S. Department of Health, Education, and Welfare. Washington, D.C.: U.S. Government Printing Office, 1967.

Kahn, Alfred. *Social Policy and Social Services.* New York: Random House, 1973.

Janchill, Sister Mary Paul. "Systems Concepts in Casework Theory and Practice." *Social Casework* 50 (February 1969).

Meyer, Carol H. "Direct Services in New and Old Contexts." In Alfred Kahn, ed., *Shaping the New Social Work.* New York: Columbia University Press, 1973.

Pincus, Allen, and Minahan, Anne. *Social Work Practice: Model and Method.* Itasca, Ill.: F. E. Peacock Publishers, Inc., 1973.

Rosenberg, N., and Brady R. *Systems Serving People.* Cleveland: Case Western Reserve University Press, 1974.

Schulberg, H. C., Baker, F., and Roen, S. R., eds. *Developments in Human Services,* vol. 1. New York: Behavioral Publications, 1973.

Teare, Robert J. "Competency and the 'Delivery Systems': Where Educators and Employees Meet," in Michael J. Austin and Philip L. Smith, eds. *Statewide Career Planning in a Human Service Industry.* Tallahassee: State University System of Florida, 1973.

Teare, Robert J., and McPheeters, Harold L. *Manpower Utilization in Social Welfare.* Social and Rehabilitation Services Grant. Atlanta: Southern Regional Education Board, 1970.

U.S. Department of Health, Education, and Welfare. "Toward a Comprehensive Service Delivery System Through Building the Community Service Center." Washington, D.C.: U.S. Government Printing Office, 1970.

Warren, Roland. *Perspectives on the American Community.* New York: Rand McNally, 1973.

Wilensky, Harold, and Lebeaux, Charles. *Industrial Society and Social Welfare.* New York: Russell Sage, 1958.

[3] Carol H. Meyer, "Direct Services in New and Old Contexts," in Alfred Kahn, ed., *Shaping the New Social Work* (New York: Columbia University Press, 1973), pp. 49–51.

REVIEW QUESTIONS—CHAPTER I

Circle the letter next to the answer of your choice.

1. Which of the following characteristics can be identified in a human service system?
   A. Inputs and outputs
   B. Boundary mechanisms
   C. Set of component parts
   D. All of the above

2. Why is it important to understand certain characteristics of people such as age, race, sex, and cultural background?
   A. People with the same characteristics behave exactly alike.
   B. Consumers are always different from the general public in behavior.
   C. These characteristics are useful in understanding consumers better.
   D. Most people are alike.

3. Being able to identify a consumer's problem(s), level of functioning, and obstacles to effective functioning will do which of the following?
   A. It will help you in achieving a better understanding of the consumer.
   B. It will reduce the time spent with each consumer.
   C. It will help you plan the appropriate services.
   D. A and C are correct.
   E. All of the above are correct.

4. From where can one get feedback about the efficiency and effectiveness of human services?
   A. Consumers
   B. Supervisors
   C. Co-workers
   D. None of the above
   E. All of the above

5. State and local public human services need to be understood from a systems perspective and should also include what other perspective, primarily?
   A. International
   B. Industrial
   C. National
   D. Religious

6. If a consumer came to you seeking help for a child who had reached a point in school where behavior problems resulted in the child's suspension from school, how would you describe the stage at which that child was functioning?
   A. Well-being
   B. Stress
   C. Problems
   D. Crisis
   E. Disability

7. If a consumer came to you for help after losing all his possessions in a flood and after a local agency had refused assistance because the consumer could not prove he had been a resident of the area for six months, what two obstacles to functioning would you say existed in this case?

    A. Personal deficiencies and environmental deficiencies
    B. Rigid laws and regulations and catastrophies
    C. Catastrophies and personal deficiencies
    D. Environmental deficiencies and catastrophies

8. The term *umbrella agency* does *not* mean which of the following?
    A. Independent human service agencies
    B. Centralized administration of services
    C. Coordinating a wide variety of services in one agency
    D. Bringing different services together for the consumer

9. In what areas of functioning would you say the consumer was experiencing problems if the consumer came to you presenting the following problems? "I have a heart condition that prevents me from doing heavy labor, but I don't have enough education to get an office job. I am applying for welfare because I don't have enough money to feed my family."
    A. Physical functioning, emotional functioning, and housing
    B. Physical functioning, educational and employment, and financial functioning
    C. Safety and security, education and employment, and spiritual and aesthetic functioning
    D. Transportation, financial functioning, and family functioning

10. When viewing consumers as a system, which of their roles is it important to recognize?
    A. They provide feedback to the agency.
    B. They seek to change agency services.
    C. They are members of a family.
    D. A and C are correct.
    E. All of the above are correct.

**Now check your answers
with the Answer key
for this chapter
at the end of the book**

CHAPTER II:
THE WORLD OF
HUMAN SERVICE WORK

INTRODUCTION

In the first chapter we emphasized the role of the consumer and the role of the agency. In this chapter attention will be given mainly to the role of the human service worker. For most of us, work occupies nearly one-third of our lives. Every day millions of men and women experience a variety of work situations, pleasures, and problems for the greater part of their waking hours. Because so much time and effort are spent at work, it is important to understand some of the factors which affect your life through work.

You have chosen human service work as the central activity around which you are organizing your life. To carry out human service work effectively, people should be committed to helping others and should find personal satisfaction in their work. The starting point for these things is examining where you work, why you work, and the kind of work you perform.

This chapter provides you with the opportunity to learn about the important factors which affect your ability to function in the world of human service work. Lesson 1 examines the characteristics of human service work settings. Lesson 2 addresses the process of establishing a work identity and the importance of developing an awareness of your own value system. Lesson 3 discusses the tasks and activities of human service work and provides the framework for understanding the nature and meaning of human service work. The overall objective of this chapter is to provide you with a comprehensive understanding of the world of human service work.

**Turn to the next page
to begin Lesson 1**

LESSON 1:
THE ORGANIZATION

One of the mechanisms our society has created to meet human needs is the human service organization. Since most human service work is carried out in a human service organization, an understanding of this physical environment, or setting, plays a crucial part in the delivering of effective human services. Successful human service work will always require the worker to deal with his own physical environment as well as with the welfare of the consumer.

While in the previous chapter we looked at the system of human service agencies, this lesson is designed to provide you with a broad understanding of your own human service agency and thereby enable you to apply systems theory to the internal operation of your agency. The goal of this lesson and the enabling activities that will help you reach this goal are presented below.

GOAL

To develop an understanding of the human service work setting by demonstrating the application of the characteristics of human service organizations to your own work-setting.

ENABLING ACTIVITIES

After completing this lesson, you will have accomplished three things:

1. Identified four characteristics of a human service organization
2. Described three primary differences between a human service organization and a non-human service organization
3. Identified possible conflict areas that exist for workers within a human service organization

Turn to Frame 1 to begin learning about the human service work setting

CHARACTERISTICS OF THE HUMAN SERVICE ORGANIZATION

Our society is characterized by a great many organizations. They may be formal organizations, such as banks, government agencies, private companies, and social welfare agencies; or they may be informal organizations, such as social clubs and recreation groups. Since you are a human service worker, your agency is probably one of many formal organizations that has been formed to deal with people's social and personal problems. To assist you in understanding your organization, let us examine the four components of a human service organization seen as a system:[1]

1. **Organization policy.** Human service organizations have policies which essentially tell you two things about the organization. First, policies tell you what the organization is supposed to to do, that is, the goals and objectives of the organization. Second, policies tell you how the organization goes about accomplishing its goals and objectives, that is, what *regulations* you as a member must observe in delivering services to consumers.
2. **Organizational structure.** In human service organizations, tasks, responsibilities, and authority are divided among various workers. Most organizations have what is called a chain of command which defines who will give orders and make decisions in each area of work activity and who will carry out the orders and decisions.
3. **Organization personnel.** This, of course, refers to the people who occupy the positions established within the organization, from the director of the organization to a clerk. Since the core activities of any human service organization center on people working with people, an organization's personnel are an important factor in assuring that goals are achieved in delivering services.
4. **Organization consumers.** Finally, there are the users or consumers of the organization's services, who are the reason for the organization's existence. The organization's policy, structure, and personnel are all based upon the knowledge of the consumers and a recognition of their needs.

Taken together, these four components combine to form a human service organization, and they must function together for the organization to operate effectively.

Turn to Frame 2

ANALYZING YOUR ORGANIZATION

You have just read a description of organization *policy, structure, personnel,* and *consumers.* Consider now how these characteristics of a human service organization apply to the organization in which you work or to the school in which you study by answering the questions in the next four frames.

(Frame 2 continued)

[1] See Harold W. Demone, Jr., and Dwight Harshbarger, *A Handbook of Human Service Organizations* (New York: Behavioral Publications, 1974); Yeheskel Hasenfeld and Richard A. English, eds., *Human Service Organizations* (University of Michigan Press, 1974); and Richard E. Boettcher, "The 'Service Delivery System' What Is It?" *Public Welfare* (Winter 1974), pp. 45–50.

Organizational policy. What are some of the goals of your agency? What is your agency trying to accomplish? Can you list four goals of your agency?

1.

2.

3.

4.

Your organization may have long-range as well as immediate goals. For example, a retardation agency may have an immediate goal of locating and providing help to retarded children in need of help who would otherwise be unassisted, and a long-range goal to help as many retarded persons as possible to become self-supporting and able to care for themselves in the community. Understanding your organization's goals will help you remember why you perform certain tasks and also help you determine how these tasks will affect the consumers and the community. Once you lose sight of the reasons for performing your tasks, they will simply become routine chores with little meaning to you or the consumer.

Now take one of the goals you listed and describe how that goal is accomplished. What program do you have in your agency to accomplish that goal? Whom does the program serve? What specific services can a consumer receive in that program?

Write in the goal:

Describe the program to accomplish that goal:

Remember: regulations that say who can or cannot be served by a given program and what services can or cannot be provided are all part of agency policy that you must observe in delivering services to consumers.

Go on now to Frame 3

FRAME 3

Organization structure. What is the "chain of command" in your agency? How are decisions made about who does what work in the agency? Do all staff members share in the decision-making process? To what extent do you have a say in determining your own work assignments? In the space below, describe a specific work assignment you have been given. Tell how the decision was made that you would be responsible for that assignment, the extent to which you shared in making that decision, and how communication went up and down the chain of command relative to that assignment.

It is important to understand the chain of command in your agency since through it work is defined and decisions are made as to who does what in the agency. Obviously, at higher levels in the chain of command a greater degree of administrative discretion exists in deciding what is to be done and how it will be accomplished than at lower levels in the organization. However, even at lower levels some discretion exists in how any given work assignment will be accomplished. The better you understand the chain of command and the more you can participate in the decision-making process the greater your contribution can be to your agency and to your consumers. Perhaps there are two questions we should always ask when engaging in a work assignment: How will this contribute to the goals and objectives of the agency? How will this help serve the consumers of the agency?

Go on to Frame 4

FRAME 4

Organizational personnel. How many different kinds of workers work in your agency? What are their responsibilities? Do they serve different kinds of consumers? Can you list three different kinds of workers in your agency (e.g., nurses, social workers) and briefly describe what they do?

1.

2.

3.

In understanding how your agency functions, it is important to know what different kinds of personnel work in the agency and how they contribute to the goals and objectives of the agency. As we better understand the roles and responsibilities of our co-workers, we come to better understand the organization of which we are a part.

Go on to Frame 5

FRAME 5

Organization consumers. Who are the consumers you serve? What kind of problems do they bring to your agency? What kinds of services do you provide to them? In the space below list as many different kinds of consumers served by your agency as possible and the services provided to them by your agency.

(Frame 5 continued)

Remember that in a human service organization such as your own agency the very existence of the organization is for the consumer. In the rush of everyday work, particularly when we get bogged down in meetings and paperwork, we lose sight of the fact that our job in the agency is to serve our consumers.

Go on to Frame 6

FRAME 6

You have just completed an exercise designed to help you better understand the organization in which you work.

As you go about the daily routine of work, it is important to remember that there are additional characteristics which further explain how organizations work. The organization functions to control the efforts of many people and to maintain a balance in dividing responsibility and authority. This is called *coordination*. The organization also seeks to control and channel a formal system for exchanging information. This is called *communication*. The organization makes rules to govern the behavior of its workers so that guidelines always exist for carrying on the business of the organization over time. This is called *continuity*. And finally, the organization sets certain requirements regarding the training and skills of its many workers so that there is a standard of quality for delivering services. This is called *competence*. All these things play a part in guiding the organization toward the successful accomplishment of its goals.

Turn to Frame 7

FRAME 7

In the previous section you learned about the characteristics of a human service organization. Now you may be asking yourself, how does a human service organization differ from any other organization? It is true that the characteristics you just studied would also apply to different kinds of organizations such as banks and large industrial firms; however, there are some basic differences. Three important differences in terms of resource base, output, and beneficiaries are noted by Demone and Harshbarger as follows:[2]

INDUSTRIAL ORGANIZATION	HUMAN SERVICE ORGANIZATION
RESOURCE BASE	
Financing for the organization is usually obtained from private sources, either individuals or corporations, and the stability of the organization is greatly affected by economic trends in the country.	Financing for the organization is usually obtained from public sources (tax monies) and the stability of the organization is not directly related to the economy in general.
OUTPUT	
The output or product of the organization is clearly defined, for example, automobiles, production, marketing. The cost of producing the product can always be easily compared to the selling cost, and the profit easily measured. The overall purpose of the organization is set by a small group of individuals, such as a board of directors, and changes are made	The output or product of the organization is not clearly defined, for example, improving the quality of life for people. The cost of producing the product is hard to determine, and the effectiveness of delivering the product is even harder to determine. Profit is very hard to determine since it lies in benefits to the consumer instead of profits to the owners.

[2] Adapted from Harold W. Demone, Jr. and Dwight Harshbarger, *A Handbook of Human Service Organizations*, New York: Behavioral Publications, pp. 26–29.

in the organization to increase profits or to survive.

The overall purpose of the organization is set by a large group of people, for example, legislators, and changes are made in the public interest.

BENEFICIARIES

The primary beneficiaries are the owners who profit financially, and the secondary beneficiaries are the staff and clients of the organization.

The primary beneficiaries are the service consumers of the organization, and the secondary beneficiaries are the staff and general public.

Turn to Frame 8

FRAME 8

You have just learned about the differences between a human service organization and an industrial organization. Based on that discussion, please think about the following questions. Write your answers to the questions and/or discuss them with your fellow students, workers, etc.

1. **Resource base.** How is your agency financed? What portion of the funds are federal, state, and local? As a public employee, what responsibilities do you think you might have that would be different from those of someone working for a private industrial organization?

2. **Output.** What product is your agency trying to produce? Who determined that this would be the right product? What are some of the ways you can determine if your product is helping consumers? How do changes come about in your organization?

(Frame 8 continued)

3. Beneficiaries. Who are the primary beneficiaries of your agencies? How do they benefit? How do you as a worker benefit?

Turn to Frame 9

FRAME 9

THE TROUBLE WITH ORGANIZATIONS[3]

Some of the resources of human service organizations are utilized in meeting consumer needs while other organizational resources simply serve to keep the organization going. Sometimes these two needs can work against each other and result in a conflict, which is soon felt by the workers and even the consumers of the organization. For example, some human service organizations are known to place more emphasis on procedures, methods, and record-keeping activities (which help maintain the organizations) as opposed to emphasizing the services and needs of consumers (which are represented as goals of the organization). In these cases, it is important to understand that these organizations are not purposely withholding services from consumers; rather, they structure themselves so that it becomes difficult to change and conflicts soon develop.

As a worker in a human service organization you need to recognize that there will be conflicts and tensions in your organization. For example, at times you may discover that rules are emphasized to such an extent that the purposes for which the rules were formulated have been forgotten. Or you may find that your desires for promotion, status, and security do not agree with those of the organization. Whether the organizational conflicts relate to consumers, to you, or to both, it is important that you not become too frustrated. On the other hand, you should also realize that sometimes rules in the organization that don't seem to make good sense to you do serve a purpose. For example, rules related to working hours, punctuality, etc., may carry a personal implication to you that the organization does not trust your behavior. However, within a large organization which employs hundreds of workers, enforcement of such rules is often necessary if the organization is to maintain control of itself and function efficiently. Remember that these problems exist to some degree in all organizations. Solving problems requires that you stay in the organization and engage in the ongoing but difficult process of seeking necessary changes in your agency.

It is always well to keep in mind that all organizations must spend part of their resources simply to keep the organization going. When an organization loses sight of its goals and objectives, it is in trouble. It is also well to remember that

[3] Bernard Gelfand, *The Window: Toward an Understanding of Human Need* (Toronto, Ontario: Training and Staff Development Branch, Ministry of Community and Social Services, undated), pp. 82–83.

rules and regulations are the laws by which organizations live. They are necessary if the organization is to maintain control of itself. When the organization becomes overly rigid, both the consumer and the worker suffer. As a member of a human service organization, it is your responsibility to abide by the rules of the organization, but it is *also* your responsibility to offer constructive criticism and to help the organization change when change is needed so that its goals and objectives can be accomplished and its consumers better served.

Turn to Frame 10

FRAME 10

Given some of the problems that naturally occur in organizations, answer the following questions from your perspective as a worker attempting to serve both the agency in which you work and the consumer.

1. What kinds of activities do you engage in that don't appear to be directed at meeting consumer needs? Can you think of ways in which these activities could help meet consumer needs?

2. What kinds of rules and regulations exist in your agency that personally frustrate you or your career goals? What do you think you, as a worker, could do to change unfair rules and regulations?

Continue to Frame 11

FRAME 11

In this lesson you looked at the characteristics of human service organizations and attempted to gain a better understanding of the agency in which you work. You examined the importance of understanding agency policy structure, personnel, and consumers. You saw how an agency strives to provide coordination, continuity, communication, and competence within its boundaries. You also gained an understanding of the resources, output, and beneficiaries of human service organizations. Finally, you looked at some of the problems you encounter within organizations. The approach you take to the problems experienced in your work will depend largely upon your values, which are the focus of the next lesson on the human service worker.

**You have now completed
Lesson 1. Go on to Lesson 2**

LESSON 2:
THE WORKER

Knowing about yourself is an extremely important part of delivering human services. While we recognize that the process of learning about your true feelings, biases, and values is a life-long activity, the delivery of human service requires all of us to spend time sorting out our feelings and reactions to the problems presented by consumers as well as to the problems presented by our agencies. Working with people who suffer from such problems as poverty, mental illness, or abuse requires all of us who really care about the needs of others to develop increasingly deeper understanding of ourselves. In addition, we all must find ways to recharge our batteries, which can often be drained by the physical and emotional needs of our consumers. Working with human problems on a daily basis also requires a clear understanding of the values we hold. These values are tested constantly by our awareness of the sometimes oppressive conditions experienced by our consumers. Knowledge of your feelings, attitudes, and values contributes to what we call your work identity, which is the primary focus of this chapter.

GOAL

You will begin the process of establishing a work identity that will successfully combine a technical knowledge of your own strengths and weaknesses with the ability to develop effective working relationships.

ENABLING ACTIVITIES

After completing this lesson, you will have done the following:

1. Reviewed some of the concrete steps you can take to begin the process of understanding yourself
2. Examined some of the factors which influence what people believe
3. Evaluated how well you understand your work and how you feel about your work

4. Recognized the process which results in *valuing* something
5. Examined five values which are basic to human service work
6. Considered how you can begin to integrate knowledge of your personal capabilities with knowledge of your work capabilities.

**Go to Frame 1
to begin this lesson**

FRAME 1

Human service work requires the establishment of relationships with other people—consumers, fellow workers, and people in the community. In dealing with people, the human service worker faces the challenging task of defining effective ways of working with others. However, it takes more than technical knowledge and skills to accomplish this. It takes an understanding of oneself. How does a worker establish an identity which successfully combines his technical knowledge with his self-knowledge? What should a human service worker be like? These questions lead to the consideration of several important issues facing any human service worker.

DEVELOPING SELF-UNDERSTANDING

In order to develop effective working relationships, it is essential for workers to possess an awareness of themselves and of the ways in which they use themselves in their relationships with others. The key to beginning this process of self-understanding is accepting and recognizing the fact that what you are will affect what you can do. Workers who understand themselves are more likely to develop a clear identity as a human service worker, which is very important in developing meaningful and productive relationships with others.

Before reviewing some concrete steps you can take to begin this process, make sure you understand what you are striving for. Self-understanding means more than simply collecting a lot of information about yourself. Just the word *understanding* itself signifies perceiving, comprehending, and knowing. Therefore, understanding yourself involves getting in touch with your feelings, attitudes, values, goals, beliefs, and ways of behaving—and this is usually a lifelong process.

How can you begin? To help you understand yourself, you can begin by trying to answer some very basic questions.[1]

1. How do I think and feel about myself?
2. How do I deal with my own fundamental needs?
3. What is my value system, and how does it define my behavior and my relationship with others?
4. How do I relate to the society in which I live and work?
5. What is my life style?
6. How do I feel and what do I believe about my work, about the consumers I work with, and about other workers I come in contact with?

Go on to Frame 2

FRAME 2

The eight questions you may ask yourself to begin the process of self-understanding are listed below. Take a few minutes to think carefully about each of these questions as they relate to you, and check one answer for each question.

(Frame 2 continued)

[1] Naomi I. Brill, *Working with People: The Helping Process* (New York: Lippincott, 1973), p. 4.

	YES	SOMETIMES	No
1. Do I have a positive view of myself? Am I OK?	—	—	—
2. Do I recognize my own needs to be respected, loved, involved, left alone, etc., and do I deal with them successfully?	—	—	—
3. Do I clearly understand how my values affect my relationships with others? For example, I think all people are basically good (value), and I give everyone a chance.	—	—	—
4. Am I involved in my community, talking with neighbors, joining clubs, going to parades, etc.?	—	—	—
5. Do I clearly understand my life style as evidenced, for example, by a fancy car, lots of clothes, few records, a modest home, etc.?	—	—	—
6. Do I like to work with people in need, such as consumers?	—	—	—
7. Do I like to work with other workers?	—	—	—
8. Do I believe that work is important? Does my work have meaning to me?	—	—	—

The rest of this lesson will provide you with some suggestions for answering these questions, in addition to discussing some related issues that are important to the human service worker.

Proceed to Frame 3

FRAME 3

WHAT PEOPLE BELIEVE

Most of the questions you just answered related to examining what you believe and how you think and behave. Since many things affect what people believe and think and how they behave, it might be helpful to consider some of the factors that have an influence on what anyone believes.

A person's *family background* for example, will affect what that person believes. If a man has been brought up in a poor, hard-working family, he might feel that getting ahead depends on a good education. On the other hand, if a person has grown up in a family which owns and operates a small but successful restaurant, this person might believe that going to college or even finishing high school is a waste of time. Such a person might believe that hard physical work and long hours in one's own business are the key to success. You can see that these two people would have very different beliefs about education, and you can see how they have been influenced by their family backgrounds.

Go on to Frame 4

FRAME 4

Can you identify any of your own beliefs which have been influenced by your family background? Read each of the following questions and check one answer for each question.

1. Do you believe that hard work will always
   be rewarded?   __ Yes   __ No

   Who helped you come to this belief?   __ father __ mother __ grand-

   parents __ aunt/uncle

   __ other (who?) _____

2. Do you believe that gaining more formal
   education is the only way to advance?   ___ Yes   ___ No

   Who helped you come to this belief?   ___ father ___ mother ___ grand-

   parents ___ aunt/uncle

   ___ other (who?) _____

These questions represent only a sample of the issues with which you need to deal if you are going to clearly understand your beliefs.

Go on to Frame 5

FRAME 5

A second influence upon a person's beliefs stems from the expectations of the groups to which the person belongs. These *group expectations* are manifested in the common groups to which people belong, such as church groups, club groups, and work groups. Church groups are a good example of how groups affect what people believe. People from religious groups sometimes have a difficult time discussing their beliefs with those outside their group because different church groups often have very different ideas about what to believe and how to behave. The groups people join will have an effect on what they believe.

The *life experiences* of a person will also influence personal beliefs. For example, if an older person has been in a nursing home for some time where no one has paid much attention to him, it might be difficult for a worker to establish a relationship with this person. The older person's experiences over a period of time have led him to believe that no one really cares about him.

A fourth influence on what a person believes comes from his *feelings about human nature*. Some people believe that others are basically bad and that they can therefore be expected to behave in the most unacceptable way possible. Other people believe that human beings are basically good but that they sometimes make mistakes. The way a person treats other people may be related to how he feels about human nature, whether he thinks people are basically good or basically bad.

Turn to Frame 6

FRAME 6

Now that you have clarified some thoughts about influences on the way you think and believe, let's try a brief exercise that will carry you one step further in getting at *who you are*.[2] Answer the following ten questions in terms of most of your own experiences and responses to people. Check one response for each question.

	YES	SOMETIMES	NO
1. Do you feel you are an open person?	___	___	___
2. Would you prefer that people do not know too much about you?	___	___	___
3. Do you feel free to tell people about yourself?	___	___	___
4. Would you get upset if someone told something about you that you preferred they did not know?	___	___	___
5. Do you like people to ask you questions about yourself?	___	___	___
6. Do you feel exposed when people seem to know too much about you?	___	___	___

(Frame 6 continued)

[2] Exercise from Eveline D. Schulman, *Intervention in Human Services* (St. Louis: Mosby, 1974), p. 9.

7. Have other people told you that you are frank?   —   —   —

8. Would you like people to know you better?   —   —   —
9. Would you feel comfortable writing or talking about your
   life experiences?   —   —   —
10. Do you feel people are prying if they ask you questions
   about yourself?   —   —   —

**When you have finished,
turn to Answer 1**

FRAME 7

FOUR QUESTIONS CONCERNING
EFFECTIVE HUMAN SERVICE WORK

Workers who understand themselves and can also understand others without losing sight of the agency's purpose are likely to be effective. In addition to understanding yourself, it is important to consider how you feel about your work. There are four questions to examine in rating yourself as a human service worker.

1. Do you understand the purpose of your position in your agency?
2. How do you feel about the consumers of your agency's services?
3. Do you mind using yourself to help others?
4. Is your approach to your work people oriented or things oriented?

Understanding the *purpose of your position* has to do with knowing how you fit into the organization which employs you. Your *feelings about consumers* are related directly to your willingness to help people in trouble. *Using yourself* depends on your ability to enter into relationships on the job, not as a friend, but as an interested and concerned employee of an organization which exists to provide services to people in need. Finally, whether you are people or things oriented will determine your willingness to deal actively with people day in and day out. The worker who would rather write reports or become a research scientist or carpenter has an approach which is things oriented rather than people oriented and might be happier in a job with less human contact. Orientation to people and things will be discussed in more detail in the next lesson, where the nature of human service work is more fully described.

Go on to Frame 8

FRAME 8

VALUING

Human service workers are continually faced with work situations which call for thought, opinion, decision, and action.[3] In almost all these situations, every action a worker takes is consciously or unconsciously based on his beliefs, attitudes, and values. One important aspect of understanding yourself is knowing your value system and how it relates to the value system of the human service professions. Values are based on beliefs, preferences, or assumptions about what is desirable or good for man.[4] Thus, values are not statements of fact but statements of how

[3] Sidney B. Simon, Leland W. Howe, and Howard Kirschenbaum, *Values Clarification: A Handbook of Practical Strategies for Teachers and Students* (New York: Hart Publishing Company, Inc., 1972), p. 13.
[4] Allen Pincus and Anne Minahan, *Social Work Practice: Model and Method* (Itasca, Ill.: F. E. Peacock Publishers, Inc., 1973), p. 38.

it *should* be. Since values grow from a person's experiences, different experiences will result in different values. These values will change as a person gains more experience and adapts to change.[5]

Values are frequently confused with goals, feelings, interests, and beliefs. In order to clarify the meaning of a value and to assist you in defining your own values, three tests are suggested for determining whether something is a value. In describing or defining a value, three requirements must be met.

1. **Choosing.** If something is a value, it must be a result of free choice. A value results when you choose from different things, after carefully considering what each means.
2. **Prizing.** When you value something you are happy with it. You prize it and respect it and are proud of it. You will share your choice with others. If you are ashamed of a choice, or would not make your position known when asked, then you don't really have a value.
3. **Acting.** Finally, when you have a value you will do something about it— it will affect your life. It will reappear on a number of occasions and will tend to become a pattern in your life.[6]

Proceed to Frame 9

FRAME 9

Values are based on a process of choosing, prizing, and acting. If you doubt whether something is a value, ask yourself whether it is (1) prized, (2) freely and thoughtfully chosen from alternatives, and (3) acted upon, repeated, and shared with others. If it is, then it is a value.

Below is a list of 16 values. Your task is to arrange them in order of their importance to you as guiding principles in your life. Study the list carefully. Then place a 1 next to the value which is most important for you; place a 2 next to the value which is second most important, etc. The value which is least important, relative to the others, should be ranked 16.

___ a comfortable life (a prosperous life)

___ equality (brotherhood, equal opportunity for all)

___ an exciting life (a stimulating, active life)

___ family security (taking care of loved ones)

___ freedom (independence, free choice)

___ happiness (contentedness)

___ inner harmony (freedom from inner conflict)

___ mature love (sexual and spiritual intimacy)

___ national security (protection from attack)

___ pleasure (an enjoyable, leisurely life)

___ self-respect (self-esteem)

___ a sense of accomplishment (making a lasting contribution)

(Frame 9 continued)

[5] Louis E. Raths, Merrill Harmin, and Sidney B. Simon, *Values and Teaching: Working with Values in the Classroom* (Columbus, Ohio: Merrill, 1966), p. 27.
[6] Ibid., p. 28.

___ social recognition (respect, admiration)

___ true friendship (close companionship)

___ wisdom (a mature understanding of life)

___ a world of beauty (beauty of nature and the arts)[7]

Turn to Answer 2

FRAME 10

Commonly Held Values of the Human Service Professions

We have discussed how beliefs are formed and the process of how values are formed. As human service workers, we all need to hold some values in common in order to work together effectively. Professions and work groups tend to establish certain values and standards of behavior which affect the ways in which workers interact with others in carrying out their work activities. If you choose to work in the human services and are people oriented, you need to be aware of some of the values held by work groups to understand your responsibilities in dealing with people.

The following are the most commonly held values in the human services:

1. **Acceptance.** Acceptance is maintaining an attitude of warm good will toward the consumer, whether or not his way of behaving is socially acceptable and whether or not it is to your personal liking.[8] Acceptance is not an opinion about a person or how he lives; it is the expression of good will toward the person irrespective of his circumstances. When you are able to accept the consumer as he is and where he is, you will be demonstrating acceptance.

2. **Tolerance.** Being tolerant is the ability of a worker to avoid making evaluations of good and bad. It is very similar to the value of acceptance. For example, when a consumer is in detention or prison or asks for help from a welfare agency, plans must be made to help the consumer to function more productively. It does no good to continue society's punishing attitude toward past undesirable behavior. A worker who helps a consumer plan for his future, rather than judging and punishing him for his past, will be acting upon the value of tolerance.

3. **Individuality.** The third value of human service work is individuality, which involves recognizing each person as being different in his own way from all others. Individuality refers to the uniqueness of each person's life style, feelings, facial expressions, problems, etc.[9]

4. **Self-determination.** Self-determination involves letting the consumer make up his own mind. For example, a person who is eligible for old age assistance from the state and who could use the money, might, nevertheless, turn it down. This is really his decision to make, regardless of what you might do if you were in his situation. Remember, however, that it is not possible for all service consumers to have total freedom in making their choices. An inmate, for example, may choose his vocational training, what he eats, and his

---

[7] Sidney B. Simon, Leland W. Howe, and Howard Kirschenbaum, *Values Classification: A Handbook of Practical Strategies for Teachers and Students* (New York: Hart Publishing Company, Inc., 1972), p. 112.

[8] Florence Hollis, *Casework: A Psychosocial Therapy* (New York: Random House, 1964), p. 14.

[9] Alan Keith-Lucas, *Giving and Taking Help* (University of North Carolina Press, 1972), p. 13.

recreation, but he may not be allowed to choose to go home for a weekend. Thus, self-determination is the consumer's right to determine his own course of action from the opportunities and limitations presented, even if it means failure.

5. **Confidentiality.** Have you ever been tempted to talk or joke about a consumer with your friend or fellow workers? Most workers have done this at one time or another, but this conflicts with the value of confidentiality. Confidentiality is your guarantee to the consumer that his personal situation will not be discussed in public. It also ensures the consumer that he will not be the subject of social conversation or gossip. However, this does not mean that information about a consumer's case cannot be shared, such as in case conferences with other workers and a supervisor, where the objective is to help the consumer.

Go on to Frame 11

FRAME 11

The five values that are basic to work in the human services are acceptance, tolerance, individuality, self-determination, and confidentiality. To check yourself on how well you understand these five values, you might try the following quiz before completing this lesson. Write in the value that is operative in each of the following descriptions. (Each value is used only once.)

_____	1. A worker assigned to a ward for the criminally insane seeks to understand each individual patient's situation.
_____	2. A worker believes that a consumer should change his approach to his family but gives the consumer the freedom to make his own mistakes.
_____	3. A worker who would like to tell a friend about a funny incident concerning a consumer decides to keep it to himself.
_____	4. A worker who outwardly believes that anyone who does not have enough sense to stay out of trouble is really bad or inadequate is denying what value?
_____	5. A worker is friendly, warm, and kind to a consumer who is physically unattractive and has no friends.

Turn to Answer 3

FRAME 12

INTEGRATING THE PERSONAL SELF WITH THE WORK SELF

Now that you are familiar with some of the values of the human service professions, it is important for you to spend some time trying to define your own value system in relation to the human service values. Remember that it is very easy to pay lip service to these values, but it is another thing to act upon them in your daily work. Also recall the three requirements for a value. For each human service value ask yourself whether it is (1) prized, (2) freely and thoughtfully chosen from alternatives, (3) acted upon, repeated, and publicly known. In addition, you might consider the following as suggestions for integrating your personal self with your work self:

1. Be aware that you are a living system of values. This system is so much a part of you that you are, more often than not, scarcely aware of its existence.

(Frame 12 continued)

2. Use all means possible to become conscious of what your values are. For example, consider how you may use the word *they*: *they* don't support their families; *they* always wear bright colors and yell too loud; *they* can never be helped to change. A worker who becomes aware of doing this has taken the first step toward understanding his or her value system and seeing how it conflicts with the human service values.
3. Strive to evaluate yourself and your values objectively and rationally. Look at their origins and the purpose they serve, and try to think about whether they will also serve this purpose for others.
4. Finally, strive to change those values that, on the basis of your evaluation, need changing so that you may use yourself more effectively in helping others.[10]

At the beginning of this lesson we stated that human service work involves establishing relationships with other people. These relationships are formed for a purpose and are based on your ability to step outside of your own personal feelings and needs and be sensitive to the needs of others.[11] In order to accomplish this, you need to establish the kind of work identity we have been discussing in this lesson. Basically this work identity involves skill in translating and integrating your own values, knowledge, and skills into your daily work behavior. Once you know who you are, how others perceive you, and are willing to accept yourself, you will be able to make effective use of yourself in relationships with others.

Proceed to Frame 13

FRAME 13

The simplest way of summarizing this lesson is to say that effective human service workers know themselves and are also aware of the opinions of others. If you don't know who you are, you will find it very difficult to influence and help others.

It should now be apparent that personal values along with values and ethics related to working with consumers will affect your reaction to changes in your agency. For example, strong feelings about the confidential nature of consumer information may be met by equally strong administrative pressures to put all relevant consumer information into a computer for planning purposes. Will your values lead you to safeguard confidential consumer information?

Before you start the next lesson, return to Frame 2 and see if you have anything to add to your answers. You might also consider discussing these questions and your answers with other students or workers to further your understanding of yourself and your work identity.

[10] Adapted from Naomi I. Brill, *Working with People: The Helping Process* (New York: Lippincott, 1973), p. 14.
[11] Allen Pincus and Anne Minahan, *Social Work Practice: Model and Method,* (Itasca, Ill.: F. E. Peacock Publishers, Inc., 1973), pp. 69–70.

ANSWERS TO LESSON 2

ANSWER 1

Look back over your answers and see if you can detect a trend. For example, do you see yourself as a helping person? Do others see you that way? Do people, rather than things, catch your attention? Are you comfortable with yourself? Do you share yourself with others to develop closer relationships?

Turn to Frame 7 for more information on these questions.

ANSWER 2

You selected the correct answer. Or did you? If your choices represent values, there is no right or wrong answer. Review your ranking. It should give you new insights into your current set of values. We emphasize *current* since future experiences may change your selection.

Turn to Frame 10.

ANSWER 3

Your answers should be as follows:

1. individuality
2. self-determination
3. confidentiality
4. tolerance
5. acceptance

If you missed any of these, return to Frame 10. If you correctly identified all five human values, congratulations! Now turn to Frame 12.

LESSON 3:
THE WORK

In addition to understanding your work setting and developing a positive work identity, it is also necessary to have a clear understanding of the work itself, or the things that workers do in the human services. Although human service work is carried out in a variety of settings with a wide range of people, it is important to recognize that there is a common foundation of knowledge, attitudes, and skills which defines the nature of all human service work. To assist in the development of your understanding of the nature and meaning of human service work, this lesson defines what human service workers do to achieve the purposes and goals of their organizations. The goal of this lesson and the enabling activities that will help you reach this goal are presented below.

GOAL

Your aim will be to develop an understanding of the nature and meaning of human service work.

ENABLING ACTIVITIES

After completing this lesson, you will have done the following things:

1. Reviewed some of the reasons why work is important in our society
2. Identified some of the worker needs which jobs fulfill
3. Examined the nature and meaning of work
4. Identified the nature and meaning of human service work
5. Recognized some of the major roles and activities involved in human service work

**Turn to Frame 1
to begin this lesson**

THE FUNCTIONS OF WORK

When most people are asked the question "Why do you work?" their first response is usually "to earn a living." However, earning money for the purchase of goods and services is only one of the functions of work. To appreciate fully the meaning of work in our society, let's examine some of the other functions which are accomplished by working.[1]

1. Work regulates activities. The pattern of work activity during the day, the week, and the month affects not only the activities of the worker while employed on the job but also his participation in nonwork activities. In addition, the patterns of activity of the worker's family are also affected. For example, the family life of a worker on the night shift in a prison is obviously affected in a different way from the family life of a worker on a regular eight to five shift.
2. Work provides the opportunity for relationships with others. The personal relationships between a worker and others who occupy related positions in an organization will frequently continue into nonwork activities. Thus, a person's friends and companions off the job are frequently his associates at work.
3. Work provides identity. Work provides one of the main answers to the question "Who am I?" "I am a psychiatric aide," "I am a correctional guard," "I am a welfare worker," include some of the responses to this question. Of course other things go into making up a person's identity, but the work a person does is one of the chief ingredients.
4. Work provides a means of human development. Work contributes to human development by helping people express themselves and giving them the opportunity to learn and demonstrate new skills. Work also helps satisfy people's social and psychological needs and provides much of the content and meaning in life.

Continue with Frame 2

The Job: Satisfying or Disappointing?[2]

Jobs are positions in particular work places such as agencies, hospitals, or institutions. An important factor to consider in any job is whether you, as the worker, will find the job satisfying or disappointing. In other words, does your job really satisfy your needs? At least twelve needs can be satisfied by a person's job:

1. Economic security satisfies the need to be assured of a steady income and an adequate standard of living.
2. Recognition and approval satisfy the needs to have one's work activities known and approved by others.
3. Mastery and achievement satisfy the need to perform well according to one's own standards and abilities.

(Frame 2 continued)

[1] Adapted from Walter L. Slocum, *Occupational Careers: A Sociological Perspective* (Chicago: Aldine, 1966), pp. 19–21.
[2] Adapted from Robert L. Darcy and Phillip E. Powell, *Manpower and Economic Education: A Personal and Social Approach to Career Education* (Denver, Colo.: Love Publishing Company, 1973), pp. 30–35.

4. Dominance satisfies the need to have some power or influence and control over things and/or people.
5. Socioeconomic status satisfies the need to provide one's family with money and material goods that measure up to community standards.
6. Self-expression satisfies the need to have personal behavior consistent with one's self-concept.
7. Affection and interpersonal relationships satisfy the need to feel accepted by other people, to be liked and loved by others.
8. A moral values scheme satisfies the need to have one's behavior consistent with some moral code in order to feel good and worthy.
9. Dependence satisfies the need to be directed by others, to avoid feeling alone and totally responsible for one's own behavior.
10. Creativity and challenge satisfy the need to meet and attempt to solve new problems.
11. Social well-being satisfies the need to help others and to have one's efforts result in benefits to others.
12. Independence satisfies the need to direct one's own behavior rather than being completely controlled by others.

Obviously, any job has both positive and negative aspects. For example, in any one job, a worker may experience friendship, a sense of accomplishment, pleasure, frustration, nervous strain, and boredom. The key to a general feeling of job satisfaction is the extent to which the job adequately meets the individual's needs. When a worker is generally satisfied with his job, he will be able to manage both the positive and the negative aspects of daily work situations.

Go on to Frame 3

FRAME 3

We have just discussed 12 of the needs that may be met in various jobs. Return to these 12 needs in Frame 2 and circle those which seem to be most important to your own job satisfaction. You may find it helpful to discuss your choices with your fellow students, workers, etc.

**When you have completed this
exercise, continue to Frame 4**

FRAME 4

Underline the correct response in the statements below:

1. When correctional guards exert influence by preventing inmates from breaking a prison regulation, they fulfill their own need for (dependence/dominance).
2. When social workers feel satisfied after helping a client with a family problem they are fulfilling the need for (social well-being/economic security).
3. When a new employee successfully completes a training program, the needs of (creativity and challenge/affection and happiness) are fulfilled.

Turn to Answer 1

FRAME 5

The Nature and Meaning of Work

Work is an activity that produces something of value for other people. It may involve physical activity, such as typing, driving, and cooking, or mental activity, such as reading, thinking, and listening.[3] However, an activity must always have a specified purpose if it is to be considered work. Consequently, a housewife caring for her children is working because she is being productive for her family and she has a specified purpose in raising her children a certain way. Writing a report regarding a particular consumer represents productive work for both the consumer and the organization and also has a particular purpose related to services for the consumer. Performing voluntary tasks in a hospital represents productive work for the community and the hospital residents and has the purpose of assisting the hospital staff and residents. Therefore, paid or not, voluntary or required, hard or easy, work is always an effort with a specific purpose which produces something of value for other people.

What are the components of work activity? What are you actually doing when you are working? In performing the activities that are part of their jobs, workers act in relation to three primary components of work activity—data, people, and things.[4] No matter where a person works or what he actually does, any job, at some time will involve the worker with information and ideas (data), with other workers and consumers (people), and with machines, equipment, or supplies (things). Obviously there are an infinite number of combinations of data, people, and things in any given job, but all are necessary components of work activity in any organization.

Go on to Frame 6

FRAME 6

We have said that the three components of work activity are data, people, and things. In the blank beside each of the statements below, write in the name of the work component being described.

_____ A. This work component involves the worker with other workers and consumers.

_____ B. This work component involves the worker with information and ideas.

_____ C. This work component involves the worker with machines and equipment.

Turn to Answer 2

FRAME 7

THE NATURE AND MEANING OF HUMAN SERVICE WORK

Human service work focuses on the interactions between people and the systems in their environment in an effort to help them solve their problems.[5] Human service work involves a vast range of activities related to data, people and things, which are performed to produce something of value for others. Since human service work requires constant interactions with people, it is important to recognize that it requires more mental and emotional involvement than many other kinds of work. Thus, human service work usually involves problem solving with consumers and

(Frame 7 continued)

---

[3] Report of a special task force to the Secretary of Health, Education, and Welfare, *Work in America* (Cambridge, Mass.: MIT Press, 1973), p. 3.

[4] Sidney A. Fine and Wretha W. Wiley, *An Introduction to Functional Job Analysis: A Scaling of Selected Tasks from the Social Welfare Field* (Kalamazoo, Mich.: W. E. Upjohn Institute for Employment Research, 1971).

[5] Allen Pincus and Anne Minahan, *Social Work Practice: Model and Method* (Itasca, Ill.: F. E. Peacock Publishers, Inc., 1973), p. 3.

fulfilling basic human needs. A great deal of effort is required in planning the strategies to resolve the problems.

You will recall that one of the major characteristics of any work activity is that there is a specified purpose. In understanding the nature and meaning of human service work, it is useful to consider its general purpose. All the activities performed by human service workers are designed, according to Pincus and Minahan, to achieve one or more of the following purposes:[6]

1. To provide material resources: Many activities in the human services are performed in order to provide people with the resources and services they need in order to survive. Tasks related to providing financial assistance, food, homemaker services, and foster home placements are all examples of activities performed to provide people with necessary material resources needed to survive.

2. To connect people with the systems that provide them with resources, services, and opportunities: One of the major purposes of human service work is connecting people with the services they need. To accomplish this purpose, human service workers engage in activities related to finding people who need services, connecting them with the appropriate resources, and making sure that the services are received.

3. To help people use their problem-solving and coping capacities more effectively: Everyone has difficulty at times in coping with the problems and frustrations of daily living, but some people find it so difficult that they develop inappropriate behaviors. Therefore, activities related to talking with, understanding, and supporting people, in addition to helping them develop plans to solve their problems are performed to achieve this purpose.

4. To serve as a resource for social control: Some human service systems have been granted the authority and have the purpose of serving as agents of social control for people whose behavior violates the laws or who are physically or mentally unable to care for themselves. Activities related to enforcing rules and regulations in providing services and maintaining security and control in settings such as prisons and mental hospitals are performed for the purpose of social control.

These four purposes of human service work are not separate from one another in practice but are related to all human service jobs. In performing your daily activities, you should be able to recognize the purpose(s) guiding each situation you are confronted with.

Turn to Frame 8

FRAME 8

All the activities of human service work are performed to achieve a specific purpose, Although each worker may have a very specific purpose in mind for a given task, there are at least four general purposes of all human service work.

1. To provide material resources
2. To connect people with the systems that provide them with resources, services, and opportunities
3. To help people use their problem-solving and coping capacities more effectively
4. To serve as a resource for social control

[6] Ibid., pp. 9–33.

Now beside each of the following statements, write the number of the purpose being accomplished.

___ A. A prison officer places an inmate in custody

___ B. A human service worker provides a woman with food stamps

___ C. A psychiatric aide discusses a patient's personal problems with him

___ D. A case worker visits a welfare recipient to explain about a new child care program

Turn to Answer 3

FRAME 9

Nine Major Roles Performed in Delivering Human Services

In order to accomplish the four general purposes of human service work, the human service worker must be competent in a range of skills related to these purposes. One useful way of organizing the skills needed to deliver human services is to look at the various roles or activities workers perform to accomplish a specific purpose. Nine major roles can be differentiated in human service work.[7] You will be given the opportunity of developing a beginning competency in all nine of these roles in the remaining chapters of this text; however, at this point it will be helpful for you to first learn what they are and how they are performed in human service systems.

The first three roles relate to the skills and activities needed to get services to people in need. These roles include: brokering, consumer advocating, and mobilizing, and are further described below:

1. **Brokering:** Brokering involves the actual physical connection between the individual(s) with a problem and the services which are needed to resolve or reduce the problem. It includes assessing the situation to identify the problem, knowing the various community resources available, preparing the individual for a positive contact with the resources available, and making sure the individual gets there and is served. Brokering also involves actively reaching out into the community to locate people with problems. It is more than providing information and making referrals.

2. **Consumer advocating.** The primary focus of consumer advocating is pleading and fighting for services for an individual whom the service system would otherwise reject. The consumer advocate literally stands in the place of the individual to bring about a change on the part of the rejecting organization in favor of the individual involved.

3. **Mobilizing.** Mobilizing involves community work directed towards bringing the people of a community together to effect changes for the better in that community. It also includes activities related to identifying specific unmet community needs and developing new facilities, resources, and programs needed to relieve these needs. It is sometimes called community organizing.

Proceed to Frame 10

---

[7] The nine roles to be discussed are adapted from Robert J. Teare and Harold L. McPheeters, *Manpower Utilization in Social Welfare* (Atlanta: Southern Regional Education Board, 1970).

FRAME 10

Which of the following activities is/are involved in brokering? Place a check beside the correct answer:

___ A. Working with the people in a community to effect changes which will relieve unmet needs.

Turn to Answer 4

___ B. Fighting on behalf of a consumer for services he is entitled to.

Turn to Answer 5

___ C. Connecting individuals with the services which have the potential for assisting them with their problems.

Turn to Answer 6

FRAME 11

You will recall from an earlier section of this lesson that all work activity involves data, people, and things and is performed to accomplish a definite purpose. The following is a list of three tasks which might be performed in the roles of brokering, mobilizing, and consumer advocating. Beside each task, see if you can write in the role that is being performed.

_____ A. Worker contacts the appropriate resource for a consumer in order to make an appointment for the consumer and advise the resource of the consumer's referral.

_____ B. Worker reports unfair treatment of a consumer to the proper source in order to initiate a review of the action.

_____ C. Worker organizes a group of clients having a common unmet need in order to help them develop the means to resolve their problems.

Turn to Answer 7

FRAME 12

The fourth, fifth, and sixth roles of human service work relate to helping consumers function more effectively. The activities include counseling, rehabilitating, and consulting, and are further described as follows.

4. **Counseling.** Counseling activities relate to teaching, coaching, supporting, or advising consumers in short-term, problem-focused situations. Counseling is based on a helping relationship between the worker and the consumer, and it is expected that the result will be improved understanding and/or skills on the part of the consumer.

5. **Rehabilitating.** This involves those worker activities which are directed towards changing or modifying a consumer's behavior using very specialized, structure-setting treatment techniques. Rehabilitating activities may range from controlling or maintaining consumers in institutional settings to the use of very specialized treatment techniques such as behavior modification and reality therapy.

6. **Consulting.** Consulting involves working with other persons or agencies to help them increase their knowledge and skills and to provide assistance in

solving consumer-related problems. Activities range from those related to giving help to those related to receiving help with work problems.

Go to Frame 13

FRAME 13

Now let's take a look at some of the tasks which might be performed in the roles of counseling, rehabilitating, and consulting. This time, match the roles on the left with the tasks on the right.

1. Consulting

2. Counseling

3. Rehabilitating

___A. Worker reassures a consumer in a stressful situation in order to provide support.

___B. Worker discusses a case situation with a co-worker in order to determine ways of planning services needed in the case.

___C. Worker leads regular group session of residents using reality therapy as the treatment modality in order to modify individual behavior.

Turn to Answer 8

FRAME 14

The last three roles of human service work relate to managing work to provide effective and efficient services. This includes work with consumers and other workers in the roles of information collecting, information managing, and supervising.

7. **Information collecting.** Information collecting includes all kinds of data-gathering activities related to service consumers. It ranges from initial interviews through monitoring and follow-up activities to update consumer service plans.

8. **Information managing.** Workers have to organize and share the information collected in their daily work. Information managing includes those activities concerned with record keeping, preparing and delivering oral and written reports, and sharing information in case conferences and other kinds of meetings with fellow workers.

9. **Supervising.** Supervising is concerned with those activities involved in maintaining staff communication, using supervision, and giving supervision. These activities keep the organization operating efficiently by making sure the necessary work is completed.

Continue with Frame 15

FRAME 15

Underline the role being performed in each of the following tasks.

1. Worker inventories the services provided to consumers at the end of each week, using case records and standard reporting forms, in order to provide a record of services for the files and program accountability. (brokering/information managing)

2. Worker assigns cases to unit staff in order to manage incoming cases. (supervising/counseling)

3. Worker interviews applicant in order to determine eligibility for services and to open or open/close case. (rehabilitating/information collecting)

Turn to Answer 9

To summarize, the nine principal roles of human service work include brokering, consumer advocating, mobilizing, counseling, rehabilitating, consulting, information collecting, information managing, and supervising. The tasks related to these roles are assigned to various levels of workers in human service organizations, with the result that many workers are performing similar activities. However, even though workers at different levels of education and experience appear to perform similar kinds of activities, it is important to recognize that these activities differ in terms of the closeness of supervision required, the extent of responsibility and decision making, and the complexity of problems engaged in.[8]

Thus understanding the nature and meaning of human service work includes the ability of each worker to have a clear understanding of his or her job. By knowing the personal needs fulfilled by your job, what activities and skills are required, and what is accomplished by the many tasks you perform, you will be providing yourself with the basis of making your work in the human services something important and personally satisfying.

Go on to Frame 17

As a way of reviewing this lesson, see if you can give an example of a task you (or another worker) might perform in each of the nine major roles. Make sure you include what activity is performed and what might be accomplished by that activity.

**Continue to the review
of the nine roles**

Roles	Activity	What Is Accomplished?
1. Brokering		
2. Consumer advocating		
3. Mobilizing		
4. Counseling		
5. Rehabilitating		
6. Consulting		
7. Information collecting		
8. Information managing		
9. Supervising		

When you have completed this exercise, take a well-deserved break, because you have now completed Chapter II. Congratulations on a job well done!

[8] Evelin D. Schulman, *Intervention in Human Services* (St. Louis: Mosby, 1974), p. 5.

ANSWERS TO LESSON 3

ANSWER 1

You should have underlined the following responses:

1. dominance
2. social well-being
3. creativity and challenge

   Return to Frame 5 and keep up the good work!

ANSWER 2

The correct answers are

A. people
B. data
C. things

   We're sure you found this easy, so proceed to Frame 7.

ANSWER 3

The correct answers are

A. 4   C. 3
B. 1   D. 2

   Get them all right? Great. Continue to Frame 9.

ANSWER 4

Sorry, but you are confusing the roles of mobilizing and brokering. Return to Frame 9 for a review and then answer Frame 10 correctly.

ANSWER 5

No—this response describes the role of consumer advocating. Return to Frame 10 and choose the correct answer.

ANSWER 6

Exactly. Brokering involves connecting people with the services they need. Continue to Frame 11.

ANSWER 7

A. brokering
B. consumer advocating
C. mobilizing

Turn to Frame 12.

ANSWER 8

Your answers should look like this:

(counseling)   <u>2</u> A. Worker reassures a consumer in a stressful situation in order to provide support.

(consulting)   <u>1</u> B. Worker discusses a case situation with a co-worker in order to determine ways of planning services needed in the case.

(rehabilitating)   <u>3</u> C. Worker leads regular group session of residents using reality therapy as the treatment modality in order to modify individual behavior.

Continue to Frame 14.

ANSWER 9

The correct answers are as follows:

1. **Information managing:** Worker inventories the services provided to consumers at the end of each week, using case records and standard reporting forms in order to provide a record of services for the files and program accountability.
2. **Supervising:** Worker assigns cases to unit staff in order to manage incoming cases.
3. **Information collecting:** Worker interviews applicant in order to determine eligibility for services and to open and/or close the case.

Get them all correct? Great! Return to Frame 16.

SUMMARY

In this chapter, issues relating to the world of human service work were addressed. Special attention was given to the concept of the human service work organization and some of its characteristics. In addition, the basic differences between human service and other service organizations, in terms of resource base, output, and beneficiaries, were discussed. The conflicts between maintaining the organization and delivering services were also identified.

This chapter placed considerable emphasis on developing a work identity. It was suggested that understanding yourself and your beliefs, values, and work was important in beginning this process. Acceptance, tolerance, individuality, self-determination, and confidentiality were identified as some of the common values of the human service professions.

The chapter concluded with a discussion of human service work that emphasized what work is and the importance of having needs met adequately in a job. We also examined the nature and meaning of human service work by identifying the nine major roles involved in delivering human services: brokering, consumer advocating, mobilizing, counseling, rehabilitating, consulting, information collecting, information managing, and supervising.

SUGGESTIONS FOR FURTHER STUDY

Further study will be needed to understand fully the components and properties of human service organizations and how these relate to effective work behavior in an organization. Additional study will also be needed in the area of developing an effective work identity, particularly in the areas of self-understanding and knowledge of values. The expanding literature on values and the process through which they are acquired should prove to be useful. Finally, additional study would prove invaluable in the area of understanding the nature and meaning of human service work. Since the concept of human services is still relatively new, there are many aspects of this concept which remain for further study. These include additional skills necessary for effective human service work, how work affects job satisfaction, and additional components of work activity itself. Additional resources in these areas are listed in the bibliography.

SUGGESTIONS FOR FURTHER READING

American Management Association. *Supplemental Readings*. AMA Supervisory Management Course, Part 1. New York, 1968.

Anastasi, Thomas E., Jr. *Face-to-Face Communication*. Cambridge, Mass.: Management Center of Cambridge, 1967.

Boettcher, Richard E. "The 'Service Delivery System' What Is It?" *Public Welfare* (Winter 1974), pp. 45–50.

Brill, Naomi I. *Working with People: The Helping Process*. Philadelphia: Lippincott, 1973.

Danish, Steven J., and Hauer, Allen L. *Helping Skills: A Basic Training Program*. New York: Behavioral Publications, 1973.

Darcy, Robert L., and Powell, Phillip E., *Manpower and Economic Education: A Personal and Social Approach to Career Education*. Denver, Colo.: Love Publishing Company, 1973.

Day, Peter R. *Communication in Social Work*. Elmsford, N.Y.: Pergamon, 1972.

Demone, Harold W., Jr., and Harshbarger, Dwight. *A Handbook of Human Service Organizations*. New York: Behavioral Publications, 1974.

Dressler, David. *Sociology: The Study of Human Interaction*. New York: Knopf, 1969.

Dubin, Robert. *The World of Work*. Englewood Cliffs, N.J.: Prentice-Hall, 1958.

Etzioni, Amitai. *The Semiprofessions and Their Organization*. London: Collier-Macmillan, 1969.

Fast, Julius. *Body Language*. New York: Lippincott, 1970.

Fine, Sidney A., and Wiley, Wretha W., eds. *Introduction to Functional Job Analysis: A Scaling of Selected Tasks from the Social Welfare Field*. Kalamazoo, Mich., W. E. Upjohn Institute for Employment Research, 1971.

Gelfand, Bernard. *The Window: Toward an Understanding of Human Need*. Toronto, Ontario: Training and Staff Development Branch, Ministry of Community and Social Services, undated.

Hasenfeld, Yeheskel, and English, Richard A., eds. *Human Service Organizations*. University of Michigan Press, 1974.

Hollis, Florence. *Casework: A Psychosocial Therapy*. New York: Random House, 1964.

Keith-Lucas, Allen. *Giving and Taking Help*. University of North Carolina Press, 1972.

Nichols, Ralph G. *Are You Listening?* New York: McGraw-Hill, 1957.

Pincus, Allen, and Minahan, Anne. *Social Work Practice: Model and Method*. Itasca, Ill.: F. E. Peacock Publishers, Inc., 1973.

Raths, Louis E., Harmin, Merrill, and Simon, Sidney B. *Values and Teaching: Working with Values in the Classroom*. Columbus, Ohio: Merrill, 1966.

Schulman, Eveline D. *Intervention in Human Services*. St. Louis: Mosby, 1974.

Shatz, Eunice, et al. *New Careers: Generic Issues in the Human Services, a Sourcebook for Trainers*. Washington, D.C.: University Research Corp., 1968.

Simon, Sidney B., Howe, Leland W., and Kirschenbaum, Howard. *Values Clarification: A Handbook of Practical Strategies for Teachers and Students*. New York: Hart Publishing Company, Inc., 1972.

Slocum, Walter L. *Occupational Careers: A Sociological Perspective*. Chicago: Aldine, 1966.

Teare, Robert J., and McPheeters, Harold L. *Manpower Utilization in Social Welfare*. Social and Rehabilitation Services Grant. Atlanta: Southern Regional Education Board, 1970.

Weissman, Harold H. *Overcoming Mismanagement in the Human Service Professions*. San Francisco: Jossey-Bass, 1973.

Work in America. Report of a special task force to the Secretary of Health, Education and Welfare. Cambridge, Mass.: MIT Press, 1973.

REVIEW QUESTIONS—CHAPTER II

Circle the letter corresponding to the answer of your choice.

1. Two components of a human service organization are organization personnel and organization structure. What are the other two components?
    A. Organization policy and organization consumers
    B. Organization systems and organization procedures
    C. Organization manuals and organization services
    D. Organization location and organization programs

2. Developing an understanding of yourself in order to serve the consumer effectively requires a personal evaluation of
    A. your beliefs.
    B. your agency's rules.
    C. your behavior.
    D. all of the above.
    E. only A and C.

3. The beliefs held by human service workers are influenced by
    A. life experiences.
    B. family background.
    C. group expectations.
    D. all of the above.
    E. none of the above.

4. The key to a general feeling of job satisfaction is the extent to which the job adequately meets the worker's needs.
    A. True
    B. False

5. Output in a human service organization differs from output in an industrial organization by
    A. being much easier to identify.
    B. costing more to produce.
    C. being harder to define.
    D. being a product for sale.

6. The resource base in a human service organization is usually provided by
    A. wealthy individuals giving to charity.
    B. private corporations making investments.
    C. the profits of public corporations.
    D. public tax funds.

7. Effective human service work primarily requires an orientation to which of the following?
    A. Things
    B. People
    C. Processes
    D. Religion

8. The process of arriving at your own values involves
    A. acting.
    B. prizing.
    C. choosing
    D. none of the above.
    E. all of the above.

9. Organizations function to control the efforts of many people and to maintain a balance in dividing responsibility and authority. What is this called?
    A. Coordination
    B. Communication
    C. Continuity
    D. Competence

10. One problem that exists in any organization and often frustrates workers is
    A. the amount of paperwork necessary to keep the organization going.
    B. too much free time.
    C. the requirement that all of a worker's time must be spent with consumers.
    D. having no career service benefits.

11. Which of the following statements is *not* correct?
    A. Work is an activity that produces something of value for others.
    B. Work is an activity performed to accomplish a specific purpose.
    C. Work is primarily physical, seldom mental.
    D. Work is composed of data, people, and things.

12. Human service work is concerned with
    A. problem solving with consumers.
    B. system interaction in the environment.
    C. very few data-related tasks.
    D. fulfilling basic human needs.
    E. only A and D.

13. Human service values include which of the following?
    A. Individuality, acceptance, and confidentiality
    B. Tolerance, rejection, and self-determination
    C. Acceptance, tolerance, and avoidance
    D. Self-determination, individuality, and selfishness

14. Which roles relate to getting services to people in need?
    A. Counseling, rehabilitating, and consulting
    B. Brokering, consumer advocating, and mobilizing
    C. Supervising, interviewing, and recording
    D. Advising, coaching, and researching

15. Which of the following is *not* one of the purposes of human service work?
    A. To serve as a resource for social control
    B. To help people use their problem solving and coping capacities more effectively
    C. To connect people with the systems that provide them with resources, services, and opportunities
    D. To emphasize group relationships and behavior as opposed to individuals

**Now check your answers
with the Answer key
for this chapter
at the end of the book**

UNIT TWO:
GETTING SERVICES
TO PEOPLE IN NEED

INTRODUCTION

One of the major goals of human service work is getting services to the people who need them. In order to accomplish this goal, human service workers reach out to people who need services, give information about available services, connect people who have problems with appropriate community resources, and make sure that these services are received by the people who need them. This process is known as brokering. In cases where people are denied services to which (they are entitled, workers frequently find they must actively protect and defend the rights of consumers. This process is known as consumer advocating.

In making sure that services are delivered to people in need workers also discover many community problems or needs that are not being met by existing resources in the community. Thus human service workers are also engaged in activities that help the people in the community work together in developing new community services so these needs or problems can be handled. This process is known as mobilizing.

Since one of your primary goals as a human service worker is to get services to people in need, this unit helps you examine three human service work roles—brokering, consumer advocating, and mobilizing. When you refer a consumer to another agency and follow-up to see that appropriate services have been provided, you are engaging in the brokering role. If you find that a consumer has been denied a service or benefit to which he is entitled, such as public assistance or social security, the activities of negotiating for the consumer are part of the advocating role. When you find, for example, that no day-care services are available for a consumer, the activities which you complete to help develop a new day-care center are part of the mobilizing role. The goal of this unit is to assist you in developing your knowledge of these roles so you will be more effective in making sure that services are delivered to the people who need them.

**Turn to the next page to learn about
the first role performed in getting
services to people in need—brokering**

CHAPTER III:
BROKERING

INTRODUCTION

Because human service agencies have grown larger and more complex in the last few years, it has become increasingly difficult for people who are not familiar with the agencies to find and use the resources that will meet their needs. Most of you are probably familiar with people who are called real estate brokers and stock brokers, so you know that a broker is generally a person who brings his client together with another party and helps him or her find and purchase goods and services. Human service workers are also brokers because they help consumers find and use the resources they need.

When you are working in the human services, you have an obligation to try and help a person who comes to you with a problem. You have a similar obligation to find people in your community who need help and are entitled to receive your agency's service but are not aware that they can get assistance with their problems. As a broker, you can think of yourself as the "person in the middle." You will be guiding, advising, and actively helping people to get the services they need. You will also be making sure that consumers do not get lost in the shuffle or give up their efforts to get help.

If you are working in a community setting, you are probably familiar with the activity of brokering. For example, if you work in a welfare agency, you probably spend a lot of your time giving consumers information and referring them to other sources for help. However, if you are working in an institutional setting ·such as a prison or a mental hospital, brokering may be a new activity to you. Just keep in mind that even though consumers who are in institutions are there for help with certain problems, they will also face some new problems living in the institution. In institutional settings, you will be looking for new problems and trying to find ways to give consumers the information and services they need.

In this chapter you will be learning about some of the basic skills you need in brokering. In Lesson 1 you will learn how to get to know the resource systems in your community. In Lesson 2 you will be introduced to some guiding principles underlying two of the main activities in brokering—giving information and referring. In Lesson 3 you will examine some techniques used in reaching out into a community to identify people who need help with their problems. The overall objective of this chapter is to assist you in learning how the role of brokering is performed to get services to people in need.

**Turn to the next page
to begin Lesson 1**

LESSON 1:
IDENTIFYING COMMUNITY RESOURCE SYSTEMS

Considerable knowledge of the resources in your community is necessary if your brokering activities are to be successful and helpful. In this lesson you will learn about the various resource systems found in most communities. The goal of this lesson and the enabling activities that will help you reach this goal are presented below.

GOAL

Given a description of a community, you will be able to identify and describe components of the various resource systems available.

ENABLING ACTIVITIES

After completing this lesson, you will have done four things:

1. Reviewed the definition of resource systems
2. Identified three kinds of resource systems and studied examples of each system
3. Considered the inadequacies of each resource system
4. Reviewed three ways of identifying and describing resources

Turn to Frame 1

FRAME 1

WHAT IS A RESOURCE SYSTEM?[1]

You will recall from Chapter 1 that an understanding of service and consumer systems is basic to effective human service work. In discussing resource systems,

(Frame 1 continued)

[1] The concepts and discussions in Frames 1 through 9 are adapted from Allen Pincus and Anne Minhan, *Social Work Practice: Model and Method* (Itasca, Ill.: F. E. Peacock Publishers, Inc., 1973), pp. 3–9.

your knowledge of systems is already proving valuable since the resource system is based on the same concepts as service and consumer systems. In fact, service systems are one of the components of resource systems.

During the early days of American society, the family was the primary system which provided people with the necessary resources to cope with their needs and problems. However, as our society grew and became increasingly complex, people became more dependent on other resource systems for assistance. Today a resource system includes services and opportunities along with the material, emotional, and spiritual resources available for help in the community. In almost all communities, this help is available from three kinds of resource systems: informal or natural resource systems, formal or membership resources systems, and societal resource systems.

Informal (Natural) Resource Systems

The first major resource system available in all communities is the informal or natural resource system. This system consists of family, friends, neighbors, co-workers, and other helpers who serve as informal sources of help in meeting needs and solving problems. The aid given through these informal relationships includes emotional support, affection, advice, and information, as well as concrete services such as baby-sitting, help in filling out forms, and assistance in locating appropriate resources.

Since today's resource systems have moved far beyond the functions originally fulfilled by the family, they have also become increasingly complex and difficult to negotiate. Relying on the informal resource system may not bring about the required assistance for several reasons:

1. A person may not have an informal helping system. For example, a person may be new to a community and not have any friends.
2. A person may be hesitant to turn to friends, relatives or neighbors for help.
3. Even if people do turn to an informal helping system, it may be unable to meet their needs. This is frequently the case in extraordinary or crisis situations, where informal helping systems may lack the resources necessary to help.

Continue to Frame 2

FRAME 2

You will recall that existing resource systems are not always able to provide the necessary resources, services, and opportunities. Can you list at least two reasons why informal resource systems may not provide the help people need?

Turn to Answer 1

FRAME 3

Formal (Membership) Resource Systems

The second major resource system is the formal resource system, which includes membership organizations and formal associations that exist to promote the mutual benefits and common interests of their members. These systems may sup-

(Frame 3 continued)

ply resources directly to members or help them negotiate with various societal systems. For example, a social club may provide recreational activities for its members in addition to helping them buy food cooperatively at a reduced rate. When formal resource organizations negotiate with societal systems, both the organization members and other people who need help may benefit. Examples of formal resource systems include labor unions, welfare rights groups, Boy/Girl Scouts, neighborhood associations, social clubs, youth clubs, better business bureaus, the American Medical Association, the National Association of Social Workers, and the National Association for Retarded Persons.

There are a variety of factors that may prevent people from receiving the necessary help from formal resource systems, including the following:

1. In some communities, such groups may not exist. There may not be a welfare rights group to help recipients in receiving adequate services from the welfare department or to inform consumers of their rights.
2. People may be reluctant to join a membership organization or association for a variety of reasons. For example, they may fail to see how it can help them or they may be unacceptable to the other members.
3. People may be unaware of the existence of a formal resource system.
4. Existing organizations may not have the necessary resources to provide services or negotiate with societal systems for members.

Turn to Frame 4

FRAME 4

Return to Frame 3 and select three inadequacies of formal resource systems. Then see if you can identify a situation illustrating each inadequacy. If you can't think of any examples, this might be a useful topic to discuss with other workers or your fellow students.

**When you have completed this
exercise, turn to Frame 5**

FRAME 5

Societal Resource Systems

The third major resource system is the societal resource system, which has been established through social legislation and voluntary citizen action to deliver services. Most people are linked to several of these systems, which include, for example, hospitals, adoption agencies, schools, day-care centers, libraries, welfare departments, social security programs, family services agencies (Lutheran, Catholic, Jewish, public, etc.), and Easter Seal centers. Some of these systems provide services through public or tax supported agencies, while others provide services through the private or voluntary agency.

Societal resource systems are the most complex of the three resource systems and are probably the most difficult to negotiate. As a result, people often encounter problems in receiving help from these systems. Some of the inadequacies of societal resource systems are the following:

1. The needed resources may not exist or may not exist in sufficient quantity to provide adequate services for all who need them.
2. The needed resource or service may not be geographically, psychologically, or culturally available to those who need it. For example, a Chicano migrant family may be hesitant to ask for help from an agency with white middle-class workers who only speak English.

(Frame 5 continued)

3. The needed resource may exist but people may not know about it or how to use it.
4. When a person is linked to more than one resource system, the systems may work at cross-purposes and trap the person in a sea of conflicting demands and messages.
5. The policies of the various societal resource systems may create new problems for people. For example, some of the requirements of being a consumer of a resource system which reduces welfare payments as soon as a consumer finds employment may create new problems such as insufficient child care resources in the family, leading to dependency on a day-care agency.

Continue to Frame 6

FRAME 6

Check the correct response about the nature of societal resource systems.

___ A. They may provide services through public and private agencies.

Turn to Answer 2

___ B. They have been established through public activities and voluntary citizen action.

Turn to Answer 3

___ C. They include family services agencies, private employment agencies, and health departments.

Turn to Answer 4

___ D. All of the above are correct.

Turn to Answer 5

FRAME 7

Now return to Frame 5 and in the section listing the inadequacies of societal resource systems, see if you can give an example of a situation illustrating each inadequacy. Also see if you can think of any additional inadequacies of societal resource systems which are not listed.

**When you have completed this
task, continue with Frame 8**

FRAME 8

In the space below, try to give examples of each of the three resource systems present in your community.

INFORMAL RESOURCES	FORMAL RESOURCES	SOCIETAL RESOURCES
1.	1.	1.
2.	2.	2.
3.	3.	3.
4.	4.	4.

Turn to Answer 6

FRAME 9

Marc S. lives in the city of Big Bend and works for the state division of mental retardation. Marc is trying to identify and classify some of the resources that are available in Big Bend, and has come up with the following list of ten community resources. How would you classify these resources? Place a check (✔) in the correct column after each resource.

(Frame 9 continued)

	INFORMAL RESOURCE SYSTEM	FORMAL RESOURCE SYSTEM	SOCIETAL RESOURCE SYSTEM
1. City of Big Bend Welfare Department	—	—	—
2. Big Bend Red Cross	—	—	—
3. A Girl Scout troop interested in volunteer work with the retarded	—	—	—
4. Federal Social Security office	—	—	—
5. A private agency that tests the retarded	—	—	—
6. A Salvation Army center	—	—	—
7. A privately owned day-care center	—	—	—
8. Relatives of retarded clients	—	—	—
9. Special classes for the retarded offered by the public schools of Big Bend	—	—	—
10. Neighbors of parents of retarded children	—	—	—

Turn to Answer 7

FRAME 10

IDENTIFYING COMMUNITY RESOURCES

How can you find out about the resources in your community? Whether you live or work in a large community or a small community, it is difficult not only for consumers, but also for workers to have a full knowledge of all the available resources. The following are some of the ways you can begin to identify and describe the resources in your community:[2]

1. **Consulting city, neighborhood, or agency directories.** Many cities have a directory published by an association to which many human service resources belong (e.g., a welfare council or a council of social agencies). In addition, some neighborhoods have guides to agencies serving neighborhood residents, and organizations such as the chamber of commerce usually publish guides that list the resources available within a community. Your agency will probably have developed some guides to resources available within the community.

2. **Developing your own resource file of community resources.** Beyond consulting directories that list available resources, you can develop a resource file of your own that is related to the common needs of consumers. In developing your own resource file, you need to know more than the fact that the resource exists. You need to know, for example, the special functions of the resource, what kinds of services are offered, and to whom they are offered. The following is a checklist of some of the important information you should collect about each resource:

    a. Name, address, phone number of resource
    b. Hours when resource can be contacted and when services are provided
    c. Types of problems handled or services offered
    d. Eligibility, including important facts about special groups served

    (Frame 10 continued)

[2] Adapted from Gertrude S. Goldberg et al., *New Careers: The Social Service Aide: A Manual for Trainees* (Washington, D.C.: University Research Corporation, 1968); and Janet Rosenberg, *Breakfast: Two Jars of Paste* (Cleveland: Case Western Reserve University Press, 1972).

3. **Visiting various resources.** Talking with workers, finding out what they are doing and how your consumers can use any of the services that are offered are other ways to find out about a community and its resources. Getting to know some of the people who live and work in a community, talking with community leaders, clergymen, volunteers who are working in various agencies, relatives of consumers, and workers in your own and other agencies are good ways to gain an understanding of each resource and what it has to offer to meet the needs of consumers.

Turn to Frame 11

FRAME 11

Alice has recently moved to the city of Flatlands, and has started working as a houseparent in a community halfway house for delinquent boys. She soon discovers that some of the boys are in need of clothes and blankets. She also finds that the boys have a lot of free time on their hands and would like to help them get part-time jobs in the community. But Alice is new to this community and has only recently started working for this agency. Can you identify two things she might do to get to know her community and the resources it contains?

1.
2.

Turn to Answer 8

ANSWERS TO LESSON 1

ANSWER 1

In your list of inadequacies of informal resource systems you may have included these: (1) a person may not have an informal helping system, (2) a person may be hesitant to turn to his informal resource system for help, and (3) the informal system may be unable to provide the necessary resources.

You might also have listed specific examples of these inadequacies or even thought of some inadequacies we did not mention.

Proceed to Frame 3.

ANSWER 2

This is partially correct. There are other correct responses in Frame 6, so return there now and select a more complete answer.

ANSWER 3

Although this statement is correct, there are also other correct statements in Frame 6. Return there now and select a better response.

ANSWER 4

True, but unfortunately not the best answer here. Return to Frame 6 and select the complete answer.

ANSWER 5

Right on! All these items reflect societal resource systems. Continue with Frame 7 and keep up the good work.

ANSWER 6

For informal resources, you should have listed such resources as family, friends, neighbors, bartenders, and co-workers.

For formal resources, you should have listed such resources as the PTA, Boy/Girl Scouts, welfare rights organizations, NAACP, and the American Medical Association.

For societal resources, you should have listed such resources as day-care centers, schools, police agencies, social security programs, and health departments.

Proceed to Frame 9.

ANSWER 7

Your answers should look like this:

	INFORMAL RESOURCE SYSTEM	FORMAL RESOURCE SYSTEM	SOCIETAL RESOURCE SYSTEM
1. City of Big Bend Welfare Department	—	—	✓
2. Big Bend Red Cross	—	—	✓
3. Girl Scout troop interested in volunteer work with the retarded	—	✓	
4. Federal Social Security office	—	—	✓
5. A private agency that tests the retarded	—	—	✓
6. A Salvation Army center	—	—	✓
7. A privately owned day-care center	—	—	✓
8. Relatives of retarded clients	✓	—	—
9. Special classes for the retarded offered by the public schools of Big Bend	—	—	✓
10. Neighbors of parents of retarded children	✓	—	—

If you did not classify all these resources correctly, you need to review Frames 1 through 8 before you go on. If you classified them all correctly, you are doing an excellent job.

Go on to Frame 10.

ANSWER 8

In order to get to know her community and the resources that are available, Alice could (1) try consulting any directories that the city of Flatlands or its chamber of commerce may have published that would list some of the resources available in Flatlands; or (2) Alice could start developing her own resource file by talking to other workers in her agency and by talking with different residents of Flatlands to find out some of the human service and non-service resources that are available. (3) Alice might also try visiting some of the other agencies in the community and get to know some of the workers in these agencies.

You have completed Lesson 1. Continue to Lesson 2 and keep up the good work.

LESSON 2:
GIVING INFORMATION
AND REFERRING

People who are not familiar with human service agencies often discover that they have a difficult time finding and using the resources that will meet their needs. Brokering is the activity in which you identify the service needs of individuals, see that they have the information they need, and see that their unmet needs are met through the provision of an appropriate community resource. In this lesson you will be learning about two of the primary activities in brokering: giving information and referring. The goal of this lesson and the enabling activities that will help you reach this goal are presented below.

GOAL

Given a description of an individual with an unmet need, you will be able to (1) identify the necessary information the individual needs to receive assistance, and (2) explain the steps you would follow in referring the individual to an appropriate resource.

ENABLING ACTIVITIES

After completing this lesson, you will have accomplished the following:

1. Recognized the process of determining an individual's unmet need
2. Identified the skills needed to understand a problem situation faced by a consumer
3. Recognized the process of preparing individuals to receive help with their unmet needs
4. Considered three questions that need to be answered before initiating a referral
5. Identified the ingredients of the process of referring an individual to another resource
6. Examined at least four ways of assisting consumers when they are having trouble getting help from another resource

Turn to Frame 1

FRAME 1

IDENTIFYING AN INDIVIDUAL'S UNMET NEEDS

How do you find out about an individual's problem or unmet need? What do you need to know about this unmet need? Several points must be considered when an individual comes to you for help with a problem or a need that is not being met.

1. Find out as much as possible about the exact need. In finding out what the exact need is, you should consider how the person came to your attention, why he is asking for help now, and how he identifies his need. While you are finding out about the specific need you should also get enough facts about the person, such as age and marital status, so you will be able to understand the nature of the problem. You will use this information later to determine the individual's eligibility for resources and services.

2. Find out what the person wants to do about the need or problem. Once you and the individual both think you understand the unmet need, you should find out how the individual feels about this need. You also have to know what, if anything, has already been done to meet this need. You should find out what the individual wants *you* to do about the need as well as what *he* wants to do.

3. Begin to determine who can handle this request best. Once you know what the need is, what the person wants to do about it, and what he expects from you, you can begin to determine whether or not your agency has the resources that will meet this need. If you find out that your agency can be of help, you can explain the services of your agency very simply and, if possible, answer questions the individual asks. If your agency does not have the necessary resources, you must begin to think about other resources that are available for help.

Go on to Frame 2

FRAME 2

An inmate in a prison has just received a letter from his family telling him that they have been threatened by their landlord with eviction. What should you do first?

1. Try to get more information on the exact need.

Turn to Answer 1

2. Find out what the inmate wanted to do about this need.

Turn to Answer 2

3. Refer the inmate to your supervisor for help.

Turn to Answer 3

FRAME 3

You have just visited Connie, a retarded citizen who lives in a community halfway house. You have both agreed that she needs to find a job and you have obtained all the background information you need on Connie and the kind of job she is looking for. What is your next step?

(Frame 3 continued)

1. Get more information on Connie's exact need.

Turn to Answer 4

2. Find out what Connie wants to do about her need.

Turn to Answer 5

3. Begin to determine who might help with this request.

Turn to Answer 6

FRAME 4

Skills Used in Identifying Unmet Individual Needs[1]

When you are trying to identify an unmet need there are some basic skills you should try to develop. Identifying an unmet need may be a simple matter because consumers often know what they need and you can help them find the appropriate resource. However, there will also be situations where it is difficult to identify the unmet need. For example, a consumer may only be able to state part of the problem or may ask for help with something other than the real problem or even avoid discussing the real problem altogether. No matter how involved or difficult the situation, there are certain skills that can be employed in identifying an unmet need, including the following:

1. Give the information the individual requests either at once or gradually, as indicated.
2. Listen, wait, and relax as needed, and above all, be yourself.
3. Emphasize the present situation and secure only the essential information from the person.
4. Try to recognize early the kind of person you are working with and continue to be sensitive to him and his needs.
5. Take hold of and use information as the person shows the interest and capacity to use help.
6. Do not pursue the deeper emotional or psychological problems that may appear, and avoid long, drawn out discussions.

Proceed to Frame 5

FRAME 5

Read the following passage and then answer the question below.

> Mr. Lane came into the office to get the addresses of some foster homes for his mother, and he seemed to be very hesitant and nervous. Kim, the worker, gave him the information he requested and listened carefully to his questions. Accepting him as deeply concerned, she gave him time to offer more and more examples of his mother's extreme behavior. He became more confident—and then suggested that his mother did not need a foster home. Kim agreed. They discussed this further, and Kim explained the services her agency could offer. Then they decided that Mr. Lane should seek the advice of a psychiatrist. Mr. Lane left, relieved that he had taken the first step in admitting something which he had been ashamed of.[2]

In the above situation, Kim was faced with a consumer who was asking for help with something other than his real problem. But Kim was able to lead Mr. Lane

(Frame 5 continued)

---

[1] Janet Rosenberg, *Breakfast: Two Jars of Paste* (Cleveland: Case Western Reserve University Press, 1972), p. 79.
[2] Ibid. Adapted from a case description.

toward recognizing the real problem or unmet need by using the skills you learned about in Frame 4. Check which skill or skills Kim used.

___ 1. Explain the function and purpose of your agency as it relates to the individual's request.

___ 2. Give the information the individual requests either at once or gradually, as indicated.

___ 3. Listen, wait, and relax as needed.

___ 4. Emphasize the present situation and secure only the essential information from the person.

___ 5. Try to recognize early the kind of person you are dealing with and continue to be sensitive to him and his needs.

___ 6. Take hold of and use information as the person shows the interest and capacity to use help.

___ 7. Do not pursue deeper problems that may appear, and avoid long, drawn out discussions.

___ 8. Kim used all of these skills.

Turn to Answer 7

FRAME 6

REFERRING

Sometimes the solution to an individual's unmet need simply involves giving information about a resource such as the address of another agency. Frequently, however, the situation will not be so clear cut and you will need to do more than provide an address and a phone number. When an individual's unmet physical, emotional, or social needs require services from another agency, you may need to make a referral. The process of *referring* is more than simply sending a person to a resource. You need to be actively involved in helping the person to find and use the resource and in staying in touch with the person to make sure that the appropriate service has been received.

In addition to identifying an individual's unmet need and deciding who can best handle this need, it is also necessary to find out if the individual is ready to accept help. Some people will be able to accept the assistance you are offering and will also be able to take the steps necessary to receive help. More often, however, people who have unmet needs will be fearful and confused and will need your assistance in understanding why they need help and what the help will do for them. There are three ways you can prepare an individual to receive help:

1. **Talking.** Discuss the individual's feelings toward getting help. Should you discover that the individual is afraid, feels guilty, or is acting hostile, you should make it possible to talk about these feelings. For example, you might say, "Let's talk about the pros and cons of this plan" or "Do you have some idea what this is going to be like?" Do not always assume that individuals have these feelings, but when they do, make it possible for them to talk.

2. **Sharing responsibility.** Involve individuals in planning how they will find and use the resource they need. You can assist individuals to see the need for getting help by working *with them* in contacting the resource (whether

it is someone in your agency or another resource). Will you make the phone call to the agency for them? Will you go with them? Do they know how to get there? Do they need to rehearse or practice what they need to do?

3. **Explaining the resources that are available for help.** Sometimes individuals will be afraid to use another resource because they do not know or understand how this resource can help them. Using your knowledge of your community's resource systems, you should explain the functions of these resources as accurately as you can. However, in doing this, it is usually *not* a good idea to discuss the details of how other agencies operate or how the individual will be treated there, because you can not always be certain this information will be accurate and up to date. By being direct, sincere, and realistic, you will be able to help the individual understand the resource and how it might assist him.

Remember that people might be hesitant to accept help from another source for many reasons. For example, the resource may be far away from where they live or it may seem large and impersonal. You should recognize when a person is not ready to accept help from another resource and use your brokering skills in preparing consumers to accept and use the help they may need.

Go on to Frame 7

FRAME 7

Fill in the blanks with the correct word to show what actions can prepare an individual to receive help.

1. _____ with the individual about his feelings toward getting help.

2. _____ the individual in planning how he will find and use the resources he needs.

3. _____ the resources that are available for help.

Turn to Answer 8

FRAME 8

Read the following passage and then answer the question below.

Jason is 19 years old and has just moved to Middle City. He dropped out of high school when he was 15, and has never worked before. Jason has located a place to live, but is now looking for a job and is not having much luck. He comes to the welfare agency and meets Seth, an intake worker. Jason reacts angrily to Seth's suggestions that he see another worker about the possibility of enrolling in a youth employment program.

Jason is not yet prepared to receive assistance with his unmet need. Can you suggest at least two ways in which Seth might prepare Jason to accept and use the help he needs?

1.

2.

Turn to Answer 9

Before initiating a referral, there are three questions you need to answer: *when*, *how*, and *where* will you refer?[3] Let's look at each of these questions so you will understand how the referral process works.

When to refer. A referral is necessary when you have identified an individual's unmet need and discovered that meeting this need requires social, health, educational, or some other community service. Thus, meeting this need may require the services of your own agency and/or another community resource. You can determine if a consumer has certain needs by (1) meeting the consumer who comes and tells about the problem, (2) observing the consumer's circumstances, or (3) locating consumers in your community with unmet needs. Referrals are made after you have identified an individual's unmet need and have decided that meeting this need will require directing the person to some community resource. In addition, you have already made certain that the individual is prepared to receive help.

How to refer. Referring consumers to a resource is not just a simple matter of telling them where that resource is located. The more important steps involved in referring are as follows:[4]

1. *Discuss* thoroughly with consumers the purpose of the referral. Let them know how and why you think this resource will be helpful.
2. *Contact* the resource to which you are making the referral. Discuss with them the important aspects of this consumer's unmet need, let them know what is expected or desired, and let them know what you have told the consumer about the resource.
3. When the referral is accepted, get an *appointment time* from the resource and give this information to the consumer or help the consumer in making the appointment.
4. Make sure consumers know the appointment time, where the resource is located, and the name of the person to see when they arrive. Offer any *support* that is needed to help the consumer keep the appointment and get the needed service.

Go on to Frame 10

Read the following passage, then answer the question below.

> George M. is 68 years old and has been in a state prison for the past twenty years. It has been determined that George is now ready to be released. But in talking with George, you discover that he has no relatives, no means of support other than Social Security, and no place to live when he is released. He makes it very clear that he does not wish to go into a boarding home. He would like to live by himself and find some way of meeting older citizens in his community.

How would you help George? Number the actions you would take in the correct sequence. Put a number 1 in front of the action you would take first, a number 2 in front of the second action you would take, etc. The first action you should take is already marked for you.

(Frame 10 continued)

[3] See Bernard Gelfand, *The Window: Toward an Understanding of Human Need* (Toronto, Ontario: Training and Staff Development Branch, Ministry of Community and Social Services, undated).

[4] Ibid., and also see Elizabeth Nicholds, A *Primer of Social Casework* (New York: Columbia University Press, 1960).

—— Get an appointment for George with some of the resources that can help him and make sure George has this information.

—— Spend time helping George to keep his appointments, possibly escorting him for his first visits.

1
— Talk with George directly about his situation, explaining the resources you might refer him to for assistance.

—— Contact the resources you and George have agreed might offer him assistance with his needs.

Turn to Answer 10

FRAME 11

Where to refer. Where you will refer a consumer depends on the resources that are available in your community and your own ability to discover undeveloped or unused community resources. You have already examined some of the ways to identify the resource systems in your community (Lesson 1). However, you will frequently discover that even your active efforts to meet a consumer's unmet need will not result in locating a service to fill this need. This is because there are gaps in service in most communities.[5] Gaps in service can occur because the needed services do not exist and also because of the ways various resources limit their services by setting very specific definitions of who will be served and how they will be served. The following case illustrates how this specialization creates gaps in services:

> Two boys, 10 and 11, are bedridden and paralyzed with muscular dsytrophy. Prognosis is death within five years. Previous aid through the Crippled Children Commission has been terminated upon diagnosis, owing to the poor prognosis and the unavailability of hospital care for purely custodial cases. After full investigation by welfare, educational, judicial, and private agency personnel, no aid was given. At last contact, the mother was caring for these boys together with her other children, in a house with no plumbing, and with no help other than that supplied by an occasional visit from a physical therapist and a volunteer neighbor who read to the boys one afternoon a week. The judge of the juvenile court reported that the marriage of the parents appeared to be in jeopardy, as a result of long physical and mental strain. Reasons given by various agencies for not extending aid were:
>
> 1. Juvenile court: no neglect or other basis for jurisdiction.
> 2. Health department: no local health department.
> 3. Welfare and relief authorities (state and county): father is employed and thus ineligible for financial assistance; suggest foster care through special educational services.
> 4. Crippled Children Commission: statute interpreted not to authorize home care.
> 5. Local school: insufficient personnel to furnish home tutoring.
> 6. State department of public instruction, special services division: locality not eligible for state-furnished special services.
> 7. Michigan Society for Crippled Children and Adults, Inc.: public agencies could help if they saw fit; private agency should not invade public agency field.[6]

(Frame 11 continued)

[5] Bernard Gelfand, *The Window: Toward an Understanding of Human Need* (Toronto, Ontario: Training and Staff Development Branch, Ministry of Community and Social Services, undated).

[6] Harold Wilensky and Charles Lebeaux, *Industrial Society and Social Welfare* (New York: Free Press, 1965), pp. 250–251.

You can see from this example that referring a consumer to a resource will not always be a simple procedure. However, since many resources are highly specialized, gaps in services are a common occurrence in many communities. The important thing to remember is *not to give up!* When you discover a service gap in trying to meet an individual's unmet need, there are at least two initial steps to take in trying to fill this gap: (1) you can *actively explore* your community for specific services and goods and (2) you can *analyze your community* to determine whether its set of resources might be interested in providing an individual service. (For example, the Lions Club or other social clubs may have an interest in providing help to a consumer.)

You will be learning more about service gaps in your community and how to fill these gaps in Chapter V, which deals with the role of mobilizing. Before you continue, stop for a minute and see if you can think of a consumer you have known who had an unmet need that could not be filled. Then see if you can think of any ways you might now try to meet that consumer's need.

**After performing this
task, go on to Frame 12**

FRAME 12

The Importance of Follow-up in Brokering

Don't forget a consumer after you have referred him to another resource! The problem of getting what one wants from a public welfare agency, a health department, an employment service, or a mental health center is no simple matter. Increasingly, if people are to get help from these resources, they need an informed guide who can help them to get what they need. Since consumers may find it difficult to get what they need, even after you have prepared them for help and have gone with them, you need to keep in touch with them to find out if they need your assistance and if the referral has been successful. If consumers need your assistance, there are several ways you can be of help:

1. **Actively representing the consumer.** When delays are unreasonable, you may have to telephone on behalf of the consumer to speed up the process. If you call a number of times and still cannot get any action, you may need to call someone with more authority to help speed up the process.
2. **Discussing problems.** Did the consumer behave in such a way that the application for assistance was refused? If so, then this needs to be discussed, asking, for example, "How did it happen?" and "What do you want from this resource?" Any problems that have occurred should be discussed with the consumer.
3. **Preparing the consumer.** Make sure the consumer was adequately prepared for the referral, and if he or she was not, find out why and then help the person try again.
4. **Straighten out difficulties.** Did the consumer have trouble filling out forms? Was there difficulty in meeting all of the eligibility requirements for the service? Is there another more appropriate resource? You need to try and straighten out such difficulties either by communicating directly with the resource or by going to your own supervisor and asking for help.

When you are dealing with other resources on behalf of a consumer, remember to be very clear about what is needed. Try to be courteous and pleasant. Do not lose control of your own emotions, but act on behalf of consumers to help them get the services they need.

Proceed to Frame 13

Eric, who is a patient in a mental hospital, has been complaining of chest pains. You have referred him to the nurse for medical attention and possible Xrays. A few days later you contact Eric to find out the results of his visit. He tells you that the nurse was very busy and was not able to set up an appointment with the doctor. Eric did not know what to do, so he has given up.

If you were the worker in this situation, what would you do?

Turn to Answer 11

ANSWERS TO LESSON 2

ANSWER 1

Exactly! The first thing you would need to do would be to find out more information about this need. Where does the inmate's family live? Why are they being threatened with eviction? What do they hope the inmate can do to help them?

Continue to Frame 3.

ANSWER 2

It is important to find out what the inmate wants to do about this need, but there is another step you ought to take first. You may want to review Frame 1 quickly before you try Frame 2 again.

ANSWER 3

This is incorrect. While you might eventually decide to send the inmate to your supervisor for assistance, you should first have a better understanding of what the inmate's exact need is. Return to Frame 2 and try it again.

ANSWER 4

No, you have already identified that Connie needs a job and you have gotten all the background information you need to help Connie get a job. You have also discussed this with Connie and she has expressed her desire to get a job. So what is your next step in helping Connie to meet this need? Return to Frame 3 and see if you can answer it correctly.

ANSWER 5

No, Connie has already talked with you and informed you of her desire to get some kind of job in the community. Return to Frame 3 and see if you can choose your next step in helping Connie meet her need.

ANSWER 6

That's correct! Your next step in assisting Connie is to begin to determine who might be most helpful with this kind of need in your community.

You are doing very well. Go right on to Frame 4.

ANSWER 7

You should have answered by checking number 8. Kim was able to lead Mr. Lane toward recognizing his real problem by using all the basic skills that are needed when you are identifying unmet individual needs.

Proceed to Frame 6.

ANSWER 8

Three ways of preparing an individual to receive help are (1) talking with the individual about his feelings toward getting help; (2) involving the individual in planning how he will find and use the resource he needs, and (3) explaining the resources that are available for help.

Proceed to Frame 8.

ANSWER 9

Some of the ways in which Seth might prepare Jason to accept and use the help he needs are (1) talking with Jason about his feelings toward getting a job and seeking help from the Welfare Department; (2) involving Jason in planning how he might find and use a resource that can help him and possibly rehearsing with Jason ways of approaching a resource for help; and (3) describing the types of resources which are available to assist him in locating a job.

Turn to Frame 9.

ANSWER 10

In proper order, the best ways to help George are as follows:

_3_ Get an appointment for George with some of the resources that can help and make sure George has this information.

_4_ Spend time helping George keep his appointments, possibly escorting him for his first visits.

_1_ Talk with George about his situation, explaining the resources you might refer him to for assistance.

_2_ Contact the resources you and George have agreed might offer him assistance with his needs.

If you had any trouble with this task, return to Frame 9 for a review. If you answered correctly, go right on to Frame 11.

ANSWER 11

Your follow-up with Eric has shown you that he needs your assistance in getting medical attention. Some of the ways you might help Eric get this service are (1) telephoning or going to see the nurse in charge and trying to enlist her support in getting an appointment as soon as possible; (2) discussing the situation with Eric to see if he behaved in such a way that his request was refused; (3) finding out whether you had adequately prepared Eric for this referral—that is, whether he knew what to do and how to get the appointment; and (4) going to your supervisor and asking for assistance in the matter. In addition to these actions, you can probably think of a number of other ways to help Eric.

**You have now completed
Lesson 2. Go on to Lesson 3.**

LESSON 3:
REACHING OUT
TO INDIVIDUALS
IN YOUR COMMUNITY

In all communities there are people with unmet needs who do not know there are resources to meet these needs. There are also people with unmet needs who know there are available resources, but for various reasons, they do not contact the resources that can help them. In this lesson you will be learning what is meant by reaching out into your community to identify and help people with unmet needs. The goal of this lesson and the enabling activities that will help you reach this goal are presented below.

GOAL

Given a community or a description of a community, you will be able to demonstrate your brokering skills by explaining the techniques you would use to reach out to identify and assist individuals with unmet needs.

ENABLING ACTIVITIES

After completing this lesson, you will have done as follows:

1. Reviewed the meaning and purpose of reaching out
2. Examined the hard-to-reach agency
3. Identified helpful ways of initiating a first contact with an individual, given a set of sample situations
4. Considered four techniques of reaching out in your community
5. Reviewed two examples showing the importance of follow-up

Turn to Frame 1

FRAME 1

REACHING OUT—WHAT IS IT?

All human service agencies and organizations have an obligation to review their programs constantly so that services to consumers can be improved. In order to do

(Frame 1 continued)

this, agencies should identify overall needs for services. Agencies also work and plan towards reaching people who are not receiving services and who may already, or shortly, be both in need and entitled to help and assistance.[1] When you are using your brokering skills to reach out to individuals in your community, you are helping your agency plan how services can be delivered to reach consumers in need.

Reaching out means *locating* the people who may need assistance, *identifying* the unmet needs of individuals in your community, and seeing that these individuals have the *information* and are *linked* with the appropriate resources that will meet their needs. The purpose of reaching out is to *identify* unmet individual needs and to *prevent* these needs from getting worse. For example, by reaching out you may be preventing a young child from an illness by helping him to get a shot he needs; or you may be identifying a patient or resident who would like to participate in some kind of recreational program but does not know how to join.

Thus when you are reaching out in a community you will be assisting in identifying the problems affecting the individuals in that community and helping them make use of the appropriate community resources as aids in solving their problems. In so doing, you are making sure that the services which your agency provides are known to the people for whom the service was developed. In addition, you are providing a service which emphasizes the prevention of more serious problems by reaching out to help with less serious problems.

Go on to Frame 2

FRAME 2

We are all involved in preventive activities in our daily lives. Can you identify the preventive activities both in daily living and in the human services for the problems below?

PREVENTABLE PROBLEMS	ACTIVITIES
DAILY LIVING	
1. Tooth decay	_____
2. Polio	_____
3. Forest fires	_____
4. Automobile accidents	_____
HUMAN SERVICES	
1. Delinquency	_____
2. Divorce	_____
3. Mental retardation	_____
4. Deterioration of muscles in the body	_____

Turn to Answer 1

FRAME 3

Hard-to-Reach Agencies

In the human services, you will frequently hear about people who are mentally ill, physically disabled, poor, or have other problems who do not use the services and resources that are available to help them. Often individuals who are blamed

(Frame 3 continued)

---

[1] Leon Ginsberg, John Isaacson, and Margaret Emery, *Syllabus on Orientation and Training of Beginning Workers to Provide Social and Rehabilitation Services*, prepared for the use of the Office of Manpower Development and Training: Department of Health, Education and Welfare, Social and Rehabilitation Service (West Virginia University School of Social Work, 1971).

for not recognizing their problems and seeking assistance are characterized as hard to reach or unmotivated. But more often, the problem of service availability rests with the hard-to-reach agency.

Many human service agencies are large, understaffed, and overworked. Although sometimes people just do not know what help is available in their community, it frequently happens that potential consumers have tried to get help but have lost their self-confidence and patience from repeated failures and frustrations in getting help. So some of the people with unmet needs in your community will be resentful, suspicious, angry, depressed, and hopeless. Others will be interested in listening to what you have to say.

To many people, human service agencies seem large, cold, and unfriendly. Therefore, human service workers should remember that the agency, the consumer, or both can be hard to reach.

Continue to Frame 4

FRAME 4

Making the First Contact

One of the most important tasks in effective outreach work is establishing the first contact with an individual in the community. This is sometimes assumed to be a difficult task since it usually means beginning a relationship with an individual you have never met before. However, establishing contact with an individual you do not know does not need to be a difficult or complicated situation. Your success will depend on your ability to communicate clearly, impress the consumer with your wish to help, and check to see that the other person understands your intentions.

The following are suggested as helpful hints to keep in mind when you are approaching an individual for the first time:[2]

1. Understand yourself and your feelings. It is important to understand your own prejudices and feelings toward individuals in your community. Remember it is easy to like and help someone who is similar to you, but it is much harder to understand the person who may do things a little differently. We all have prejudices and feelings. When you are reaching out, you need to be aware of yourself and to understand what makes another person behave differently from the way you or others behave.
2. Approach the individual openly. Explain who you are and your reason for being available to be of help. Try to pick a time to approach a person when nothing much is going on so that other activities will not be a distraction.
3. Try to understand people, their behavior, and their unmet needs. Show that you accept individuals as they are. Show that you care about their problems and are interested in helping.
4. Do not offer help too quickly. Take the time to try and understand the individual's unmet need before you rush to offer solutions. Help individuals to discover their own solutions to the problem. Also make an effort to get to know individuals by encouraging them to talk about their needs.
5. Know what you can and can not do. Be aware of what you can do to help an individual and of when you should go to other resources for help. Do not feel that everything must be done by yourself!

Proceed to Frame 5

---

[2] Adapted from Janet Rosenberg, *Breakfast: Two Jars of Paste* (Cleveland: Case Western Reserve University Press, 1972), pp. 63–65.

Which of the following are examples of helpful ways of initiating a first contact with an individual consumer who may have an unmet need? After each example, circle the words that tell whether you think it is helpful or not.

A. Telling a person who needs welfare that you think people
   on welfare are basically lazy.   Helpful   Not helpful
B. Finding out about a patient's need for recreation and
   telling her you can not guarantee she will get what she
   needs, but that you will do as much as you can to help.   Helpful   Not helpful
C. Trying to start a conversation with a juvenile offender
   while he is playing cards with a fellow offender.   Helpful   Not helpful
D. Yawning when a young unwed mother expresses her feel-
   ings about putting her child up for adoption.   Helpful   Not helpful
E. Noticing that a consumer is getting very angry with the
   receptionist, and taking the time to talk with the con-
   sumer and try to understand the reasons for her anger.   Helpful   Not helpful

**Turn to Answer 2 to
see how well you did**

REACHING-OUT TECHNIQUES

You will recall from the previous lesson that the basic steps involved in identifying an individual's unmet needs are to (1) find out as much as possible about the exact need, (2) find out what the person wants to do about the need or problem, and (3) begin to determine who can help and what information will be most successful in solving this need. These steps are usually followed when an individual comes to you for assistance; however, when you are reaching out, *you* are the one who is trying to find the people who need assistance. While you will still be using these basic principles once you have located an individual with an unmet need, the key skill in reaching out is *finding* those individuals who need assistance. This process is also called case finding.

The following are four examples of techniques that are used to locate and engage individuals who can not express or accept their need for help, those who have given up their efforts to get help, and those who do not know about the available resources for help.

1. **Informal discussion with community residents.** Be active in your community! Get to know as many people as you can so that they in turn can get acquainted with you. You may only spend a few minutes with people, telling them who you are and just getting to know them. Some people may at first be hesitant to discuss their problems with you. A good way to help them get to know you and what you are doing is by showing you are interested. Then they will be more willing to share their problems with you and receive your assistance. Do not try to force yourself on people, but do try and demonstrate your sincerity in wanting to help.

2. **Observation.** Be a good observer while you are working in your community. What do residents say to other residents? Do you notice any individuals who seem to have unmet needs that they may not recognize? By just watching individuals in their daily activities, you may be able to identify those who have problems or needs with which you may be able to help.

3. **Interviews and questionnaires.** Your agency or your supervisor may ask you to interview various people in your community to find out what their prob-

(Frame 6 continued)

lems are. They may also provide you with a set of specific questions they would like community residents to answer. By interviewing various individuals and asking them specific questions on behalf of your agency, you will be able to discover what problems and needs are affecting people and also to begin providing them with information that will help them in handling these problems.

4. **Contacts with staff in your own and other agencies.** When you see other workers in meetings or even while you are working, you might make it a habit to inquire whether they know of any individuals who may be having some problems. Other workers, including volunteers, clerical staff, your co-workers, or your supervisor, may know of individuals who have problems and may suggest that you make an effort to offer your assistance.

**Once you feel you have a good grasp
of some of the techniques used in
reaching out, proceed to Frame 7**

FRAME 7

Read the following example and then answer the question below.

Art is a worker in the state welfare department. While visiting the home of Mrs. Lane, a food stamp recipient, he asked if she knew of anyone who needed the services of a new program that provided meals and transportation for elderly citizens. Art learned that Mrs. Lane's parents and great-aunts were in need of such services.

Which of the reaching-out techniques was Art using in this example?

A. Observation.

Turn to Answer 4

B. Interviews and questionnaires

Turn to Answer 7

C. Informal discussion with a community resident

Turn to Answer 9

D. Contacts with staff in his own agency

Turn to Answer 11

FRAME 8

We have just discussed four examples of techniques you can use to reach out in your community. One of these techniques is listed below. Can you name the other three techniques?

1. Interviews and questionnaires
2.
3.
4.

Turn to Answer 6

FRAME 9

Read the following passage and then answer the question below.

Marty is an aide at a local clinic of the state health department. Although he is not assigned to work in the reception area, he passes through it several times a day. One day he noticed a woman he remembered seeing in the waiting area for the last few days. He also noticed that she was wandering around looking dazed and bewildered. Even though Marty did not work in

(Frame 9 continued)

the waiting area, he began to think about going over to the woman to see if there was anything he could do to help.

Which of the following statements best describes what Marty should do in this situation?

A. Marty has observed an individual who probably feels lost and confused. Even though he does not work in the waiting area, he should reach out and offer to help this individual.

Turn to Answer 3

B. Marty has observed an individual who is lost and confused. But Marty is not assigned to work in the waiting area of the clinic, and should get back to his assigned duties.

Turn to Answer 5

FRAME 10

The Importance of Follow-up in Reaching Out

Remember our dicussion of the importance of follow-up as a part of the referral process? Follow-up is also very important when reaching out. After initiating a contact with an individual, it is important to follow-up on your initial contact. Follow-up is also used when individuals show no interest, hold back, or express anger at your attempts to contact them. You need to pursue and visit individuals again, even if they show no interest, and especially if you think they have an unmet need that requires assistance.

Remember that it takes time for trust to develop and for an individual to engage in receiving assistance. So try to maintain your contacts with individuals by talking with them when and where you can. Assure them that you are interested in them and want to understand them. Express conviction about what you have to offer. Make it known that you regard the individual's feelings and problems as real and important. And stick to presenting the facts, do not make promises you can not keep.

Proceed to Frame 11

FRAME 11

Check the correct response.

Suppose you are contacting an individual for the first time who expresses anger at being bothered again by "one of those people who always promises to help with problems but never comes back." Which one of the following would you do?

___ A. Say you are sorry you bothered the person and never go back.

Turn to Answer 12

___ B. Suggest that perhaps you have come at an inconvenient time, but offer to return when it is more convenient.

Turn to Answer 8

___ C. Agree that it must very annoying to have people break their promises, but try to express conviction about what you are offering and show you are sincere in wanting to get to know the individual.

Turn to Answer 13

___ D. Tell the person you are sick and tired of trying to help people who act like that and you can see why no one has ever kept a promise to help.

Turn to Answer 10

___ E. Both B and C, to help maintain contact with this individual.

Turn to Answer 14

ANSWERS TO LESSON 3

ANSWER 1

There are different answers that can be given as preventive activities for daily living. Here are a few:

1. Tooth brushing and flouridation of the water supply
2. Vaccination and oral medication
3. Using water to put out campfires and stripping your cigarette butt
4. Defensive driving and driver training courses

In the human services, there are also many different approaches to preventing disability or emotional problems. Your answers might look like this:

1. Youth recreation programs
2. Marriage counseling
3. Prenatal care of mothers (before the baby arrives)
4. Physical therapy and regular exercise

Continue to Frame 3.

ANSWER 2

You should have circled the following:

A. Not helpful
B. Helpful
C. Not helpful
D. Not helpful
E. Helpful

If you missed *any* of these, you need to return to Frame 4 for a review.
If you answered all of these examples correctly, you are doing an excellent job! Proceed to Frame 6.

ANSWER 3

Right on the money! Marty has used the technique of observation to discover an individual who needs assistance. The best thing for Marty to do would be to reach out by introducing himself to this woman and finding out if there is anything he can do to help her.

Go on to Frame 10.

ANSWER 4

Perhaps a review of Frame 6 will assist you in understanding that Art is not using the technique of observation in this situation.

ANSWER 5

We don't think this is the best approach for this situation. Even though Marty is not assigned specific work in the waiting room, he has observed an individual who may need assistance. The best thing for Marty to do would be to reach out and offer to help this individual.

You may want to review Frame 6 before you go on to Frame 10.

ANSWER 6

Four techniques you can use to reach out in your community are (1) interviews and questionnaires, (2) informal discussions with community residents, (3) observation, and (4) contacts with staff in your own and other agencies. Were you able to state these techniques? If so, well done—go on to Frame 9. If not, return to Frame 6 for a review before you go any further.

ANSWER 7

No, Art is not interviewing Mrs. Lane, nor is he using a questionnaire. Return to Frame 6 and review it very carefully before you try Frame 7 again.

ANSWER 8

While this is one possible answer, there is also another acceptable solution to this situation. Return to Frame 11 and select a more complete answer.

ANSWER 9

Excellent! Art is talking informally with Mrs. Lane and is using this opportunity to find out if she knows of any residents in the community who are in need of a new program that is being developed.

Turn to Frame 8.

ANSWER 10

If you respond like this, you will only be confirming this individual's distrust and suspicion of people who want to help him. You are also not making much of an effort to try and understand why this individual might feel this way.

You need to review Frame 10 very carefully before you try Frame 11 again.

ANSWER 11

Did we catch you napping?!? Art is not using the technique of contacting staff in his own or another agency—perhaps you would do well to review Frame 6 before you try Frame 7 again.

ANSWER 12

If you understand the importance of follow-up in all of your brokering activities, you know that this is not a good way to respond to this kind of situation. Return to Frame 10 for a careful review of the importance of follow-up in reaching out.

ANSWER 13

While this is a very acceptable solution to this situation and shows that you understand the importance of follow-up in your reaching out activities, there is also another acceptable solution contained in Frame 11. Return there now and see if you can choose the complete answer.

ANSWER 14

Very well done! You have demonstrated an excellent understanding of the importance of follow-up in your reaching out activities.

You have now reached the end of lesson 3 which is also the end of the chapter on brokering. For those who are ready, a short review of this chapter is provided at the end of this lesson. If you have any doubts, return to Lesson 1 and review the material on identifying community resource systems before you begin the review questions.

SUMMARY

Chapter III described some of the basic principles of brokering which is the activity used in connecting people with the services which will meet their needs. In the first lesson we discussed the resource systems found in most communities. These included the informal resource system, consisting of family, friends, and co-workers, the formal resource system, consisting of membership organizations or formal associations that exist to promote the mutual benefits and common interests of their members; and the societal resource system, which has been established through social legislation and voluntary citizen action to deliver services. We also recognized the inadequacies of each resource system relative to the problems people may encounter in trying to receive help. Finally, we reviewed some of the procedures which can be used to identify the resource systems in your community (such as consulting various directories).

In the second lesson, special attention was given to two of the primary activities in brokering—giving information and referring. The steps and skills used in identifying an individual's unmet needs were first described to assist you in identifying whether a consumer needs information and/or a referral. Referrals occur when an individual's unmet needs require the provision of an appropriate community resource. The referral process involves preparing the consumer to receive assistance, discussing the purpose of the referral, contacting the appropriate resource, helping the consumer in making an appointment, providing any support the consumer may need to get services, and following up to make sure the consumer has received the services he or she is entitled to. The lesson concluded with a discussion of service gaps which may occur because the needed services do not exist or because of the ways various resources may limit their services to consumers. In this regard, we stressed the importance of actively exploring your community to fill service gaps and representing and assisting those consumers who may be having trouble receiving help from existing resources.

The third lesson was concerned with the brokering activity of reaching out to locate people who may need assistance and to prevent their problems and needs from getting worse. We noted that agencies and other resource systems frequently seem large and cold to the consumer and may be hard to reach. Attention was given to ways of making an initial contact with a community resident with such guidelines as understanding yourself, approaching individuals openly, trying to understand them, not rushing to offer help, and being aware of your limitations in helping. Examples of techniques to use in reaching out included informal discussions with community residents, observation, interviews, questionnaires, and contacts with staff in your own and other agencies. The lesson concluded with a discussion of the importance of follow-up in reaching out.

SUGGESTIONS FOR FURTHER STUDY

If you are interested in further study of the basic principles of brokering, you should include an investigation of alternative schemes for categorizing and analyzing community resource systems. Making distinctions between informal, formal, and societal types is only one way of analyzing resource systems and may not prove useful from your perspective. Further study will also be necessary for a full understanding of the various resource systems and the inadequacies of each.

Expanding your knowledge of brokering should also include attention to communication skills, since these are basic to the process. It may also be helpful to locate various case studies which illustrate the process of reaching out to help consumers meet their needs. (Some of these can be found in the book by Riessman et al., listed below.) Additional study will develop your ability to diagnose the unmet needs of consumers and thereby improve your brokering skills.

SUGGESTIONS FOR FURTHER READING

Carney, Frank J., Mattick, Hans W., and Callaway, John D. *Action on the Streets.* New York: Association Press, 1969.

Gelfand, Bernard. *The Window: Toward an Understanding of Human Need.* Toronto, Ontario: Training and Staff Development Branch, Ministry of Community and Social Services, undated.

Ginsberg, Leon, Emery, Margaret, and Isaacson, John. *Syllabus on Orientation and Training of Beginning Workers to Provide Social and Rehabilitation Services.* West Virginia University School of Social Work, 1971.

Goldberg, Gertrude S., Kogut, Alvin B., Lesh, Seymour, and Yates, Dorothy. *New Careers: The Social Service Aide: A Manual for Trainees.* Washington, D.C.: University Research Corporation, 1968.

Hamilton, Gordon. *Theory and Practice of Social Casework.* New York: Columbia University Press, 1951.

Johnson, David W. *Reaching Out: Interpersonal Effectiveness and Self-actualization.* Englewood Cliffs, N.J.: Prentice-Hall, 1972.

Klenk, Robert W., and Ryan, Robert (eds.). *The Practice of Social Work.* Belmont, Calif.: Wadsworth, 1970.

Lowy, Louis. *Training Manual for Human Service Technicians Working with Older Persons, Part II: Trainees.* United Community Services of Metropolitan Boston, 1968. (Available through Boston University Bookstores.)

Nicholds, Elizabeth. *A Primer of Social Casework.* New York: Columbia University Press, 1960.

Pincus, Allen, and Minahan, Anne. *Social Work Practice: Model and Method.* Itasca, Ill.: F. E. Peacock Publishers, Inc., 1973.

Reissman, Frank, Cohen, Jerome, and Pearl, Arthur. *Mental Health of the Poor.* New York: Free Press, 1964.

Rosenberg, Janet. *Breakfast: Two Jars of Paste.* Cleveland: Case Western Reserve University Press, 1972.

Schulman, Lawrence. *A Casebook of Social Work with Groups: The Mediating Model.* New York: Council on Social Work Education, 1968.

Spergel, Irving. *Street Gang Work: Theory and Practice.* Reading, Mass.: Addison-Wesley, 1966.

Weissman, Harold. *Individual and Group Experiences in the Mobilization for Youth Experience.* New York: Association Press, 1969.

Wilensky, Harold, and Lebeaux, Charles. *Industrial Society and Social Welfare.* New York: Free Press, 1965.

REVIEW QUESTIONS—CHAPTER 3

Circle the letter corresponding to the answer of your choice.

1. Three resource systems found in most communities are
    A. informal, formal, and societal.
    B. informal, natural, and formal.
    C. human service, nonservice, and private.
    D. formal, membership, and societal.

2. Which of the following will help you identify and describe the resources in your community?
    A. Developing a community resource file
    B. Identifying the needs of consumers
    C. Consulting city, neighborhood, and agency directories
    D. Getting to know people who live and work in the community
    E. A, C, and D

3. (Giving information/Referring) is the process whereby an individual's physical, emotional, or social needs are met through the discovery and provision of an appropriate community (resource/action).
    In order of appearance, the responses in parentheses in the above statement should be
    A. Giving information; resource
    B. Giving information; action
    C. Referring; resource
    D. Referring; action

4. Which of the following is *not* a possible inadequacy of a community resource system?
    A. The resource may not be geographically available to those who need it.
    B. The resource may be funded from public and private sources.
    C. People may be unaware of the existence of the resource.
    D. The resource may not have the capability to provide adequate services.

5. If there are no resources in your community to meet the needs of an individual consumer you should
    A. try to discover undeveloped or unused community resources that might be able to meet the need.

B. tell the consumer he or she is expecting too much from you and your agency.

C. give up and tell the consumer to make the best of the situation.

D. B and C above.

E. A, B, and C above.

6. Membership organizations and associations that exist to promote the mutual benefits and common interests of their members are

A. included in the societal resource system.

B. illustrated by resources such as welfare agencies, police departments, and mental health hospitals.

C. part of the formal resource system.

D. included in the private service resource system.

7. _____ means keeping in touch with a consumer after you have referred him to another resource to find out if the referral has been successful.

A. Information giving

B. Planning

C. Brokering

D. Follow-up

8. Talking with a consumer about his feelings toward getting help, involving him in planning how to find and use the resource he needs, and explaining the resources that are available for help are ways of

A. getting to know your community's resources.

B. preparing an individual to receive help.

C. filling in service gaps.

D. identifying an individual's unmet needs.

9. Suppose you live in a community which has the following resources: a health clinic, a community mental health center, a welfare agency, an Easter Seal center, a women's club, and a Lions Club. These resources are part of the

A. informal resource system.

B. societal resource system.

C. formal resource system.

D. systems in A and C.

E. systems in B and C.

10. Assume you are a counselor in a training school for female youthful offenders. You are talking with Sally, one of the youths you supervise, and are trying to identify whether she has any needs or problems that you might be able to help her with. Which of the following steps would you try to follow in identifying Sally's unmet needs?

A. Find out what, if anything, Sally wants to do about her needs.

B. Find out as far as possible what her exact needs or problems are.

C. Begin to determine who might be able to assist Sally.

D. A and C are correct.

E. All of the above are correct.

11. The process of referring involves

A. identifying the consumer's need(s).

B. contacting the appropriate resource.

C. follow-up.
D. preparing the consumer to receive help.
E. all of the above.

12. Cathy L. has recently been deserted by her husband and has been left with four children to support. Although she has been unable to find a job, she is receiving some assistance from the local welfare department. But Cathy has just learned that she needs to be hospitalized, and she has no way to pay the expenses or to have her children taken care of. How would you help Cathy? To answer, first number the actions you would take in order of their importance, placing a number 1 in front of the action you would take first, a 2 in front of the next action, etc., and then choose your answers from those listed below.

___ Talk with Cathy directly about her situation, explaining the resources you can refer her to for assistance.
___ Get an appointment for Cathy with some of these resources and make sure she has this information.
___ Spend some time helping Cathy keep the appointments. Offer her your support, possibly by going with her for her first visits with these resources.
___ Contact the resources you and Cathy have agreed might be able to help her with her problem.

Choose your answer from the following:
A. 4, 3, 2, 1
B. 1, 3, 4, 2
C. 3, 1, 4, 2
D. 2, 3, 4, 1

13. If you discover that a referral has been unsuccessful, what are some of the steps you can take to help the consumer get the services he needs?
    A. Lose your temper with the referral source.
    B. Try calling someone with more authority at the resource location to help speed up the process.
    C. Make sure the consumer was adequately prepared for the referral.
    D. Discuss with the consumer why the referral has been unsuccessful.
    E. B, C, and D above.

14. A hard-to-reach agency is one where people with unmet needs have tried to get help and have been refused or frustrated repeatedly in their attempts.
    A. True
    B. False

15. Which of the following are examples of techniques you can use to reach out in your community?
    A. Interviews and questionnaires
    B. Contacts with staff in your own agency
    C. Informal discussions with community residents
    D. A and C
    E. All of the above

16. Which of the following can help initiate a first contact with a consumer who may have an unmet need?
    A. Promising a mental patient that you are going to be able to cure all his problems

B. Telling a person who you know needs financial assistance that anybody who receives welfare is just "basically lazy"

C. Finding out about an inmate's desire to work on completing his high school diploma and telling him you can't guarantee anything, but you'll see what you can do to help

D. A and C

E. All of the above

17. When an individual shows no interest, holds back, or expresses anger at your attempts to initiate a contact, you need to

A. contact the appropriate resource system.

B. maintain contact with him and try again.

C. promise your agency's assistance.

D. leave him alone.

18. Beverly Weeks is a resident in a training center for retarded citizens. Beverly has been living at the center for almost two months now, and refuses to leave her cottage for anything except her meals. Suppose you are a worker at the center but are not specifically assigned to supervising Beverly. Which of the following statements *best* describes what action you should take?

A. Beverly is probably still very frightened and confused in her new surroundings. But you are not specifiaclly assigned to Beverly, so you should simply carry on with your own duties.

B. Even though you are not specifically assigned to Beverly, you should try to talk with her and encourage her to participate in some of the activities at the center.

C. You should report Beverly's refusal to participate in any activities to your supervisor.

Now check your Answers with the Answer key for this chapter at the end of the book

CHAPTER IV:
CONSUMER ADVOCATING

INTRODUCTION

Workers in the human services sometimes find it necessary to intervene on behalf of a consumer in order to make sure consumers are provided with the resources to which they are entitled. When consumers are denied a service that they need, and when you *know* that they are entitled to that service, you are faced with a difficult decision. Should you try to defend the consumer's right to service, or should you just keep quiet and accept things as they are? Even though there are risks involved, workers are now being encouraged to defend and fight for the rights of consumers in need. Unfortunately it has not always been that way, but there is a growing recognition on the part of the courts, legislators, and professionals themselves that the rights of consumers as well as any other group should be protected through the role of advocating.

An advocate is one who pleads the cause of another, one who argues for a cause or a proposal. Lawyers are advocates when they fight for their clients and defend their legal rights before courts of law. In this chapter you will be learning some basic concepts and principles of advocating as a human service role. However, this chapter is only a beginning introduction to a very complex activity.

In the human services, advocating is a special kind of pleading for an individual consumer—a willingness to fight for the individual. Advocating means standing up for individuals and being willing to do what is necessary to uphold their rights. While advocating does not mean making unreasonable demands on human service agencies, it does emphasize protecting and defending the rights of individuals by using recognized legitimate means in their behalf.

Advocating is a challenging activity for any human service worker. In fact, it is so challenging that many workers are afraid of this activity since it means they must speak out and confront human service agencies and institutions, sometimes even at the risk of losing their jobs. When advocating, one may expect differences of opinion. This chapter introduces you to some of the basic skills involved in persuading and applying appropriate kinds of pressure on behalf of a consumer. In Lesson 1 you examine some basic techniques of advocating, such as pressuring and utilizing consumer grievance procedures. Since the protection of consumer rights is an important part of understanding advocating, in Lesson 2 you are introduced to some of the legal and human rights that are being defined and recognized for human service consumers. The overall objective of this chapter is (1) to introduce you to some of the basic issues and principles involved in defending a consumer's rights to service and (2) to illustrate some of the basic legal and human rights of human service consumers.

**Turn to the next page
to begin Lesson 1**

LESSON 1:
TECHNIQUES OF ADVOCATING

When consumers are confronted with a situation where they are denied services to which they are entitled, it may be necessary for the human service worker to engage in the role of advocating. In this lesson you will be reviewing some of the techniques of advocating that are used in efforts to settle grievances or disputes between consumers and the human service system. The goal of this lesson and the enabling activities that will help you reach this goal are presented below.

GOAL

Given a description of a consumer in need of an advocate, you will be able to identify and describe two techniques that could be used with other agencies or other individuals in defending the consumer's rights to service.

ENABLING ACTIVITIES

After completing this lesson, you will have accomplished the following:

1. Reviewed three reasons why human service consumers sometimes need advocates
2. Examined three factors that are considered in making the decision to begin advocating
3. Identified three guidelines for using advocating technique
4. Identified the components of the persuading technique
5. Considered three different techniques for persuading, using examples
6. Reviewed five helpful hints to remember when you are persuading
7. Identified the difference between persuading and pressuring
8. Examined two techniques that are used in the pressuring technique

**Turn to Frame 1
to begin this lesson**

THE NEED FOR CONSUMER ADVOCATING

In their efforts to get services to people in need, workers sometimes discover situations where there is a conflict between a consumer's needs and what an institution or agency is willing or able to do to meet that need. Usually there are three reasons why these situations can occur in delivering human services:

1. **The attitude of human service agencies and institutions.** Often, the institutions and agencies with which individual consumers must deal are far from willing to provide services or even consider grievances which are brought to their attention. In fact, they are sometimes overtly negative, hostile, or secretive in concealing or distorting information about rules, procedures, and even office hours.[1]

2. **What consumers know and feel about human services.** Many people who need help from human service agencies and institutions are too uninformed, too apathetic, or feel too powerless to do anything when services are denied them or when they are not being served satisfactorily. Many will not exercise their rights, press for their needs, or appeal actions against them unless someone acts as their advocate. And if human service workers do not assume this activity, it is very likely that no one will.[2]

3. **The wrongs suffered by consumers.** In addition to being denied and uninformed about the services, consumers suffer other "wrongs" that they cannot "right" themselves. For example, some are harassed, some are "spied on," some are in institutions where they do not belong, and some are forced to work while they are responsible for child rearing.

You can see from these situations and probably from your own experience that individuals who need help from the human services cannot always get this help on their own. They need someone to take their side and advocate for them.

Move to Frame 2

In the human services, it is sometimes necessary for workers to assume the role of advocates on behalf of consumers who are not being served satisfactorily. Circle those reasons listed below which contribute to advocating as an important worker activity.

A. Many people with unmet needs are not familiar with human service agencies and feel too powerless to do anything when services are denied or delivered unsatisfactorily.

B. Some human service agencies are, for various reasons, reluctant to provide services to just "anyone" who may need them, and they can make it very difficult for some people to get the help they need.

C. Even though most human service agencies seek to make services available for anyone in need, consumers come in contact with agency workers who either refuse to help or are ignorant about how to help.

(Frame 2 continued)

---

[1] Charles Grosser, *New Directions in Community Organization: From Enabling to Advocacy* (New York: Praeger, 1973), p. 197.
[2] Scott Briar, "The Current Crisis in Social Casework," *Social Work Practice 1967* (New York: Columbia University Press, 1967).

D. Consumers sometimes suffer 'wrongs' that are unjust or unnecessary in order to receive services, and are not always aware of ways in which they can right these injustices.

Turn to Answer 4

FRAME 3

How to Make the Decision to Advocate

Advocating is only one of many ways of making sure services are delivered to people in need. Making the decision to turn to advocating on behalf of an individual consumer requires careful consideration of several factors.

First: The worker needs to make certain that the complaint, action, or decision is a legitimate grievance; unreasonable or unjustified demands should not be made on behalf of the consumer. If a worker is not sure about the merits of a consumer grievance, it is wise to check with a supervisor or other workers familiar with the situation before starting to advocate.

Second: It must be decided whether advocacy is necessary. Have other means of solving the problem been tried? Is the need sufficiently important that strong measures are warranted?[3] Is advocating the most useful activity that can be applied in this situation? Before advocating, other means of resolving the problem should always be explored because the problem may be a result of a misunderstanding or a lack of information.

Third: Before advocating, the worker needs to discuss the problem thoroughly with the consumer and get his or her consent. This is especially important if the advocating actions require identifying the consumer by name to other sources. Of course in some instances, getting a consumer's consent may be hard to do either because of the difficulty the consumer is having or because the consumer is simply unable to understand his or her situation. In these situations you may not be able to get the consumer's consent, but whenever possible, the worker should always try to discuss future actions with the consumer and receive his or her support, understanding, approval, and participation.

The three steps above should always be taken before advocating. If the advocating process is initiated as soon as the consumer encounters difficulty, then the worker runs the risk of pursuing an unjustified complaint and alienating agency representatives who may be innocent of any wrongdoing.

Go on to Frame 4

FRAME 4

Check the correct response.

You should decide to begin advocating

A. after you have discussed the situation with the consumer and have both agreed it is necessary.

Turn to Answer 2

B. as soon as a consumer encounters difficulties in getting a service he needs.

Turn to Answer 3

C. after you have tried other available means of solving the problem situation.

Turn to Answer 6

(Frame 4 continued)

[3] Florence Hollis, *Casework: A Psychosocial Therapy* (New York: Random House, 1972), p. 307.

D. after you have made certain the complaint or grievance is legitimate.

Turn to Answer 8

E. under conditions in A, B, and C.

Turn to Answer 9

F. under conditions in A, C, and D.

Turn to Answer 10

FRAME 5

Marcy's 8-year-old daughter is not feeling very well, so Marcy takes her to the county health clinic. She is told that her daughter needs to be admitted to the hospital immediately for some extensive tests. Marcy wants to stay with her daughter in the hospital since the child is very upset, but the head nurse refuses her request. When Marcy comes to you for help, you

A. tell Marcy not to worry and immediately call the head of the nursing department at the hospital to complain about the situation.

Turn to Answer 1

B. find out if the hospital allows parents to stay with their children. Discuss this with Marcy and decide the first thing you should both try to do is to discuss the situation again with the head nurse.

Turn to Answer 5

C. tell Marcy not to worry and that you will check on the child to make sure she is OK.

Turn to Answer 7

FRAME 6

You can see that making the decision to advocate on behalf of a consumer requires careful thought on your part. Before you learn some of the techniques of advocating, see if you can write in the space below the three factors you need to consider before making the decision to advocate:

1.
2.
3.

If you have any trouble recalling these three factors, return to Frame 3 for a quick review.

Proceed to Frame 7

FRAME 7

ADVOCACY GUIDELINES

One of the biggest difficulties for many workers to overcome in advocating is their fear that they will be refused when they confront any agency with a problem situation. An important guideline for overcoming this fear is to make it easy for the agency to say "yes" to your request. If workers make an effort to practice the following three guidelines when advocating, they will have a better chance of getting a positive response to their request from an agency:[4]

(Frame 7 continued)

[4] Adapted from Janet Rosenberg, *Breakfast: Two Jars of Paste* (Cleveland: Case Western Reserve University Press, 1972), p. 83.

Knowing the agency or resource well. The worker should know who to contact and how. In most advocating situations, the first person to contact would be the one who was responsible for the unfavorable situation or decision. If satisfactory results are not obtained from this person, the worker's own supervisor may be able to help. And if the situation is still unsatisfactory, other administrators and officials who may be in a position to help with the situation can be contacted. The important thing to remember is to know as much as possible about the resouce involved.

Being clear about the complaint or grievance. This is important no matter what technique of advocating is being employed. The complaint or grievance should be stated very clearly so that the person who is receiving the complaint will fully understand the problem.

Being clear about what is being requested for the consumer. Finally, in any advocating situation it is important to state very clearly what actions are needed for the consumer. It is also important to discuss the situation with the consumer before others are approached with the request or complaint.

Go on to Frame 8

FRAME 8

Eric is a patient in a state mental hospital. Mike, an aide assigned to Eric's ward, has been talking with Eric about his complaint that the doctors and other staff have been very cruel to him and treating him unjustly.

Mike is immediately outraged that a patient feels this way. He notices a doctor walking down the hall and rushes up to him saying, "I am going to be forced to go to the superintendent unless you and the rest of this staff start showing Eric that you care about him and respect him as an individual." Mike is stunned when the doctor says he does not have much time to discuss this right now and then walks away.

Can you think of any reasons why Mike's attempts at advocating on behalf of Eric have failed? Write them in the space below and then turn to Answer 12:

FRAME 9

THE TECHNIQUE OF PERSUADING

There are several different techniques employed in advocating. One common technique is persuading, something with which you are already familiar. For example, when a girl begs her father for a new dress, or a woman urges her neighbors to work together to establish a recreation center for young people, or a dormitory supervisor urges students to keep the noise down so others can study, they are all engaged in persuading. Thus, when a worker seeks to influence someone to carry our a particular action or a decision by pleading or appealing to their reason or emotion, the technique of persuading is being employed.

Before we discuss the components of persuading,[5] you should keep in mind that these components will apply to both oral and written persuasion, although our discussion will emphasize oral persuasion.

(Frame 9 continued)

---

[5] See Elton Abernathy, *The Advocate: A Manual of Persuasion* (New York: McKay, 1964); Wayne C. Minnick, *The Art of Persuasion* (Boston: Houghton Mifflin, 1957); and Lynn Surles and W. A. Stanbury, *The Art of Persuasive Talking* (New York: McGraw-Hill, 1960).

1. When trying to persuade someone to change a decision or take an action, it is first necessary to clearly state the problem. The problem is the unsatisfactory condition or difficulty which needs to be changed. It is important to plan carefully what will be said and to be certain the listener has an accurate understanding of the problem.

2. Discuss the problem. When discussing the problem, all the important facts should be presented. This will help the other person understand more about the situation and why it needs to be changed. The facts about the problem include the worker's observations of the situation, discussions with the consumer, discussions with other staff, and letters which may have been written to people about the situation. When discussing the problem, it is also important to try to keep emotions under control, and to show other people that you understand their position or why they may have acted the way they did.

3. After discussing the problem situation, the solution to the problem or the action desired should be stated. The solution to the problem should be one both the worker and the consumer have discussed. It should also be one that can be reasonably expected to win support, without sacrificing the rights of the consumer. When stating the proposed solution to the problem, a few comments should also be made regarding what will happen if the solution is not agreed to by the other person.

4. Finally, everything that has been discussed and agreed on should be briefly summarized. Restate the problem, the major facts, and the suggested or agreed upon solution. It is also helpful to involve the other person in finding a solution to the problem situation which is mutually agreeable.

Now that you have reviewed the four components of the technique of persuading it is very important to remember that they should be applied in proper order. *First*, state the problem; *second*, discuss the problem; *third*, state the proposed solution; *fourth*, summarize the agreement, if any.

Proceed to Frame 10

FRAME 10

Check the correct response.

Which of the following would you regard as an example of the persuading technique of advocating?

A. A supervisor ordering a worker to complete his case records.

Turn to Answer 11

B. An administrator sending a memo to his staff announcing a holiday.

Turn to Answer 13

C. A worker interviewing a consumer to obtain background information.

Turn to Answer 14

D. A worker urging the welfare department to assist a consumer who has been refused food stamps.

Turn to Answer 15

FRAME 11

Read the following narrative, and then answer the question below.

Roy is a welfare aide at the public welfare office. Doris, one of Roy's clients, calls him telling him she is about to be evicted from her apartment

(Frame 11 continued)

because she is a month behind in her rent. Doris explains that she has been unable to get past the landlord's secretary to try to explain her situation.

Roy call Mr. Mann, who is Doris' landlord. He says, "Mr. Mann, I am calling you regarding one of your tenants, Doris S. I understand Doris is about to be evicted from her apartment, and I think if you are fully aware of her situation, you will find that eviction may not be necessary." Roy then explains to Mr. Mann that Doris is no longer employed, but will be receiving a public assistance check within the next week which she will be using to pay her rent. They then discuss some of the details relating to Doris' situation.

Roy is trying to persuade Mr. Mann to change his decision to evict Doris from her apartment. Do you think Roy has clearly stated the problem situation to Mr. Mann?

A. Yes
B. No

Turn to Answer 16

FRAME 12

Roy clearly stated the problem to Mr. Mann when he said, "I understand Doris is about to be evicted from her apartment, and I think if you are fully aware of her situation, you will find that eviction may not be necessary." Roy started the second part of his persuading effort by discussing Doris' situation with Mr. Mann so that he would be able to understand why Doris should not be evicted. Let's continue to follow Roy's efforts at persuading Mr. Mann.

During their discussion, Roy explained to Mr. Mann that Doris was behind in her rent payments because her past public assistance payments would not cover all of her recent expenses. However, she would be receiving her check within the week. Roy concluded their discussion saying, "I have discussed this situation with Doris, and we both feel that she should not be evicted since she will be paying her past due rent by the end of this week. We would like you to allow Doris to stay in her apartment, and we assure you the rent will be payed."

Mr. Mann assured Roy that an exception would be made now that he was aware of Doris' situation. Roy thanked Mr. Mann for his time and understanding but did not hang up before he restated their agreement regarding Doris' situation.

Go on to Frame 13

FRÁME 13

Go back to Frame 12 and underline the statement which shows how Roy employed the third part of persuading—stating his solution to the problem or stating the action he desired Mr. Mann to take. When you have completed this task, turn to Answer 18.

FRAME 14

Is the following statement true or false? Refer back to Frame 12 if you need to.

Although Roy was successful in persuading Mr. Mann to change his decision about evicting Doris, he forgot to make use of the fourth part of

(Frame 14 continued)

persuading, that is, to summarize briefly what they had discussed and agreed to regarding Doris.

A. True

Turn to Answer 20

B. False

Turn to Answer 25

FRAME 15

Three Ways to Use the Persuading Technique[6]

Using the four components of persuading, there are a number of different ways to swing people to accept the proposed solution to an unsatisfactory situation. Three ways of using the technique of persuading are given below. You will probably be able to think of others based on your own experience and observations.

1. **Finding a common ground.** This approach begins by finding out where the worker and the other person agree. For example, both might find out that they agree, first, that the consumer has a problem and, secondly, that they want to find some way to remedy the situation. After both have agreed on something, the worker begins slowly to reveal the facts about the problem and to describe the situation. For example, the worker might say, "But here is something I'd like you to think about" or "Here is a good example of what we have been discussing." If the person doesn't want to listen or shows signs of discomfort, wait for another time to try again.

2. **Putting your cards on the table.** In situations that are obviously not going to be remedied by finding a common ground or when the worker feels more comfortable being straightforward and honest, showing one's true feelings can be very useful and persuasive. The worker might say, for example, "I know you disagree with me, but I want you to know exactly where I stand."

3. **The blunt assault.** This approach is really an extension of the cards-on-the-table strategy. It is a very difficult procedure and it does *not* work in most situations. In fact, it should only be used when other ways of persuading have been tried and when the problem is an outright denial of a consumer's rights to service. The worker might say, for example, "I'm going to be blunt with you. I'm opposed to your decision in every way. I'll do everything I can to change it. Here's why I'm going to fight."

Proceed to Frame 16

FRAME 16

Let's review the three ways of persuading by using three sample advocating situations. Read each situation, then check which persuading technique is being used.

Situation 1. A consumer clearly eligible to receive health care has been denied treatment at the county health clinic. The worker goes directly to the supervisor responsible for this action and says the following:

"I'm not going to waste any time. You have denied Mrs. Haney services she is entitled to, and I am going to do whatever is necessary to see that she receives the treatment she is supposed to get."

(Frame 16 continued)

[6] Adapted from Lynn Surles and W. A. Stanbury, *The Art of Persuasive Talking* (New York: McGraw-Hill, 1960), pp. 49–63.

In this situation the worker is using the persuading technique of

__ A. common ground

__ B. cards on the table

__ C. blunt assault

Situation 2. A worker is calling another agency to try to get some information that has been denied to one of his consumers. The receptionist answering the phone says that obtaining this information is impossible. The worker says the following:

> "I sympathize with you. You know I run into many of the same problems where I work. We've got so many consumers and so many records that it gets pretty difficult to keep up with all the details somebody wants about a particular consumer."

In this sitaution, the worker is using the persuading technique of

__ A. common ground

__ B. cards on the table

__ C. blunt assault

Situation 3. A worker is calling a representative of another agency about a consumer who has been denied the opportunity of visting his young son being detained by the juvenile authorities. The worker says to this representative:

> "I'm going to be very frank with you. Mr. Blink has been trying to visit his son for the past three days and his requests have been repeatedly refused. I'd like you to understand that I am calling to see that Mr. Blink is granted the opportunity to see his son as soon as possible."

In this situation, the worker is using the persuading technique of

__ A. common ground

__ B. cards on the table

__ C. blunt assault

Turn to Answer 19 to see how well you did

FRAME 17

General Hints on Persuading

You should now have a good understanding of how the technique of persuading is employed in advocating on behalf of an individual consumer. In addition, it may be helpful to remember the following hints when persuading someone to change an action or a decision:

1. Always try to be sincere and speak with conviction.
2. Look the other person in the eye.
3. Avoid negative appeals; do not start out by telling people you know they are not interested in the problem or you know that the only reason they are listening to you is because they are being forced to.

(Frame 17 continued)

4. Do not do all the talking; let the other person tell you how he or she sees the problem and what he or she thinks an acceptable solution is. Request the person's advice.
5. Control your emotions—try not to show anger or irritation.[7]

Go right on to Frame 18

FRAME 18

THE TECHNIQUE OF PRESSURING

There are times when efforts at persuading will not be successful in correcting or changing a consumer's situation. When this happens, one can use the alternative technique of pressuring.[8] Pressuring involves the use of some kind of *forceful action* on behalf of the consumer and implies bold and vigorous efforts. Pressuring is a very powerful technique, and considerable caution should be exercised in using it since it can create hostility and resistance in the people involved. Pressuring should be used only when

1. Other means of advocating have been tried, such as persuading, and have failed to get the actions desired,
2. there is considerable evidence that an injustice has occurred, and
3. it appears reasonable to assume that there is a chance of succeeding with this technique of advocating.

Before we discuss some of the different ways pressuring is used in advocating, it is very important to note that your use of pressuring will require strong support and a great deal of assistance from your supervisor and other workers. If your supervisor is unwilling to give you the support needed to use the pressuring technique, then you should carefully reconsider the consequences of proceeding with this technique since your job within the agency will be less secure without the supervisor's support.

Grievance Procedures

One example of a pressuring technique is making use of any formal procedures that have been adopted by your agency for handling consumer grievances. Some human service agencies, such as welfare and mental health agencies, provide the opportunity for consumers who are dissatisfied with the actions of the agency to make a formal appeal to agency officials asking that conditions or decisions affecting them be changed. When agency officials receive notice of this appeal, they will usually give the consumer a chance to present his case at a hearing before representatives of the agency or other designated officials. Many consumers are not even aware of their right to appeal or challenge decisions affecting them, so if your agency has any consumer grievance procedures, you should be sure your consumers know and understand that they have this right.

What are the usual steps in utilizing consumer grievance procedures?[9] Con-

(Frame 18 continued)

---

[7] Ibid.

[8] See Florence Hollis, *Casework: A Psychosocial Therapy* (New York: Random House, 1972), p. 159.

[9] Adapted from Department of Health and Rehabilitative Services, Florida Division of Family Services, *Fair Hearing Manual* (Tallahassee, October 15, 1971); and Joel F. Handler, "Justice for the Welfare Recipient: Fair Hearings in AFDC—the Wisconsin Experience," *Social Service Review* 43, no. 1 (March 1969): 12–34.

sumers and/or their workers may decide to appeal an action when consumers are dissatisfied with the services they are receiving or are denied services to which they are entitled. After the decision is made to appeal, the consumer and/or his worker makes a verbal or written request for a hearing. Usually a request for a hearing is accompanied by a written summary which gives all the necessary information relating to the consumer's challenge. This summary generally includes the following information:

1. Consumer's name and address
2. Statement of the specific action or decision being challenged
3. Statement of the consumer's current situation and how this relates to the challenge being made
4. Concluding statement describing why the challenge should be accepted

The consumer will then be notified of the time and place of the hearing. Most procedures give consumers the right to represent themselves or have someone else (e.g., a worker, an attorney) represent them, and also the right to bring any additional people they need for support. When the hearing is held, all the information and facts relating to the claim will be examined by the agency representatives and the consumer. The consumer will then be notified of the decision reached as a result of the hearing. Should the consumer not be satisfied with this decision, there is usually some provision for making one other appeal to a higher level official.

Proceed to Frame 19

FRAME 19

Pressuring differs from persuading in that it involves

A. understanding the other side's position.

Turn to Answer 17

B. forceful action.

Turn to Answer 21

C. an appeal to reason.

Turn to Answer 24

FRAME 20

Pressuring should be used only when (check those that apply)

A. __ there is a very clear injustice or violation involved.

B. __ there is a chance of succeeding with persuading techniques.

C. __ all other techniques have failed.

D. __ the consumer will not give his consent to advocating activities.

E. __ it can be determined that there is a good chance of succeeding.

Turn to Answer 22

FRAME 21

Check the correct response.
    Pressuring is an advocating technique that should be used

A. whenever you see any situation where it might be tried.

Turn to Answer 23
(*Frame 21 continued*)

B. with a great deal of caution.

Turn to Answer 26

C. with strong support and a great deal of assistance from your supervisor.

Turn to Answer 27

D. when a consumer is dissatisfied with agency decisions affecting him.

Turn to Answer 29

E. only in cases of B and C.

Turn to Answer 30

F. only in cases of A and D.

Turn to Answer 31

FRAME 22

A request for a hearing is usually accompanied by a written summary. Check which of the following are *not* included in this summary.

1. ___ Consumer's name and address

2. ___ Copy of all the consumer's records the agency has on file

3. ___ Statement of the specific action or decision being challenged

4. ___ Picture of the consumer

5. ___ Statement of the consumer's current situation and how this relates to the challenge being made

6. ___ Detailed description of all of your contacts and observations of the consumer

7. ___ Concluding statement describing why the challenge should be accepted.

Turn to Answer 28

FRAME 23

The Last Resort

One other example of the pressuring technique of advocating is using other community resources—individuals or groups—to bring pressure to bear on the consumer's behalf.[10] For example, a lawyer could be contacted for the consumer if the person's rights are being violated. Often just a telephone call from a lawyer expressing interest in a particular case will be enough to convince someone they are acting without respect for a consumer's rights. Other uses of resources include contacting city or county officials and state legislators. As with other pressuring techniques, these methods also require that you work closely with your supervisor and other workers to make certain you are using the most effective means of assisting the consumer in getting the services he needs.

You have now completed Lesson 1—congratulations! You can see that there are a number of ways to defend and fight for the rights of consumers, and that making the decision to advocate requires very careful consideration and preparation. If you feel you have a good grasp of the techniques of advocating, proceed to Lesson 2 where you will be learning about some of the basic rights of human service consumers. However, if you think you need to review this lesson, turn back to Frame 1 before going on to Lesson 2.

[10] Florence Hollis, *Casework: A Psychosocial Therapy* (New York: Random House, 1972), p. 159.

ANSWERS TO LESSON 1

ANSWER 1

Sorry, but if this is the action you would take, your attempt to help Marcy would probably fail. Before you decide to begin advocating on behalf of any consumer, you should (1) try other means of solving the problem, (2) discuss the situation with the consumer and get the person's consent, and (3) make certain the complaint or grievance is legitimate. Return to Frame 5 and see if you can choose the correct action you should take in this situation.

ANSWER 2

This is one factor you have to consider before making the decision to begin advocating. But what are the other two factors? Return to Frame 3 for a review, and then answer Frame 4 correctly.

ANSWER 3

No—the decision to begin advocating is one that requires you to carefully consider the consumer's situation. You need to reread Frame 3 very carefully before you try Frame 4 again.

ANSWER 4

You should have circled A, B, C, and D. If you answered correctly, you have a good understanding of why consumers sometimes need worker advocates. Go right on to Frame 3 and keep up the good work.

If you had any trouble with Frame 2, return to Frame 1 for a quick review before you go to Frame 3.

ANSWER 5

Excellent! This action shows you are carefully considering Marcy's situation and are first making an attempt to solve her problem by discussing the situation again with the head nurse. You are also involving Marcy in your actions and both of you are making certain that her complaint is legitimate. You've demonstrated a good understanding of the three factors that are important to consider before any advocating begins. Go on now to Frame 6.

ANSWER 6

This is one factor you need to consider before making the decision to begin advocating. But what are the other two factors? Return to Frame 3 for a review, then answer Frame 4 correctly.

ANSWER 7

This response demonstrates that little effort is being made to understand Marcy's situation and indicates a patronizing attitude towards Marcy by attempting to exclude her involvement. Return to Frame 1 and start this lesson again.

ANSWER 8

This is one factor you need to consider before making the decision to begin advocating. But what are the other two factors? Return to Frame 3 for a review, then answer Frame 4 correctly.

ANSWER 9

A and C are correct, but B is incorrect. Advocating is *not* the activity to turn to as soon as a consumer runs into difficulties in getting a service he needs. You have to consider other factors carefully before you begin advocating. Return to Frame 4 and select the correct response.

ANSWER 10

Right you are! These are the three factors you need to consider before making the decision to begin advocating. Turn to Frame 5.

ANSWER 11

No, if a supervisor is "ordering" a worker to complete his case records, he is making no effort to persuade or appeal to the worker to complete this task. Reread Frame 9 before you try Frame 10 again.

ANSWER 12

Some of the reasons Mike's attempts at advocating on behalf of Eric failed are as follows: (1) Mike did not take the time to find out from Eric what specific actions he felt were cruel and unjust, who specifically was treating him unjustly, and what he wanted changed. (2) Mike was also unsuccessful because he did not make any effort to find out exactly who he should contact. Running to the first doctor he saw in the hall made it likely that his efforts would fail. (3) Mike also failed to check whether Eric's complaint was legitimate before he made his hasty and irresponsible decision to begin advocating.

Did you think of any other reasons why Mike's efforts failed? We hope so, since this situation is a good example of the need to consider a consumer's situation carefully before you begin advocating. It is also a good example of what can happen when you fail to practice the three basic principles of any advocating technique.

Go on now to Frame 9 to learn about the advocating technique of persuading.

ANSWER 13

This is definitely *not* an example of persuading. This administrator is merely announcing a holiday and is in no way trying to persuade anyone to do anything. Return to Frame 9 and review what is meant by persuading before you try Frame 10 again.

ANSWER 14

Sorry, but this is not an example of the persuading technique. This worker is collecting background information on a consumer and is not engaged in trying to influence the consumer or change a decision or action.

Return to Frame 9 for a review before you try your hand at Frame 10 again.

ANSWER 15

Excellent! Urging the welfare department to assist a consumer who has been refused food stamps is very definitely an example of the persuading technique of advocating.

Turn to Frame 11 and keep up the good work.

ANSWER 16

Yes, Roy has done a good job of clearly stating the problem situation to Mr. Mann. Return to Frame 11 and see if you can underline exactly where Roy made his clear statement of the problem to Mr. Mann, and then go on to Frame 12.

ANSWER 17

No, persuading involves making an effort to understand the other side's position, but this is usually *not* the case when pressuring is being employed. Return to Frame 18 for a review of pressuring before you try Frame 19 again.

ANSWER 18

You should have underlined the following sentence: "We would like you to allow Doris to stay in her apartment and can assure you the rent will be payed."

Here Roy is telling Mr. Mann his solution or the action he desires Mr. Mann to follow. If you had any trouble identifying this statement, you may want to review Frame 9. Go on to Frame 14.

ANSWER 19

Situation 1. You should have checked C, blunt assault since this worker is not taking any time to find any common ground, nor is he simply trying to be frank and honest and lay his cards on the table. He is bluntly saying to this supervisor that he is opposed to the decision that denied a consumer treatment and that he is going to fight the decision in any way he can.

Situation 2. You should have checked A, common ground, since this worker is starting his persuading efforts by trying to find where he and the receptionist can agree before he starts to reveal the facts concerning the consumer who needs the information.

Situation 3. You should have checked B, cards on the table, since this worker is being straightforward and frank concerning Mr. Blink's situation and what action needs to be taken.

How well did you do? You should have answered all three of these situations correctly. If you did, you understand some of the different ways persuading can be used to advocate. Go on to Frame 17 to learn some helpful hints to remember no matter what technique of persuading you are using.

If any of your answers to the situations in Frame 16 were incorrect, you should review Frame 15 before going on to Frame 17.

ANSWER 20

Are you sure you read the last paragraph in Frame 12?? Roy did remember to make use of the fourth part of persuading by restating what he and Mr. Mann had agreed to before they hung up. This is a very important part of any persuading effort. If you still feel a little uncertain, you may want to go back to Frames 9, 11 and 12 for a review. If not, go right on to Frame 15.

ANSWER 21

Correct! Pressuring differs from persuading in that it involves the use of *forceful action*. In persuading, the emphasis is on understanding the other side's position and appealing to reason. Go right on to Frame 20.

ANSWER 22

You should have checked A, C and E, as the factors that should be considered before any pressuring activities begin. Review Frame 18 if you had any trouble here; otherwise, continue to Frame 21.

ANSWER 23

No!! Pressuring is a very powerful technique of advocating and must be used with a great deal of planning and caution. Should you think there is a need for it, you should discuss the situation with your supervisor and fellow workers. Return to Frame 18 for a careful review.

ANSWER 24

No, *persuading* and *pressuring* involve making appeals to reason in order to change decisions and actions. Return to Frame 18 for a review of pressuring before you try Frame 19 again.

ANSWER 25

Right you are! Roy did remember to use the fourth part of persuading before they hung up by restating what he and Mr. Mann had agreed to regarding Doris. Good work. Turn to Frame 15.

ANSWER 26

You are partially correct—but there is one other thing to remember when pressuring is being used. Return to Frame 21 and select a more complete answer.

ANSWER 27

You are partially correct—but there is one other thing to remember when pressuring is being used. Return to Frame 21 and select a more complete answer.

ANSWER 28

You should have checked 2, 4, and 6 as items that are *not* included in a written summary for a hearing. Review Frame 18 if you answered incorrectly, otherwise turn to Frame 23.

ANSWER 29

Sorry, but pressuring is not the advocating technique that is chosen just because a consumer is dissatisfied with agency decisions affecting him. There are other activities and other techniques of advocating that should be utilized *before* it is decided to turn to the pressuring technique.

Review Frame 18, then answer Frame 21 correctly.

ANSWER 30

Right!! Pressuring is an advocating technique that should be used with a great deal of caution *and* with strong support and a great deal of assistance from your supervisor. Turn to Frame 22.

ANSWER 31

You are way off the mark with this answer. Remember that pressuring is a very powerful technique, and since it relies on the use of force, it must be used with a great deal of caution. You would be well advised to return to Frame 18 for a very careful review of the technique of pressuring, before you answer Frame 21 correctly.

LESSON 2:
BASIC RIGHTS OF HUMAN SERVICE CONSUMERS

Until very recently, it was commonly taken for granted that if someone became a human service consumer, it would not be unusual for that person to lose or be deprived of some basic rights. For example, correctional inmates, the retarded, the mentally ill, and welfare recipients have often been denied basic rights and privileges that we take for granted. Today, however, there is a growing awareness of the need to recognize and define some of the basic rights of human service consumers, and to make sure these rights are upheld in all service settings.

In this lesson, you are introduced to some of the basic rights that are being defined and recognized for human service consumers. However, before you begin this lesson, you should realize that many consumer rights presently depend on where a person lives and the nature of the services being recieved. This lesson describes consumer rights in very general terms. The goal of this lesson and the enabling activities that will help you reach this goal are presented below.

GOAL

When you finish this lesson, you will be able to explain two kinds of rights, and to identify at least six basic rights that should be guaranteed to all human service consumers.

ENABLING ACTIVITIES

After completing this lesson, you will have done four things:

1. Reviewed the meaning of a right
2. Identified the difference between the two types of rights
3. Demonstrated your knowledge of the rights of consumers in five different human service settings
4. Considered six basic rights that should be guaranteed to all human service consumers.

Turn to Frame 1 to begin this lesson

FRAME 1

WHAT ARE RIGHTS?

What does it mean when we say human service consumers have rights? What does it mean to say that all men have rights? Generally, a right is something which belongs to a person because of a law, tradition, or nature.[1] But in order to understand fully what rights are, it is necessary to know the difference between the two major types of rights—legal rights and human rights.[2]

A legal right belongs to a person because it has been established by the government, the legislature, the courts, or some other policy-making organization. The most important thing to remember about legal rights is that they are *enforceable* and recognized by a law or policy. A human right is a right which belongs to people simply because they are human beings. Not all human rights are recognized or upheld by laws. Human rights may be thought of as moral rights, or rights which people *ought* to have. Some human rights are also legal, that is, they are recognized by law and enforceable, but many that are not recognized by law are not enforceable even when they are denied or violated.

An easy way to distinguish between these two kinds of rights is to remember that legal rights are *what is*, while human rights are *what ought to be*.

Turn to Frame 2

FRAME 2

Choose the correct response.

A right is something which belongs to a person because of

A. law.

Turn to Answer 4

B. favor.

Turn to Answer 5

C. tradition.

Turn to Answer 6

D. nature.

Turn to Answer 7

E. A, C, and D.

Turn to Answer 10

FRAME 3

In this lesson, you will learn that certain rights are guaranteed to all consumers of human services. However, you will discover that there are very few such rights. Since the concern with consumer rights is only recent in the human services, there is a great deal of variation in definitions of these rights. Whether or not human service consumers can enjoy the legal and human rights to which they are entitled depends largely on where they live and the decisions of local officials.[3] While

(Frame 3 continued)

[1] *Webster's New World Dictionary of the American Language*, College Edition.
[2] For a discussion of legal and human rights, see Maurice Cranston, *What Are Human Rights* (London: Bodley Head, 1973), pp. 5–7.
[3] Elizabeth Ogg, *Securing the Legal Rights of Retarded Persons* (New York: Public Affairs Committee, Inc., 1973), p. 4.

important decisions have been made in some states, most states still do not recognize or guarantee many rights to human service consumers. However, it is important for you to recognize that in many states advocates for human service consumers (e.g., lawyers, interested citizens in the community, workers) and even the consumers themselves are actively involved in attempts to ensure all consumers equal protection under the law.

To give you some idea of the legal and human rights of human service consumers, the next few frames describe these rights as they are being defined in five major human service settings. The rights of five groups of human service consumers are discussed: (1) the retarded, (2) mental patients, (3) inmates in correctional settings; (4) welfare recipients, and (5) youthful offenders.

Go on to Frame 4

FRAME 4

Some Basic Rights of the Retarded

Of the 6 million persons labeled mentally retarded, approximately 250,000 are confined to residential institutions. Many of these persons receive inadequate or no treatment and others do not even receive safe custodial care. Thousands of involuntarily confined residents daily perform institution maintaining labor—without any compensation—which would otherwise require the hiring of regular employees. It has further been estimated that of the 7 million children identified as handicapped, only 40 percent receive appropriate education. Despite occasional improvements in their situation, the mentally retarded have traditionally been relegated to second-class status in our society.[4]

Let's now look at some of the legal and human rights that are being recognized and defined for the retarded.

Right to treatment. There have been several court decisions on the right of institutionalized retarded residents to receive adequate treatment. Several of these decisions have held that the retarded have a right to adequate medical treatment and assistance in acquiring and maintaining those life skills which enable them to cope more effectively with the demands of their own person and their environment.

Right to least restrictive alternative. Several court decisions have held that people should not be institutionalized if services and programs in the community can provide them with adequate habilitation. Changes are now underway to secure community care as a right for all retarded persons.

Right to education. Most states have mandatory provisions for the education of retarded people who do not live in institutions; however, this does not always mean that these laws are observed and implemented. For example, there have been several recent cases in the courts where retarded young people have been denied education in the public schools, and these cases have reaffirmed the right of the retarded to an education. In addition, a recent court decision has held that retarded people who are residents in institutions also have the right to some kind of education, whether it is provided by the institution or by the public school system.

Protection from abuse. Several court decisions have held that physical punishment will not be permitted in an institution. In addition, other decisions have upheld the right of the retarded not to receive medication as a form of punishment.

Right to marry and right of choice regarding sterilization. Many states have

(Frame 4 continued)

---

[4] Mental Health Law Project, *Basic Rights of the Mentally Handicapped* (Washington, D.C., 1973), p. 2.

laws that in some way restrict the right of the retarded to marry and rear children. In some instances, there are laws that prevent the retarded from having children by surgery, or sterilization. In practice, however, most of these laws have rarely been enforced. Some laws that prevent the retarded from having children have been struck down by the courts; but generally the courts have not had the opportunity to do so, although some state legislatures are beginning to repeal such laws regarding marriage and having children.

Payment for working. All retarded residents in institutions are now entitled to fair wages for any work they may perform for the upkeep of the institution, provided it is work for which the institution would otherwise have to pay an employee.

Go on to Frame 5

FRAME 5

Although some of the rights of the retarded are not recognized in every state or in every institution, it is important for you to be familiar with the meaning of these rights. For example, the right to the least restrictive alternative means

A. a retarded person should not be institutionalized if there are other services and programs in the community that can meet his needs.

Turn to Answer 2

B. that when a retarded person is institutionalized, he should have the right to receive treatment that will keep him in good physical health.

Turn to Answer 8

FRAME 6

Sharon lives in the state of Florida and works in an institution for the retarded. In this state, the retarded have the right to be protected from physical abuse. This means that Sharon can hit a resident for disciplinary purposes only when she feels that it is necessary.

A. True

B. False

Turn to Answer 1

FRAME 7

Alice is a resident in an institution for the retarded. She is required to see that all beds are made and floors swept in her unit each day. Is she entitled to a fair wage for this responsibility?

A. Yes

B. No

Turn to Answer 11

FRAME 8

The right to treatment means that

A. each resident should be kept in good physical health.

Turn to Answer 3
(Frame 8 continued)

B. each resident should be helped to develop daily living skills to his full ability.

Turn to Answer 9

C. no resident should be prevented from having children through surgery.

Turn to Answer 12

D. both A and B.

Turn to Answer 13

FRAME 9

Some Basic Rights of Mental Patients

. . . There are, right now, nearly three-quarters of a million patients in this nation's mental hospitals. . . . Many of them will be physically abused, a few will be raped or killed, but most of them will simply be ignored, left to fend for themselves in the cheerless corridors and barren back wards of the massive steel and concrete warehouses we—but not they—call hospitals. Each day thousands will die or be discharged, and other thousands will take their place.

. . . Almost all mental patients are poor or black or both, and most of them are old. Less than 5 percent of those patients are dangerous to themselves or to others. They are put away not because they are, in fact, dangerous, but because they are useless, unproductive, "odd" or "different." . . . For years, mental patients have been stripped of their liberties and dignity.[5]

The following are some of the legal and human rights that are being recognized and defined for patients in mental health settings:

Right to treatment. Many states have provisions that entitle mental patients to medical care and treatment, but most of these provisions are not very well defined, that is, they do not clearly specify what care and treatment means. All mental patients should be entitled to the medical, social, educational, and rehabilitative services necessary to bring about their early release, and specific standards for adequate treatment should be clearly defined.

Right to communication and visitors. A number of states have provisions which guarantee patients the rights to communicate by *sealed* mail with anyone inside or outside the hospital and to receive visitors. Some states also grant patients absolute rights to private communications with their attorney, the courts, and their physicians. However, many states also allow the superintendent of the hospital or the physician to restrict visitors and communication if they think the welfare of the patient will thereby be served.

Right to payment for working. Mental hospitals are required to pay a minimum wage to patients who work in the hospitals. If patients do not want to work, they cannot be forced to work. If they perform tasks which would have to be done by a hospital employee, then these tasks are considered to be work that requires payment.

Right to personal property, adequate clothing, and funds upon discharge. A very limited number of states provide patients with the right to a court hearing and legal counsel before their personal possessions and funds are confiscated by the hospital. However, some states do grant patients the right to control and have possession of their personal property (such as clothing) while they are hospitalized. A number of states require that released patients be provided with suitable clothing

(Frame 9 continued)

---

[5] Bruce J. Ennis, *Prisoners of Psychiatry: Mental Patients, Psychiatrists, and the Law* (New York: Harcourt Brace Jovanovich, 1972), pp. vii–viii.

upon discharge along with enough money for transportation to their home. They should also be provided with job training, public assistance, job placement, and housing, but this varies from state to state.

Protection from abuse. Many states expressly prohibit the physical abuse of patients and allow physical restraints to be used only to prevent physical injury to themselves or others. Some mental hospitals use treatment techniques such as shock therapy, and patients usually do not have the right to refuse this kind of treatment. Consent for this kind of treatment can usually be given by a relative of the patient or by the hospital superintendent. However, many advocates of the rights of mental patients maintain that patients who have *not* been declared legally "incompetent" should have the absolute right to refuse treatments such as shock therapy.

Sterilization. You will recall that sterilization is a surgical method used to prevent a person from having children. There are still some states that authorize the sterilization of some mental patients, but these patients must be given the right to a hearing, the right to be represented by an attorney, and the right to appeal the decision before sterilization is authorized.

Proceed to Frame 10

FRAME 10

Check which of the following statements is *not* true regarding a mental patient's right to treatment.

A. ___ All mental patients should be entitled to the medical, social, educational, and rehabilitative services that are necessary to bring about their early release.

B. ___ Specific standards for adequate treatment of mental patients are clearly defined in every state.

C. ___ Most states entitle mental patients to some form of medical care and treatment.

Turn to Answer 15

FRAME 11

In the state of Texas, all mental patients have an absolute right to private (uncensored) communications with their attorneys and with the courts. This means that

A. any worker may check these communications to make sure there are no complaints or charges against the hospital or its staff.

Turn to Answer 17

B. no one has the right to restrict or to read these communications without the patient's permission.

Turn to Answer 19

FRAME 12

Brian lives in Pennsylvania and is an aide in one of the state's mental hospitals. In this state, mechanical restraints are not allowed unless they are necessary to prevent a patient from harming himself or others when being moved from one place to another, or unless the restraints are ordered by a physician.

(Frame 12 continued)

Suppose one of the patients on Brian's ward has disobeyed one of the nurses by refusing to take his medication. The nurse orders Brian to put this patient into a straitjacket until he decides to take his medicine. Is this a violation of this patient's rights?

A. Yes

Turn to Answer 21

B. No

Turn to Answer 22

FRAME 13

Some Basic Rights of Inmates in Correctional Institutions

As an institution, our penal and "correctional" system is an abject failure. The conditions in America's jails and prisons virtually ensure psychological impairment and physical deterioration for thousands of men and women each year. Reformation and rehabilitation is the rhetoric; systematic dehumanizatian is the reality. Public attention is directed only sporadically toward the subhuman conditions that prevail in these institutions, and usually only because the prisoners themselves have risked many more years in confinement, and in some cases even their lives, to dramatize their situation by protest.[6]

Let's now review some of the basic rights of inmates that are beginning to be recognized in various parts of the United States.

Freedom from cruel and unusual punishment. Inmates have an absolute right to be free from cruel and unusual punishment; however, this is a right that is easy to state but often difficult to enforce because different standards are used to define what constitutes such punishment. Generally there are three tests that are applied to determine whether a punishment is cruel and unusual: (1) Does the punishment shock the conscience of a civilized society? (2) Is the punishment unnecessarily cruel? and (3) Does it go beyond what is necessary to achieve a legitimate aim of the correctional institution? Using these three tests, various states have decided that inmates have the right not to be confined in solitary for an excessive period of time, the right to a reasonable opportunity for physical exercise, and the right to be free from any physical or corporal punishment.

Right to communication. Most states have established for inmates the right to communication with the outside world, especially with attorneys, courts, and government officials. However, there are still limitations in most states regarding the free flow of written correspondence and reading materials. Most states give prison officials the right to read all the nonlegal materials and personal correspondence of an inmate and to withhold or censor these materials if they feel it is necessary. Often, inmates are not informed that their communication has been withheld or censored, and they are thus denied any opportunity to challenge these actions.

Right to medical treatment. Lack of adequate medical, dental, and psychiatric care is usual in many correctional institutions. However the general rule today is that inmates have a right to be provided with medical treatment. It should be noted that in most instances, the inmate is not considered the final judge of what medical treatment is necessary. The courts will usually believe the testimony of prison officials and doctors that treatment was adequate. Inmates should also

(Frame 13 continued)

have the right to be protected from sexual assault and to receive education and training while in the prison, but these rights are guaranteed in very few states.

Right to use available procedures for review of complaints. Inmates have a right to use available administrative procedures for review of their complaints. For example, many prisons provide for an internal review of the complaints registered by inmates. Inmates also have the right to challenge prison conditions in the courts, but they do not have the right to appear in court to present evidence or to argue their case.

Notice of rights. Some states have recognized the right of inmates to receive adequate advance notice concerning the kind of conduct that will result in discipline and/or punishment. Regarding prison disciplinary hearings, very few courts or states have been willing to specify inmate's rights; however, some have held that the inmate is entitled to a written notice of the charges against him, a record of the hearing, the right to cross-examine witnesses, the right to call witnesses in his own behalf, the right to counsel, and the right to receive in writing the list of reasons which led to a decision.

Right to organize. The right of inmates to organize and to present their collective demands for changes in prison practices is still being tested in the courts. Presently, most states will not tolerate political organizing, petitioning, or group meetings of inmates if the purpose of these meetings poses a danger to the security and discipline of the prison.

Go to Frame 14

FRAME 14

You have just reviewed six rights that only recently have been defined for inmates in correctional settings. In discussing the right of inmates, it is important to keep in mind that an inmate, because he has been convicted of a crime, must expect to lose certain liberties. But an inmate does *not* lose his citizenship, nor should he be deprived of any rights that are not expressly (or necessarily) taken from him by law.[7] Keeping this in mind, let's test our understanding of the rights to which inmates *are* or should be entitled to.

Inmates have an absolute right to freedom from cruel and unusual punishment. Check which of the following rights would be included in the right to freedom from cruel and unusual punishment.

A. ___ The right to receive education and training

B. ___ The right to a reasonable opportunity for physical exercise

C. ___ The right to be free from physical abuse and punishment

D. ___ The right to adequate medical treatment

E. ___ The right not to be confined in solitary for an excessive period of time

Turn to Answer 18

FRAME 15

Suppose you are a correctional guard working in a prison in a state which clearly recognizes the right of an inmate to receive adequate medical treatment. Joe is an inmate in your tier (cell block) and comes to you complaining of severe stomach pains. You are busy doing a report at the time and scheduled to go off duty in a

(Frame 15 continued)

---

[7] Steven Wisotsky, "Equal Justice Under Law," *The Florida Bar Journal* 47, no. 7 (July 1973): 464–466.

few hours. So you tell Joe to wait until the next shift comes on and tell the night guard, since you do not have time to be concerned about it. Have you violated or denied Joe his right to receive adequate medical treatment?

1. Yes

2. No

Turn to Answer 14

FRAME 16

"Notice of rights" means which of the following:

A. An inmate receiving advance notice of what conduct will result in discipline or punishment

Turn to Answer 16

B. An inmate receiving written notice of any charges against him

Turn to Answer 20

C. An inmate is entitled to organize a group meeting for political purposes

Turn to Answer 23

D. A and B

Turn to Answer 24

FRAME 17

Some Basic Rights of Welfare Recipients

Welfare is a major problem in American society today. Everyone—radicals and reactionaries, conservatives and liberals, welfare administrators and recipients—agrees that the present welfare system is unsatisfactory. The system does not provide enough for poor perons to live with any semblance of adequate housing, nutrition, health, or dignity. The way in which it is administered under existing laws and regulatons ferquently breaks up families, fosters dependency, and destroys the spirit and self respect of those who must accept welfare to survive. Poor people are being hurt.[8]

Consider, for example, "the unemployed head of a family, for whom the 'price' of the meager benefits with which he somehow keeps his family alive is loss of human dignity through something called 'investigation of eligibility,' which begins with the assumption that he is irresponsible and dishonest. . . . Or the mother deserted by her husband, who is denied aid for her dependent child because her relationship with a man to whom she is not married has offended the morality of welfare regulation."[9]

The legal and human rights of welfare recipients are more clearly defined than the rights of other groups of human service consumers. This is because (1) there have been numerous cases in the courts that have defined and upheld some of the rights of welfare recipients and (2) the welfare program was one of the first of the human services to experience the pressure of organized consumers (welfare

(Frame 17 continued)

[8] Timothy J. Sampson, *Welfare: A Handbook for Friend and Foe* (Philadelphia: United Church Press, 1972), p. 12.
[9] Richard C. Allen, *Legal Rights of the Disabled and Disadvantaged* (Washington, D.C.: U.S. Department of Health, Education and Welfare Social and Rehabilitation Service, 1969), p. 2.

recipients and other low-income people) who formed a national organization called the National Welfare Rights Organization. The strength of this organization can be found in local groups where one of its main goals is to make sure the legal and human rights of welfare recipients and other low-income people are protected.

The National Welfare Rights Organization has set forth a "Bill of Welfare Rights." Some of the legal rights included in this listing, which have been upheld by the courts, are given below.[10]

1. The right to fair and equal treatment, free from discrimination based on race, color, or religion.
2. The right to apply for any welfare program and to have that application put in writing.
3. The right to have the welfare department make a decision promptly after application for aid (generally held to be within 30 days).
4. The right to be told in writing the specific reason for any denial of aid.
5. The right to a hearing if requested before a check can be reduced or cut off and before medical aid is affected.
6. The right to appeal a denial of aid and to be given a fair hearing before an impartial referee.
7. The right to get welfare payments without being forced to spend the money as the welfare department wants.
8. The right to have the same constitutional protections that all other citizens have.
9. The right to be told and informed by the welfare department of all rights, including the ways to make sure the welfare money will be received.

Turn to Frame 18

FRAME 18

The legal and human rights of welfare recipients are more clearly defined than the rights of other groups of human service consumers. Which of the following would be a reason for this?

A. Welfare recipients have had a national consumer organization which seeks to protect consumer's rights.

Turn to Answer 28

B. Welfare recipients and other low-income people are isolated.

Turn to Answer 29

C. There have been numerous court cases that have defined and upheld the rights of welfare recipients.

Turn to Answer 30

D. Welfare recipients have rarely been denied any of the rights they are entitled to.

Turn to Answer 32

E. A and C.

Turn to Answer 33

F. None of the above.

Turn to Answer 36

[10] Timothy J. Sampson, *Welfare: A Handbook for Friend and Foe* (Philadelphia: United Church Press, 1972), p. 137.

Check which of the following is *not* a legal right of welfare recipients.

A. __ The right to fair and equal treatment, free from discrimination based on race, color, or religion

B. __ The right to apply for any welfare program and to have that application put in writing

C. __ The right to receive assistance without having to answer questions about who their relatives are

D. __ The right to get welfare payments without being forced to spend the money as the welfare department wants

Turn to Answer 25

FRAME 20

Some Basic Rights of Youthful Offenders

In this section you will learn about some of the basic rights of youths who are accused of being delinquent and/or beyond control.

> Children have a special place reserved for them in our system of criminal justice. Our juvenile laws are founded on the ideal that children should receive from the state, care, training, and treatment—all designed to rehabilitate them and prepare them for adulthood. . . . Unfortunately, the treatment of the juvenile offender in this country's history has been deplorable. The minor has received neither the legal protections accorded to adults nor the special care and treatment postulated for children.[11]

You may be interested in the following statement which was made 40 years ago, and is similar to comments that are made today regarding the rights of youth:

> . . . it becomes evident that children are still commonly detained in jails all over the country; that there is an absence of adequate facilities for detention in many jurisdictions; that detention homes are sometimes little better than jails; that all too commonly, policies of intake and discharge of children are inadequate; that the wrong kind of children are detained; that children are confined for too long periods; in short, that which is technically known among social workers as "good casework standards" are too often lacking in the treatment of these children.[12]

Let's now take a look at some of the changes which are occurring today regarding the basic rights of youth.

Right to an explanation of the charges in language the youth can understand. When a law violation or other juvenile problem is reported and the case cannot be settled informally, a full explanation of the charges should be given to the youth and his or her parents. This is a right guaranteed to all youth who are formally accused of a law violation or other juvenile problem.

Right to a hearing to determine custody status. This means that if a youth is detained, he has a right to a hearing before a judge or referee that will decide

(Frame 20 continued)

[11] Leonard Edwards, "The Rights of Children," *Federal Probation* XXXVIII, no. 2 (June 1973): 34–5.
[12] Frederick Ward, "Juvenile Detention," *Crime and Delinquency* 13, 1 (January 1967): xxii.

whether he will continue to be detained. This hearing should take place as soon as possible (usually within 24 hours after the youth has been formally charged).

Right to counsel. The right to be represented by an attorney, or to have one appointed by the court and paid for by the state if the youth and his parents are unable to afford one, has been established. However, this right is clearly established only in the trial, or fact-finding, and sentencing phases of delinquency proceedings. The laws in different states vary as to whether this right is essential in all phases of juvenile proceedings.

Right to be taken to a specific facility and have parents notified. This right applies when a youth is formally accused of a law violation or other juvenile problem and is taken into custody. A specific facility would be, for example, a detention center. This is a right that is accorded to youths by most juvenile courts.

Right to a review. The current trend in this area is for a closer review of case progress after the case has been settled. This means that if the youth remains in the community, a review is made to determine (1) whether treatment efforts have been effective and (2) when the youth can return to the community. This is not an established right of all youthful offenders, but several states are moving in this direction.

Right to treatment. Some states have provisions that entitle youthful offenders to treatment and care that will give them an opportunity to be rehabilitated. However, most of these provisions tend to define treatment and care in terms of psychiatric treatment and counseling, and specific standards for adequate treatment are not clearly defined. Presently, youthful offenders are not guaranteed a right to treatment, whether they are institutionalized or whether they remain in the community. Advocates for youthful offenders are currently trying to secure a recognition of a juvenile's right to treatment, but the trend is this area is to try to get state legislatures and the courts to ensure that youthful offenders are not deprived or denied an opportunity to develop into mature, law abiding citizens.

Proceed to Frame 21

FRAME 21

Regarding youthful offenders who are formally accused of a law violation, the right to an explanation of charges means that the youth is entitled to

A. a full explanation of what unlawful actions he is being accused of.

Turn to Answer 26

B. adequate treatment and care.

Turn to Answer 27

C. have these charges explained to his or her parents.

Turn to Answer 31

D. be immediately released.

Turn to Answer 34

E. A and C.

Turn to Answer 35

FRAME 22

Jody is a worker in a detention center where youths are held after they have been formally charged with an offense. Margaret S. is brought to the center on Monday, having been charged with illegal possession of drugs. Jody explains to Margaret

(Frame 22 continued)

what she has been charged with and what these charges mean, but then leaves to check on another youth at the center. Margaret is still at the center on Friday, and Jody discovers that Margaret's parents have not been notified and that Margaret has not been told how long she will be detained at the center.

Check which of the following are rights that Margaret has been denied.

A. __ Right to review

B. __ Right to a quick and speedy trial

C. __ Right to a hearing to determine custody status

D. __ Right to have her parents notified where she is and what the specific charges are

Turn to Answer 39

FRAME 23

Some Basic Rights of All Human Service Consumers

You have seen that our courts and legislatures are beginning to recognize many of the basic rights of persons who are consumers of various kinds of human services. This is resulting in two important trends regarding advocating activities of human service workers: (1) Administrators in the human services are now beginning to realize that they can no longer rely solely on their own judgment or choice in their decisions regarding consumers,[13] and (2) human service workers and other community persons who are interested in the welfare of human service consumers are beginning to realize that something can be done when a consumer's rights are unjustly denied.

Since many types of human service consumers have not been discussed in this lesson, some understanding will be gained by looking at several of the basic rights that many think *should* be guaranteed to *all* consumers of human services, regardless of the setting in which they are receiving services.

Right to due process. All consumers of human services should have the right to due process. This right would assure consumers protection in their efforts to defend themselves in any area of the human services. It would require that the fate of consumers not be decided in closed chambers and that consumers be advised of any charges or actions against them. It would also require that consumers have the right to challenge any evidence against them, introduce witnesses in their behalf, and be provided with counsel (an attorney). While some rights of due process are guaranteed to some human service consumers, others are still having to fight for recognition of this right.

Civil rights. Some states have recognized that human service consumers are entitled to the same constitutional protections that all other citizens possess. For example, the right to be free from discrimination based on race, religion, or sex should be guaranteed to all consumers. They should also have the right to be free from discrimination based on their status as human service consumers (for example, when they are applying for a job or trying to get an education). Currently, these rights are greatly restricted in settings concerned with corrections, mental health, and mental retardation.

Community services. All consumers of human services should enjoy the same privileges as any other citizen, such as the right to adequate food and nutritional care, the right to enjoy the community through intellectual, recreational, and

(Frame 23 continued)

---

[13] South Carolina Department of Corrections, *The Emerging Rights of the Confined* (Columbia: The Correctional Development Foundation, Inc., 1972).

cultural activities, and the right to be trained to have a job, earn an adequate living, and receive equal pay for equal work. Generally speaking, these rights are not guaranteed to many consumers of human services.

Dignity. Consumers of human services should have the right to be treated with respect for their individual importance. They should not be treated as objects of pity or hopeless burdens on society. Some states are slowly beginning to recognize this as a right of human service consumers.

Privacy. All human service consumers should have the right to be treated in a way which does not invade their privacy. They should have the right to receive assistance without having to answer personal questions, such as being required to give the names of their friends. This right would be necessarily somewhat restricted in settings such as correctional situations but should be recognized as much as possible in other human service settings.

Confidentiality of records. Nothing in an agency's or institution's record of a consumer should be disclosed to anyone without the consumer's expressed consent or a court order. To date, very few states recognize this as a right, and it is commonly overlooked in the correctional setting.

Religious freedom. This is a right that needs to be recognized for all human service consumers, but especially for those in institutional settings. Consumers should be guaranteed the right to practice their own religion, unless the institution can show that it would be seriously threatened by the practice.

Notice of rights. All consumers of human services should be guaranteed the right to be advised of their rights and to have these rights explained to them in language they can understand. While this is recognized in welfare settings and situations concerning youthful offenders, it is not yet fully guaranteed to all consumers of human services.

Proceed to Frame 24

FRAME 24

Sara has applied to the welfare office for financial assistance. A worker in the office has discovered that Sara lives in a commune and associates with juveniles who have been delinquent in the past. Based on this information, Sara's application for assistance is denied. If the right of _____ was recognized in her state, then this decision would be a violation of this right.

Choose your answer from those listed below.

A. Due process

Turn to Answer 37

B. Dignity

Turn to Answer 38

C. Privacy

Turn to Answer 40

D. Religious freedom

Turn to Answer 42

FRAME 25

Fill in the blanks with the correct responses and then turn to Answer 41.

If the right to confidentiality of records was guaranteed to all human service consumers, it would mean that nothing in a consumer's record could be disclosed to anyone without the consumer's _____ or a _____.

To check your understanding of some of the basic rights that should be guaranteed to all human service consumers, see if you can list at least five of them in the space below. If you have any trouble remembering these rights, return to Frame 23 for a review.

1.

2.

3.

4.

5.

  After you have completed this task, go right on to Frame 27 to complete this lesson.

Before you leave this lesson, you should recognize that the rights of human service consumers are undergoing constant change. Since there are decisions being made each day, keep in mind that parts of this lesson may be outdated by the time you have completed it.

  You have an obligation to make sure your consumers are aware of their rights and to do everything you can to make sure their rights are not denied. You also have an obligation to find out the specific rights that are recognized in your state and in your agency, so that you can be more effective in your advocating activities as you work to make sure that services are delivered to people in need.

  You have now completed this lesson which is also the end of the chapter on consumer advocating. If you are ready for the review questions on this chapter, go now to the end of Chapter IV. However, if you have any doubts, return to Lesson 1 and review the techniques of advocating and the rest of this chapter before starting the review questions. In addition to reviewing the content of this chapter, you may want to discuss the issues of advocacy more thoroughly with your supervisor, instructor, and/or colleagues. There may be some consumer rights with which you disagree. You may find that more rights need to be guaranteed for all consumers. In any event, advocating involves knowledge and skills which should be tested through discussion and under supervision before you are able to feel confident about your competence in advocating.

ANSWERS TO LESSON 2

ANSWER 1

Of course you said this statement was false! If the state of Florida recognizes the right of the retarded to be protected from physical abuse, Sharon most certainly does *not* have the right to hit a resident even if she thinks it is necessary. If you answered this question correctly, proceed to Frame 7. However, if by chance you missed this question, you need to review Frame 4 before you go any further.

ANSWER 2

You are correct.

The right to the least restrictive alternative means that a retarded person should not be institutionalized if there are other services and programs in the community that can meet his needs. Remember, however, that this is not a legal right for all retarded citizens.

Turn to Frame 6 and keep up the good work.

ANSWER 3

You are partially correct, but a careful review of Frame 4 will show you there is another correct answer that should be included. Return there now, and then complete Frame 8 correctly.

ANSWER 4

That's one-third of the answer! Return to Frame 1 for a quick review and then see if you can answer Frame 2 with the complete response.

ANSWER 5

No, favors have nothing to do with rights. Return to Frame 1 and read it carefully before you try to answer Frame 2 correctly.

ANSWER 6

That's one part of the answer, but there is a more complete answer contained in Frame 2. Return there now, and then answer this question correctly.

ANSWER 7

Well, that's part of the answer, but there's more to it than just nature. Return to Frame 1 for a review, and then answer Frame 2 correctly.

ANSWER 8

Sorry, but you were asked about the meaning of the right to the least restrictive alternative, and you answered in terms of the right to treatment. You may want to review Frame 4 before you answer Frame 5 correctly.

ANSWER 9

Yes, the right to treatment does mean that each resident should be helped to develop skills to his full abilities. But the right to treatment also includes something else. Return to Frame 8 and select the complete answer.

ANSWER 10

Excellent! A right is something which belongs to a person because of a law, tradition, or nature. Proceed to Frame 3.

ANSWER 11

Yes, all retarded residents in institutions are now entitled to fair wages if they perform work for the upkeep of the institution provided someone else would ordinarily be paid to do the work. Continue to Frame 8.

ANSWER 12

No, this has nothing to do with the right to treatment. You need a careful review of Frame 4 before you answer Frame 8 correctly.

ANSWER 13

Right again! The right to treatment for the retarded means that each resident should be kept in good physical health and should be helped to develop his skills to his full capabilities. Keep in mind though, that this right is not yet recognized in every state nor in every institution for the retarded. But many states are moving in the direction of recognizing this as a right of all retarded citizens.

Now turn to Frame 9 to learn about some of the basic rights of mental patients.

ANSWER 14

Yes, in this situation, if you decided that Joe should not be allowed to attend sick call, and your only reason was that you were busy and did not want to be bothered about it, then you were denying Joe his right to receive adequate medical treatment. We might also add that even if you are working in a state that clearly does not give inmates in correctional settings the right to adequate medical treatment, you as a human service worker, should try to see to it that the inmates get the medical treatment they need.

Continue to Frame 16.

ANSWER 15

You should have checked B. Specific standards for adequate treatment of mental patients are *not* clearly defined in every state. Even though many states do have provisions that entitle mental patients to medical care and treatment, most of these provisions are not clearly defined and do not set specific standards that should be followed.

If you answered this question correctly, you are doing very well and should continue to Frame 11. If you missed this answer, you might find that a review of Frame 9 would be helpful before you proceed.

ANSWER 16

Well, you are partially correct, but notice of rights also includes something else. Return to Frame 13 for a quick review of the rights of inmates in correctional settings before answering Frame 16 correctly.

ANSWER 17

Absolutely not! If a state recognizes the right of mental patients to have private communications with their attorneys and the courts, this means workers are violating a patient's rights if they check these communications to make sure there are no complaints or charges against the hospital or its staff. Return to Frame 9 for a careful review, and then answer Frame 11 correctly.

ANSWER 18

You should have checked B, C, and E, as rights which are included in an inmate's right to freedom from cruel and unusual punishment. If you missed any of these, return to Frame 13 for a review before proceeding to Frame 15. If you answered correctly, well done; go directly to Frame 15.

ANSWER 19

Right you are! You are doing an excellent job of understanding some of the basic rights of mental patients. Continue to Frame 12 and keep up the good work.

ANSWER 20

You've got part of the answer, but you need to return to Frame 16 and find a more complete answer to what notice of rights means for inmates in correctional settings.

ANSWER 21

You are correct with this choice. In this situation, putting a patient in a strait-jacket simply because the person has refused to take a medication is in violation of the individual's rights. However, if this refusal to take medications can lead to uncontrollable behavior which may be harmful to the patient or others, some restrictions may be needed. For example, the patient can be denied canteen privileges or ground privileges. Mechanical restraints are usually unnecessary for such patient behavior. Now turn to Frame 13 to learn about some of the basic rights of inmates in correctional settings.

ANSWER 22

Sorry, but if you read this Frame carefully, you would realize that this answer is incorrect. If the state of Pennsylvania recognizes the right of mental patients to have mechanical restraints used only if they are necessary to prevent the patient from harming himself or others when being moved from one place to another, or if they are ordered by a physician, then the nurse's actions in this situation are in violation of this patient's rights.

Read Answer 21 and turn to Frame 13.

ANSWER 23

No, this has nothing to do with notice of rights. Return to Frame 13 for a careful review of some of the basic rights of inmates in correctional settings before answering Frame 16 correctly.

ANSWER 24

Excellent! Notice of rights means that an inmate will receive adequate advance notice of what conduct will result in discipline or punishment and also written notice of any charges against him. You are doing fine, take a well deserved break before going on to Frame 17 where you will learn about some of the basic rights of welfare recipients.

ANSWER 25

You should have checked C. Welfare recipients do *not* have the right to receive assistance without having to answer questions about who their relatives are, since this may affect their level of assistance. If you answered correctly, you've done a good job in learning about some legal rights of welfare recipients, and you should continue to Frame 20. However, if you answered Frame 19 incorrectly, you should probably review Frame 17 before going on to Frame 20.

ANSWER 26

You are partially correct. If you will return to Frame 21 and review the choices again carefully, you should discover one other correct answer to this question.

ANSWER 27

Sorry, but this is incorrect. A review of Frame 20 would be very helpful to you before you try answering Frame 21 correctly.

ANSWER 28

While this answer is correct, there is another reason that the legal and human rights of welfare recipients are more clearly recognized and defined than the rights of other groups of human service consumers. Return to Frame 18 and see if you can locate this other reason.

ANSWER 29

If you selected this response as a reason that the legal and human rights of welfare recipients are more clearly defined than the rights of other groups of human service consumers, then you need a very careful review of Frame 17 before you try to answer Frame 18 correctly.

ANSWER 30

That's one half of the answer! Perhaps you need to review Frame 17 quickly before selecting the complete answer to Frame 18.

ANSWER 31

Yes, when a youth is formally accused of a law violation or juvenile problem, the right to an explanation of charges does mean that the youth has the right to have these charges explained to his or her parents. But it also includes another basic right. Return to Frame 21 and see if you can select the complete answer.

ANSWER 32

Sorry, but this is not a reason why the rights of welfare recipients are more clearly defined than the rights of other groups of human service consumers. Return to Frame 17 for a review before you try Frame 18 again.

ANSWER 33

You are correct! Continue to Frame 19 and keep up the good work.

ANSWER 34

Are you sure you read Frame 20 carefully? If you did, then you would not have selected this as an answer to Frame 21. Perhaps a review of Frame 20 would clarify what the right to an explanation of charges means for youthful offenders.

ANSWER 35

Correct again! The right to an explanation of charges means that the youth is entitled to a full explanation of what unlawful actions he is being accused of and is also entitled to have these charges explained to his or her parents. Continue to Frame 22.

ANSWER 36

Your selection of this answer indicates that you need to review Frame 17 carefully before you try Frame 18 again.

ANSWER 37

Sorry, but due process is not the correct choice here. Return to Frame 23 for a review, and then answer Frame 24 correctly.

ANSWER 38

While the denial of Sara's application for aid might be viewed as a disregard of her right to dignity, there is a better answer to this situation. Return to Frame 23 for a review, and you'll have no trouble answering Frame 24 correctly.

ANSWER 39

You should have checked C and D. Margaret was denied her right to have her parents notified of where she was and what she was charged with. She was also denied her right to a hearing (which should take place as soon as possible, and preferably within 24 hours) to determine her custody status. If you had no trouble with this Frame, continue to Frame 23.

ANSWER 40

Correct! If this state recognized a welfare recipient's right to privacy, then the decision to deny Sara's application for aid would be in definite violation of this right. Turn to Frame 25.

ANSWER 41

If the right to confidentiality of records was guaranteed to all human service consumers, it would mean that nothing in a consumer's record could be disclosed to anyone without the consumer's *expressed consent* or a *court order*. Proceed to Frame 26.

ANSWER 42

You are way off base with this answer. A review of Frame 23 is in order before you try Frame 24 again.

SUMMARY

In this chapter special attention was given to the need for consumer advocacy and related techniques. We identified the legal and human rights of human service consumers along with the reasons that the advocating role is sometimes necessary. Attention was given to the factors which must be considered in deciding whether or not advocating is needed. For example, one must consider the particular agency which is related to the consumer grievance, the grievance itself, and the consumer's needs.

Two specific techniques of advocating, persuading, and pressuring, were discussed in detail. Different ways of applying the techniques were described along with the advantages and disadvantages of each. Special attention was given to basic principles and helpful hints in the use of the advocating process; for example, thoroughly understanding the situation, securing the understanding and permission of the consumer, gaining support of the supervisor, choosing the appropriate advocating technique, and applying the technique properly.

In discussing consumer rights, attention was given to the difference between legal rights and human rights. Examples of both were discussed in connection with five human service settings. Six basic rights were identified that should be guaranteed for all human service consumers.

SUGGESTIONS FOR FURTHER STUDY

To understand fully the process of effective advocating, one needs further study of such subjects as the difficulty of determining the need for the advocating role in specific case situations, how to gather support from various sources in applying advocating techniques, and how to ensure the most protection for both the consumer and worker in the process.

Further study will also be needed for the worker to be able to identify situations where discrimination or denial of services is being directed, not at individual consumers, but at entire groups or categories of consumers. This is generally described as "class discrimination," and the process of advocacy takes on new dimensions in such situations. Quite often when a worker identifies a situation where a number of consumers with similar characteristics (e.g., unwed mothers) are being denied services, advocacy techniques can be used most effectively by helping the entire group rather than by working case by case. However, the responsibility for pursuing this type of advocacy, generally called systems advocacy, usually lies beyond the responsibility of the worker because it involves negotiating for dramatic changes in agency policies and procedures or even in laws. The worker can learn, through further study, how to discriminate between these different kinds of situations so that the attention of agency administrators can be directed to class discrimination if this is where they need to take appropriate action.

Further study will also be needed in the area of consumer rights, since this area is constantly changing with new laws being made, court cases being decided, and policies that affect the rights of consumers being revised. The professional journals in human service areas and the information pamphlets and newsletters of state and federal human service agencies should provide an excellent resource in this area.

SUGGESTIONS FOR FURTHER READING

"A Right To Treatment for Juveniles?" *Washington University Law Quarterly*, V. 1973: 157–196.

Abernathy, Elton. *The Advocate: A Manual of Persuasion.* New York: McKay, 1964.

Allen, Richard C. *Legal Rights of the Disabled and Disadvantaged.* Washington,

D.C.: U.S. Department of Health, Education, and Welfare, Social and Rehabilitation Service, 1969.

Briar, Scott. "The Current Crisis in Social Casework." In *Social Work Practice 1967*. National Conference on Social Welfare. New York: Columbia University Press, 1967, pp. 19–32.

Cloward, Richard A., and Elman, Richard M. "Advocacy in the Ghetto." *Transaction* 14 (April 1969): 27–35.

Cranston, Maurice. *What Are Huamn Rights?* London: Bodley Head, 1973.

Edwards, Leonard. "The Rights of Children." *Federal Probation* XXXVIII, no. 2 (June 1973): 34–41.

Eldefonso, Edward. *Law Enforcement and the Youthful Offender: Juvenile Procedures*. New York: Wiley, 1967.

Ennis, Bruce J. *Prisoners of Psychiatry: Mental Patients, Psychiatrists and the Law*. New York: Harcourt Brace Jovanovich, 1972.

Ennis, Bruce, and Siegel, Loren. *The Rights of Mental Patients*. New York: Richard W. Baron, 1973.

Florida Division of Family Services. *Fair Hearing Manual*. Tallahassee: Department of Health and Rehabilitative Services, October 15, 1971.

Fraenkel, Osmond K. *The Rights We Have*. New York: Crowell, 1971.

Grosser, Charles. *New Directions in Community Organization: From Enabling to Advocacy*. New York: Praeger, 1973.

Handler, Joel F. "Justice for the Welfare Recipient: Fair Hearings in AFDC—The Wisconsin Experience." *Social Service Review* 43, no. 1 (March 1969): 12–34.

Hollis, Florence. *Casework: A Psychosocial Therapy*. New York: Random House, 1972.

Kittrie, Nicholas N. "Can the Right to Treatment Remedy the Ills of the Juvenile Process?" *Georgetown Law Journal* 57, no. 4 (March 1969): 848–885.

Law, Sylvia. *The Rights of the Poor*. New York: Avon Books, 1974.

Mental Health Law Project. *Basic Rights of the Mentally Handicapped*. Washington, D.C., 1973.

Minnick, Wayne C. *The Art of Persuasion*. Boston: Houghton Mifflin, 1957.

Ogg, Elizabeth. *Securing the Legal Rights of Retarded Persons*. New York: Public Affairs Committee, Inc., 1973.

Parker, Frank J. *The Law and the Poor*. New York: Orbis Books, 1972.

Prigmore, Charles S., and Davis, Paul R. "Wyatt v. Stickney: Rights of the Committed." *Social Work* 18, no. 4 (July 1973): 10–18.

Pyfer, John F. "The Juvenile's Right to Receive Treatment." *Family Law Quarterly* VI, no. 3 (Fall 1972): 279–320.

Rogers, William D. *Manual of Rights of Patients*. Tallahassee: Department of Health and Rehabilitative Services, Division of Mental Health, January 1974.

Rosenberg, Janet. *Breakfast: Two Jars of Paste*. Cleveland: Case Western Reserve University Press, 1972.

Rudovsky, David. *The Rights of Prisoners*. New York: Avon Books, 1973.

Sampson, Timothy J. *Welfare: A Handbook for Friend and Foe*. Philadelphia: United Church Press, 1972.

Segal, Robert M., ed. *Advocacy for the Legal and Human Rights of the Mentally Retarded*. University of Michigan Publications Distribution Service, February 1973.

South Carolina Department of Corrections. *The Emerging Rights of the Confined*. Columbia, South Carolina: The Correctional Development Foundation, Inc., 1972.

Surles, Lynn, and Stanbury, W. A. *The Art of Persuasive Talking*. New York: McGraw-Hill, 1960.

Weinstein, Noah. *Legal Rights of Children*. Reno, Nevada: National Council of Juvenile Court Judges, 1973.

Wineman, David, and James, Adrienne. "The Advocacy Challenge to Schools of Social Work." *Social Work* 14 (April 1969): 23–32.

Wisotsky, Steven. "Equal Justice Under Law." *Florida Bar Journal* 47, no. 7 (July 1973): 464–466.

REVIEW QUESTIONS—CHAPTER 4

Circle the letter corresponding to the answer of your choice.

1. When should advocating begin?
   A. After discussing the situation with the consumer and receiving his consent
   B. As soon as a consumer has difficulty getting a service he needs
   C. After other means of solving the problem situation have been tried
   D. After making certain the complaint or grievance is legitimate
   E. A, C, and D above

2. Which of the following are techniques used in consumer advocating?
   A. Referring and persuading
   B. Persuading and pressuring
   C. Pressuring and mobilizing
   D. Mobilizing and referring

3. Assume that you are a worker in a welfare agency. Jack S., one of your clients, calls you and is very upset because he hasn't received a wheelchair that was promised to him over a month ago by another agency. You fail to ask Jack S. who it was that promised him the wheelchair, but you decide to call someone you know at the other agency. So you call the other agency and clearly state what Jack's problem is and what he needs. Two weeks later, you discover that Jack still doesn't have his wheelchair. This is because you have forgotten to practice which of the following basic principles of advocating?
   A. Being clear about the complaint or grievance
   B. Knowing who to contact about the problem and how to contact him
   C. Being clear about what you want for Jack

4. Which of the following would you regard as examples of a worker using the persuading technique of advocating?
   A. Urging a management company not to evict a consumer because of past due rent
   B. Referring a consumer to another agency that might help him when the first agency you referred him to refused
   C. Appealing to your supervisor to allow a consumer to participate in an activity group
   D. A and C above

5. The four steps of the persuading technique of advocating are listed below. Indicate the correct order in which they should be taken, using numbers 1 to 4.

   ___ Discuss the problem.

   ___ Clearly state the problem.

   ___ Summarize what has been discussed and agreed on.

   ___ State your solution to the problem or the action desired.

Choose your answer from the following:

    A. 3, 2, 4, 1
    B. 1, 2, 4, 3
    C. 2, 1, 4, 3
    D. 2, 1, 3, 4

6. Which of the following would be uses of the advocating technique of persuading?
    A. Pressuring and threatening
    B. Common-ground approach and blunt assault
    C. Consumer grievance procedures and legal aid
    D. Referring and follow-up

7. You are calling John French, a supervisor at the local welfare office, to try to persuade him to change his decision not to give financial assistance to one of your consumers. You begin by saying, "Mr. French, I know you disagree with me, but I am going to be very frank with you—" What persuading technique are you using?
    A. Cards on the table
    B. Blunt assault
    C. Consumer grievance procedures
    D. Common ground
    E. Direct approach

8. The advocating technique of pressuring differs from that of persuading because in pressuring
    A. the use of forceful action is involved.
    B. trying to understand the other side's position is involved.
    C. strong support and a great deal of assistance from your supervisor is required.
    D. A and C are correct.
    E. A, B, and C are correct.

9. When a consumer makes a formal appeal to agency officials with your help to challenge a decision or action affecting him and to request a hearing, this is an example of the advocating technique of
    A. persuading agency officials.
    B. legal aid.
    C. consumer grievance procedures.
    D. blunt assault.

10. Which of the following are examples of a worker using the pressuring technique of advocating?
    A. Contacting a lawyer to represent a consumer who has been unjustly denied a service
    B. Deciding with a consumer to contact a state legislator on behalf of the consumer
    C. Using agency grievance procedures to appeal unfavorable decisions
    D. A, B, and C
    E. None of the above

11. All human service consumers are guaranteed the same legal and human rights.
    A. True
    B. False

12. The kind of right that is enforceable and recognized by the law is called
    _____; a right that people ought to have but is not
    always recognized by the law is called _____.
    A. legal; human
    B. human; legal
    C. basic; policy
    D. legal; basic

13. If a state recognizes that a retarded person should not be institutionalized
    when there are other services and programs in the community that can meet
    his needs, this is called
    A. a right to treatment.
    B. a right to the least restrictive alternative.
    C. a right to education.
    D. freedom of choice.
    E. community service.

14. Which of the following statements is/are *not* true regarding a mental pa-
    tient's right to treatment?
    A. Most states entitle mental patients to some form of medical care and
       treatment.
    B. All mental patients have the right to be paid for the work they perform
       for the upkeep of the institution.
    C. Specific standards for adequate treatment of mental patients are clearly
       defined in every state.
    D. B and C (are not true).
    E. All of the above (are not true).

15. Which of the following groups of human service consumers must by law
    expect to lose some of their civil liberties?
    A. The aged
    B. Dependent children
    C. Welfare recipients
    D. Inmates in correctional settings
    E. All of the above

16. Inmates in correctional settings have an *absolute* right to
    A. freedom from cruel and unusual punishment.
    B. organize political groups.
    C. free communication with the outside world.
    D. education and treatment.
    E. all of the above.

17. Which is the only group of human service consumers to organize their own
    national organization to protect their rights
    A. Inmates in correctional settings
    B. Welfare recipients
    C. Mental patients
    D. Youthful offenders

18. Which of the following is/are the legal right of welfare recipients?
    A. The right to fair and equal treatment, free from discrimination based on race, color, or religion
    B. The right to apply for any welfare program and to have that application put in writing
    C. The right to get welfare payments without having the welfare department dictate how the money will be spent
    D. All of the above

19. Which of the following statements is *false* regarding the rights of youthful offenders?
    A. All youthful offenders are entitled to an explanation of any formal charges against them.
    B. All convicted youthful offenders are guaranteed a clearly defined right to treatment.
    C. If a youth is detained by legal officials, he or she has the right to a hearing to determine custody status.
    D. Youths who are formally accused of a law violation have the right to an attorney when they are brought to trial.

20. It is generally agreed that *all* human service consumers *should* be entitled to which of the following rights?
    A. Right to due process
    B. Right to dignity
    C. Right to religious freedom
    D. B and C above
    E. All of the above

**Now check your Answers with the Answer
key for this chapter at the end of the book**

CHAPTER V: MOBILIZING

INTRODUCTION

Mobilizing is community work in which the people of a community are brought together to effect changes for the better in that community. Mobilizing involves working with community problems or unmet needs and is the activity used to try and do something about these unmet needs.

Workers who engage in mobilizing activities are trying to help community residents make their communities better places in which to live. We all know that the resources and services currently available in our communities do not always relieve all the needs of the people in that community. Residents may need day care, recreation, better housing, or additional help for juvenile delinquents, and existing services do not always respond to relieving these needs. Mobilizing involves the process either of encouraging existing service agencies to work together to deal with an unmet community need or of creating a new resource that will meet the need.

In this chapter you will be learning about the organizing skills required for effective community work, including how workers begin to identify unmet needs in a community and get to know a community. You will also examine the basic organizing steps used in helping community groups solve problems. The overall objective of this chapter is to assist you in learning how mobilizing is used in building support and making changes in a community in order to deal with unmet community needs.

Turn to the next page to begin Lesson 1

LESSON 1:
IDENTIFYING UNMET COMMUNITY NEEDS AND TAKING ACTION

In this lesson you will learn what unmet community needs are and how to identify them. You will also learn the basic steps of mobilizing and how it is used to gather support in the community to change or modify services. The goal of this lesson and the enabling activities that will help you reach this goal are presented below.

GOAL

Given an actual community situation or a description of a community situation, you will be able to explain how you would begin to identify the unmet needs of the community.

ENABLING ACTIVITIES

After completing this lesson, you will have done six things:

1. Reviewed what is meant by unmet community needs
2. Examined at least five areas of knowledge needed to understand a community
3. Reviewed the meaning of mobilizing
4. Identified the major objectives of mobilizing
5. Identified the primary types of community groups that may serve as mechanisms for mobilizing
6. Considered five basic steps to follow in mobilizing for change

Ready? Turn to Frame 1
and begin this lesson

WHAT IS AN UNMET COMMUNITY NEED?

Hopefully, a need involves a problem that can be solved. When we talk about unmet needs in community work, we are talking about needs or problems in the community that are not being met or relieved by existing community resources (e.g., no recreational program to keep potentially delinquent teenagers off of the streets or no program to help idle patients in a hospital keep physically fit). We know that individuals in our communities have many needs which often can be met by previously existing or newly developed services. In mobilizing, we are looking beyond individual needs and trying to examine these needs or problems at the local community level. The mere statement of a need by a single consumer, community resident, or worker does not necessarily mean that a real unmet community need exists.

How are unmet community needs identified? Learning about any community (its people, organizations, and problems) is a continuous process. To gain knowledge of a community it is usually important to contact organized groups in the community who are interested in problems your agency wishes you to work on. For example, a civic group may be concerned about the lack of recreational facilities. Or it may be necessary to recruit persons who are not affiliated with groups but who can play an important role in seeking change, for example, parents of children with special learning disabilities whom the local school system has ignored.

Whatever the community's unmet needs may be, it is important to know something about established groups in the community. It is also important to be *out* in the community—which includes talking with residents and human service consumers and their friends and observing their activities. There are five questions to keep in mind when trying to identify unmet community needs:

1. What do the residents say the problems are?
2. What do the residents talk about to each other?
3. Do the stated problems and the conversations reflect the same concerns?
4. How do nonresidents in the community, merchants, professionals, etc., see the problems?
5. What are the different points of view regarding the problems, and is there any common ground?

Remember that different groups or individuals may view or define the same problem in different ways. For example, the merchant whose windows are regularly broken may speak of "young hoodlums," the school social worker may be concerned about "teenage gangs," and parents may talk about their kids having "no place to play." All these people are talking about the same *general* problem in different ways. The worker will want to find out, in such a case, what is happening in the community that results in juvenile delinquency. Is it lack of parental control, lack of recreation facilities, or what? Only by being in the community and finding out more about the real nature of the problem and the needs can a worker begin to discover what can and should be done.

Go on to Frame 2

Underline the proper words in parentheses, and then turn to Answer 2.

Mrs. Betty R. needs day-care services for her children in order to hold a job.
(Frame 2 continued)

No low-cost day-care programs exist in her community. Mrs. R. is experiencing an individual need that is being (met/unmet). The provision of daycare services is a community need that is (met/unmet).

FRAME 3

We have said that there are five key questions to remember in pinpointing unmet community needs. Read the following paragraph and then answer the questions below.

> Hank is a human service worker who makes it a habit to "hang out" in the places frequented by community residents. When he does so, he listens carefully to conversations to find out what the residents seem to be most concerned about. He also engages many of them in conversations, asking them how they see the problems in the community, making mental notes as to whether statements of the problems are the same things they talk about in their conversations. From this Hank sizes up what he thinks the unmet needs of the community are.

Hank has remembered to keep only some of the five key questions in mind as he goes about searching for unmet community needs and has forgotten others. Beside each question below, place a check mark (✔) if Hank has remembered the question and an X if he has forgotten it.

___ 1. What the residents say are the problems in the community

___ 2. What the residents talk about

___ 3. Whether the stated problems and the conversations are the same

___ 4. How nonresidents in the community, merchants, professionals, etc., see the problem

___ 5. What the different points of view are and whether there is any common ground

Turn to Answer 3

FRAME 4

THE STRUCTURE OF COMMUNITIES

Learning about a community is an important first step in finding out what unmet community needs exist. Whether the community in which you work is a town or neighborhood, you should be familiar with various community structures, such as social service agencies, educational agencies, and consumer groups, as these can be valuable resources for seeking new approaches to solving community problems. You should know *how* to contact them and *who* to contact. If your community is a hospital, a prison, or another kind of institution, you should also be familiar with the particular structures that exist, such as social services, volunteer services, and recreation services.

To acquire a better idea of these various community structures, carefully study the two charts that follow. After you have done so, place a check mark beside the organizations or services you are familiar with in your own community, whether it is a neighborhood or an institution.

Turn to Frame 5

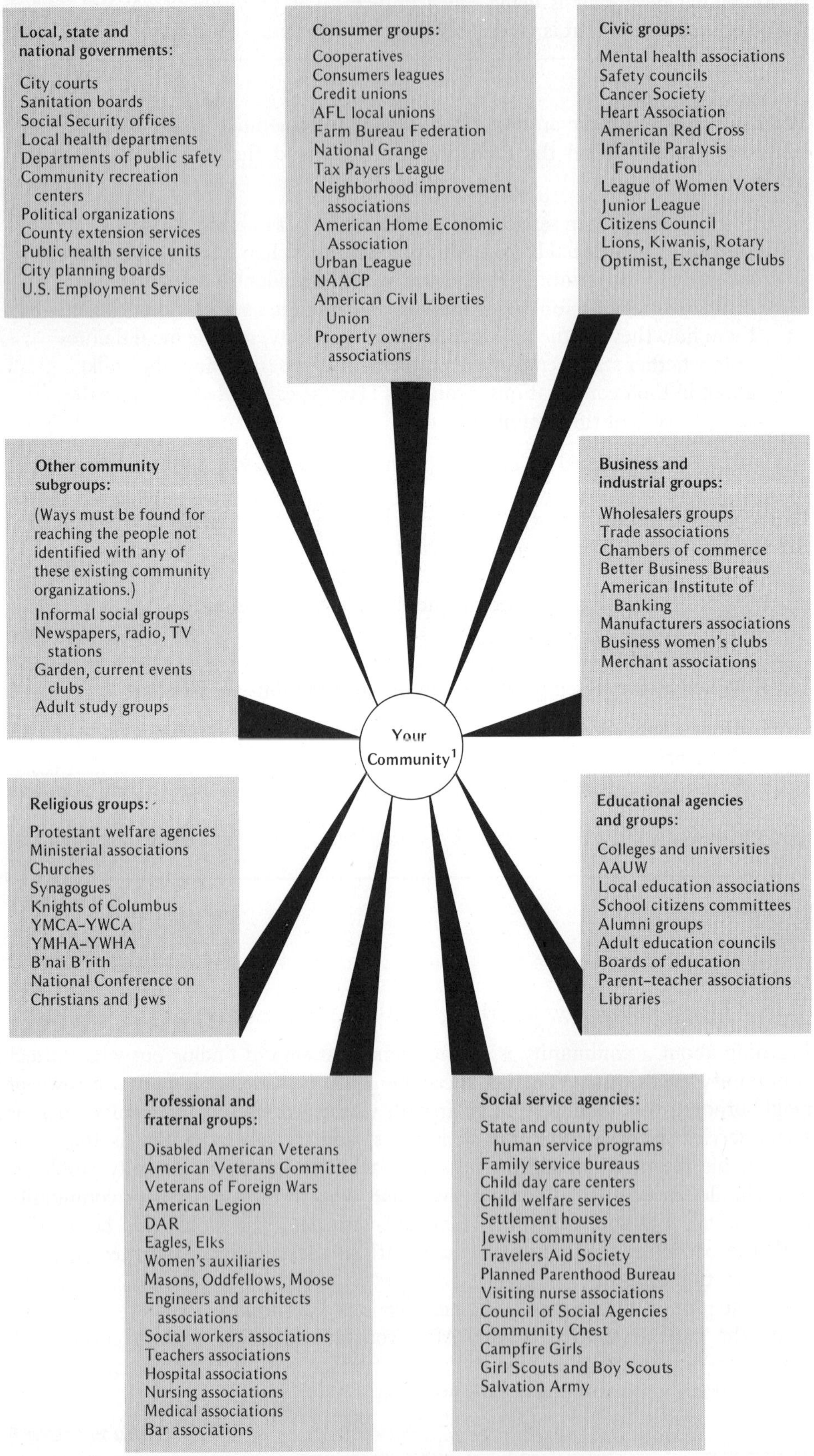

Local, state and national governments:

City courts
Sanitation boards
Social Security offices
Local health departments
Departments of public safety
Community recreation
  centers
Political organizations
County extension services
Public health service units
City planning boards
U.S. Employment Service

Consumer groups:

Cooperatives
Consumers leagues
Credit unions
AFL local unions
Farm Bureau Federation
National Grange
Tax Payers League
Neighborhood improvement
  associations
American Home Economic
  Association
Urban League
NAACP
American Civil Liberties
  Union
Property owners
  associations

Civic groups:

Mental health associations
Safety councils
Cancer Society
Heart Association
American Red Cross
Infantile Paralysis
  Foundation
League of Women Voters
Junior League
Citizens Council
Lions, Kiwanis, Rotary
Optimist, Exchange Clubs

Other community subgroups:

(Ways must be found for
reaching the people not
identified with any of
these existing community
organizations.)

Informal social groups
Newspapers, radio, TV
  stations
Garden, current events
  clubs
Adult study groups

Business and industrial groups:

Wholesalers groups
Trade associations
Chambers of commerce
Better Business Bureaus
American Institute of
  Banking
Manufacturers associations
Business women's clubs
Merchant associations

Your Community[1]

Religious groups:

Protestant welfare agencies
Ministerial associations
Churches
Synagogues
Knights of Columbus
YMCA-YWCA
YMHA-YWHA
B'nai B'rith
National Conference on
Christians and Jews

Educational agencies and groups:

Colleges and universities
AAUW
Local education associations
School citizens committees
Alumni groups
Adult education councils
Boards of education
Parent-teacher associations
Libraries

Professional and fraternal groups:

Disabled American Veterans
American Veterans Committee
Veterans of Foreign Wars
American Legion
DAR
Eagles, Elks
Women's auxiliaries
Masons, Oddfellows, Moose
Engineers and architects
  associations
Social workers associations
Teachers associations
Hospital associations
Nursing associations
Medical associations
Bar associations

Social service agencies:

State and county public
  human service programs
Family service bureaus
Child day care centers
Child welfare services
Settlement houses
Jewish community centers
Travelers Aid Society
Planned Parenthood Bureau
Visiting nurse associations
Council of Social Agencies
Community Chest
Campfire Girls
Girl Scouts and Boy Scouts
Salvation Army

[1] Edwin F. Hallenbeck, "Who Does What in Your Town", *Adult Leadership* 4 no. 1 (May 1955).

Fig. 2

Turn to Frame 6

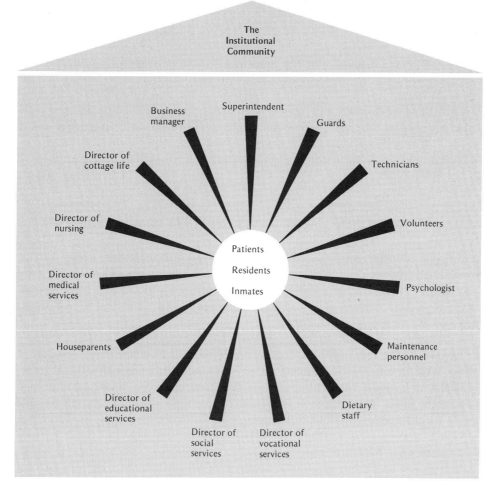

Fig. 3

Turn to Frame 7

FRAME 7

Sometimes it is difficult to view an institution (mental hospital, prison, training school for retarded, halfway house for delinquent youths) as a community. However, institutions are like total communities in that they provide life-supporting services for consumers and such necessities as food, shelter, clothing, recreation, and safety.[2] Total institutional communities were established to meet the needs of consumers in terms of rehabilitation and the needs of society in terms of socially controlling people who can not cope with the pressures of life.

If there are no rooms or lounge areas where an individual can be alone or meet others, such a situation in the institutional community could reflect an unmet need. The same can be noted if the consumers are not allowed to have their own personal clothing in contrast to prison uniforms or hospital clothes. Unmet needs in an institution may also relate to improving the quality of treatment, creating or expanding recreational and occupational programs, and improving the level of staff training.

(Frame 7 continued)

[2] Erving Goffman, *Asylums: Essays on the Social Situation of Mental Patients and Other Inmates* (Garden City, N.Y.: Doubleday, 1961).

Resources available to the institutional community include volunteer services, occupational therapy, recreational therapy, social services, and psychological services. These resources are as important to an institutional community as religious, educational, and social service resources are to a neighborhood or geographic community.

You can see the large and challenging task that any worker would have in trying to identify actual unmet needs in a community. There is no simple method for performing this task. Now that you have some understanding of the components of a community and how unmet community needs are identified, continue with Frame 8 to learn how mobilizing is used to deal with unmet community needs.

FRAME 8

WHAT IS MOBILIZING AND WHAT SHOULD IT ACCOMPLISH?

Mobilizing means to assemble community resources and make them ready for use to deal with unmet community needs. We begin by identifying the unmet needs, and then our goal is to do something about these needs. Mobilizing is the activity designed to *link resources with unmet community needs*. But this is not always easy.

Many groups in our communities do not make their needs known (e.g., children in need of health care) and some occasionally resist help when it is offered (e.g., alcoholics). It can also be difficult to get community resources to work together to deal with a need (e.g., getting a prison staff to develop an inmate rehabilitation program). Some resources need help in working with others (e.g., schools and police) and some are resistant to changing policies or services. Also, in the human services, we are always searching for better ways to find out who needs services, where they are needed, and why.

In addition to helping existing agencies work together, mobilizing also involves activities related to developing a new service. For example, the development of a new day-care center for children might involve mobilizing the support of parents, churches, fund raisers, the welfare and health departments, merchants, and other resources in the community. Mobilizing for community support requires attention to all the aspects of community life.

When engaging in mobilizing community interests, there are a number of different objectives related to addressing unmet needs. Mobilizing activities are designed to accomplish one or more of the following:

1. Making existing community resources known and easily *accessible* to the community (e.g., finding recreational equipment for use on hospital wards to help patients relate to each other)
2. Getting existing community resources to either *change* their present services or *work together* in dealing with the unmet need (e.g., encouraging schools to develop teenage counseling programs before students are expelled)
3. Bringing existing needs *to the community's attention* in an effort to gather support and acceptance (e.g., elderly residents in need of a "meals on wheels" program)
4. Working for the *establishment of new services* when all other alternatives have been exhausted (e.g., developing a new Big Brother program for delinquent youth)

(Frame 8 continued)

You can see that trying to bring community resources and people together may mean either supporting and working with existing community resources or creating a new service to relieve the need.

Turn to Frame 9

FRAME 9

Check the correct response.
   Mobilizing refers to which of the following activities?

A. Identifying unmet community needs

Turn to Answer 5

B. Meeting individuals in the community with problems and assisting them in finding help

Turn to Answer 7

C. Developing new services or linking presently available services together to meet community needs

Turn to Answer 8

FRAME 10

Place a check mark beside those explanations below which describe why it is often difficult to bring community resources to bear on fulfilling unmet community needs.

__ 1. Too many community groups make their needs known.

__ 2. Some community groups resist help when it is offered.

__ 3. Community resources are often changing the types of services they offer.

__ 4. Community resources often wish to work alone.

__ 5. Few community groups make their needs known.

Turn to Answer 4

FRAME 11

Place a check mark beside those statements below which refer to the objectives of mobilizing, and then turn to Answer 6.

__ 1. To bring a need to the attention of the community in order to obtain acceptance and support of fulfilling the need
__ 2. To help families and groups learn how to obtain services for their needs
__ 3. To gather and give information to consumers and agencies about unmet needs
__ 4. To convince existing community resources to change their services or work together in relieving an unmet need
__ 5. To publicize existing community resources and make them more easily accessible to residents of the community
__ 6. To help organize welfare rights groups, protest movements, etc.
__ 7. To encourage the development and establishment of new services needed in the community

As a human service worker in a community halfway house for delinquent girls, you are amazed to find that there are no job-preparation and training courses offered in your community. Since many of the girls in your halfway house have no experience in finding or keeping a job, you have decided to mobilize some of the community leaders and seek out some of the relevant resources to promote a new program of job training for youth in the community. Answer the following questions as a way of indicating how you would proceed.

1. How would you determine the need?

2. How would you bring existing resources together?

3. How would you gather community support and acceptance?

Turn to Answer 1

Mechanisms and Activities For Mobilizing Groups

A number of mechanisms are used to mobilize support in the community, most of which involve working with some kind of *community group*. Organizing community residents to solve a community problem is the main activity in mobilizing. When a worker brings two or more people together, he or she is using group work activities.

There are many different kinds of community groups, some already formed, others organizing for the purpose of solving a particular community problem. The typical kinds of groups a worker may encounter include the following:

1. Councils of representatives from existing community organizations
2. Committees of interested individuals not necessarily affiliated with any organized group, operating permanently or formed for the specific purpose of solving an unmet community need
3. Existing organizations in the community, such as school boards, city commissions, neighborhood organizations, etc.
4. Existing consumer groups, such as welfare rights organization, patient or inmate councils, parents of retarded or delinquent youth, etc.

All these groups may be involved in a number of activities related to the community, such as making decisions or recommendations, giving advice, studying problems, and effecting changes in the community. So the *group* is an important mechanism used in mobilization efforts.

Steps in mobilizing. We know that no two communities are alike in their unmet needs and how they deal with them. But there is a basic plan workers can keep in mind when mobilizing for change. When attempting to deal with an unmet community need by bringing together fragmented and isolated services or creating

(Frame 13 continued)

new services, it is important to plan activities in the community. Not all workers follow these steps in their community work, but these steps do show you one approach to planning and organizing certain work activities related to the community. Once a worker has identified an unmet community need, some of the steps in mobilizing for change might include the following:

1. First find out if there is an existing service that can meet the need (e.g., a local community action agency may have a free transportation service to the food-stamp office of which community residents are unaware).
2. If there is an appropriate service or program, find out if the need can be met through an existing service organization by making the organization aware of the need (e.g., a number of patients in a mental hospital may request that a basic reading program be started, and the volunteer coordinator, once aware of the problem can start one).
3. If there is no existing service and no organization immediately capable of providing the service, help get one started by recruiting a group of interested people to work on solving the problem.
4. If a group of interested people is organized to work on the problem of meeting a community need, make sure the group represents the largest possible number of community organizations and interested parties related to the problem at hand.
5. Whether working with an existing organization or organizing a group, help develop a plan of action by gathering support in the community and involve the largest possible number of people and groups in the community who might make a contribution.

Turn to Frame 14

FRAME 14

Which of the following groups would probably be formed for the purpose of solving a specific unmet community need?

A. A city commission

Turn to Answer 9

B. A committee

Turn to Answer 11

C. A club

Turn to Answer 12

FRAME 15

Wanda P. is a psychiatric aide in a mental health hospital. She is concerned about the lack of opportunities for patients on her ward to take trips outside the hospital. Within the hospital, there is a patient activity group which was established by the hospital superintendent some time ago to act in an advisory capacity to hospital staff regarding patient activities (e.g., recreation, home visits). Wanda goes to this group and discusses the problem with them, hoping they may be interested in requesting a field-visit program for patients. What type of group is Wanda working with?

Turn to Answer 10

FRAME 16

In order to help get a service or program started to meet a need, which of the following should you do?

A. Develop a plan of action.

Turn to Answer 13

B. Recruit residents to form a group which will work toward solving the problem.

Turn to Answer 14

C. Gather support in the community.

Turn to Answer 15

D. A and B above.

Turn to Answer 16

E. A, B, and C above.

Turn to Answer 17

FRAME 17

In conclusion, if you find an existing service or an organization capable of providing the service in your community that can meet a need, your task would be to gather support in the community for this service. If, however, there is no organization in the community capable or willing to fill the need, your task would be to help get such a service established. Community support would be needed, and a group could be formed to plan ways to meet the need or solve the problem.

Go on now to Lesson 2 to examine some of the skills used in mobilizing a community to deal with unmet community needs.

ANSWERS TO LESSON 1

ANSWER 1

The most important step in the mobilizing process is a careful determination of community needs. It makes little sense to mobilize a wide range of community resources if a related program or service already exists or if the girls in your halfway house are the only ones in need. If only your girls need the service, a small program in the halfway house itself could be developed, with as much community involvement as necessary.

The answers to how you would proceed are as follows:

1. How would you determine the need? Meetings with high school guidance counselors, employment service counselors, and chamber of commerce representatives might provide you with preliminary information on the extent of the need for specialized job training in the community.
2. How would you bring existing resources together? Once you have been able to at least estimate the number of girls who could benefit and the number of employers who would support the program, with some documentation, an interagency task force could be established by the local social planning agency or by your own agency.
3. How would you gather community support and acceptance? After several meetings of the task force, representatives are better able to identify resources and usually more prepared to share their own resources. Significant community leaders could then be approached for financial support and/or moral support. A campaign to educate the public through news releases, public speaking, brochures, etc., could also be an approach to gathering community support.

As you can see, the process of mobilizing involves the use of organizing and planning skills as well as of skills in working with groups.
Return now to Frame 13.

ANSWER 2

You should have underlined the words *unmet* and *met*, since Mrs. R's need for low-cost day-care was not being met, although the community need for day-care

165

was being met. There may be many reasons for the fact that Mrs. R's need is not being met. When several cases such as hers are found by human service workers or others in a community, it is time to mobilize resources to deal with this as an unmet community need.

Return now to Frame 3.

ANSWER 3

Hank has remembered questions 1, 2, and 3. He has neglected, however, to find out how nonresidents, merchants, professionals, etc., see the problems; consequently, he has no basis to compare their perceptions to community residents. If you had trouble with this question, go back and review Frame 1 before going on to Frame 4. Otherwise, proceed directly to Frame 4.

ANSWER 4

You should have checked 2, 4, and 5, since many groups do not (a few do) make their needs known, and community resources are often resistant to changes in the policies and types of services offered. This makes it difficult to identify unmet needs, and also to mobilize resources to meet those needs that are identified.

Turn to Frame 11.

ANSWER 5

Identifying unmet needs in a community is the activity which must take place before mobilization can begin.

Return to Frame 8 and review the material presented there before answering Frame 9 correctly.

ANSWER 6

You should have checked statements 1, 4, 5, and 7. Statements 2 and 3 are objectives of the brokering functions, while statement 6 is an objective of the advocating function. Mobilizing objectives include making known resources accessible, getting resources to change their services or coordinate with other resources, gathering support and assisting in establishing new services—all to help meet unmet community needs.

Return to Frame 12.

ANSWER 7

When a human service worker is meeting people with problems in the community and helping them obtain assistance he or she is performing a brokering function, as distinct from a mobilizing function.

Return to Frame 8 and review the material presented there before selecting the correct response to Frame 9.

ANSWER 8

This is correct. Mobilizing refers to the activity of developing new services or linking present services to fulfill an unmet community need.

Return now to Frame 10 and continue the good work.

ANSWER 9

No, a city commission is a group of individuals already formed to handle the business of a city. It would not be formed on a temporary basis.

Return to Frame 13 and review the material presented there before answering Frame 14 correctly.

ANSWER 10

If you answered "an existing consumer group" you are right! It was not necessary for Wanda to form a committee or a council. Nor was it necessary for her to go to an official organization of any kind since a consumer group interested in dealing with such a problem already existed within her community (the hospital). If you answered anything else, go back and review Frame 13 before going on to Frame 16.

ANSWER 11

Right! Committees can be formed on permanent and temporary bases to work toward the solution of a problem. Other community groups are formed, for the most part, to handle long-term problems.
   Return to Frame 15 and answer that question.

ANSWER 12

A club is usually formed around a common interest in some activity and not for solving specific community problems.
   Since you had trouble here, return to Frame 13 for a review before answering Frame 14 correctly.

ANSWER 13

This is only partially correct, since it is only one of the possible answers given.
   Return to Frame 13 for a review, and then answer Frame 16 correctly.

ANSWER 14

Yes, but you are only partly correct. There are other equally correct responses to this question.
   Return to Frame 13 for a review, and then answer Frame 16 correctly.

ANSWER 15

This is a correct response, but there are other equally correct responses.
   Return to Frame 13 for a brief review before answering Frame 16 correctly.

ANSWER 16

You are two-thirds correct if you chose this answer. Although both these responses are correct, there is also another action you should take.
   Therefore, return to Frame 16 and select the proper answer.

ANSWER 17

Well done. To help get a service or program started which will meet a need, you should develop a plan of action, gather support, and recruit residents to form a group that will be responsible for either establishing a new community service or bringing together existing resources to meet the need.
   Return now to Frame 17.

LESSON 2:
MOBILIZING IN
YOUR COMMUNITY

In this lesson you will be reviewing some of the principles and skills of mobilizing. You will learn about participation in group meetings and the process of helping community groups solve problems. Such information will help you develop some of the skills you need to mobilize in your community. The goal of this lesson and the enabling activities that will help you reach this goal are presented below.

GOAL

Given a description of an unmet need in your community, you will be able to demonstrate your understanding of the skills needed to mobilize support in the community to solve the problem.

ENABLING ACTIVITIES

After completing this lesson, you will have accomplished four things:

1. Distinguished the difference between a formal and an informal meeting
2. Identified important skills of group meetings
3. Reviewed different roles that you can play when working with community groups
4. Examined six stages of group problem solving.

Turn to Frame 1 to begin this lesson

FRAME 1

PREPARING FOR AND PARTICIPATING
EFFECTIVELY IN COMMUNITY MEETINGS

Most community work will require a familiarity with the skills needed to prepare and participate in both formal and informal meetings.

(Frame 1 continued)

Formal meetings are those in which the transaction of business proceeds according to set ground rules, for example, only one person will talk at a time, anyone may submit a proposal or make a motion, the proposal must be discussed, and the majority rules when a vote is taken. *Informal meetings* are those in which the transaction of business proceeds by informal group discussion involving usually three or more persons. Informal meetings involve a face to face meeting of the group, and discussion is carried out without fixed rules. All group members are expected to participate in the discussion, and one person usually assumes the role of the discussion leader. Informal meetings have a definite subject for discussion, that is, the group does not simply engage in casual conversation.

Many of you have already developed some of the skills used to participate in these meetings in your roles as parents or other active participants in your community. Since it is impossible for us to cover all the skills needed, we will talk about five of the more important ones: (1) getting people to come to a meeting, (2) setting up a meeting, (3) achieving major goals at the first meeting, (4) developing and distributing an agenda, and (5) keeping a group moving toward its goals.[1]

Getting people to come to a meeting. This can be a very difficult job. You may be asked to recruit people and get them interested. First you should visit each person you are trying to involve, explain the purpose, and tell the person why it is important that he or she attends. This is particularly important if it is the person's first meeting or if you have never met the person before. Talking with people to persuade them to come to a meeting can be very time consuming. Once the group is established, one way to cut down on the time involved is to appoint a committee to recruit people for the meeting. Another way is to ask each group member to bring a friend who has a contribution to offer. People are more likely to attend if a friend asks them to come.

Here are some helpful hints to remember in trying to get people to attend a meeting:

1. Explain the purpose of the meeting and why it is important for the person to attend, and do this in person if possible.
2. Make your request far enough ahead of time to allow the person to make arrangements to attend.
3. Follow up with a note or phone call just prior to the meeting.
4. Thank each person who attends and acknowledge their contribution.
5. Do not "write off" a person you have invited who doesn't show up. Try again—there may have been a very good reason why the person couldn't attend.

Setting up a meeting. If you are asked to set up a meeting or help others to set up a meeting, you should have a check list of things to do based on questions such as the following:

1. Does everyone know where and when the meeting is being held? Have reminders been sent out?
2. Are there enough seats for everyone?
3. Are there name tags or cards identifying each person? If there are no tags, is there another way for people to be introduced to each other?
4. Are there copies of the agenda for everyone? If not, can the agenda be put on a big poster or blackboard?

(Frame 1 continued)

---

[1] These skills may be found in Gertrude S. Goldberg, Alvin B. Kogut, Seymour Lesh, and Dorothy Yates, *New Careers: The Social Service Aide: A Manual for Trainees* (Washington, D.C.: University Research Corporation, 1968).

5. Has someone been selected to take notes at the meeting so decisions and discussions are not lost?
6. Will a report of the meeting be sent both to people who attended and to those who couldn't come?
7. Do you have printed material from your agency to hand out? If not, are you prepared to tell the group something about you and your agency's services?
8. Have other people been encouraged to participate in the meeting and been given the necessary help?

Obviously, there will be some things you will want to add to this list or change, depending on the particular meeting you are setting up. The important thing is to make sure questions like these are taken care of when you are setting up a meeting.

Achieving major goals at the first meeting. Certain things have to happen at the first meeting of a group if it is to have a chance for success in launching a program. Participants need to experience some accomplishments early in the process, and it is important to set realistic goals that can be easily achieved. The following six goals for group members relate to the meeting process itself and are, therefore, good ones to start out with:

1. People should get acquainted and exchange points of view.
2. Group members should agree on what they will tackle first.
3. The group should agree on how it will tackle the problem.
4. People should be given responsibilities for working on the problem.
5. The group should agree on the time and place for the next meeting.
6. The members should make plans for involving other interested people in the the next meeting.

Go on to Frame 2

FRAME 2

For the following list of meeting activities, put F next to those that are more commonly found in formal meetings and I next to those more often found in informal meetings.

1. __ There is a definite subject for discussion.

2. __ A chairperson is chosen to preserve order and help keep the meeting moving.

3. __ The group participates, for the most part, in casual conversation.

4. __ There is usually a discussion leader.

5. __ When a vote is taken, the majority rules.

6. __ More than one person may be talking at the same time.

7. — All group members are expected to participate in the discussion.

Turn to Answer 2

FRAME 3

A regular membership meeting of a committee of community residents to discuss past progress and future actions would be a meeting of the _____ type, while a luncheon meeting of agency executives with a mutual interest would probably be the _____ type.
    Choose the correct answers (in order of appearance).

(Frame 3 continued)

A. informal, formal.

Turn to Answer 6

B. formal, informal.

Turn to Answer 8

FRAME 4

If you had the responsibility for getting ten specific people to come to the first meeting of a newly formed committee on developing day-care services, the best way for you to proceed would probably be to

1. send personalized letters explaining the purpose of the meeting.

Turn to Answer 10

2. visit each person to explain why they are needed.

Turn to Answer 12

3. call them personally explaining their potential role.

Turn to Answer 13

FRAME 5

Suppose one of the persons you contacted for the meeting mentioned in the previous frame is a Mr. Cranston, who, even after indicating his interest and promising to attend, did not show up. As time for the next meeting approached, you could either go by and see Mr. Cranston again and invite him to the meeting or you could assume he was really not interested, as indicated by his absence from the first meeting, and spend your time working with people you know you could depend on.

**Decide which you think is the
best course of action, and then
turn to Answer 3**

FRAME 6

When setting up a meeting, you should be sure to perform certain activities, eight of which we have noted. In the space provided, state the two activities that will inform everyone at the meeting of what is going to happen and will also help people who did not attend the meeting.

1.

2.

**Once you have identified these
activities, turn to Answer 4**

FRAME 7

If a group is to be successful in launching its program, project, etc., which of the following should occur at the first meeting? Check those that apply:

1. __ Group members should agree on the problem which has first priority.

2. __ Members should get acquainted and exchange points of view.

3. __ The group should agree on how it will tackle the first problem.

(Frame 7 continued)

4. __ Members should identify other persons who should be involved in the next meeting and plan how to bring them in.

5. __ Members should be given responsibilities for working on the problem with the first priority.

6. __ The group should agree on the time and place for the next meeting.

Turn to Answer 1

FRAME 8

There are two additional skills used in participating in group meetings:

Developing and distributing an agenda. It is important to develop and distribute an agenda for each meeting. The written agenda usually includes a list of things to be discussed by the group. You can make up the agenda before the meeting, or a committee of group members can make it up. If everyone has a copy of the agenda at the meeting, it will help people stick to the topics and know what is going to happen next. Topics that are not on the agenda can also be discussed, but the agenda will give the group an idea of where they are going. It is very important to avoid making the agenda too long because this can result in too little time being spent on important topics.

Keeping the group moving toward its goals. Some things to remember for keeping a group going in their efforts to solve community problems are listed below.

1. The more people involved in the planning and leadership group, the more likely you are to have an ongoing, active group.
2. Seeing a problem through and then moving on to another one not only maintains interest but increases involvement in community affairs.
3. Taking time at the end of the meeting to plan for the next one is a good way to get people interested in participating in it and in coming again.
4. Bringing new people into the group helps members feel that it is worth being part of the group.
5. Time should be allowed for all members to take part in discussions.
6. Members should take increasing amounts of responsibility for the group as time goes on. You should be available for advice and direction, but leadership should usually be assumed by the members as soon as it is feasible.

Turn to Frame 9

FRAME 9

An agenda, or list of topics to be discussed at a meeting, is useful in which of the following ways?

A. It helps participants know what will happen during the meeting.

Turn to Answer 5

B. It eliminates nonproductive discussion, since only topics on the agenda may be discussed at the meeting.

Turn to Answer 7

C. It helps give direction to the meeting.

Turn to Answer 9

D. A and C above.

Turn to Answer 11

E. A, B and C above.

Turn to Answer 14

Mrs. Pope is the leader of a local committee aimed at trying to provide services for unmarried mothers. She has been successful in leading this committee in the accomplishment of many tasks. She has delegated many of her responsibilities to other members and has involved many of them in planning and directing projects. She also sees to it that new people continue to be invited to join the group. Name below at least two other ways in which Mrs. Pope is probably helping to keep this committee active and moving forward in solving the problems of unwed mothers.

1.

2.

3.

**After citing at least two ways
above, go on to Answer 18**

FRAME 11

YOUR VARIOUS ROLES IN COMMUNITY WORK

In working with different community groups, you may have to play a number of different roles, depending on the type of group, your style of working, how you handle groups, and what assignment your agency has given you to work on with the group. A worker will probably even play different roles with the same group. It is important to decide which of the following roles will be most useful to the community group in achieving its goals:

Organizer. If you are trying to recruit community residents or establish a pressure group to work for quicker action on some community problem, you will be organizing. You will have an active role and will be persuading, urging, and convincing. You may also need to lead the first group meeting until the group has selected its own leader.

Enabler. Enabling involves helping a group to function better by encouraging the development of a leadership within the group. You may give the group information, offer suggestions and examples, keep records of group meetings by recording actions and decisions, and help the group acquire information and consider different plans of action. Your objective is to encourage the group to be independent of you, to develop its own leadership, and to make its own decisions and plans.

Gatekeeper. The gatekeeper attempts to keep communication channels open by encouraging the participation of others or by proposing limits on the flow of communication so that others will have a chance to participate. The gatekeeper may also praise, agree with, and accept the contribution of others.

Tension reliever. When conflicts arise within the group, the worker should try to resolve differences between members and relieve tension. Good ways of doing this are by using humor and by temporarily changing the topic of discussion.

Follower. The follower goes along with the movement of the group, more or less passively, accepting the ideas of others and serving as an audience in group discussion and decisions.

Go on to Frame 12

FRAME 12

Which one of the following roles attempts to keep communication open among group members?

A. Enabler

Turn to Answer 16

B. Organizer

Turn to Answer 20

C. Gatekeeper

Turn to Answer 22

D. None of the above

Turn to Answer 24

FRAME 13

If you are giving group members information or suggesting methods of action with the goal of helping the group become independent by developing its own leadership and making its own decisions and plans, you are acting as

A. enabler.

Turn to Answer 15

B. organizer.

Turn to Answer 17

C. gatekeeper.

Turn to Answer 19

D. follower.

Turn to Answer 21

FRAME 14

Explain below the role of a tension reliever, and then proceed to Answer 26.

FRAME 15

MAJOR STAGES OF GROUP PROBLEM SOLVING

As you work with others to solve community problems or meet community needs, you should try to follow some basic steps which will assist you in helping groups function effectively. The following are some basic steps.

1. **Clarify the problem and obtain information.** Help the group spell out the problem by getting complaints, preferences, and facts from the people experiencing the problem. Make sure everyone has a clear understanding of the problem. Decide what information is needed to make the problem clear, and determine ways to get this information.

(Frame 15 continued)

2. **Set up goals.** Help group members decide what result they want, what is to be done, and what change needs to be made.

3. **Find alternative solutions.** Think of ways to solve the problem and discuss different possibilities. Check each possible solution and then decide which is the best.

4. **Plan and organize for action.** Putting the plan into operation involves gaining approval from those in authority, overcoming resistance, and using resources. Keep lines of communication open since people must understand what has been done, what is being done, and what is going to be done. Encourage the group to perform their tasks with as little of your assistance as possible.

5. **Evaluate progress as you go along.** Based on what steps should be taken according to the plan of action, determine what steps have been taken and what the results have been. If something did not work, find out why. Decide what changes in plans have to be made as a result of what has happened.

6. **Follow up on the action.** Are people carrying out their responsibilities on time? If the community said it would act, has it done so? What did the group learn about getting things done? What should be done differently next time? By gaining information from all those involved in the mobilizing effort about the success of the plan and unmet needs, the group is led into another problem-solving process in which new problems and needs are defined.

Go on to Frame 16

FRAME 16

In your work with community groups, you will often be helping the group solve problems. What is the first step in this process?

A. Discussing possible solutions

Turn to Answer 23

B. Helping the group clarify the problem

Turn to Answer 25

C. Helping group members decide what results they wish to achieve

Turn to Answer 27

FRAME 17

Once you are sure that all group members clearly understand the problem, what is the next task in the problem-solving process?

A. Deciding what result is desired

Turn to Answer 28

B. Identifying ways to solve the problem and deciding on the best way

Turn to Answer 29

C. Acting on solving the problem

Turn to Answer 30

FRAME 18

Assume you have proceeded through the first four phases in the problem-solving process with a group working on the development of a recreational program in your

(Frame 18 continued)

institution. You have helped the group spell out the problem so that they all understand it clearly; they have decided on the results they want, the best ways to solve the problem, and have put a plan into action. What final two things remain for the group to do to complete their plan of action?

1.

2.

**After you have stated these last
two Activities, go on to Answer 31**

ANSWERS TO LESSON 2

ANSWER 1

You should have checked all the items. If you had any trouble, return to Frame 1 for a review before going on to Frame 8.

ANSWER 2

You should have put I next to items, 1, 4, 6, and 7 and F next to items 2, 3, and 5. Informal meetings also have a definite subject under discussion, with all taking part and one person assuming the role of leader. If this does not occur, little will be accomplished. Since informal meetings have no set ground rules, a leader is needed to maintain an orderly, though very flexible, procedure.

Return to Frame 3.

ANSWER 3

The best course of action would be to go by and visit Mr. Cranston again. His absence at the first meeting may have been unavoidable. However, *do not* question him about why he did not attend. It is sufficient to say that he was missed and you hope he can make the upcoming meeting. To "write him off" because he missed the first meeting would be a mistake, in that Mr. Cranston may well have the potential to make valuable contributions to the group. If you answered incorrectly go back and review Frame 1 before going on to Frame 6.

ANSWER 4

Two of the key activities in preparing for a meeting are the following:

1. Preparation of an agenda for everyone
2. Preparation of a meeting report to be sent to all those who attended and did not attend

Hopefully, you are able to list all eight of the tasks that are necessary in setting up a meeting.

Go on now to Frame 7.

ANSWER 5

Yes, this is one way in which an agenda may be useful, but there are other ways.
Return to Frame 9 and identify one or more of these other uses for an agenda.

ANSWER 6

No, you have them reversed. A committee would conduct formal meetings while these agency executives are meeting informally.
Return to Frame 1 for a brief review and then answer Frame 3 correctly.

ANSWER 7

No, topics which are not on the agenda may also be proposed for discussion. Such topics can be productive if members feel they are important enough to discuss.
Return to Frame 8 for a brief review and then answer Frame 9 correctly.

ANSWER 8

Right you are. A committee would hold formal meetings while these executives would be holding an informal meeting with no ground rules, although one of them may have been the leader in setting up the meeting and making sure something is accomplished at the meeting.
Return now to Frame 4.

ANSWER 9

This is correct, but it is only a partial answer to this question. Return to Frame 9 and answer the question correctly.

ANSWER 10

No, sending letters is not necessarily the best way to get people to attend meetings, particularly a first meeting. It should only be used as a last resort, although it is a good way to remind people of the meeting once they have been contacted in other ways.
Return to Frame 1 for a review before answering Frame 4 correctly.

ANSWER 11

Correct. An agenda may be useful in helping members know what is going to happen at a meeting as well as for giving direction to the meeting.
Return now to Frame 10 and keep up the good work.

ANSWER 12

Excellent! By taking the time to visit each individual on a personal basis, explaining the purpose of the meeting and the importance of their attending, you are conveying to that person that he or she is important and needed by the group.
Continue to Frame 5.

ANSWER 13

This may be a useful second alternative, but it is not the best method. Calling may also be a useful way of reminding the person of the meeting.
Return to Frame 1 for a review before answering Frame 4 correctly.

ANSWER 14

You are only two-thirds correct since you have included an erroneous response in your answer.
Return to Frame 8 for a review before answering Frame 9 correctly.

ANSWER 15

Well done! The enabler helps the group function better and become independent.
Go on now to Frame 14.

ANSWER 16

No, the enabler helps the group function independently.
Return to Frame 11 for a review before answering Frame 12 correctly.

ANSWER 17

This is close, but not correct. The organizer helps establish groups to work on solving community problems. Once the group is formed and has selected a leader, the organizer shifts to become more of an enabler.
Return to Frame 11 for a review and then select the correct answer to Frame 13.

ANSWER 18

In addition to her success in keeping this committee moving forward, Mrs. Pope is probably also helping the committee to do the following:

1. See problems through to a solution and then move on to another one
2. Take time at the end of each meeting to plan for the next one
3. Plan meetings so that there will be time for all members to participate if they so desire

Did you state at least two of the above? If so, go on to Frame 11. If not, review Frame 8 briefly before going on to Frame 11.

ANSWER 19

This is not the best choice. Return to Frame 11 for a review before answering Frame 13 again.

ANSWER 20

The organizer establishes groups by recruiting residents to work on solving problems.
Return to Frame 11 for a review of the five major roles before answering Frame 12 correctly.

ANSWER 21

No, the role of follower is a passive role. The follower rarely provides information or advice.
Return to Frame 11 for a review before choosing the correct answer to Frame 13.

ANSWER 22

This is correct. The gatekeeper's role is to keep the channels of communication open among members of groups by encouraging and facilitating participation of all members.
Return now to Frame 13.

ANSWER 23

It would be difficult to fulfill this task until the problem has been clarified by the group.
Return to Frame 15 for a review and then answer Frame 16 correctly.

ANSWER 24

Sorry, but there was a correct answer among the three choices given. Return to Frame 11 for a review and then select the correct role described in Frame 12.

ANSWER 25

Good show! The first stage in problem solving is to help the group clarify the problem. This can be accomplished by obtaining information, complaints, etc., from those experiencing the problem.

Return to Frame 17 and continue the lesson.

ANSWER 26

The tension reliever helps resolve differences between group members. You may have to assume this role whenever conflicts arise between group members causing a blockage of action or decision making.

Return now to Frame 15.

ANSWER 27

Group members would have a difficult time deciding on the result they wish to achieve before they know what the problem is.

Return to Frame 15 for a review before answering Frame 16 correctly.

ANSWER 28

Yes, once the problem is clear, and before ways are identified for solving the problem, it is necessary to decide on what results are desired to alleviate the problem.

Return to Frame 18.

ANSWER 29

The task of identifying those methods to be used in solving the problem should not be taken up until another task is completed.

Return to Frame 15 for a review and then answer Frame 17 correctly.

ANSWER 30

This would be a premature action. Before planning and organizing for action, methods for solving the problem should be identified and discussed.

Return to Frame 15 for a review of the stages in problem solving and then answer Frame 17 correctly.

ANSWER 31

In order to find out whether or not the group is accomplishing what it set out to accomplish, there must be a continuous evaluation of the progress made to date. Lastly, follow-up action is needed to check on the solution to the problem. This will lead to information about how effectively the problem-solving process has worked and will identify additional unmet needs in the community, thereby setting in motion another problem-solving process.

You have reached the end of Chapter V which is also the end of Unit Two. You should be ready to turn to the summary and short review of Chapter V, which is found at the end of this lesson. If you have any doubts, return to the beginning of the chapter for a review of both lessons before starting the summary and review questions.

SUMMARY

This chapter was designed to describe the major tasks and strategies of mobilizing within the community. Particular attention was given to the process of identifying unmet community needs and taking effective action to meet those needs. Particular attention was also given to strategies involved in organizing and working with community groups.

The important first step of mobilizing is the identification of unmet community needs, whether the community is a neighborhood or an institution. Once an unmet need has been identified, the process of mobilizing begins with specific steps to be taken in order to link resources with unmet community needs. It was pointed out that the primary task in mobilizing, whether working to make an existing service more accessible or working to create a new service, is to develop a plan of action by gathering community support and involving as many people and groups as possible who can make a contribution.

Human service workers who engage in mobilizing activities usually work with community or staff committees, and they must be aware of the different kinds of meetings, the skills necessary for working with groups, and the common mobilizing roles assumed by workers engaged in the process. Specific attention was directed to the six stages of problem solving with groups, beginning with helping the group define the problem and concluding with what is involved in following up on the action.

SUGGESTIONS FOR FURTHER STUDY

Most of the literature available on mobilizing will come from the field of social work related to community organization and from the areas of sociology concerned with the structure of communities and the process of community development. Further study is needed in order to refine your organizing skills. For example, the activity of identifying unmet community needs should receive further study in terms of client analysis and needs assessment. Further exploration should be made into the area of developing information sources in the community and into the area of identifying and utilizing indigenous leadership in the community. Several books by Saul Alinsky are helpful in this area.

Understanding community power structures is also very important and needs additional study. There is a wealth of literature in this area, largely from the fields of sociology and political science. The works of such authorities as Floyd Hunter, Peter Rossi, Robert Dahl, Scott Greer, and Roland Warren, to name only a few, will provide helpful perspectives on community power structures. This is an important area of further study for human service workers who carry out mobilizing activities, since decisions are often made through a political process involving trade-offs between various power groups and not always in the humanitarian tradition of the "common good."

Further study also is indicated in the area of effective work with groups, specifically the process of group dynamics. Much attention is given to this area in the fields of psychology and sociology. Another important area relates to working with community groups which require particular organizing strategies. In organizing some groups one may have to concentrate on short-term problem-focused activities, for example, in starting a Boy's Club, while other groups can be organized around some ongoing community involvement, such as an organization for neighborhood improvement. The role of the mobilizer will differ, and the strategies employed will vary, depending upon the nature of the group.

SUGGESTIONS FOR FURTHER READING

Alinsky, Saul. *Reveille for Radicals*. New York: Random House, 1969.

Brager, George. "Organizing the Unaffiliated in a Low-Income Area." *Social Work* 8 (April 1963): 34–40.

Cox, Fred M.; Erlich, John L.; Rothman, Jack; and Tropman, John E.; eds. *Strategies of Community Organization*. Itasca, Ill.: F. E. Peacock, Publishers, Inc., 1970.

Dahl, Robert. "Critique of the Ruling Elite Model." *American Political Science Review* (June 1958).

Dahl, Robert L. *Who Governs?* New Haven: Yale University Press, 1961.

Dunham, Arthur. *The New Community Organization*. New York: Macmillan, 1970.

Goffman, Erving. *Asylums: Essays on the Social Situation of Mental Patients and Other Inmates*. Garden City, N.Y.: Doubleday, 1961.

Goldberg, Gertrude S.; Kogut, Alvin B.; Lesh, Seymour; and Yates, Dorothy. *New Careers: The Social Service Aide: A Manual for Trainees*. Washington, D.C.: University Research Corporation, 1968.

Greer, Scott. *The Emerging City*. New York: Free Press, 1962.

——— *Governing the Metropolis*. New York: Wiley, 1962.

Hallenbeck, Edwin F. "Who Does What in Your Town?" *Adult Leadership*, 4 (May 1955).

Hunter, Floyd. *Community Power Structure*. Garden City, N.Y.: Doubleday Anchor Books, 1963.

Kiester, Dorothy J. "Mobilizing Resources to Meet the Needs of Children." *Public Welfare* 21 (January 1963)

Kramer, Ralph M., and Specht, Harry. *Readings in Community Organization Practice*. Englewood Cliffs, N.J.: Prentice-Hall, 1969.

Lowy, Louis. *Training Manual for Human Service Technicians Working with Older Persons, Part II: Trainees*. United Community Services of Metropolitan Boston, 1968. (Available through Boston University Bookstores.)

Ross, Murray. *Community Organization*. New York: Harper & Row, 1955.

Rossi, Peter H. "Community Decision Making." *Administrative Science Quarterly* 7 (March 1957): 415–443.

Sieder, Violet M. *The Rehabilitation Agency and Community Work: A Source Book for Professional Training*. Washington, D.C.: U.S. Department of Health, Education, and Welfare, Vocational Rehabilitation Administration (March 1966).

Stein, Maurice R. *The Eclipse of Community*. New York: Harper & Row, 1960.

Warren, Roland. *The Community in America*. Chicago: Rand McNally, 1972.

Weissman, Harold. *Community Development in the Mobilization for Youth Experience*. New York: Association Press, 1969.

REVIEW QUESTIONS—CHAPTER V

Circle the letter corresponding to the answer of your choice.

1. Assume that you work in a local office of the division of mental retardation. After working there for a short time, you begin to get the feeling that the mentally retarded in your community are not obtaining many services provided in other communities in the state. How would you go about trying to confirm feelings?

    A. Study model programs in other parts of the state.

    B. Question residents who have retarded children.

C. Visit and observe activities at community agencies presently providing services for the retarded.

D. B and C above.

E. None of the above.

2. What other methods could you use to help confirm your feelings about needed services for the retarded in your community?

A. Question doctors, lawyers, businessmen, and other professionals in the community.

B. Attempt to identify the common problems that emerge from the conversations of the residents.

C. Compare what the parents of retarded have told you to the common problems discussed by residents.

D. B and C above.

E. A, B, and C above.

3. Now take a moment to reflect on your own community (your home town, a local community, or an institution in which you work) and think of one unmet need of the residents in that community.

Have you thought of one? Okay, then write it in the space below:

Assuming that fulfillment of the unmet need you mentioned above is your goal, what action would you take first?

A. Help start a service or program in the community to meet the need.

B. Develop a plan of action.

C. Find out if there is an agency or program that could develop a service to meet the need.

D. Find out if there is an existing agency in the community that can provide the services necessary to fulfill the unmet need.

4. Whether or not there is an agency in the community capable of fulfilling the unmet need you have identified, what is your major task as a mobilizer?

A. Gather support in the community.

B. Set up a committee or council to handle the problem.

C. Help develop a plan of action involving as many residents as possible who are capable of making a contribution.

D. A and C.

E. A, B, and C.

5. Assuming that no local agency could gear up to meet the need, with which of the following groups or agencies could you probably work in attempting to mobilize the community to fulfill the need you identified in Question 3?

A. The local school board

B. A committee or council composed of those residents capable and willing to make contributions

C. The local community action agency

D. The local welfare office

E. B and C

6. As a mobilizer, what would your objective be if you found that many persons in your community needed a service that was available but were not receiving the service?

    A. Gather support for the agency providing the service.
    B. Establish a similar service that will reach these people.
    C. Help make the service known and more easily reached.
    D. Tell them they had to use the service.
    E. A and C.

7. Suppose that during a luncheon meeting of some representatives from local agencies you explain the unmet need you have identified and ask for their support. After a brief discussion, several of them tell you that they will help in any way they can. This was what type of meeting?
    A. Formal
    B. Informal
    C. Committee
    D. None of the above

8. Which of the following activities would occur at an informal meeting?
    A. When a vote is taken, the majority rules.
    B. One person speaks at a time.
    C. All group members participate in the discussion.
    D. All proposals made are thoroughly discussed.
    E. C and D.

9. Assume you are the chairperson of a local committee to work on fulfilling the need you have identified in Question 3. After getting people to come to the meeting and setting it up, you are now involved in chairing the first meeting. Which of the following skills should you have to effectively run the meeting?
    A. Developing and distributing an agenda
    B. Attempting to attain the six major goals of a first group meeting
    C. Keeping committee members headed toward the major goals
    D. A and C above
    E. A, B, and C above

10. Which of the statements listed below should be your major goals at the first meeting mentioned in Question 9? Choose your answer from those listed below the statements.
    1. Obtain agreement among committee members on what should be accomplished first.
    2. Make sure the committee sees each problem through before moving on to another one.
    3. Make sure people get acquainted and exchange points of view.
    4. Obtain agreement from committee members on how they will tackle the first problem.
    5. Delegate responsibilities for working on the first problem.
    6. Be sure only topics on the agenda are discussed.
    7. Be sure the time and place for the next meeting are agreed upon and plans are made for bringing other people to the next meeting.

    Choose your answer from the following:
    A. 2, 4, 5, 6, 7
    B. 1, 3, 4, 5, 7
    C. 1, 2, 4, 5, 7
    D. 2, 3, 4, 6, 7
    E. 1, 3, 4, 5, 6

11. Which of the methods listed below is (are) ways of keeping a group functioning effectively (toward goal attainment)?
    A. Bring new people into the group.
    B. Restrict the number of members involved in the planning and leadership group.
    C. Allow all members to take part in discussions and assume responsibility for progress.
    D. A and C above.
    E. A, B, and C above.

12. One of the roles played in working with a community group is the role of enabler. What is the responsibility of this role?
    A. Control the flow of communication so everyone can participate.
    B. Help the group get organized to deal with the problem.
    C. Listen to different points of view giving support as needed.
    D. Help the group become independent and develop its own leadership.
    E. None of the above.

13. Another role played in working with a community group is the role of gatekeeper. What is the responsibility of this role?
    A. Control the flow of communication so everyone can participate.
    B. Help the group get organized to deal with the problem.
    C. Listen to different points of view giving support as needed.
    D. Help the group become independent and develop its own leadership.
    E. None of the above.

14. Once again assume you are working with a community group organized to help fulfill the unmet need you identified in Question 3. Your task is to get the group together so that it will become effective in solving problems as they arise. Which of the following activities should you undertake in order to assist in problem solving?
    A. Help group members decide what result they want.
    B. Help the group clarify the problem.
    C. Think of ways to solve the problem.
    D. A and C above.
    E. A, B, and C above.

15. Another basic step to group problem solving is to plan and organize for action. Which of the actions listed below could you take to help the group plan and organize for action?
    A. Keep lines of communication open.
    B. Encourage the group to perform their tasks with as little of your assistance as possible.
    C. Bring in outside consultants to tell the group the best strategy to pursue.
    D. A and C above.
    E. A, B, and C above.

16. Once a plan has been developed for solving a problem and the group has organized for action, what else should be done in order to be sure the problem is solved and the next problem is identified?
    A. Help group members decide the result they want.
    B. Evaluate progress toward problem solution.
    C. Follow up on the action taken.
    D. A and C above.
    E. B and C above.

**Now check your Answers with the Answer
key for this chapter at the end of the book**

UNIT THREE:
HELPING CONSUMERS TO FUNCTION MORE EFFECTIVELY

INTRODUCTION

Everyone has difficulty at times in coping with the problems and frustrations of daily living, but some people find it so difficult that they develop inappropriate or deviant behavior with which they require assistance. Generally speaking, in our society there are two approaches to assisting people with their behavioral and emotional problems. One approach involves short-term help in solving personal problems. Another approach involves ongoing long-term assistance with abnormal or more deviant behaviors which may require an institutional setting to effect control and change.

In dealing with consumers who have developed inappropriate or deviant behavior, human service workers are trying to bring about some kind of behavioral change in the consumer. This may involve supporting, counseling, helping, and coaching the consumer in an effort to convey the knowledge and develop the basic skills needed to solve the personal problems encountered in daily living. In maintaining or controlling the consumer in an institutional setting, various treatment techniques are used in an effort to bring about explicit changes in the consumer's behavior.

Since one of the primary goals of human service work is helping human service consumers function more effectively, this unit includes some of the activities and basic skills needed to achieve this goal. Three primary roles are performed by human service workers in accomplishing this goal: counseling, rehabilitating, and consulting. The goal of this unit is to assist you in broadening your understanding of these roles so you will be more effective in helping consumers solve the problems of daily living and change, or modify, their inappropriate or deviant behavior.

CHAPTER VI: COUNSELING

INTRODUCTION

The ability to help others effectively is one of the most important skills needed in delivering human services. Counseling is the process in which workers coach, help, and support consumers so they will be better able to deal with and solve their personal problems. Counseling is based upon a helping relationship in which you, as the helper, try to promote and improve the functioning of consumers. For example, you may help consumers in very specific ways through financial counseling or job counseling. You may also help consumers in more general ways by giving advice, by coaching, or by spending some time talking and being with them to offer your support and guidance.

Since helping others is such an important activity in the human services, this chapter discusses ways of giving useful help. The lessons in this chapter emphasize four areas that are necessary for effective helping: (1) basic helping skills, (2) building helping relationships, (3) coaching human service consumers, and (4) counseling groups of human service consumers.

Learning how to be an effective helper involves knowing a great deal about yourself as well as about the appropriate skills. Therefore, this chapter provides some guidelines and suggestions to consider as you develop your capacity for helping others. Although the focus is on counseling as a process of building helping relationships with individuals and groups, remember that helping can begin the first time you meet a consumer. Even if you do not have the opportunity to build long-term helping relationships, you can utilize the skills discussed in this chapter in your many brief contacts with human service consumers.

Share your thoughts about this chapter with others. As you discuss and perhaps argue about some of the issues presented, you will be increasing your understanding of what it means to help others. The overall objective of this chapter is to assist you in learning how to use counseling skills in order to be helpful to others.

Turn to the next page
to begin Lesson 1

LESSON 1:
HELPING SKILLS

Helping others is a very personal process. Therefore, this lesson provides some guidelines for beginning the process of understanding yourself. This lesson also introduces the communication skills necessary for effective helping. The goal of this lesson and the enabling activities that will help you reach this goal are presented below.

GOAL

Given a description of a worker attempting to help a consumer, you will be able to identify which of the worker's characteristics are regarded as strengths and which as weaknesses in a given relationship with a consumer, and you will be able to categorize the communication elements in the situation as either verbal or nonverbal.

ENABLING ACTIVITIES

After completing this lesson, you will have accomplished four things:

1. Explained the meaning of helping
2. Reviewed common characteristics in effectively helping others and identified strengths and weaknesses
3. Identified five main elements of successful verbal communication
4. Named six main elements of successful nonverbal communication.

Turn to Frame 1 to begin this lesson

FRAME 1

WHAT IS HELPING?

Helping is something offered by one person to another in such a way that the helped person can make use of it to achieve some measure of self-fulfillment.[1] Helping takes place in a relationship between two or more people and begins the moment they meet for the purpose of helping.

Effective helping requires the ability of the helper to reach out to others based on a clear understanding of his or her own personal strengths and weaknesses. Thus, as a helper, your chief tool in helping others will be yourself and the qualities you bring to your relationships with consumers who need help. Learning how to be an effective helper begins with the process of personal discovery, developing self-understanding and learning how to communicate effectively with another person.

Turn to Frame 2

FRAME 2

Which of the following best describe the meaning of helping?

___ A. Help is something offered by one person to another.

Turn to Answer 1

___ B. Help is offered in a way that the helped person can make use of it.

Turn to Answer 2

___ C. Help is offered so that the helped person can achieve some measure of self-fulfillment.

Turn to Answer 3

___ D. A, B, and C.

Turn to Answer 4

___ E. Only A and C.

Turn to Answer 5

FRAME 3

Some Guidelines to Follow in Self-understanding

Effective helping is a complex process requiring a variety of skills. One basic skill required is self-understanding. To help others we must all start with what we have, begin with what we are. A good way to understand yourself is to try taking an honest look at yourself. In this section, we hope to assist you in this process by discussing some common characteristics that are considered necessary in order to help others. There are certain qualities, attitudes, and approaches to life that are generally possessed by people who are skillful in helping others. While there is no one best kind of helper, just as there is no one best kind of teacher or salesman, there are certain common characteristics which contribute to effectiveness.[2] In developing self-understanding, the helper can become flexible and better able to control and direct his or her behavior with others.

(Frame 3 continued)

---

[1] Alan Keith-Lucas, *Giving and Taking Help* (University of North Carolina Press, 1972), p. 15.
[2] Stanley C. Mahoney, *The Art of Helping People Effectively* (New York: Association Press, 1967), pp. 86–99.

Some common characteristics that are usually considered necessary in order to help others are as follows:

Desire to help. The deep feeling that we really want to help and the conscious intention to use ourselves in the most helpful manner possible are indispensable attributes of the helping person.

> Example remark: "I stayed nearby knowing that she was very upset and might need my support."

Faith in others and ourselves. To be effective, a helper needs a deep conviction that people do have inner resources which they can develop and use to resolve their problems.

> Example remark: "While progress was very slow in the beginning, I knew that a retarded boy like Jimmy could learn to dress himself."

Sensitivity. This consists of a harmonious blending of the intellectual and the emotional, and ability to be aware of another person's feelings and needs.

> Example remark: "I began our counseling sessions very informally, since it was apparent that Karen was shy and apprehensive about our clinic."

Tolerance for frustration. We experience frustration when our progress toward a goal is blocked. We need to set goals that we can reasonably expect to attain.

> Example remark: "I was frustrated by the lack of concentration which Tommy displayed in learning how to read his school books, so I began reading magazines with him and his reading improved significantly."

Self-awareness and a readiness to learn. Mature helping persons are aware and accepting of their strengths and weaknesses in helping others and are ready to learn to improve themselves.

> Example remark: "Every year I try to attend one workshop which will help me learn more about myself, and I also try to enroll in one evening class to learn more about my field."

In addition to the common characteristics of effective helpers, you also need to look at some characteristics of ineffective helpers. In this process, it is important to remember that we are all human and, therefore, we all have some negative and unhelpful ways of relating to consumers.

Punitive, judgmental, and rejecting attitudes. A person who functions with these attitudes tends to view people as being "good" or "bad" and their behavior as either "right" or "wrong." More attention is given to determining *whether* people should be helped than *how* they can be helped. Thus, these attitudes reflect an absence of concern about the needs of the consumer.

> Example remark: "This consumer is an alcoholic and all alcoholics are bad and unworthy of our help."

Overcritical attitudes and unrealistic expectations. These are associated with an eagerness for someone else to succeed and a lack of faith that they will be able to do so without prodding or pushing.

> Example remark: "This consumer is poor and needs to be called everyday to see if she has applied for a job."

Overinvolvement. If we are going to help others, then we must become involved with others. However we can become too involved with others so that it interferes with our capacity to be of help.

> Example remark: "I spent three nights a week and every weekend with this physically disabled consumer, but he never improved."

Oversimplification. This happens when one regards consumer problems as simple and easy to solve, when upon investigation, the problems are really quite complicated. It refers to making decisions and reaching conclusions in an impulsive manner, without reasonable consideration of the issues and factors involved.

> Example remark: "I've seen the problems this consumer has many times before, so I'll try the same approach to solving the problem as I've used before."

Go on to Frame 4

FRAME 4

Place an X next to the characteristics which could be considered *strengths* in helping others.

___ A. Desire to help

___ B. Good health

___ C. Faith in others and ourselves

___ D. Overcritical attitudes

___ E. Sensitivity

___ F. Self-awareness

___ G. A college degree

___ H. Tolerance for frustration.

Turn to Answer 7

FRAME 5

Place an X next to the characteristics that are usually weaknesses in attempting to help others.

___ A. Overinvolvement

___ B. Overweight

___ C. Overreaction

___ D. Oversimplification

___ E. Overcritical attitude and unrealistic expectations

___ F. Sensitivity

___ G. Judgmental and rejecting attitudes

Turn to Answer 6

Communication Skills in Helping

Success as a helper also depends on skills in communicating with others. Communication is much more than a matter of words—it is a function of common meanings and shared experiences. When the meanings that exist for the helper are the same as those of the consumer, the feeling of understanding and being understood results. When meanings fail to overlap, communication breaks down and misunderstandings occur.[3]

As a helper, you will be responsible for establishing and maintaining good communication in any relationship. People make impressions quickly of the person with whom they are communicating. Therefore, what you say and how you say it play a very important part in establishing a meaningful relationship. You will need to develop good skills in the two types of communication—verbal and nonverbal.

In verbal communication, or oral communication with words, phrases, or sentences, the consumer may tell you his problems in a straightforward manner, he may abruptly change the subject, or he may ignore your question and answer another, perhaps an unspoken one. The primary elements of successful verbal communication in a helping relationship include the following skills:[4]

1. Using a common language base (standard language, dialect, slang, jargon) and stating things simply
2. Listening and understanding what is being said as well as what is not being said
3. Asking open-ended questions and giving clarification and feedback
4. Being aware of the use of intonation, inflection, and volume of voice
5. Detecting whether or not the verbal messages are consistent with the nonverbal messages

Nonverbal communication is speaking without words. The consumer may speak to you in many ways—through the way he or she is dressed; his or her facial expressions; where and how he or she sits; his or her body movements, such as nervous twitches, hand or foot motion, the direction and intensity of gaze, coughing, throat clearing, and frequent face touching.[5] There may be a big difference between a person's words and his nonverbal communications. Therefore, it is necessary to explore new ways to use nonverbal communication in a constructive manner with consumer. As Simons and Reidy (1971) have stated:

> If you remain in the room with him and accept all these nonverbal communications, you may say to him what he needs most to hear and what perhaps no one else has ever said to him despite the fact that he has acted nonverbally with them just as he is acting now with you. You may tell him that you sense, despite all he is saying, that he is angry with you. You may express your own wonder that he can speak calmly of his mother while at the same time he is crushing and kneading his empty cigarette pack. You may point out that you wish he would look at you, and that you wonder if he is afraid or ashamed to. It is quite possible

[3] Arthur Combs, Donald L. Avila, and William W. Purkey, *Helping Relationships: Basic Concepts for the Helping Professions* (Boston: Allyn & Bacon, 1971), pp. 248–49.

[4] Leon Ginsburg, Margaret Emery, and John Isaacson, *Syllabus on Orientation and Training of Beginning Workers to Provide Social and Rehabilitative Services* (West Virginia University School of Social Work, 1971).

[5] Joseph Simons and Jeanne Reidy, *The Human Art of Counseling* (New York: Herder and Herder, 1971), p. 53.

that addressing yourself to his significant nonverbal communications may be the way to reach this person at the level where his concern really lies.[6]

In order to establish good communication, you should know the six main elements of successful nonverbal communication.

1. Concentrate on what you are doing, not on what you are saying. Learn to control yawning, finger tapping, looking at your watch, and other nonverbal behaviors that generally express boredom and/or impatience.
2. Convey interest in the consumer with eye contact.
3. Be aware of the fact that different cultures may utilize different gestures.
4. Try to keep words and behavior consistent. If you want to show empathy and support, don't turn your back on the consumer.
5. Be aware of agency environment (lighting, desks, etc.) as elements of nonverbal communication to the consumer.
6. Look at the other person when you speak and be aware of his nonverbal communications.[7]

Go on to Frame 7

FRAME 7

Test your understanding of the five elements of effective verbal communication by matching the element with the occurrence.

1. Questioning and answering effectively	___A. Consumer speaks loudly and quickly.
2. Using common language	___B. Consumer describes everyone's feelings but his own.
3. Detecting verbal and nonverbal consistency or inconsistency	___C. Worker asks, "How does that make you feel?" "We can work on that together."
4. Being aware of intonation	___D. When consumer uses slang expressions, helper uses them also.
5. Listening to what is said and not said	___E. Consumer indicates how he values worker's help but repeatedly reaches for the office door in order to leave.

Turn to Answer 8

FRAME 8

The following exercise tests your ability to distinguish between verbal and nonverbal communication.

If the communication is verbal, write V in the blank. If nonverbal write NV.

___ 1. Coughing

___ 2. "Please listen"

___ 3. Direction and intensity of consumer's gaze

___ 4. "Stop that!"

___ 5. Nervous twitches

___ 6. The way the consumer is dressed

Turn to Answer 9

---

[6] Ibid., p. 54.

[7] Leon Ginsberg, Margaret Emery, and John Isaacson, *Syllabus on Orientation and Training of Beginning Workers to Provide Social and Rehabilitation Services* (West Virginia University School of Social Work, 1971).

FRAME 9

The fact that you are letting a person unburden his problems on you is enough. Relax. Take it easy and drink your coffee. It is important to try to finish that crossword puzzle while he talks.

___ A. True

___ B. False

Turn to Answer 10

ANSWERS TO LESSON 1

ANSWER 1

You are correct in saying that helping is something offered by one person to another; however, helping involves much more than this. Return to Frame 1 for a review and then answer Frame 2 correctly.

ANSWER 2

You are correct in saying that helping is offered in a way that the helped person can make use of it; however, there is much more to effective helping than this. Return to Frame 1 for a review before you select the correct answer to Frame 2.

ANSWER 3

You are correct in saying that helping is offered so that the helped person can achieve some measure of self-fulfillment, but there are other things involved in helping which are included in Frame 2. Return to Frame 2 and select the complete answer.

ANSWER 4

Right! Helping is something offered by one person to another in such a way that the helped person can make use of it to achieve some measure of self-fulfillment. Go on to Frame 3 and keep up the good work you've started.

ANSWER 5

You have correctly identified only two elements of what is meant by helping. There is one more element contained in the question in Frame 2, so return there now and choose the complete answer.

ANSWER 6

The common characteristics you should have selected that are usually weaknesses in helping others are as follows:

A. Overinvolvement
D. Oversimplification
E. Overcritical attitudes and unrealistic expectations
G. Judgmental and rejecting attitudes

If you missed any of these, go back to Frame 3. If you got them all right, go on to Frame 6.

ANSWER 7

The characteristics which could be considered strengths in helping others are as follows:

A. Desire to help
C. Faith in others and in ourselves
E. Sensitivity
F. Acceptance of one's limitations
H. Tolerance for frustration

Did you get them right? If so, you are doing an excellent job. Move on Frame 5.
Did you miss some of the strengths? Read over the correct answers again, and then try Frame 5.

ANSWER 8

Your answers should be

_4_ A.
_5_ B.
_1_ C.
_2_ D.
_3_ E.

If you missed any of these, return to Frame 6. Otherwise proceed to Frame 8.

ANSWER 9

The verbal communications:

2. "Please listen"
4. "Stop that!"

The non-verbal communications:

1. Coughing
3. Direction and intensity of consumer's gaze
5. Nervous twitches
6. The way the consumer is dressed

If you missed any, go back to Frame 6. If you go them all right, go on to Frame 9.

ANSWER 10

The correct answer is B, false. While actual practice situations are usually much more complex than this simplified example, you should at least have a beginning understanding of communication skills.

Hopefully you also have a desire to seek additional information to supplement the introduction provided in this lesson.

You have now completed Lesson 1. Proceed to Lesson 2.

LESSON 2:
BUILDING HELPING RELATIONSHIPS

In Lesson 1 you examined some of the self-knowledge and communication skills you need to become an effective helper. This lesson shows how these skills contribute to building helping relationships and what it means to be able to give help, and provides some practice principles to apply to the helping process. The goal of this lesson and the enabling activities that will help you reach this goal are presented below.

GOAL

Given a description of a worker attempting to develop a helping relationship with a consumer, you will be able to identify whether the necessary characteristics of a helping relationship are present, which factors of helping are being used, and what practice principles of helping are being applied.

ENABLING ACTIVITIES

After completing this lesson, you will have done the following:

1. Examined four long-range purposes of the helping relationship
2. Identified and described five characteristics of a helping relationship
3. Reviewed three factors of helping that are used in building helping relationships
4. Explained four ways of working within the helping process
5. Considered at least five practice principles that are useful in building helping relationships

**Ready? Turn to Frame 1
and begin this lesson**

LONG-RANGE PURPOSES OF THE HELPING RELATIONSHIP[1]

When you are helping a consumer, the goals and purposes you are seeking to accomplish have a very important influence on your behavior. Frequently, however, when you are actively engaged in the helping process, you may have a tendency to get overly involved with the details of the situation and lose sight of your long-range purposes for the relationship. This is why it is very important to have a clear understanding at all times of your purposes in helping a consumer.

Generally your overall purpose in any helping relationship is to help a person (or a group) make choices about a problem or situation and about the help they are willing to take regarding this problem or situation.[2] Contained within this overall purpose are at least four fundamental long-range purposes that can be used as guidelines for determining whether or not you are really helping a consumer. Although at times your primary concern may be with just one or two of these purposes, you should not lose sight of the others if you are going to be really helpful. If you become overly concerned with one purpose and exclude the others, your efforts at successful helping will probably be greatly reduced. The four long-range purposes of helping are given below:

To help the consumer become more realistic. One purpose of any helping relationship is to help the consumer understand himself and others better and function in a manner consistent with this knowledge. Being realistic means becoming aware of and accepting what *is* before making decisions about what *should be.*

To help the consumer feel more self-confident and adequate. A second purpose of any helping relationship is to help the consumer in developing a faith in his capacity to do what has to be done. This means helping the consumer feel "I can" more often than "I can't," and "I am" more often than "I am not." It also means helping the consumer feel "I am good" and "I am important."

To help the consumer become more self-directing. A third purpose of the helping relationship is to help the consumer to assume responsibility for his own life. This means helping him make decisions, solve problems, take actions on his own, and be willing to accept the consequences of these actions and decisions. This also involves helping a person develop and use his capacities to the fullest.

To help the consumer value life itself. A final purpose of the helping relationship is to assist the consumer to become enthusiastic about life and valuing the "here and now." This also involves developing a realistic understanding of the joys and sorrows we all experience in life.

**Turn to Frame 2 to see how well
you understand the four long-range
purposes of the helping relationship**

Which of the following statements is *not* correct?

____ A. The purposes a helper seeks to accomplish in a helping relationship with a consumer have a very important influence on the behavior of the helper.

(Frame 2 continued)

[1] See Stanley C. Mahoney, *The Art of Helping People Effectively* (New York: Association Press, 1967), pp. 19–27; and Arthur W. Combs et al., *Helping Relationships: Basic Concepts for the Helping Professions* (Boston: Allyn & Bacon, 1971), p. 165.

[2] Alan Keith-Lucas, *Giving and Taking Help* (University of North Carolina Press, 1972), p. 47.

___ B. An effective helper should always try to focus on only one long-range purpose in each helping relationship.

___ C. To be most effective, a helper must try never to lose sight of the five long-range purposes of helping relationships.

Turn to Answer 4

FRAME 3

Generally, the *overall* purpose of any helping relationship is to help an individual (or a group) make choices about

___ A. a problem.

Turn to Answer 7

___ B. a situation.

Turn to Answer 9

___ C. the help they are willing to take.

Turn to Answer 11

___ D. only A and C.

Turn to Answer 13

___ E. A, B, and C.

Turn to Answer 14

FRAME 4

One of the four long-range purposes of a helping relationship is to help the consumer feel more self-confident and adequate. This means

___ A. helping the consumer become more realistic.

Turn to Answer 2

___ B. helping the consumer feel "I can," "I am," and "I am important."

Turn to Answer 5

___ C. helping the consumer feel "I can't" and "I am not important."

Turn to Answer 8

FRAME 5

Helping a consumer make decisions, solve problems, take actions on his own, and be willing to accept the consequences of these actions best describes which of the long-range purposes of the helping relationship?

___ A. Self-directing

Turn to Answer 1

___ B. Self-destructing

Turn to Answer 3

___ C. Self-confidence

Turn to Answer 6

___ D. Valuing life

Turn to Answer 10

FRAME 6

One purpose of any helping relationship is to help the consumer understand himself and others better and function in a manner consistent with this knowledge. This describes the long-range purpose of helping the consumer to become more

_____.

**Fill in the blank with the correct
response and then turn to Answer 12**

FRAME 7

THE CHARACTERISTICS OF A HELPING RELATIONSHIP

Helping relationships are special ones. They differ from the kinds of relationships people encounter in most of their daily lives. Most ordinary experiences are dialogues in which both parties seek personal satisfaction. In the helping relationship, one party determines to set aside his own needs temporarily to help another. This, in itself, makes the helping relationship distinct from ordinary ones.[3]

The helping relationship is a unique relationship with special qualities and characteristics that you, as the helper, must understand.[4]

Mutuality. The helping relationship is a mutual and not a one-way relationship. The consumer and the worker both bring things to the helping relationship, and so the success or failure of the relationship depends as much on the consumer as it does on the worker. This is especially important for you, as the helper, to recognize, since some agency workers tend to blame the consumer if things go wrong or if a relationship is not established.

Honesty. The helping relationship is not necessarily always pleasant and friendly. Any worker who attempts to keep a relationship always on a pleasant and friendly level, regardless of the circumstances, has not developed a true helping relationship with a consumer. For example, many workers fear that their relationship with a consumer will be irreparably damaged if they have to do anything the person will not like or if they have to tell the consumer something he or she does not want to hear. True helping relationships are characterized by a sincere and honest interest in the consumer, and this may sometimes mean that anger, hostility, or disagreement will be expressed.

Feelings. The helping relationship involves feelings as well as knowledge. In addition to having the knowledge and skills required for helping, in a true helping relationship, the worker is committed to working _with_ the consumer. This means that the worker treats the consumer as someone who, in spite of having problems, has feeling and opinions. The worker recognizes these as important and empathizes with the consumer.

Immediacy. The helping relationship takes place in the here and now. Since the helping relationship is limited in time and scope, the worker must be concerned with what is happening in the present. The worker must be aware not only of _what_ is said, but also of _why_, _when_, and _how_ it is said, both by himself and by the consumer.

(Frame 7 continued)

[3] Arthur W. Combs et al., _Helping Relationships: Basic Concepts for the Helping Professions_ (Boston: Allyn & Bacon, 1971), p. 214.

[4] Alan Keith-Lucas, _Giving and Taking Help_ (University of North Carolina Press, 1972), pp. 47–65.

Tolerance. The helping relationship must be nonjudgmental. The worker in a helping relationship is not there to judge, approve, or disapprove. In a true helping relationship, the worker will demonstrate to the consumer that they are fellow human beings, both capable of making mistakes. Thus, the worker demonstrates that he is not superior to the consumer, but is there to give the consumer help.

Proceed to Frame 8

FRAME 8

A true helping relationship is always

___ A. friendly.

Turn to Answer 15

___ B. one way.

Turn to Answer 16

___ C. mutual.

Turn to Answer 17

___ D. without feeling.

Turn to Answer 19

FRAME 9

Sue has just received a memo from her supervisor informing her that Rose Martin, a consumer she has been helping, has failed to report her salary increase and that the agency is considering cutting off her assistance grant since she has violated agency regulations.

Sue has made it a point to have a very pleasant and friendly relationship with Rose, and has never had to deny her any assistance she needed. But she now decides that her relationship with Rose will be seriously damaged if she tells her this news in person, so she writes Rose a letter instead. Do you think that Sue has built an effective helping relationship with Rose?

___ A. Yes

Turn to Answer 22

___ B. No

Turn to Answer 23

FRAME 10

The helping relationship includes both _____ and _____.
   Choose your answer from the following.

___ A. approval, disapproval

Turn to Answer 18

___ B. feeling, knowledge

Turn to Answer 20

THREE FACTORS USED IN BUILDING HELPING RELATIONSHIPS[5]

How do you establish the kind of helping relationship that has just been described? Remember that the relationship is the medium through which help is offered, it is *not* help itself. Unfortunately, there are no easy formulas or steps to follow in giving help to a consumer. However, by your words, feelings, and actions, you convey to a consumer a sense of *reality, empathy,* and *support.* In the paragraphs below, we discuss each of these separately. Keep in mind that in giving help, these three factors can be conveyed separately, together, and in any order.

1. **Reality.** A sense of reality involves accepting the importance of the consumer's problem or difficulty, facing the problem as it actually is, and making an effort not to ignore it or offer quick solutions. Telling a consumer "things will be all right" when you know this is not the case, is an example of how workers frequently keep consumers from facing their problems and thus block the establishment of a helping relationship.

   How do you know when to introduce reality? Reality is appropriate when there is sufficient understanding established between the worker and the consumer to assure the consumer that he is not being threatened. Reality is also appropriate if it can be expressed in terms the consumer will understand. This means being concrete and immediate, responding to the problems which brought the consumer into the relationship in the first place. Finally, the introduction of reality is appropriate when you, as the helper, are prepared to support the consumer in facing the reality. Becoming realistic may also mean becoming self-directed, and this involves helping consumers become aware of the fact that we are all responders to the conditions of life; we are also active agents of change. A sense of reality is probably the hardest of the three factors to maintain in a helping relationship, but it is a very necessary element of giving useful help.

2. **Empathy.** The second factor that must be conveyed in giving useful help is empathy. Empathy means feeling *with* the consumer without becoming caught in that feeling and losing your own perspective on the problem. It involves your ability to enter into the consumer's feeling, to experience it, and, therefore, to know and understand its meaning. This type of understanding refers to the ability of the worker to "step into the shoes" of the consumer. Basically, empathy means conveying "I know this must hurt."

3. **Support.** Support has two forms in giving help—material support and emotional support. Material support is what the helping visibly gives to the consumer, for example, money, education, medicine, and technical assistance. Emotional support includes your assurance to the consumer that you are there to help him and will not desert him if he disappoints you or makes an unwise decision; conveying to the consumer "I am here to help you if you need me, so you need not face this alone." It should be apparent that support and empathy are closely related and that both are usually needed to form an effective helping relationship.

Our discussion of these factors does not tell you how to give specific help, but it should provide some idea of how to approach a situation and how to look at your

(Frame 11 continued)

[5] Ibid., 70–88.

own helping efforts. For example, if you encounter a helping situation that has been unsuccessful, you can ask yourself the following three questions to find out what might have gone wrong:

1. Have I been able to face reality with this person, or have I glossed over the truth and offered false reassurance?
2. Have I been able to feel and express real empathy?
3. Have I offered real support, or has it been conditional support ("I'll do this as long as you don't do. . . ?")

An honest and thoughtful answer to each of these questions may give clues regarding what has gone wrong in a particular situation. Just remember that effective helping involves, at a minimum, three factors—reality, empathy, and support.

Move to Frame 12

FRAME 12

Which of the following statements best describes what is involved in conveying empathy as a helping factor?

___ A. The ability to help a person solve a problem for himself

Turn to Answer 25

___ B. The ability to listen

Turn to Answer 26

___ C. The ability to know or experience what another person is feeling

Turn to Answer 27

FRAME 13

Which of the following remarks do you think best conveys a sense of reality as a helping factor?

___ A. "Don't worry, things are going to work out just fine."

Turn to Answer 21

___ B. "This is the way it is."

Turn to Answer 24

FRAME 14

After each of the following statements, mark M if it is an example of material support, E if it is an example of emotional support, and X if it is not an example of any kind of support.

A. Spending extra time with a consumer who has just agreed to place her severely retarded child in an institution. ___
B. Ceasing all contact with a consumer after you have had a disagreement regarding the amount of financial assistance he is entitled to receive. ___
C. Locating a foster home for an elderly citizen. ___

Turn to Answer 28

WAYS OF WORKING WITHIN THE HELPING RELATIONSHIP[6]

There is no one best method of helping people. In fact, the ways in which effective helpers work are almost as varied as the personalities of the helpers. Each of the many different ways of helping a consumer is based on the presence of the three helping factors—a sense of reality, empathy, and support. The appropriate method to use in conveying these factors to build a helping relationship depends on (1) the worker's self-awareness and his or her beliefs; (2) the people the worker must work with; (3) the particular needs of the consumer; (4) the time available to build a helping relationship; and (5) the special demands imposed upon the worker in the agency.

There are at least three general areas of concentration in building a helping relationship. While conveying a sense of reality, empathy, and support, a helper may choose to work with the consumer's environment, with the individual consumer alone, or with a group.

1. **Changing the Environment.** This means focusing the helping efforts on changing some aspect of the physical world in which the consumer lives. Usually, changing the consumer's environment involves working with the people who are part of that environment (family, neighborhood, school, physician, other agency staff members, etc.). Since this often includes a number of people, helpers normally work directly with the person who has come for help in order to reach others in his or her environment.

2. **Face-to-Face, One-to-One Relationships.** This refers to establishing a helping relationship with an individual consumer, and involves accepting him as he is, giving him any information he needs, and helping him solve his personal problems. As with the other ways of helping, this also involves conveying empathy, a sense of reality, and a feeling of support.

3. **Relationships in Groups.** One of the most effective ways in which people can help one another is through the formation of groups. The process of working to help groups of consumers involves building helping relationships both with the group and with each individual in the group. You will be learning more about counseling and helping groups of consumers in Lesson 4 of this chapter.

Each of the above ways of working to build a helping relationship with human service consumers has its own advantages and drawbacks, and the selection usually depends on the helper, the needs of the consumers, and the agency or setting in which the helping will occur.

Go on to Frame 16

Check the three general ways of working to build a helping relationship with human service consumers.

(Frame 16 continued)

[6] Arthur W. Combs et al., *Helping Relationships: Basic Concepts for the Helping Professions* (Boston: Allyn & Bacon, 1971), pp. 272–287.

__ A. Through relationships in groups

__ B. Through relationships with your supervisor

__ C. Through other people

__ D. Through changing the environment

__ E. Through the prescription of drugs

__ F. Through one-to-one relationships

__ G. Through changing your job title

Turn to Answer 29

FRAME 17

You have just learned that there are many different ways to help a consumer. Check the four things that determine the method you would use to give help to a consumer.

__ A. The length of time you have been working in your agency

__ B. Your knowledge of yourself and your beliefs

__ C. The people you work with (your supervisor, other workers, etc.)

__ D. Where you live

__ E. The particular job you have in the agency

__ F. How many children you have

__ G. The needs of the consumer

Turn to Answer 30

FRAME 18

PRACTICE PRINCIPLES USEFUL IN HELPING[7]

The following general practice principles are suggestions for helping. They are not intended to be rules or guarantees of success in helping a consumer or a group of consumers. In combination with all the other factors you have just examined, they are important things to consider in the process of becoming an effective helper.

Respond to Feeling in Addition to Literal Content. This means centering your attention and responding to what the consumer is trying to tell you both non-verbally and verbally. For example, in some situations you might need to say something to the consumer such as the following: "You are telling me this as if you wanted to do it, yet you don't sound like this is what you want or like."

Hold Fast to Your Function as a Helper. Do not take over the consumer's decisions, but also do not allow him to control your approach to helping. This simply means that you, as the helper, should not control the use which the consumer makes of the helping relationship. But it also means that the consumer should not be allowed to control your actions or to set conditions on the help you will be giving him. For example, if the consumer wants you to "tell" him what to

---

[7] Alan Keith-Lucas, *Giving and Taking Help* (University of North Carolina Press, 1972), pp. 109–135.

do or to make a decision for him, your response should be one that will help the consumer make decisions for himself and take the responsibility for those decisions. **Help the Consumer Express What He Wants and Work with Him to Get What He Can.** This is expressed in the statement "This is what you are saying you really want; now let's see how much of that is possible." Once you have helped the consumer express his problem and what he wants, you must then help him to face the reality of what the problem is and what can be reasonably done to solve it.

Keep the Problem Clear. Restate the consumer's problem from time to time as you see it. The point here is to try and maintain contact with the consumer, using such comments as "It seems to me that you are saying. . . ." or "It seems to me we have agreed that your problem looks like this." This is a good way to make sure that you and the consumer are hearing and understanding each other and are not going off in different directions.

Know When to Refer. Know enough about the obvious signs of severe mental illness either to refer to a doctor or to stay out of the situation. While anyone who is in trouble or cannot solve a personal problem is, in a sense, mentally disturbed, there are some people who will have such severe problems or who will be so far removed from reality, that they may need something more than you can offer them in a helping relationship. When you think you are dealing with a person who may need something more than helping, do not hesitate to get your supervisor's advice and the advice of other people you work with.

Go on to Frame 19

FRAME 19

Sally has been placed in a foster home and has been rejecting all the attempts of her foster parents to be kind to her and love her. Mrs. Graves, Sally's welfare worker sat down with Sally one day and said, "Sally, I know how hard it must be for you to be away from your mother, and you must really want to be with her. But you do realize that your mom is going to be very sick for the next few months and that she just won't be able to take care of you. So, the only thing your mom could do was to make sure you were taken care of until she gets better."

Mrs. Graves is using which of the following practice principles of helping?

— A. Recognizing that Sally is in need of something more than the helping process

Turn to Answer 31

— B. Responding to Sally's nonverbal communications

Turn to Answer 33

— C. Helping Sally understand what she wants and then helping her face what she can have

Turn to Answer 34

FRAME 20

The statement "It seems to me that you are saying you want to visit your mother at the nursing home, but there's something you can't put your finger on that's holding you back" demonstrates the practice principle of

— A. restating the consumer's problem from time to time as you see it.

Turn to Answer 32

(Frame 20 continued)

___ B. not allowing the consumer to control any of the conditions of help.

Turn to Answer 35

___ C. recognizing an obvious sign of severe mental illness.

Turn to Answer 36

FRAME 21

You have now completed the lesson on building helping relationships. Congratulations! Before you go on to Lesson 3, we would like to leave you with one final thought on helping relationships:

> Helping others to help themselves is not always easy, and it is seldom simple. Like many other things that we do it requires motivation, understanding, and effort from us if we want to do it effectively. It requires not only our intention to use ourselves in a way that will be beneficial to another, but also our willingness to engage in some hard and honest thinking and wondering about ourselves and others. How effective we will be in helping others to help themselves will depend largely upon how successful we are in becoming realistic, self-confident, self-directing, self-actualizing, and rejoiceful of life ourselves. Our examples will usually speak louder than our words.[8]

If you feel you have a good understanding of some of the principles used in building helping relationships, proceed to Lesson 3 to learn about coaching human service consumers. If you need a review, return to Frame 1.

[8] Stanley C. Mahoney, *The Art of Helping People Effectively* (New York: Association Press, 1967), p. 27.

ANSWERS TO LESSON 2

ANSWER 1

Excellent! Helping a consumer make decisions, solve problems, take actions on his own, and be willing to accept the consequences of these actions best describes the long-range purpose of helping the consumer to become more self-directing.

Continue with Frame 6 and keep up the good work.

ANSWER 2

Helping the consumer feel more self-confident and adequate is not the same as helping him to become more realistic. This is another long-range purpose of a helping relationship. A review of Frame 1 is in order before you select the correct response in Frame 4.

ANSWER 3

A review of Frame 1 is in order to clarify the four long-range purposes of the helping relationship. After you have reviewed Frame 1, you are certain to answer Frame 5 correctly.

ANSWER 4

The only incorrect statement in this Frame is B—which states that an effective helper should always try to focus on only one long-range purpose in each helping relationship, and this is obviously incorrect. To be most effective in helping, you, as the helper, should try *never* to lose sight of the four long-range purposes of helping relationships, with each consumer you are helping.

Continue to Frame 3.

ANSWER 5

That's correct! The long-range purpose of helping a consumer feel more self-confident and adequate means helping him feel "I can," "I am," and "I am important." Continue to Frame 5.

ANSWER 6

Sorry, but you've got the long-range purposes of the helping relationship confused —return to Frame 1 for a careful review, and then answer Frame 5 correctly.

ANSWER 7

Helping an individual (or group) make choices about a problem is only one component of the overall purpose of any helping relationship. What are the others? Return to Frame 1 if you need a review, and then answer Frame 3 correctly.

ANSWER 8

Your selection of this response indicates you are in need of a careful review of Frame 1, so return there now before you select the correct answer to Frame 4.

ANSWER 9

Helping an individual (or group) make choices about a situation is only one component of the overall purpose of any helping relationship. What are the others? Perhaps a review of Frame 1 will assist you in answering Frame 3 correctly.

ANSWER 10

No. The long-range purpose of valuing life refers to helping the consumer to be enthusiastic about life and to value the here and now. Return to Frame 1 for a review and then select the correct response to Frame 5.

ANSWER 11

Helping an individual (or group) make choices about the help they are willing to take is but one of the components of the overall purpose of any helping relationship. A review of Frame 1 would assist you in selecting the complete answer to Frame 3.

ANSWER 12

Helping the consumer understand himself and others better and function in a manner consistent with this knowledge describes the long-range purpose of helping the consumer to become more *realistic*.
    Proceed to Frame 7.

ANSWER 13

You are two-thirds correct but have overlooked one of the components of the overall purpose of any helping relationship. Return to Frame 3 and choose the complete answer.

ANSWER 14

Right! The overall purpose of any helping relationship is to help an individual (or group) make choices about a problem, a situation, and the help they are willing to take. Nice work. Proceed to Frame 4.

ANSWER 15

No deal! A true helping relationship is *not* necessarily always friendly. In fact, if you, as the helper, make this a goal in your helping efforts, then you can not build a true helping relationship with a consumer.
    Return to Frame 7 for a review and then select the correct answer in Frame 8.

ANSWER 16

Incorrect. Any relationship that is one way is *not* a helping relationship. Return to Frame 7 for a very careful review of the characteristics of a helping relationship before you try Frame 8 again.

ANSWER 17

We agree. A true helping relationship is always a mutual or a sharing relationship between the consumer (helpee) and the worker (helper).

Good work. Proceed to Frame 9.

ANSWER 18

Incorrect. Remember that one of the characteristics of a helping relationship is that it is nonjudgmental. This means the worker is *not* there to judge, approve, to disapprove.

Return to Frame 10 and select the correct answer.

ANSWER 19

Sorry, but this is an incorrect response. A true helping relationship is one with feeling and with knowledge. Return to Frame 7 for a review and then answer Frame 8 correctly.

ANSWER 20

Right you are! The helping relationship is one of feeling as well as knowledge. Continue with Frame 11.

ANSWER 21

Of the two statements, this one does not express or describe the helping factor of reality. In fact, it expresses just the opposite. It is saying, "You don't need to face your problem; If you don't think about it, it will go away."

Return to Frame 11 for a review of the reality factor and then answer Frame 13 correctly.

ANSWER 22

Sorry, but we think Sue has failed to build an effective helping relationship with Rose. Review Frame 7 which discusses the characteristics of a helping relationship, and then turn to Answer 23, which explains why Sue has not established a helping relationship.

ANSWER 23

If you agree with the material discussed in Frame 7, then this is the correct choice. The reason Sue has failed to establish a helping relationship with Rose is her fear that their relationship would be damaged if she had to tell her that the assistance grant was being cut off. Sue is focusing too much attention on keeping things "pleasant and friendly" no matter what the circumstances, and this is not a characteristic of a helping relationship.

Now turn to Frame 10.

ANSWER 24

You've done an excellent job of applying what we have discussed about the factor of reality in helping. "This is the way it is" is a statement that expresses what a sense of reality means in helping.

Continue to Frame 14 and keep up the good work!

ANSWER 25

No, that's not the correct answer. You selected a definition of reality. Perhaps a review of Frame 11, which discusses empathy, would assist you in answering Frame 12 correctly.

ANSWER 26

We do not think this is the best answer here. Empathy does involve some listening, but it *also* involves the ability to know or experience what another person is feeling; that is, it is the ability to feel *with* someone, without becoming caught up in that feeling and losing your own perspective. Therefore, you should have selected answer C as the correct response to Frame 12.

Continue to Frame 13.

ANSWER 27

Correct! You selected C, empathy as the ability to know or experience what another person is feeling. You are also aware that empathy includes experiencing the feeling without becoming caught up in it and losing your own perspective.

Move right on to Frame 13.

ANSWER 28

A. Spending extra time with a consumer who has just agreed to place her severely retarded child in an institution. E: an example of emotional support.
B. Ceasing all contact with a consumer after you have had a disagreement regarding the amount of financial assistance he is entitled to receive. X: not an example of any kind of support.
C. Locating a foster home for an elderly citizen. M: an example of material support.

Have any trouble? Hope not. If you did, review Frame 11 before going on to Frame 15. If you answered correctly, you deserve a pat on the back. Return to Frame 15.

ANSWER 29

You should have checked A, C, D, and F as the three general ways of working within the helping relationship. You can see that helping in the human services will require choosing what kind of role you are going to play in order to give the most useful help.

Proceed now to Frame 17.

ANSWER 30

You should have checked B, C, E, and G, as some of the things that determine the method you will use to give help to a consumer. Get them all right? Great! Go on to Frame 18. If you missed any answers, you ought to review Frame 15 before continuing to Frame 18.

ANSWER 31

Incorrect. There is no indication that Sally needs something more than a helping relationship. Sally is having trouble facing the reality that she can't be with her mother right now, and Mrs. Graves is trying to help Sally recognize this. Return to Frame 19 and select the correct answer.

ANSWER 32

Right you are! This demonstrates an attempt to make sure the worker (helper) and the consumer are hearing and understanding each other and aren't going off in different directions.

Return to Frame 21 and complete this lesson.

ANSWER 33

We do not think this is the best answer here. Although Mrs. Graves may have noticed that Sally's nonverbal communication was saying she was unhappy, Mrs. Graves is taking a more obvious step in helping. She is trying to help Sally face the reality of her situation. Return to Frame 19 and select the best answer.

ANSWER 34

Agreed. Mrs. Graves is trying to help Sally understand that what she *wants* and what is *possible* are two different things, and that Sally must try to adjust to what is possible.

Now turn to Frame 20.

ANSWER 35

No, you are confusing two different practice suggestions for building helping relationships. A review of Frame 18 will assist you in selecting the correct answer to Frame 20.

ANSWER 36

Did we catch you asleep?? There's nothing in this statement that even remotely suggests a severe mental illness. Review Frame 18 and then answer Frame 20 correctly.

LESSON 3:
COACHING CONSUMERS

In addition to building helping relationships, the counseling process also involves helping individuals and groups learn the skills and abilities they need to improve their own daily functioning. This activity can be called coaching, and is similar to some of the activities performed by athletic coaches who help the individuals on their team develop the special talents and skills they need to perform effectively in their daily activities. In this lesson, you will be introduced to some basic methods of applying your skills to coaching adult consumers. The goal of this lesson and the enabling activities that will help you reach this goal are presented below.

GOAL

Given a description of consumers who need help in learning basic skills to improve their daily living, you will be able to (1) determine from their needs what skills they need and (2) describe some of the initial ways to begin coaching the consumers in these skills.

ENABLING ACTIVITIES

- After completing this lesson, you will have done five things:

  1. Identified four characteristics of a learner
  2. Explained how to build a helping relationship in coaching
  3. Reviewed the four basic steps of coaching
  4. Identified two reasons for using evaluation in coaching
  5. Listed at least five helpful hints to remember when you are coaching

Turn to Frame 1

COACHING AND THE CONSUMER

Coaching can be defined as training by instruction, demonstration, and practice. As a human service worker you will need to develop good coaching skills to help consumers learn how to cope with problems they encounter in their daily living, for example, family budget problems, finding a job, preventing health problems, or staying out of trouble with the law.

It is important to note that in coaching both adults and children, it is necessary to have a respect for their past living experiences. In addition, they will learn best when the skills taught have an immediate usefulness to them. Therefore, you should give consumers a chance to decide what skills they need to know and help them relate these skills to their present experiences. Consumers as learners have four main characteristics:

1. Consumers have *experience* in living.
2. Consumers have a *readiness* to learn different things because they are facing new and different tasks.
3. Consumers are *sensitive to failure* and may have to overcome personal doubts and fears about their ability to learn.
4. Consumers are interested in the *immediate usefulness* of new knowledge.

When coaching consumers, it is important to remember these special characteristics of a learner. It is also important to note that coaching involves imitation. While we noted in a earlier lesson the importance of the consumer determining his own approach to solving problems, in this lesson we are emphasizing the consumer as a learner and thereby indicating that coaching involves the process of the consumer imitating the worker's performance in order to learn how to cope with a particular daily living problem.

**When you feel you have a good
understanding of the material
in Frame 1, proceed to Frame 2**

The Coaching Relationship

When you are coaching, you are dealing with the world of *information*. You are trying to help the consumer discover how to use information, for example, about jobs, child rearing, and homemaking, to function more effectively in his daily life. In order to coach a consumer about ways of doing things, you will be trying to build a special kind of helping relationship. Although there are many different styles and techniques of coaching, the same three factors used to build helping relationships should also be conveyed to the consumer in coaching:

1. **Reality.** Be yourself—be real. Accept the consumer and his problem as important.
2. **Empathy.** Try to understand the consumer from his own point of view—put yourself in his shoes.
3. **Support.** Remember that each consumer is an individual with many feelings. Show interest, trust, respect, and support for the consumer by showing him him you believe he *can* learn.

Go on to Frame 3

Fill in the blanks with the correct response in the statements below.
There are four main characteristics of the consumer as learner:

1. The consumer has _____ in living.

2. The consumer has a _____ to learn different things because he is facing different tasks.

3. The consumer is sensitive to _____ and may have to overcome his doubts and fears about learning.

4. The consumer has an interest in the _____ usefulness of new knowledge.

Turn to Answer 1

Consumers as learners learn best by *doing* and *practicing* as well as by drawing upon their own experiences. For example, you should not necessarily expect a delinquent youth to learn how to occupy his time constructively by giving him a book on the subject. For the most effective learning, the youth should first be shown how to plan his free time and then be allowed to practice various recreational activities on his own. Be available to answer questions, but give the youth a chance to try it on his own.

Learning will also be easier for consumers when new things are presented in terms of their own past experiences. For example, if you are helping an adult who has been out of work learn how to find a job, you might talk with him about his previous job and how he found it. Then, based on his past experiences, you can help him decide what type of job he would like and then coach him in learning how to find another job and how to be interviewed.

Proceed to Frame 5

Which of the following answers is correct?

___ A. Consumers learn best by doing.

Turn to Answer 2

___ B. Consumers learn easily when new skills are explained in terms of their own experiences.

Turn to Answer 4

___ C. Both A and B.

Turn to Answer 5

___ D. None of the above.

Turn to Answer 6

As we have just described, consumers learn best by doing and by having new skills presented in terms of their own experiences. When you are coaching, it is also important to remember that learning should be focused on the *problem*. For example, do not try to show a person how to plan well balanced meals if he or she is out of work and has no money to buy groceries. Help the person deal with the problem at hand—in this case, getting some food and finding a job—and then focus on coaching in additional skills that may be useful.

Continue to Frame 7

FRAME 7

If you were going to coach a group of adult welfare recipients in basic homemaking skills, which of the following would you do?

___ A. Tell them to read a basic home economics textbook.

Turn to Answer 3

___ B. Tell them what the ideal home should be like so they can learn to run their home properly.

Turn to Answer 7

___ C. Find out first their experiences in homemaking and what problems they are having now.

Turn to Answer 8

FRAME 8

BASIC STEPS TO FOLLOW IN COACHING[1]

When you and a consumer have decided what the problem area is and what skills are needed, you can begin to plan your coaching activities. For coaching a consumer, four basic steps are suggested to assist you in helping the consumer develop the skills he needs.

1. **Introducing.** Before you engage a consumer in any coaching activities, discuss or introduce the purpose of the activity. Guard against showing dismay or disappointment at any poor or slow performance; make certain the consumer will have a chance for success in the activity or skill; and show your interest and enthusiasm.
2. **Explaining.** In explaining an activity, skill, or knowledge area, you should be short, clear, and concise. Repeat words or phrases only when they are needed to emphasize an important point. Get to the point quickly so that the consumers can begin to practice and participate as soon as possible.
3. **Demonstrating.** This means actually showing the consumer how to do the skill or activity. You should adapt your demonstration to the consumer's level of understanding and ability, using words and actions that will call attention to important details. Avoid detailed demonstrations, but try and demonstrate the whole activity at least once so that your continuing efforts in coaching will have meaning for the consumer.
4. **Participating.** Involve the consumer in practicing and participating with you in the activity, either during the demonstration or at the end.

Continue to Frame 9

[1] See J. W. Moore, *The Psychology of Athletic Coaching* (Minnesota: Burgess Publishing Company, 1970); and Thomas A. Tutko and Jack W. Richards, *Psychology of Coaching* (Boston: Allyn & Bacon, 1971).

RESOURCES TO USE IN COACHING

Once you have decided what and how you will coach, there may be a need for some background research for information and materials. There are three main sources where you can go to get information and materials.

The first and most important source is *the agency where you work*. For example, you may get information from your supervisor and the other workers. Many agencies already have materials prepared that you can use, and some agencies have their own library. Find out about the resources in your own agency, as this can save you time and provide a lot of information.

The second source is *your local library*. If you do not know where it is or how to use it, you might ask one of your co-workers or your supervisor to help you.

The third source is *other agencies and local businesses* in your community. For example, suppose you have a group of consumers who all need coaching in how to find a job. You might find information on this subject from another agency, such as the employment service or from local businesses which may have pamphlets or other materials on the subject.

Turn to Frame 10

Read the following paragraph and then answer the question below.

> Wayne is a worker in a community correctional center for adult male offenders. Hank is one of the offenders whom Wayne supervises, and Hank is now eligible for parole. But Hank is terrified at the thought of leaving. He doesn't know how to get a job, where to look for one, or how to conduct himself during a job interview.
>
> Wayne decides to try to assist Hank by coaching him in various ways of finding and securing a job. In their first coaching session, Wayne demonstrates to Hank some of the procedures and skills he will need during a job interview. Wayne gives a very lengthy, detailed description of the job interview, and then ends the coaching session, feeling quite confident that he has provided Hank with most of the skills he will need for a successful job interview. Wayne is quite surprised when he learns that Hank has had more than four opportunities for job interviews, but has turned them all down.

Wayne's efforts at coaching have not been very successful. This is probably due to the fact that

__ A. Wayne has not given Hank enough practice or rehearsing for a job interview.

__ B. Hank is not very intelligent and will probably never be able to handle himself in a job interview.

__ C. Wayne has shown interest in Hank, but has failed to adapt his demonstration to Hank's individual needs.

__ D. Wayne has basically neglected to follow the basic steps.

__ E. Hank is not interested in getting a job.

Check those that apply and then turn to Answer 10

FRAME 11

THE IMPORTANCE OF EVALUATION IN COACHING

How do you know whether the way you are coaching is helping the consumer? How do you know if the consumer will have any additional learning needs? If you evaluate your coaching activities you should be able to answer these questions. Evaluation means to determine how effective your coaching has been with a consumer. Evaluation is an important part of coaching, because it enables you to assess (1) your own efforts, (2) the progress the consumer is making, and (3) what additional coaching is needed.

The best way to use evaluation in coaching is to *actively involve consumers* in the process. For example, you might ask consumers for their reactions to what you have been doing. Have they understood what you have been demonstrating? Was anything unclear? Do they feel confident in what they have learned? Are there any other skills they can identify that will help them to perform better?

Other criteria can also be used. Did the consumer get a job after the coaching experience? Did the consumer save money after lessons in family budgeting? Did the potentially delinquent youth plan his time sufficiently to stay out of trouble over the past year? These and other criteria can be used to evaluate your coaching effectiveness.

Turn to Frame 12

FRAME 12

Why should you make an active effort to evaluate your coaching activities?

___ A. You need to find out what progress, if any, you and the consumer are making.

Turn to Answer 9

___ B. You need to know if the consumer likes you.

Turn to Answer 11

___ C. You need to determine if the consumer needs any additional coaching.

Turn to Answer 12

___ D. You need to make certain that the consumer is following your instructions accurately.

Turn to Answer 13

___ E. Both A and C.

Turn to Answer 14

___ F. A, C, and D.

Turn to Answer 15

FRAME 13

HELPFUL POINTS TO REMEMBER IN COACHING

Successful coaches have always developed their style of coaching based on their experiences and their observations of others. Although there is no one source that has identified all the skills and knowledge a good coach needs, the following list has been selected for your special attention. Examine them, organize them in your own

(Frame 13 continued)

way, and apply them when you think they are appropriate. Add your own ideas to this list and make necessary changes based on your own experiences in coaching human service consumers.

1. Do not put too much pressure on a consumer to learn faster than his or her abilities will allow.
2. Be generous with praise, and do not hesitate to repeat and repeat again.
3. Develop special learning exercises that will motivate the consumer to work hard at learning how to solve the problem.
4. Work with the consumer in whatever way is best for that particular individual.
5. When a consumer has established his or her own best way of dealing with a problem, interfere as little as possible.
6. Do not forget that the consumer needs to recognize the practical value of what you are coaching.

Turn to Frame 14

FRAME 14

Indicate which of the following would not be helpful in coaching.

___ A. Pressure a consumer to learn as fast as possible.

___ B. Be generous with praise.

___ C. Once a consumer has established his or her own best way of dealing with a problem, make sure it is exactly what you have taught the person.

___ D. Remember that a consumer needs to recognize the practical value of your coaching.

___ E. Motivate the consumer and work *with* him or her in a way most suited to that individual.

Turn to Answer 16

ANSWERS TO LESSON 3

The correct answers are as follows:

1. The consumer has a vast *experience* in living.
2. The consumer has *readiness* to learn different things.
3. The consumer is sensitive to *failure* and may have to overcome his doubts and fears about learning.
4. The consumer has an interest in the *immediate usefulness* of new knowledge.

Did you miss any? If so, go back and read Frame 1. If you got them all right, move on to Frame 4.

ANSWER 2

You selected A, consumers learn best by doing, and you are partially correct. But consumers also learn easily when new skills are explained and taught in terms of their own experiences. Return to Frame 5 and choose the complete answer.

ANSWER 3

Sorry, but this is exactly what you should *not* do. Return to Frames 4 and 6 for a review before you answer Frame 7 correctly.

ANSWER 4

B is correct, but the *best* answer would have been C, both A and B. True, consumers learn easily when new skills are explained in terms of their own experiences, but consumers *also* learn best by practicing and doing.

ANSWER 5

Very good! Consumers *do* learn best by doing, and they also learn easily when new skills are explained in terms of their own past experiences. You're doing a nice job in understanding the consumer as a learner. Proceed to Frame 6.

ANSWER 6

Sorry, but this selection is incorrect. A review of Frame 4 is in order before you answer Frame 5 correctly.

ANSWER 7

No, this is not the best answer in this situation. Remember that coaching will be most effective when it is presented in terms of the adult's past experience and when it focuses on immediate problems. Return to Frame 7 and answer correctly.

ANSWER 8

Great! You've applied your knowledge of the adult learner very nicely. Proceed now to Frame 8 and learn some of the basic steps to follow in coaching.

ANSWER 9

That's half the answer. You have overlooked one other important reason why evaluation is important in coaching. Return to Frame 12 and select the complete answer.

ANSWER 10

You should have checked answers A, C, and D as some probable reasons that Wayne has not been a very successful coach. You can probably think of a number of other reasons. This situation simply demonstrates the importance of following the basic steps of coaching when you are trying to teach a consumer certain ways of doing things.
    Proceed to Frame 11.

ANSWER 11

Incorrect. You do not evaluate your coaching activities to see how popular or well liked you are. Review Frame 11 before you try Frame 12 again.

ANSWER 12

You've got half of it, so a careful rereading of Frame 11 will show you there is one other important reason for evaluating your coaching activities. Return to Frame 12 and select the complete answer.

ANSWER 13

This is not a primary purpose of evaluation. In evaluation, your primary concern is to find out how well the consumer is progressing. Consumers have the right to follow and adapt your instructions in ways that are most helpful to them personally. Return to Frame 11 for a review.

ANSWER 14

Right on! Evaluation will assist you in determining the progress you and the consumer have made, and it will also aid you in identifying any additional areas in which the consumer may need coaching.
    Go right on to Frame 13.

ANSWER 15

You have included one incorrect answer with this choice. Answer D is not a primary purpose of evaluation. Return to Frame 12 and choose the correct answer.

ANSWER 16

You should have checked A and C as things which are *not* helpful in coaching. If you had any trouble with this question, review Frame 13.

You have now completed Lesson 3 and have made a good start in examining the basic knowledge and skills necessary for becoming an effective and useful helper. If you are ready, continue to Lesson 4, where you will be learning about some of the skills you need when you are counseling groups of human service consumers.

LESSON 4:
COUNSELING GROUPS OF CONSUMERS

Quite often the problems experienced by human service consumers can be handled successfully in groups. This allows consumers to share similar problems with each other, and even to help each other in resolving their problems. In this lesson you will be learning how to organize and work with activity groups. The goal of this lesson and the enabling activities that will help you reach this goal are presented below.

GOAL

Given a description of consumers with similar problems, you will be able to explain (1) how to organize those consumers into an activity group, and (2) how to help group members solve their problems so they can live or work together more effectively.

ENABLING ACTIVITIES

After completing this lesson, you will have accomplished the following:

1. Stated the definition of a group
2. Described two different kinds of groups and two different kinds of settings where you might organize groups
3. Examined five guidelines to remember that will help you in getting to know a group of people
4. Named two elements basic to organizing a new group and five hints to remember in planning an activity with a group
5. Examined at least four basic principles to remember when you are working with an activity group
6. Explained three ways of helping a group meet their needs

Turn to Frame 1
to begin this lesson

FRAME 1

WHAT IS A GROUP?

People tend to form groups naturally to satisfy their needs for belonging and for interacting with others. Thus, we might think of our family, our neighbors, and our friends as different groups.

As a human service worker, you can make use of groups to help people solve their common problems. In the human services, the term *group* means more than just any collection of individuals, such as those in a waiting room. A group that you might be working with in the human services is a collection of individuals participating with each other and with a worker to accomplish some specific objective by being together.[1] You should also remember that group members will usually share some common or similar problems and interests. For example, you might be organizing or working with a group of consumers who are having problems budgeting their money, or you might be working with a group of consumers who are trying to develop some recreational activities for themselves.

Turn to Frame 2

FRAME 2

Read each statement below and write in the blank whether the statement is true or false.

_____ 1. Using our definition of a group, neighbors within the community constitute a group.

_____ 2. Any collection of individuals, such as people watching a movie, would be considered a group in human services.

_____ 3. The term *group* carries a special meaning in human services.

_____ 4. In human services we think of a group as being a collection of individuals working together and with a worker to achieve a specific objective.

Turn to Answer 2

FRAME 3

Different Kinds of Groups and Different Settings

Specially trained psychiatrists, psychologists, and social workers often use groups to help treat people who are suffering from psychological problems. Such a group, usually referred to as a *therapy group*, tends to focus more on the growth and/or change of its individual members. Therapy groups are formed to provide play therapy for children, geriatric remotivation therapy, marital counseling, etc. Although you may be assisting a mental health specialist in such areas, as a human service worker you will probably be working more often with *activity groups*.

In an activity group consumers are helped to solve a common problem related to everyday living. A group of consumers, for example, may need child-care services while they are enrolled in a work-training program. The members of an activity group may be healthy or they may be seriously disturbed. For example, you may be working with a group of patients or inmates in an institution, or you may be work-

(Frame 3 continued)

---

[1] Margaret E. Hartford, *Groups in Social Work* (New York: Columbia University Press, 1972).

ing with a group of neighborhood residents who are all concerned about common community problems. You should always remember that no matter what kind of group you are working with, you will be trying to identify group problems and to solve common problems. Even when working with seriously disturbed consumers, you should remember that you will be helping them solve common problems, such as handling the frustration that may accompany the process of learning how to weave a basket, and not necessarily treating them for severe psychological disturbances.

The two settings in which you will be working with groups are institutions and communities. Hospitals, schools, prisons, and halfway houses are examples of institutions where consumers share common problems. Groups of community residents who are welfare recipients are examples of community groups where consumers share a variety of everyday living problems. In either case, your job will be to identify the problem or problems, identify the consumers sharing the problem, and work toward helping to establish the group.

Go on to Frame 4

FRAME 4

Fill in the blanks with the correct words.

In human services, there are two kinds of groups that you should be able to recognize. The first kind of group is made up of consumers who are experiencing severe psychological problems. This kind of group is called a _____ group. The second kind of group is made up of consumers who share some kind of common problem about everyday living. This kind of group is called an _____ group.

Turn to Answer 1

FRAME 5

GETTING TO KNOW A GROUP

If you recognize that a problem is common to a number of consumers with whom you are working, you may wish to help these consumers form a group in which they can work toward solving that problem together. On the other hand, there may be a group already in existence that needs your help in solving their problems. Establishing contact with potential group members or with groups that are already formed requires planning. In either case, there are some basic principles to remember that will help you make contact with these consumers and get to know them.[2]

1. Approach the group of consumers *openly*, explaining who you are and your purpose. You also need to have a goal in mind, such as improved climate on the ward, improved neighborhood appearance, or greater participation in health department services.
2. Do your *homework*. Know what to look for and what to expect, that is, find out important information about the consumers, both before you meet with the group and during the first few meetings.

---

[2] See Frank J. Carney, Hans W. Mattick, and John D. Callaway, *Action on the Streets* (New York: Association Press, 1969); and Irving Spergel, *Street Gang Work: Theory and Practice* (Massachusetts: Addison-Wesley, 1966).

3. Approach the group of consumers when they can give you enough *time* and attention, so you can explain your interest.
4. Have a sense of *humor*, especially if you are met with a cold, hostile silence. You will also need to have considerable patience, particularly if the group decides to "test you out" to see if you are really committed to helping them.
5. Remember that the group will respond positively to you only if you consistently demonstrate through *word and deed* what you can do to help the group.
6. Be a *good observer* of the group. Try to learn as much as you can about the group, what they do, what activities seem to interest them most, and what their needs and aspirations are.

Turn to Frame 6

FRAME 6

Alex is a psychiatric aide in a hospital. He has noticed that several patients in his ward have complained about the lack of recreational activities at the hospital. He would like these patients to get together to form an activity group and, perhaps, to plan some recreational activities.

Check the step below that Alex should take to make contact with potential group members.

— 1. Go to each patient who has complained and tell them that he has heard them complaining about the lack of recreational activities.

Turn to Answer 7

— 2. Go to each patient personally and openly seek his or her thoughts about forming a new recreation group.

Turn to Answer 6

— 3. Post a notice on the bulletin board telling them that he is organizing a group.

Turn to Answer 5

FRAME 7

Sherrie is a family service aide. She is aware of a group of welfare recipients in a local housing project who are meeting regularly to try and develop child-care resources so they can attend a training program. Sherrie is given permission to attend one of their meetings by one of the group members. When she arrives and begins to explain who she is and why she is there, the group members are sullen and hostile toward her. Of the three choices below, check the one which is the best response for Sherrie to make.

— 1. Sherrie should maintain a sense of humor and not show that she is upset or angry as she tries to win the group over.

Turn to Answer 3

— 2. Sherrie should tell the group that they are being rude and unappreciative of her help.

Turn to Answer 4

— 3. Sherrie should leave immediately and forget about helping this group.

Turn to Answer 8

ORGANIZING GROUPS AND PLANNING ACTIVITIES

In organizing and working with activity groups, it is important to remember that while you are helping the group resolve problems, you are also helping the members have a sense of belonging and improve their skills in getting along with each other. Therefore, it is important for each group member to participate fully. To accomplish this, you need to look for (1) the *individual* interests and problems of each group member, and (2) the *common* interests and problems of most of the group.[3] Once you have focused attention on the problems facing the group, joint participation can begin.

As a human service worker, you will find that engaging in an *activity* will be the most useful means of communicating with the group. Through activities, group members can have fun, seek companionship, find relief from boredom and fatigue, and develop better ways of working and living together. The following five guidelines may help when you are organizing and working with activity groups.

1. If the activity is to be conducted successfully, both the planning for it and the performance of it should be done *with* the group rather than *for* them.
2. You should use an activity which will bring about personal reactions among the group members.
3. If you show anxiety about the necessity for controls on the range of allowable group activities, the individuals will begin to test your limits. Be firm and fair.
4. You should be imaginative and flexible in your planning with the group.
5. You should be sure to obtain the necessary facilities, staff approval, and advice if you need it.

Turn to Frame 9

Leon is a cottage parent in a halfway house for delinquent boys. Several boys in his cottage are having problems getting along with each other, and Leon would like to get them involved in an activity group. After identifying the group members, Leon decides that he will take them on a camping trip because he enjoys camping and believes that all boys enjoy outdoor activities. Do you think this is a wise decision?

— Yes   — No

**Explain your answer, and
then turn to Answer 10**

Josie works in a training center for retarded children. She is working with a group of children to help them plan field trips outside the institution. In one of the group meetings, the children ask Josie to take them on a trip to the library the next day. Josie quickly agrees to do so. Do you think this is a wise decision on Josie's part?

— Yes   — No

**Explain your answer, and
then turn to Answer 11**

[3] George M. Beal, Joe M. Bohlen, and T. Neil Raudabaugh, *Leadership and Dynamic Group Action* (Iowa State University Press, 1962).

Working as Group Leader

Working with groups of consumers to help them solve common problems requires the development of certain skills. To be an effective group worker and/or group leader, it is important for you to build and maintain a positive relationship with the group. The following are some basic techniques and guidelines that may be useful.[4]

1. **Be on Time.** You should try to arrive early. Being on time will set an example of responsibility and will also provide you with the opportunity of greeting and observing group members as they arrive.
2. **Relax But Also Act Interested.** A relaxed posture and a pleasant speaking voice will help create a nonthreatening climate. Try not to slouch or gaze out the window. Instead, make an effort to show an interest in the group, frequently looking around the group at each member.
3. **Identify the Activity.** Introduce, explain, demonstrate, and participate in the activity. Try to involve all group members as rapidly as possible. Clarify terms and words by asking for definitions and explanations.
4. **Enforce the Rules.** Do this without bossing or demanding a level of precision which destroys the fun. Also, remember to be generous with praise and encouragement.
5. **Maintain Interest.** Try to stop the activity while group interest is still high. This will help the members to look forward to their next meeting.
6. **Request Feedback.** Find out how the group liked the activity. Begin to identify leadership within the group, so that future direction may come more from the group itself.
7. **End on Time.** A partial function of activity groups is to assist members to plan their time better. Prompt conclusions will help members to carry over what they are learning into their daily routines.

Turn to Frame 12

Marilyn is a correctional officer in an institution for women. She works with a group of inmates who have been organized to plan and participate in leisure time activities. A local hair stylist has consented to meet with the group and show them how to fix the latest hair styles. Marilyn arrives early for the meeting to make sure all the equipment is ready for the evening's activity. After the meeting starts, she explains that everyone will have an opportunity to have her hair done and she helps the members choose partners to work with. During the meeting, Marilyn goes around the room complimenting the group members on what a good job they are doing. At the end of the scheduled time, Marilyn reminds the group that it is time to quit for the evening, even though several group members complain. Marilyn quickly points out that the group meetings must be limited to two hours, but perhaps their guest could return for a future meeting. As everyone leaves, Marilyn checks with the group members informally to determine if everyone had a good time.

Identify which of the seven principles of being a good group leader Marilyn applied by checking the appropriate items.

(Frame 12 continued)

---

[4] See Janet P. Murray and Clyde E. Murray, *Guidelines for Group Leaders* (New York: Whiteside, Inc., and Morrow, 1954); Henry Swift and Elizabeth Swift, *Community Groups and You* (New York: John Day Company, 1964); and Charles F. Tarr, *Group Counseling: Models and Methods* (State Division for Youth, New York, undated).

___ A. She arrived early.

___ B. She acted interested.

___ C. She involved everyone as soon as possible.

___ D. She enforced the rules without being bossy but also gave praise.

___ E. She stopped the activity while group interest was still high.

___ F. She checked to see if everyone had a good time.

___ G. She ended on time.

Turn to Answer 9

FRAME 13

Helping Groups Meet Their Needs

It is important while planning and participating in activities with a group to be sensitive at all times to helping both individual members and the group as a whole to solve problems and meet needs. Whether a group is problem focused or concentrates more on activities, you can help solve problems and meet needs by remembering to do the following.

1. Be available and accessible to the group.
2. Ask the group questions that show you are interested and want to help. ("Who has a problem?" "What can I do to help?" "What do you think we should do now?")
3. Provide information and guidance to the group on matters where they need help or support. Such matters include finding jobs, family problems, needs that are not being met in the institution, and helping the group or an individual prepare to leave an institution.
4. Help members assume more and more responsibility for the direction and activities of the group.

Remember also to be aware of whether you need the assistance of other staff members or professionals. In addition, the knowledge and skills needed for effectively helping groups meet their needs will require learning about communication patterns within the group and studying group dynamics. This lesson serves only as a very preliminary introduction to group work, and we hope that you will use the bibliography at the end of this chapter to expand your own knowledge and understanding of this important activity.

Turn to Frame 14

FRAME 14

Charlie is a correctional officer in a community correctional facility. He is working with a group of inmates who are in a work-release program. The purpose of the group is to discuss the common problems the men are having in work-related areas, such as unfair supervisors and job discrimination. During one of the meetings, several of the group members approach Charlie for advice on how to handle a particular problem. Charlie responds by telling the group members that he doesn't know. Later in the meeting, another group member asks Charlie if the plant manager where several of the members work could be invited to the next meeting. Charlie responds by saying, "Don't bother me now, I'm filling out my daily report."

Throughout the meeting, Charlie is preoccupied with other matters and does not participate in the discussion.

   1. What mistakes did Charlie make? (Explain your answer.)

   2. What advice could you give Charlie to help him become a better helper?

Turn to Answer 12

FRAME 15

When you are working with groups, you will make mistakes, but do not be discouraged! By making mistakes, you will be able to learn more about yourself and more about the group. Group members want a worker who is interested in them, who likes them and is their friend, and who enjoys doing what they are doing.

You have now completed Lesson 4, which is also the end of Chapter VI. If you feel you have a good understanding of counseling, proceed to the summary and review questions found at the end of this chapter. However, if you think you need a review, return to Lesson 1 and, starting with the material on helping skills, review Chapter VI before answering the review questions.

ANSWERS TO LESSON 4

Groups of consumers experiencing severe psychological problems are called *therapy* groups. Groups of consumers sharing some kind of common problems concerning everyday living are called *activity* groups. If you filled in both blanks correctly, you are doing very well! Go on to Frame 5. If not, go back and review Frame 3 before going on to Frame 5.

ANSWER 2

You should have answered as follows:

1. *False.* We generally do not think of neighbors living together as a group since they have not necessarily been brought together to accomplish some specific objective.
2. *False.* Since there must be some common interest or problem associated with groups, a collection of people who happen to be in the same place at the same time, is *not* a group.
3. *True.* It is important to remember that the term "group" has a special meaning in the human services.
4. *True.* This is exactly what is meant by the term "group" in the human services.

   You should have answered all of these correctly. If you did, nice work. Continue to Frame 3. If you missed any, you need to review Frame 1 before continuing to Frame 3.

ANSWER 3

Very good! You remembered that a sense of humor should be maintained even when the group is hostile.
   Go on to Frame 8.

ANSWER 4

If Sherrie does this, the group will be convinced that she really is not interested in their problems. Go back over Frame 5 before trying Frame 7 again.

237

ANSWER 5

As a first step in this example, this action would probably be unsuccessful. If Alex did this, he might not get a response from the patients, since he did not take the trouble to get to know them first, find out about their problems and interests, and let them know he was interested in helping. If you checked this item go back and review Frame 5 *carefully* and then answer Frame 6 correctly.

ANSWER 6

Great! This is probably what Alex should do first. This allows him to break the ice with the patients and begin to get to know them. He can then begin to help them get organized. Go on to Frame 7.

ANSWER 7

We doubt whether this action would be profitable. It would probably frighten the patients and they might think they were going to be punished for complaining. If you checked this item go back and review Frame 5 *carefully* before you try Frame 6 again.

ANSWER 8

Dangerous! If Sherrie leaves the meeting she probably loses any chance of being able to work with this group in the future. Go back over Frame 5 before trying Frame 7 again.

ANSWER 9

You should have checked all the principles listed. If you had any trouble with this question, review Frame 11. If you answered correctly, continue to Frame 13 to learn how to help a group meet its needs.

ANSWER 10

If you answered *no*, you are correct. Why? Because Leon did not take time to find out what the interests of the group were. Instead, he planned an activity *for* the group, not *with* the group. If you missed this question, review Frame 8. If you answered correctly, go on to Frame 10.

ANSWER 11

If you answered *no*, you are correct. Why? Josie neglected to check and see if a visit to the library could be arranged and to see if she had permission to take the boys away from the training center. If the trip didn't work out, the boys would be disappointed and lose faith in their worker. If you missed this question review Frame 8. If you answered correctly proceed to Frame 11.

ANSWER 12

Charlie ignored all three ways to help the group solve problems and meet needs by (1) not being able to provide information to the group, (2) not being available to talk to group members, and (3) not participating in the group meeting.

If you were able to identify all these areas or additional areas where Charlie failed, and can tell him how to correct his mistakes, great! If not, please review Frame 13.

Return to Frame 15.

SUMMARY

This chapter on counseling includes some of the basic principles which are used in developing effective helping relationships with consumers. In the first lesson we defined the helping process and indicated that as a human service worker it is necessary for you to be aware of your strengths and weaknesses in order to participate effectively in the helping process. In addition, considerable awareness of the communication process is needed in any helping relationship, especially an understanding and skillful use of verbal and nonverbal communication.

In the second lesson we described the process of building relationships, which is a basic component of the counseling role. Since all counseling activities in the human services are oriented toward a specific goal or set of goals, we identified four of the more common purposes for establishing a helping relationship including helping consumers become more realistic, more self-confident, more self-directing, and more appreciative of the potentials of life. The basic characteristics of the helping relationship were described and related to the needs for a sense of reality, empathy, and support in the processes of change through environment, through one-to-one relationships, and through group work. This lesson concluded with a description of five practice principles of effective counseling, including responding to both feeling and verbal content, maintaining your helping role, helping the consumer express his problems and needs, periodically restating the problem, and referring more complicated consumer problems to other workers or specialists.

In the third lesson, we wanted you to begin to apply the knowledge you acquired in the first two lessons to the process of *coaching* consumers. In order to do this, you needed to know about the learning process as it affects human service consumers as well as about the attributes of a coaching relationship, including the sense of reality, empathy, and support, which are found in all helping processes. Included in the lesson were four basic steps in the coaching process and some of the reasons for evaluating this process. The lesson concluded with additional practice principles related to pressuring and praising the consumer, motivating and pacing in learning and problem solving, and the practical nature of the coaching process.

The fourth lesson emphasized the skills needed to work with groups of consumers effectively. We defined a human service group and identified the two major types—therapy groups and activity groups. Special attention was given to the skills needed in contacting consumers for the purpose of forming a group, including openly approaching the group, doing your homework, and having a sense of humor. These were related to the worker's efforts to identify the individual interests and common interests of the group members. Additional principles were noted relating to the effective functioning of a group worker, including being on time, giving praise, and enforcing rules. The lesson concluded with a discussion of how the worker assists the group in solving its own problems, with special emphasis on the role of the worker in helping the members of the group assume more and more responsibility for the direction and activities of the group.

By now it should be apparent that we have defined counseling in the human services as a process requiring skills in self-awareness, relationship formation, coaching, and group work. Through further study and experience you might want to adapt this definition to suit your own work perspective.

SUGGESTIONS FOR FURTHER STUDY

Since we have provided only an introduction to the role of counseling, further study should include an analysis of other therapies. The reader's attention is directed to rehabilitation therapy (physical, occupational, speech, dance, music, etc.); remotivation counseling related to deinstitutionalization; and client-centered counseling as developed by Rogers and Carkuff.

Expanding your knowledge of counseling will also require attention to the stages of human development from birth to death, including biological, psychological, sociological, and cultural explanations of human behavior. Human behavior will also need to be understood in terms of group influences, including that of the family, neighborhood, community, peer group, and work group. Human behavior can also be evaluated in terms of various theories of personality, which also require further study. And finally, you will need to acquire additional knowledge of the range of behavior disorders as noted in the field of abnormal psychology. The following suggestions for further reading should help you explore additional areas of knowledge related to counseling.

SUGGESTIONS FOR FURTHER READING

Anderson, Ralph E., and Carter, Irl E. *Human Behavior in the Social Environment.* Chicago: Aldine, 1974.

Beal, George M., Bohlen, Joe M., Raudabaugh, J. Neil. *Leadership and Dynamic Group Action.* Iowa State University Press, 1962.

Brill, Naomi. *Working with People.* Philadelphia: Lippincott, 1973.

Carkuff, R. *The Art of Helping: A Guide for Developing Helping Skills for Parents, Teachers and Counselors.* Amherst, Mass.: Human Resource Development Press, 1972.

Collins, Alice A. *The Human Services: An Introduction.* Indianapolis: Odyssey Press, 1973.

Combs, Arthur W., Avila, Donald L., and Purkey, William W. *Helping Relationships: Basic Concepts for the Helping Professions.* Boston: Allyn Bacon, 1971.

Ginsberg, Leon, Emery, Margaret, and Isaacson, John. *Syllabus on Orientation and Training of Beginning Workers to Provide Social and Rehabilitation Services.* West Virginia University School of Social Work, 1971.

Hartford, Margaret E. *Groups in Social Work.* New York: Columbia University Press, 1972.

Holler, Ronald F., and DeLong, George M. *Human Services Technology.* St. Louis: Mosby, 1973.

Keith-Lucas, Alan. *Giving and Taking Help.* University of North Carolina Press, 1972.

Kidd, J. R. *How Adults Learn.* New York: Association Press, 1959.

Konopka, Gisela. *Group Work in the Institution.* New York: Association Press, 1970.

——— *Social Group Work: A Helping Process.* Englewood Cliffs, N.J.: Prentice-Hall, 1963.

Lowe, Robert. *The Growth of Personality: From Infancy to Old Age.* New York: Penguin Books, 1972.

Luft, Joseph. *Group Processes: An Introduction to Group Dynamics.* Palo Alto, Calif.: National Press Books, 1970.

Lyle, Mary S., and Van Horn, Rua. *Homemaking Education Program for Adults.* Washington, D.C.: U.S. Government Printing Office, undated.

Mahoney, Stanley C. *The Art of Helping People Effectively.* New York: Association Press, 1967.

McCurdy, Harold Grier. *The Personal World: An Introduction to the Study of Personality.* New York: Harcourt Brace Jovanovich, 1961.

Moore, J. W. *The Psychology of Athletic Coaching*. Minnesota: Burgess Publishing Company, 1970.

Murray, Janet P., and Murray, Clyde E. *Guidelines for Group Leaders*. New York: Whiteside, Inc., and Morrow, 1954.

Perez, Joseph F. *The Initial Counseling Contact*. New York: Houghton Mifflin, 1968.

Perlman, Helen Harris. *Social Casework: A Problem Solving Process*. University of Chicago Press, 1957.

Rogers, Carl. *Client-Centered Therapy*. Boston: Houghton Mifflin, 1951.

Schulman, Eveline D. *Intervention in Human Services*. St. Louis: Mosby, 1974.

Schwartz, William. "Social Group Work: The Interactionist Approach." In Robert Morris, ed., *Encyclopedia of Social Work*, vol. II (New York: National Association of Social Workers, 1971) pp. 1252–1263.

Simons, Joseph, and Reidy, Jeanne. *The Human Art of Counseling*. New York: Herder and Herder, 1971.

Spergel, Irving. *Street Gang Work: Theory and Practice*. Mass.: Addison Wesley, 1966.

Swift, Henry, and Swift, Elizabeth. *Community Groups and You*. New York: John Day Company, 1964.

Tarr, Charles F. *Group Counseling: Models and Methods*. State Division for Youth, New York, undated.

Tropp, Emanuel. "Social Group Work: The Developmental Approach." In Robert Morris, ed., *Encyclopedia of Social Work*, vol. II (New York: National Association of Social Workers, 1971) pp. 1246–1252.

Tutko, Thomas A., and Richards, Jack W. *Psychology of Coaching*. Boston: Allyn & Bacon, 1971.

REVIEW QUESTIONS—CHAPTER VI

Circle the letter corresponding to the answer of your choice.

1. Which of the following *best* describes the meaning of helping?
    A. Helping is something offered by one person to another in such a way that the helped person can make use of it to achieve some measure of self-fulfillment.
    B. Helping is something material, like money or clothing, that a human service worker gives to a consumer.
    C. Helping is something intangible, like advocating or mobilizing, that a human service worker does by himself.
    D. Helping is something given by a human service worker to a consumer in a very impersonal, formal relationship.

2. Which of the following statements is false?
    A. The chief tools in helping others are good communication skills and your own self-understanding.
    B. There is only one effective way of giving useful help to a consumer.
    C. There are certain qualities, attitudes, and approaches that are common to all good helpers.
    D. Helping begins the moment two people meet for the purpose of helping.

3. Which of the following are characteristics that may be *weaknesses* in effectively helping others?
    A. Judgmental attitudes
    B. Sensitivity and faith in others

C. Tolerance for frustration

D. Oversimplification and unrealistic expectations for the consumer.

E. A and D

4. Which of the following are attitudes that are generally considered *strengths* in effectively helping others?

A. A college degree and overcritical attitudes toward the consumer

B. Sensitivity, desire to help, and faith in others and ourselves

C. Overinvolvement and oversimplification

D. Impulsive decision making and overinvolvement

5. Which of the following would be important for successful verbal communication in helping?

A. Be very clear about what you want to say.

B. Be receptive to feedback from the consumer.

C. Make an effort to see that your message is related to the consumer's immediate needs.

D. B and C are correct.

E. All of the above.

6. Which of the following would be important in establishing successful nonverbal communication?

A. Concentrate on what you are saying, not on what you are doing.

B. Listen attentively and be interested in the consumer.

C. Try to keep your words and behavior consistent.

D. B and C.

E. All of the above.

7. Next to each of the six communications below, write V for verbal and NV for nonverbal, and then choose your answer from beneath the list.

1. Appearance of clothing
2. Clarifying unclear messages
3. Clearly relating your message to the consumer's needs
4. Facial expressions
5. Giving feedback
6. Hand movements

Choose your answer from the following:

A. NV, NV, V, NV, NV, NV

B. NV, V, V, NV, V, NV

C. V, NV, NV, V, V, V

8. Effective helping relationships should always

A. be pleasant, one-way, and judgmental.

B. focus only on feelings, the consumer's past, and the worker's superiority to the consumer.

C. be tolerant, allow for two-way communication, and allow for the expression of anger or disagreement.

D. focus only on the past and ignore consumer's feelings and opinions.

E. include both C and D.

9. The long-range purposes of the helping relationship are to help the consumer

A. become less realistic, more self-directing, and feel inadequate.

B. value life, become more realistic, self-directing, and self-actualizing.

C. feel "I can't" and "I am not important," and focus on what "should be."

D. be unwilling to make his own decisions, to value life, and to accept "what is."

10. The three factors used in building helping relationships are listed in column 1 below. Descriptions of each of these factors are listed in column 2 below. Write the correct description next to each helping factor, and then choose your answer from the choices listed below.

Column 1	*Column 2*
1. Sense of reality	a. Material and emotional assurance to the consumer conveying "You don't have to face this alone"
2. Empathy	b. The consumer's problem as it actually is ("This is it")
3. Support	c. Feeling with the consumer and conveying "I know this must hurt"

Choose your answer from the following:

A. c, a, b

B. b, a, c

C. b, c, a

11. Using the helping factors of a sense of reality, empathy, and support, there are several different ways of working within the helping relationship. These include which of the following?

A. Changing the environment and changing your job title

B. One-to-one and group relationships

C. Prescribing drugs and building relationships with your supervisor

D. Focusing on nonverbal communications and offering quick solutions to a consumer's problem.

12. When you are building helping relationships, which would be generally useful?

A. Respond to feeling rather than to literal content.

B. Take over the consumer's decisions, but allow the consumer to control the approach you use.

C. Help the consumer express what he wants and then work with him toward what he can reasonably have.

D. Restate the consumer's problem from time to time as you see it.

E. A, C, and D.

13. You are a worker in a detention center for youthful offenders. James has run away from home and is brought to the center by a police officer. If you are going to try to build a helping relationship with James and help him to do something about his behavior, which of the following should you do?

A. Try to help James face the facts of his situation: He has done something illegal; he might be sent to a correctional school; he might be placed on probation.

B. Make an effort to prevent James from expressing any anger he may feel towards you, his parents, or other workers.

C. Convey to James that you are there to help him if he wants help and won't desert him if he makes another mistake.

D. A and C.

E. All of the above.

14. Assume that you are working in the welfare department. You have been talking with Mrs. Francis, a mother receiving financial assistance for the past few weeks, to try and help her with the many problems she is facing since her husband deserted her and their five children. In your conversations, you keep trying to find out why her husband deserted her and why she had behaved with such hostility toward her children before her husband left. You are surprised when Mrs. Francis fails to show up for her next three appointments.

Which of the following is the *major* mistake you are making in your effort to build a helping relationship in this situation?
   A. Focusing on the past instead of being concerned with what is happening in the present
   B. Trying to be consistently pleasant and friendly
   C. Passing judgments on the childrens' behavior
   D. Not referring Mrs. Francis to a psychiatrist for assistance

15. Which of the following statements is false?
   A. Adults and children are most interested in the immediate usefulness of new knowledge and skills.
   B. Adults and children learn best by doing and practicing.
   C. Adults and children are rarely sensitive to failure and have few doubts about their ability to learn.
   D. Learning will be easier for an adult and child when new things are presented in terms of their own past experiences.

16. Coaching a consumer will depend on your understanding of which of the following?
   A. Consumer's needs and interests
   B. Consumer's living situation
   C. Past experiences of the consumer
   D. Kinds of content that may serve the consumer's needs
   E. All of the above

17. Which of the following are the four basic steps to follow in coaching?
   A. Talking, describing, rehearsing, and demonstrating
   B. Introducing, explaining, demonstrating, and participating
   C. Discussing, questioning, practicing, and explaining

18. In coaching it is important to _____ your activities and to _____ the consumer in the process.
   A. plan, reject
   B. demonstrate, ignore
   C. evaluate, involve

19. If you are coaching parents in basic child-rearing skills, you should
   A. tell them to read a textbook on home repair.
   B. introduce and explain the skills you are coaching.
   C. tell them how "ideal" parents ignore their children.
   D. demonstrate the skills and involve the parents in practicing the skills.
   E. do B and D.

20. In the human services, a group is a collection of individuals participating with each other and with a worker to accomplish some specific objective by being together.
    A. True
    B. False

21. Assume you are a houseparent in a training school for youthful offenders. The youths in your cottage have only recently arrived, but you find they are all having difficulty in getting along and in following the rules. So you decide you'd like to form some kind of activity group. Since you don't know the youths very well yet, the best way to start this group would be to do which of the following?
    A. Go to each youth and tell him you're interested in helping him adjust to his new situation.
    B. Find out what activities seem to interest the youths.
    C. Tell the youths that they are being rude and unappreciative of the help the institution is offering them.
    D. A and B.
    E. A, B, and C.

22. Which of the following would be helpful when you are organizing an activity group?
    A. Involve the group in planning and doing the activity.
    B. Be very structured and rigid in your planning with the group.
    C. Try to use an activity which won't result in any personal reactions from the group members.
    D. Show anxiety about any necessity for rules or controls for group members or the activity.

23. Which of the following statements is false?
    A. To be effective, a group leader should be on time and greet each group member personally.
    B. An effective group leader should be generous with praise and encouragement.
    C. An effective group leader should demand high levels of precision performance from the group.
    D. An effective group leader should stop the group activity while interest is still high in the activity.

24. When you are counseling groups of human service consumers, it is important to try to help the group meet its needs. Which of the following would represent an effective way of helping to meet group needs?
    A. When a group member asks you a question about an activity or a problem, respond: "Don't bother me now . . . I'm filling out my daily report."
    B. Ask the group "What do you think we should do now?" and "What can I do to help?"
    C. Try to be available and accessible to the group.
    D. B and C.
    E. All of the above.

Now check your answers with the Answer key for this chapter at the end of the book

CHAPTER VII: REHABILITATING

INTRODUCTION

In addition to offering consumers useful help, human service workers are engaged in activities that are designed to bring about a change in the behavior patterns, habits, and perceptions of individuals and groups. For people who are less responsive to the traditional counseling process, workers use a variety of rehabilitating techniques that are designed to structure and set limits on consumers' environments so that they will be able to change their socially abnormal or inappropriate behavior. The underlying assumption of rehabilitating is that behavior is learned and that inappropriate behavior needs to be unlearned and/or reshaped. By working intensively with consumers in specialized environments, rehabilitating techniques are used to change behavior in very specific ways. In rehabilitating, worker activities are planned and directed toward modifying or changing a consumers' abnormal or inappropriate behavior using techniques of treatment that are very specialized and involve setting limits on inappropriate behavior.

This chapter introduces three examples of rehabilitating techniques usually used with groups of human service consumers who are unable to respond to the counseling process. Such consumers include the following groups, among others.[1]

1. **Mentally Ill.** Many people who are mentally ill need both medication and very specialized living arrangements. The mentally ill who are institutionalized are very often far removed from reality, and, therefore, their treatment usually consists of specialized methods designed to change their behavior.
2. **Mentally Retarded.** Here we are referring to the severely retarded and those who cannot express themselves at all. The moderately retarded or people of low intelligence may also be included, in the sense that they can usually respond to a supportive relationship and some form of helping.
3. **Children.** Although counseling and therapeutic techniques for changing behavior can be useful, children also respond to more structured techniques for changing behavior, that is, to techniques requiring the structured types of relationships which we will be discussing in this chapter.

[1] Alan Keith-Lucas, *Giving and Taking Help* (University of North Carolina Press, 1972), pp. 152–158.

4. **The Senile.** Aged persons who have become senile also are in need for something more than counselng. They too can frequently be helped through a structured type of relationship.

5. **Those Suffering from Character Disorders.** These are people who, although they have not lost all touch with reality and are not mentally ill in a medical sense, have become so wholly self-centered that all their energies are directed towards their own immediate advantage. People who have committed crimes usually fall into this group, and they often provide a real challenge to our rehabilitating skills since they frequently lack an initial desire to change.

There are so many rehabilitating techniques used to help these and other groups of consumers that we could not possibly cover them all in this text. Therefore, we have chosen three frequently used techniques as examples: (1) parenting, (2) reality therapy, and (3) behavior modification. These techniques emphasize therapy as a learning process and are employed in a range of human service settings. Other techniques, which explain abnormal behavior in terms of physical, psychic, or pathological factors are not included; however, references for investigating other techniques are included in the chapter bibliography.

A puzzling, sometimes frustrating finding related to the successful rehabilitation of certain human service consumers is the fact that no matter which technique is employed, one-third of the consumers will get better, one-third will stay the same, and one-third will get worse.[2] Thus, the role of rehabilitating is by no means clearly defined. We are still searching for the most effective ways of analyzing and changing problem behaviors.

Before you begin this chapter, it may be helpful to know something about the general steps employed by trained therapists in the treatment process. The effective application of these steps requires considerable experience and education, but it is important for you to be aware of the process in which you will be offering assistance. The eight general steps include:[3]

1. **Inventory of the Problem Areas.** Obtain the range of problems as seen by the consumer and the therapist.

2. **Problem Selection and Contract.** Reach a verbal or written agreement with the consumer concerning the specific problem area needing the most attention, and help the consumer with this process if the consumer initially appears incapable of identifying the problem.

3. **Conditions Controlling the Problem.** Denote those specific behaviors of the consumer that constitute the essential elements of the problem area, and determine the frequency and magnitude of these behaviors.

4. **Resources Available for Treatment.** Determine what resources may be used to modify behavior (consumer and his environment, worker and agency, etc.).

5. **Goals.** Specify the treatment goals or behavioral objectives of the treatment plan.

6. **Identification of Techniques.** Select the appropriate techniques to be used in achieving the treatment goals.

7. **Application.** Use the selected appropriate techniques in the treatment.

---

[2] See Bernard Berelson and Gary A. Steiner, *Human Behavior: An Inventory of Scientific Findings* (New York: Harcourt Brace Jovanovich, 1964), pp. 287–289.

[3] See Edwin J. Thomas, "Social Casework and Social Groupwork: The Behavioral Approach," in *Encyclopedia of Social Work*, vol. II (New York: National Association of Social Workers, 1971), p. 1233; and Derek Jehu, *Behavior Modification in Social Work* (London: Wiley Interscience, 1972).

8. **Assess Treatment.** Obtain information concerning the effectiveness of treatment.

You will not become a skilled therapist in any of these techniques when you finish this chapter, but you will be able to recognize and understand the value and effective application of three rehabilitating techniques useful in changing specific behaviors—parenting, reality therapy, and behavior modification. You will also be able to help other workers who are using these techniques to change a person's behavior. The various techniques and definitions will become more meaningful when you are able to observe them in use by trained practitioners in human service agencies. The overall objective of this chapter is to help you to recognize and understand the value and effective application of these rehabilitating techniques.

**Proceed to the next page
and begin Lesson 1**

LESSON 1:
THE REHABILITATING TECHNIQUE OF PARENTING

In this lesson you will learn about the rehabilitating technique of parenting. Based on the traditional role of father or mother, this technique is used to give people the experience of being loved, cared for, and disciplined, in an effort to change their behavior. The goal of this lesson and the enabling activities that will help you reach this goal are presented below.

GOAL

When you finish this lesson, you will be able to explain the two main methods that are used in parenting and to list at least three limitations of the parenting technique.

ENABLING ACTIVITIES

After completing this lesson, you will have accomplished the following:

1. Identified the aim of the parenting technique
2. Named four human needs fulfilled through parenting
3. Explained three ways a worker uses the method of "caring" in parenting
4. Defined the method of "disciplining" and explained four characteristics of good discipline
5. Reviewed four ways workers who function as parents should behave so they can obtain the best results
6. Explained three limitations of the parenting technique

Are you ready? Well, ready or not . . .

Proceed to Frame 1 and begin this lesson

FRAME 1

PARENTING: DEFINITION AND RATIONALE

Parenting includes the processes of helping children and adults grow emotionally, teaching cultural approaches to living, and encouraging the attainment of basic standards of adult individuality and responsibility.[1] In the human services, parenting as a treatment technique is used by adults other than the person's real parents to provide the consumer with the experience of being loved, cared for, and rehabilitated through discipline in a parental way. Parenting can be useful to a range of consumers including the juvenile delinquent, the mentally ill, the aged, and inmates in correctional institutions. When used with these groups, it is a way of helping them control their impulses, fears, anxieties, and the acting out of their feelings in unacceptable ways. It also gives these people the experience of being loved and cared for. Thus, the aim of parenting is to provide a caring, structured relationship until a person is able to develop enough self-reliance to accept the necessary demands of living.

Proceed to Frame 2

FRAME 2

Parenting in the human services is carried out by

A. the natural parents.

Turn to Answer 2

B. mature adults other than the consumer's natural parents.

Turn to Answer 4

FRAME 3

Which of the following examples reflect an activity which could be a part of the parenting technique? Make your choices and then turn to Answer 6.

___ 1. A worker holds closely a child who has just been told that she must change foster parents.
___ 2. A worker shares a cigarette or piece of gum by passing it through the cell bars to an inmate in an institution.
___ 3. A worker makes an elderly person comfortable upon the person's arrival in a nursing home for the first time.
___ 4. A worker disciplines a delinquent youth, after repeated violations of the rules of a halfway house, by sitting down with the youth and discussing the violations.
___ 5. A worker walks down the ward with a mentally ill woman who has been denied permission to leave the ward and discusses her frustrations.

FRAME 4

The Human Needs Fulfilled by Parenting

We have assumed that certain consumers need someone who can fulfill the role of a parent, and you may be wondering why anyone but a child would have this need. One reason is that he or she may have missed one of the most important things we

[1] See Christopher Beedell, *Residential Life with Children* (New York: Humanities Press, 1970).

all need in growing up—parents who love us and who teach us how to behave. Many people living in human service institutions have in one way or another missed this important opportunity. Therefore, the parenting technique in their treatment represents one way to meet these needs. The following are some of the needs that can be fulfilled through parenting:[2]

1. **The Need for Security.** We all have a need to feel secure and stable—financially, emotionally, and physically. Parenting is designed to give a person the experience of receiving the care and comfort that help him feel secure.

2. **The Need for Responsibility and Limits.** We all need a relationship with a responsible person who functions on a rational level and behaves in acceptable ways. This provides an opportunity to learn and accept limitations on one's own behavior. Parenting is designed to provide a structured environment that shows a person where the limits are and how to behave in appropriate ways within these limits.

3. **The Need for Learning To Cope with Frustrations and Problems.** We all encounter endless frustrations and problems in our daily living. But in order to find logical solutions to these difficulties we need to learn how to cope with these problems. Parenting serves as a way of teaching a person to find logical solutions to his problems and frustrations.

4. **The Need To Be a Self-directed Person.** We all have the need to lead our own life, make our own decisions, and manage our own relationships with other people. Parenting is designed to help a person lead his own life more completely by deliberately attempting to help the person develop acceptable and responsible ways of behaving.

Go on to Frame 5

FRAME 5

PARENTING AS CARING

The two main methods that are often used concurrently in the parenting technique are *caring*, or showing affection, and *disciplining*, or training. A worker can display affection while showing a concern for training through disciplining. Keeping this in mind we shall first discuss caring, or showing affection.

The actual experiences in which the individual is provided with care, affection, and comfort will, of course, depend upon the needs of the particular individual and his situation. Providing these experiences through the following forms of caring will help create and strengthen acceptable behavior.[3]

1. **Showing Acceptance.** When the worker makes an effort to relate to the consumer and by specific actions shows an interest in the consumer as an individual, that is, not just as another case, the worker is showing acceptance.

    Example remark: "I usually meet the consumer in the waiting room since the route to my office is cold and uninviting."

(Frame 5 continued)

---

[2] See Ibid. and also Joseph Bird and Lois Bird, *Power to the Parents* (Garden City, N.Y.: Doubleday, 1972), and Sister Mary Charles Keane, *The Housemother: A Member of the Institutional Team* (Washington, D.C.: National Conference of Catholic Charities, 1954).

[3] See Christopher Beedell, *Residential Life with Children* (New York: Humanities Press, 1970); and John B. Liebrock, *Manual of Skilled Houseparentry* (Philadelphia: Whitmore Publishing Company, 1967).

2. **Providing Sound Physical Care.** Making certain that simple food and drink, warmth, and bodily comfort are provided serves as another way of caring or showing affection.

> Example remark: "When children are admitted to a halfway house, we make sure that they have enough clothing, a clean bed, and a chance to bring in some of their own furniture."

3. **Making Sure the Individual Understands the Present Situation.** People who are placed in an unfamiliar environment, such as a halfway house, a prison, or a mental institution, feel very uncertain and unsettled. Caring or showing affection is demonstrated by helping the person understand both the situation and what will be expected of him or her.

> Example remark: "We always accompany retarded persons to their first meal so that we can show them the way and make sure they understand their new surroundings."

Proceed to Frame 6

FRAME 6

The two major methods used in parenting involve

A. loving and warmth.

Turn to Answer 1

B. guidance and training.

Turn to Answer 3

C. discipline and caring.

Turn to Answer 5

D. training and discipline.

Turn to Answer 10

FRAME 7

In which of the following ways does the worker who is employing the parenting technique show that he cares for the consumer? Check those that apply.

___ 1. Helping the consumer understand his or her situation and what will be expected of him or her

___ 2. Making decisions for the consumer

___ 3. Showing acceptance

___ 4. Providing physical care for the consumer

___ 5. Giving the consumer money to spend.

Turn to Answer 8

FRAME 8

PARENTING AS DISCIPLINING

One of the main methods used in parenting is training through discipline. Discipline is important because no group of people can share or work together without the presence of some rules and regulations.[4] Basically, discipline involves structuring learning. Thus in parenting, discipline is viewed as a plan of training that stresses a positive approach and also includes direction and control.

When we use the word *discipline* many people immediately think of punishment, especially physical punishment. But discipline and punishment are not the same; the difference lies in the goal of discipline. Planned discipline focuses on developing a structure that will provide opportunities for learning acceptable ways to behave and for coming to grips with important problems. Punishment by itself does not mean a plan of training, but simply refers to correcting offenses or infractions. When we say that training through discipline is a primary method of parenting, we are saying that the concern is with setting goals, letting the consumer know what is expected, and praising small efforts toward acceptable goals. This is in contrast to punishing failures.

With this understanding of discipline, we can now discuss some of the characteristics or qualities of positive training through discipline in parenting.[5]

1. **Planning.** Good discipline is planned. By knowing about the person's problems, interests, and abilities, the worker can develop a plan of discipline that will be suited to the person's needs.

   > Example remark: "Bobby always knows that if he leaves this room messy, he will lose special privileges in the halfway house."

2. **Setting Limits.** Good discipline lets the person learn about setting limits. The person needs to know how he should behave and the consequences of inappropriate behavior. He also needs to be free to practice, to have choices, to make mistakes, and to blow up once in awhile.

   > Example remark: "Patients who wander off the ward soon discover that they will not be able to eat until everyone else is fed."

3. **Firmness and Fairness.** Good discipline is firm, fair, and consistent. This means sticking to what you say, especially when you are being tested to see if you meant what you said. It also means being fair and not picking at little things. Overlook what you can, but when there is something serious, get to the bottom of it. Being consistent means holding to the same practices and rules with a given individual.

   > Example remark: "While inmates know that privileges will be denied when they are caught smoking in the chapel, this does not mean I cannot offer them a cigarette when I see them on the grounds."

4. **Verbalizing.** Good discipline allows for verbal expression. If a person is able to get his or her feelings out verbally, and has a chance to talk things over with someone, it saves a lot of resentment.

   > Example remark: "While I bring it to the children's attention if they fail to sign out, I always chat with them in the lounge in order to learn the reasons for their failure."

Go on to Frame 9

---

[4] See E. Lakin Phillips and Daniel Wiener, *Discipline, Achievement, and Mental Health* (Englewood Cliffs, N.J.: Prentice Hall, 1972), p. 3.

[5] See Ibid., pp. 28–42, and John B. Liebrock, *Manual of Skilled Houseparentry* (Philadelphia: Whitemore Publishing Company, 1967), pp. 32–35.

FRAME 9

Disciplining as a method of parenting refers to which of the following?

A. Punishment

Turn to Answer 7

B. A plan of training to learn direction and control

Turn to Answer 11

C. Correcting offenses

Turn to Answer 13

FRAME 10

The worker using discipline, as a major method of parenting, uses it to help the consumer learn to do which of the following?

A. Set goals

Turn to Answer 9

B. Know what is expected

Turn to Answer 12

C. Take steps toward fulfilling acceptable goals

Turn to Answer 14

D. A and C above

Turn to Answer 16

E. A, B and C above

Turn to Answer 18

FRAME 11

In order to help the consumer learn where his limits are, the worker should allow which of the following on the part of the consumer. Check those that apply.

__ 1. Consistent misbehavior

__ 2. Practice on his own.

__ 3. Making mistakes

__ 4. Constant frustration

__ 5. Showing anger once in awhile

__ 6. Having choices.

Turn to Answer 15

FRAME 12

You should now be able to explain what disciplining means and what the four major characteristics of good disciplining are. Think of these now, and if you are unable to define *disciplining* or name its *four characteristics*, return to Frame 8 for a review before going on to Frame 13. If you can state these in your own words, go right on to Frame 13.

FRAME 13

Guidelines for Effective Parenting

The parenting technique will generally have the most positive results if you, as the worker, follow these guidelines.[6]

"1. Try to *be at your best* at all times—mentally, socially, physically, and emotionally.
2. Try *not to be too critical* of a consumer's efforts. Rather aim to instill the hope that the consumer can and will perform better.
3. Deal with the consumer in a manner that is *fair and understandable*, through a friendly but businesslike attitude.
4. Watch *what you say* and *how you say it*, so that mistakes are not reinforced and so that the consumer is corrected and then encouraged to perform correctly."

Proceed to Frame 14

FRAME 14

As a human service worker, which of the guidelines stated below should you follow when working with a consumer in a parenting relationship? Check those that apply.

___ 1. Deal with the consumer fairly and in a way that is understandable to him or her.

___ 2. Be at your best at all times.

___ 3. Watch what you say and how you say it.

___ 4. Continually emphasize mistakes of the consumer.

___ 5. Use positive criticism so the consumer believes he can and will perform better, but refrain from being too critical.

___ 6. Try to be at your best when working with the consumer.

Turn to Answer 20

FRAME 15

LIMITATIONS OF THE PARENTING TECHNIQUE

At the beginning of this chapter, we emphasized that rehabilitating techniques do not work with every human service consumer. Further, they do not always work every time they are used. With a basic understanding of how parenting works, it is now appropriate to discuss some of the limitations associated with the parenting technique.[7]

1. Because many people have a confused or poor understanding of the counseling process that was discussed in Chapter VI and limited understanding of the different rehabilitating techniques, parenting is sometimes chosen because it

(Frame 15 continued)

---

[6] John B. Liebrock, *Manual of Skilled Houseparentry* (Philadelphia: Whitmore Publishing Company, 1967), pp. 84–89.
[7] Alan Keith-Lucas, *Giving and Taking Help* (University of North Carolina Press, 1972), pp. 164–168.

seems to be either the easy way out or the only method they feel comfortable using.

> Example remark: "I keep a close watch over the delinquent kids on that ward because all they need is a strong person to control them."

2. Parenting requires a good deal of knowledge, sensitivity, and patience. Since good parenting is personally rewarding to the worker, it is very hard to give up the role. Thus we must be very careful in deciding who needs parenting and who will act as the parent.

> Example remark: "I always take care of the old ladies on that ward, although I know they can take care of themselves."

3. The parenting relationship has a tendency to attract those who consciously or unconsciously enjoy power over others. Thus we must be very sure of our motives before we engage in the parenting technique, since the major responsibility in this relationship lies with the worker.

> Example remark: "Those retarded children need me to watch over them all the time since they can not be trusted."

4. It is very difficult to decide who is in need of parenting. In fact, almost anyone can decide that another is in need of parenting, since there are few standards we can follow that will tell us when someone needs this kind of treatment.

> Example remark: "Disciplining him with solitary confinement is good for him, although it might be more helpful for him to see the counselor on a regular basis."

These are some of the limitations of the parenting technique. There are many situations where parenting is a very useful and helpful way of dealing with people who have problems in behaving in acceptable ways. The main thing to remember is that before you engage in the parenting technique you need to examine your own motives carefully and be very sure that this is the best technique available to help the consumer change his behavior.

Proceed to Frame 16

FRAME 16

For many reasons it is usually very easy for the worker to enter into a parenting relationship. Check the reasons for this in the list below.

___ 1. The worker may feel more comfortable with the parenting technique than with others that seem more complicated.

___ 2. The worker receives little gratitude but avoids a lot of anguish by choosing this method.

___ 3. It is easy to decide who needs parenting since there are clear standards to follow in deciding who needs it.

___ 4. It gives the worker a feeling of power.

___ 5. The good parent often receives a lot of gratitude for his efforts.

Proceed to Answer 19

FRAME 17

Before choosing the parenting technique, the worker should answer which of the following questions? Check those that apply.

___ 1. Will the consumer benefit from this treatment more than from some other treatment?

___ 2. Am I choosing this treatment because it is the one I am most comfortable using?

___ 3. Do I have a need to feel powerful?

___ 4. Do I have the necessary knowledge, sensitivity, and patience to employ this treatment effectively?

___ 5. Do I need a lot of gratitude for my efforts?

Turn to Answer 17

FRAME 18

You have now completed Lesson 1. Hopefully, you have a beginning understanding of the characteristics and limitations of the parenting technique. If you wish to learn more about this useful technique of rehabilitating, refer to the bibliography at the end of this chapter. Go on now to Lesson 2 for information regarding another technique of rehabilitating known as *reality therapy*.

ANSWERS TO LESSON 1

ANSWER 1

This answer is only partially correct. Return to Frame 5 for a review, and then answer Frame 6 correctly.

ANSWER 2

No, the parenting role is *not* carried out by the consumer's natural parents but is assumed by a mature human service worker. The natural parents may have either given up their responsibilities or were unable to carry them out effectively.

Return to Frame 1 for a review, and then go on to Frame 3.

ANSWER 3

This answer is only partially correct. Return to Frame 5 for a review before answering the question in Frame 6.

ANSWER 4

Right you are. The parenting role is assumed by a mature human service worker in order to provide the consumer with experiences he or she has missed in life.

Return now to Frame 3 and continue the lesson.

ANSWER 5

This is correct. The major methods used in parenting are loving or caring for consumers and training them to control their emotions and behave maturely through the use of discipline tempered by love.

Go on now to Frame 7.

ANSWER 6

All of these examples should have been chosen since they all reflect activities often associated with the parenting technique. If you omitted one or more, review them before moving on to Frame 4.

ANSWER 7

Although to some people discipline and punishment mean the same thing, this is not the case when discipline is used as a method in parenting. Return to Frame 8 for a review before answering Frame 9 correctly.

ANSWER 8

You should have checked numbers 1, 3, and 4. Giving money and making decisions for others reduce your effectiveness in attempting to establish a parenting relationship, and also reduce the consumer's pride and ability to establish an effective relationship. Return to Frame 5 for a review if you had trouble here. If not, go on to Frame 8.

ANSWER 9

Yes, helping the consumer learn to set goals is one of the reasons for employing the method of discipline in parenting. However, other reasons are also stated in Frame 10. Return to Frame 8 for a review of the major concerns of the worker who employs disciplining as a parenting method, and then answer Frame 10 correctly.

ANSWER 10

Training through the use of discipline is one of the major methods used in parenting but there is another method that must be used together with training.

Return to Frame 5 and review the material there before choosing the correct answer to the question in Frame 6.

ANSWER 11

Precisely. Disciplining as a method of parenting refers to a plan of training which includes correction and control, but which also focuses on developing for the consumer a structure that will provide opportunities for learning acceptable ways of behavior and the ability to come to grips with important problems. Go right on to Frame 10.

ANSWER 12

Helping a consumer learn to know his limits, how to live within them, and how to accept responsibility are only some of the valuable lessons taught using the method of disciplining listed in the question in Frame 10. Return there now, and select the proper answer after rereading all the answers.

ANSWER 13

Although correcting offenses or infractions is part of disciplining, the major aspect of disciplining as it applies to parenting is as a means toward helping the consumer attain self-control and direction. Return to Frame 8 for a review and then answer Frame 9 correctly.

ANSWER 14

Yes, helping the consumer learn to take steps toward fulfilling acceptable goals is an important concern of the worker using the discipline method. However, there are other important concerns listed in Frame 10. Return there now and identify these concerns and then answer the question correctly.

ANSWER 15

Your answers were 2, 3, 5 and 6? Well done. The consumer, in order to become effective at learning to live within his limits, should be allowed to practice on his own; make mistakes and learn to correct them; have choices between two or more proper ways of behaving; and show his anger once in a while, to avoid frustration and inner tension. Go on now to Frame 12.

ANSWER 16

You have identified two of the major concerns of the worker using discipline as a method in the parenting process. However, there are others. Review Frame 8, and then answer Frame 10 correctly.

ANSWER 17

You should have checked all five questions. You may wish to use these questions as a guide when trying to decide whether or not to use the parenting treatment. When using it, your answers should be as follows:

Question 1: "Yes"
Question 2: "Not unless it will be useful to the consumer"
Question 3: "Not necessarily"
Question 4: "Yes"
Question 5: "I don't think so—but I do need some thanks"

Return to Frame 18.

ANSWER 18

Well done, all three of these are major concerns of the worker employing the method of discipline. Punishment does not mean a plan of training but simply correcting offenses or infractions of rules. Disciplining as a method of the parenting technique, therefore, does not refer to punishment but to all the concerns mentioned in this question. Return now to Frame 11, and continue the good work.

ANSWER 19

The answers were numbers 1, 4, and 5. The worker must beware of entering the parenting relationship and checking his motives since there are often many emotional reasons that would tend to make the worker desire such a relationship which may be detrimental to the consumer. If you had any trouble here, return to Frame 15 for a review. If not, go on to Frame 17.

ANSWER 20

Your answers should have been numbers 1, 2, 3, 5, and 6. You should *try* to be at your best mentally, emotionally, socially, and physically; use positive criticism whenever necessary; watch what you say and how you say it; and deal fairly and in a way that is understandable to the consumer. If you had trouble with any of these, review Frame 13. If not go on to Frame 15.

LESSON 2:
THE REHABILITATING TECHNIQUE OF REALITY THERAPY

In this lesson you will be learning about the rehabilitating technique of reality therapy. Like parenting, reality therapy is a way of structuring a person's environment so that he can have an opportunity to change his behavior. But unlike other treatment techniques, reality therapy assumes that all people with psychiatric problems are suffering from the *same* problem, which is the inability to fulfill essential emotional needs resulting in irresponsible behavior. Therefore, in reality therapy the goal is to help people learn or relearn how to behave responsibly. The goal of the lesson and the enabling activities that will help you reach this goal are presented below.

GOAL

When you finish this lesson you will be able to explain the three basic procedures that are used in reality therapy and to list at least three limitations of the technique.

ENABLING ACTIVITIES

After completing this lesson, you will have done five things:

1. Examined the aim of reality therapy
2. Reviewed the four major principles of reality therapy
3. Identified the three basic procedures of reality therapy
4. Examined the four steps usually followed in a reality therapy session
5. Considered some of the limitations of reality therapy

**If you are ready, proceed to
Frame 1 and begin this lesson**

FRAME 1

THE AIM OF REALITY THERAPY[1]

Reality therapy is a treatment technique developed primarily by Dr. William Glasser to help individuals and groups change their unacceptable behavior. It is used most frequently with juvenile delinquents, mental patients, and disturbed children, and is also used with problems ranging from nervous headaches to obesity. No matter how people express their problems, the reality therapist believes that everyone who needs treatment suffers from the same basic problem: an inability to fulfill essential emotional needs. As people unsuccessfully attempt to fulfill their needs, they all deny the reality of the world around them and thus act irresponsibly. It is when a person's emotional needs are fulfilled that problem behavior should disappear. Thus the primary aim of reality therapy is to help people develop acceptable behavior by accepting the responsibility for their actions and by learning how to fulfill their needs appropriately.

We might also mention that in institutional settings, where there are a number of people who have similar kinds of problems, reality therapy is usually most effective when it is applied in group sessions. Although individual therapy is still used, there is an increasing trend toward the use of the techniques of group treatment.

Continue to Frame 2

FRAME 2

The reality therapist believes that people have emotional problems caused by their inability to fulfill their needs and also believes that this inability causes these people to

A. deny reality.

Turn to Answer 1

B. act irresponsibly.

Turn to Answer 2

C. both A and B.

Turn to Answer 5

FRAME 3

The primary aim of reality therapy is to change unacceptable behavior by teaching the person to accept the responsibility for his actions and to fulfill personal needs. Which of the following dialogues is the best example of this aim?

A. Worker: Ann, why are you late for this morning's session?
    Ann: I'm not that late. Besides, I came as fast as I could.
  Worker: Well, do better next time or something will have to be done.

If you think this dialogue is the best example, turn to Answer 3

(Frame 3 continued)

---

[1] All material in this lesson has been drawn from William Glasser, *Reality Therapy: A New Approach to Psychiatry* (New York: Harper & Row, 1965). The hypothetical dialogues used as examples are taken from training materials developed by the Florida Division of Youth Services, Bureau of Group Treatment, which are unpublished and undated.

B. Worker: What are you doing Ann?
     Ann: Coming in late.
  Worker: What happens when you are late?
     Ann: I guess you get mad. I suppose I may miss something important too.

**If you think this dialogue is the
best example, turn to Answer 6**

FRAME 4

MAJOR PRINCIPLES OF REALITY THERAPY

There are four major principles underlying reality therapy. The first concerns the concept of basic emotional needs. In reality therapy, everyone is viewed as having two basic emotional needs: (1) the need to love and be loved and (2) the need to feel worthwhile about oneself and others. In working with consumers, the key to fulfilling these basic needs is the consumer's involvement with someone for whom he or she cares and who the consumer feels cares in return.

When people have not learned early in life acceptable means of fulfilling these needs, they may be driven to unrealistic and unacceptable actions to fulfill their needs. Then they will feel upset and confused and will become increasingly unable to behave realistically or responsibly. The reality therapist hopes to teach these people how to recognize their needs and, subsequently, how to change their behavior in order to fulfill their needs with realistic, acceptable behavior.

The second principle of reality therapy is that only present or future behavior can be changed. In reality therapy sessions, the focus is present behavior, or what the person is doing now. Of course present behavior can also include activities closely preceding the time of the session. Thus, the reality therapist asks *what*, not why, and focuses on current behavior.

Turn to Frame 5

FRAME 5

Following a reality therapy session which took place last week in which a group member was late, which behavior could be changed?

A. A group member would be able to change the unacceptable tardiness which occurred at the meeting the previous week.

Turn to Answer 7

B. A group member would be able to change an unacceptable plan to be late for the next meeting.

Turn to Answer 9

FRAME 6

Everyone has basically two essential emotional needs that must be fulfilled in order to feel emotionally mature. One of these needs is to love and be loved. State the second essential need below, and then turn to answer 10.

FRAME 7

Which of the following questions would the reality therapist be likely to ask his consumers?

A. Why did you act that way?

Turn to Answer 4

B. How do you feel when you are in that situation?

Turn to Answer 8

C. What do you do when that happens?

Turn to Answer 11

FRAME 8

A third principle of reality therapy is that it only deals with reality. This means that attention is directed to actions and events as they exist in fact, not as they were or should have been.

The fourth principle is responsibility. Responsibility is the ability to fulfill one's needs and to do so in a way that does not deprive others of the opportunity to fulfill their needs. A responsible person can give and receive love, and behaves in ways resulting in feelings of self worth and worth to others. Thus, the consumer must learn to accept responsibility for his own behavior, and to accept the consequences associated with the behavior. This is reality, and it must be accepted if the consumer hopes or plans to change unacceptable behavior.

Turn to Frame 9

FRAME 9

Which of the following is the major concern of reality therapy?

A. Those who have not learned to lead responsible lives

Turn to Answer 12

B. Labeling people who are mentally ill or delinquent

Turn to Answer 13

C. Those who have lost the ability to lead responsible lives

Turn to Answer 14

D. A and B

Turn to Answer 15

E. A and C

Turn to Answer 17

FRAME 10

THE PROCEDURES OF REALITY THERAPY

Now that you are familiar with some of the basic concepts of reality therapy, you are ready to learn how it works. Therapy is a special kind of teaching or training which attempts to accomplish in a relatively short, intense period growth and understanding which should have been accomplished during earlier stages of human growth and development. Irresponsible behavior requires learning about acceptable, realistic behavior in order to fulfill needs. The specialized learning situation of reality therapy is made up of three separate but related procedures.

(Frame 10 continued)

1. **Involvement.** The therapist must become so involved with the consumer that the consumer can begin to face reality and see how his behavior is unrealistic. This involves the development of a trusting relationship and is the most difficult phase of the treatment. It is important for the therapist to be a very responsible person and strong enough to reject the consumer's request for sympathy.

2. **Rejection of Unreality.** The therapist must reject the behavior which is unrealistic, but still accept the consumer and maintain the involvement. The therapist helps consumers realize that they are responsible for their own behavior. In reality therapy, the concern is with the consumer's behavior, not necessarily attitudes or feelings. Along with this, the therapist freely gives praise when the consumer acts responsibly, and shows disapproval of irresponsible behavior.

3. **Learning.** The therapist must teach consumers better ways to fulfill their needs within the confines of reality. When consumers admit that their behavior is irresponsible, the last phase of learning or relearning begins. Here consumers can rely on the therapist's experience to help them learn more effective ways of behaving. When they can express their behavior in responsible ways, therapy is nearing an end.

While these are the three basic procedures that are used in reality therapy, it is difficult to actually separate them in practice. In practice, reality therapy can only be viewed as a whole process. It is only after all the pieces are put together that the full process can be appreciated.

These three procedures can now be translated into the basic steps generally followed in reality therapy. First the therapist helps the consumer *identify* his or her behavior. Once this has occurred, the therapist usually helps the consumer do one or both of the following:

1. He helps the consumer make a value judgment about his or her behavior. For example, the consumer may say, "I'm not supposed to do that."
2. He helps the consumer identify the consequences of the behavior. For example, the consumer may conclude, "When people do that, they usually get into trouble."

At this point in the therapy, the therapist helps the consumer formulate alternative plans for changing to behavior which the consumer judges to be appropriate. Throughout the entire process, the therapist is warm, subjective, and personal with the consumer.

When the therapy reaches the final stage of planning, the therapist will be open and honest with the consumer. Should the consumer select a plan for behavioral change which the therapist considers inappropriate, the therapist will state these feelings to the consumer and assist in formulating more appropriate alternatives. The following dialogue illustrates these procedures. An eight-year-old boy has just stolen some cherries and has the following conversation with his dad on the way home.

Dad: Bob, what do you have in your pocket?
Bob: Just some cherries.
Dad: Where did you get the cherries?
Bob: Down in Mr. Miller's orchard.

Dad: Did he give them to you?
Bob: No.
Dad: How did you get them?
Bob: Well, I sort of took them.   (Identifies his behavior)
Dad: What do we call that, Bob?
Bob: I guess it's kind of stealing.   (Identifies behavior)
Dad: Is that what you are supposed to do?
Bob: No.   (Makes a value of judgment of his behavior)
Dad: What happens when little boys take things that don't belong to them?
Bob: They get in trouble.   (Identifies the consequences of his behavior)
Dad: What else?
Bob: People get mad at them and then they don't trust them anymore.

(Identifies consequences)

Dad: Is that what you want, Bob?
Bob: No.   (Makes a value judgment of the consequences of his behavior)
Dad: Well what do you think you could do?
Bob: Not steal any more cherries.   (Begins to formulate an alternative plan)
Dad: What about the ones in your pocket?
Bob: I guess I ought to take them back.   (Formulates alternative plan)
Dad: Is that all?
Bob: Yeah, I could throw them over the fence.   (Formulates alternative plan)
Dad: Would that make it right?
Bob: No.
Dad: Well then, what are you going to do?
Bob: I guess I ought to give them back to him and say I'm sorry.

(Formulates a plan)

Dad: That's a good idea, Bob. When are you going to do it?
Bob: I guess I could do it now.   (Formulates a plan)
Dad: Is there any way I can help you?
Bob: Sort of. I'm afraid of Mr. Miller. Will you go with me and just be there beside me?   (Formulates a plan)
Dad: Of course, Bob. Let's go.

Turn to Frame 11

FRAME 11

In order to become effectively involved with the consumer during the first phase of treatment, human service workers using reality therapy principles should be able to do which of the following? Check those that apply.

— 1. Be very sympathetic.

— 2. Accept the consumer as he is.

— 3. Reject any desire to become emotionally involved with the consumer.

— 4. Become emotionally involved with the consumer; show empathy.

— 5. Reject requests for sympathy.

— 6. Be responsible.

Turn to Answer 20

FRAME 12

In order to reject the unrealistic behavior of the consumer and yet maintain his involvement with him, which of the following does the reality therapist do?

A. Helps the consumer realize and accept the fact that he is responsible for his own behavior

Turn to Answer 16

B. Shows his concern mainly for the consumer's attitudes and emotions

Turn to Answer 19

C. Gives praise when the consumer acts responsibly

Turn to Answer 23

D. A and C above

Turn to Answer 26

E. A, B, and C above

Turn to Answer 28

FRAME 13

In reality therapy, the therapy process is nearing a close when which of the following occurs?

A. The consumer is able to admit his behavior is irresponsible.

Turn to Answer 18

B. The consumer begins to express his behavior in responsible ways.

Turn to Answer 22

C. The therapist becomes emotionally involved with the consumer.

Turn to Answer 24

FRAME 14

In practice, reality therapy becomes which of the following?

A. A separate process with three distinct procedures

Turn to Answer 21

B. An integrated process

Turn to Answer 25

C. Exclusively a group process

Turn to Answer 27

FRAME 15

Remember the four steps usually followed in a reality therapy session (see dialogue in Frame 10)? To see if you understand these steps, try the following exercise. Ask your supervisor, trainer, or instructor to set up a typical situation you might encounter where reality therapy would be employed. Then, with another worker or student, take turns playing the roles of a worker and a consumer using the principles of reality therapy. Discuss what happens with the participants.

Continue with Frame 16

LIMITATIONS OF REALITY THERAPY

Before completing this lesson, it is important to note some of the problems and consequent limitations in the use of reality therapy. Since reality therapy requires a special emphasis on the present, its effectiveness rests on the ability of the therapist to use it at the time the consumer shows a need for it. This sometimes requires stopping what you are doing in order to meet the consumer's needs and, of course, this is not always possible.

Secondly, reality therapy used with consumers in an institution or in a caseload (individually or in groups) has been most successful when the worker has some control over the consumers. This is easier when the consumer is confined to an institution. In terms of a caseload, when the technique is used with law offenders who are on parole, the conditions of parole serve as a form of control. However, when a worker has limited control, as in a welfare setting, reality therapy may be difficult to employ successfully.

A third limitation of reality therapy is that its techniques sometimes permit the consumer to give the outward appearance of great change, when in fact he or she is really "playing a game" with the therapist by behaving appropriately in the setting. This limitation implies that there is a type of consumer who is most suited to this kind of treatment and suggests that reality therapy is probably a useful technique only with certain groups of human service consumers.

These problems represent only a few of the limitations in the use of reality therapy. It should be reemphasized that no rehabilitating technique works for everyone, and some are more successful with one type of consumer than another.

These introductory descriptions of reality therapy should help you when you are working with a therapist. In addition, to gain further insights about the therapeutic process, you should seek the supervision of a trained therapist.

Go on to Frame 17

Check the correct response.

Which one of the following is a limitation of reality therapy?

___ A. It is usually most successful when the worker has some control over the consumer.

Turn to Answer 31

___ B. It emphasizes the past and, therefore, requires a great deal of time on the part of the worker.

Turn to Answer 30

___ C. It works well with most human service consumers.

Turn to Answer 29

ANSWERS TO LESSON 2

This is only half the answer. The reality therapist believes that people who are unable to fulfill their essential needs will soon begin to deny reality, and this then leads to a final sign that these people have emotional problems. Return to Frame 1 for a review of the reality therapist's view and then answer Frame 2 correctly.

ANSWER 2

Yes, indeed, the reality therapist does believe that the final outcome of a person's inability to meet his essential needs is to act irresponsibly. However, such people are also involved in a specific mental problem. Return to Frame 1 for a review and then select the correct response in Frame 2.

ANSWER 3

Incorrect. In this dialogue, the worker has already identified Ann's behavior as unacceptable and confronted her. Ann's reply indicates she disagrees. When the worker then avoids pursuing the matter further, nothing has been accomplished to help Ann identify her own behavior and its consequences. Turn to Frame 4.

ANSWER 4

Since the past is ignored as irrelevant, the reality therapist is not interested in why something happened in the past, only what the consumer is doing now that is causing his inability to fulfill his emotional needs.

Return to Frame 4 for a review and then answer Frame 7 correctly.

ANSWER 5

This is correct. The reality therapist believes that the root of all emotional problems is an inability of the individual to fulfill his essential needs and that this, in turn, leads to a denial of the reality of the world around him, resulting ultimately in irresponsible behavior by which others realize he may have problems. Return now to Frame 3.

ANSWER 6

Right. You observed that the worker helped Ann identify her unacceptable behavior and accept personal responsibility. Continue with Frame 4.

ANSWER 7

You said the group member would be able to change behavior that occurred a week ago. While he or she might certainly plan how to avoid repeating such an action, the act itself has already occcured and can never be changed. Review Frame 4, and then turn to Answer 9.

ANSWER 8

Feelings are not the focus of reality therapy so the therapist would not ask this question.

Return to Frame 4 for a review, and then find the proper question in Frame 9.

ANSWER 9

Good choice. Behavior which a person is presently performing or plans to perform is the only behavior the person can logically change. Now return to Frame 6.

ANSWER 10

In addition to being able to love and being loved, everyone has a need to feel worthwhile to themselves and to others. Although these are concepts that are used a great deal, they almost defy definition. Only when you are feeling them do you know their true meaning, and even then you are probably unable to define them in words. Return now to Frame 7.

ANSWER 11

Yes, this is the type of question a reality therapist would ask a consumer since he is interested in changing *present behavior*, not past or future feelings or behavior.

Return to Frame 8 and keep up the good work.

ANSWER 12

Yes, but you have neglected to identify another group of people with whom reality therapy is concerned.

Return to Frame 9 and find that other group.

ANSWER 13

No, reality therapy is not concerned with labeling people as mentally ill or delinquent.

Return to Frame 1 and review the lesson.

ANSWER 14

Although you have identified one of the groups with whom reality therapy is concerned, you have neglected to identify the other one in Frame 9. Return there now, and select the correct answer.

ANSWER 15

This is only partially correct. The reality therapist does not view people with problems as mentally ill, delinquent, or by any other label, but merely as evidencing irresponsible behavior. Return to Frame 9 and answer correctly.

ANSWER 16

Yes, this is correct but there is another, more complete response to the question. Return to Frame 12 and locate that response.

ANSWER 17

Well done, the reality therapist places no label on people with problems. He sees them as merely evidencing irresponsible behavior caused by the fact that they failed to learn responsibility or lost the ability to lead responsible lives for some reason. Return to Frame 10 and continue the lesson.

ANSWER 18

Although this is a major forward step in the therapy process, it does not signify that therapy is coming to a close, only that it is progressing well.

Return to Frame 10—you need a brief review of the procedures before answering the question to Frame 13 correctly.

ANSWER 19

The reality therapist, as you learned earlier, is not concerned with attitudes and feelings, but with *behavior*. You should review Frames 4 and 10 before answering the question in Frame 12 again.

ANSWER 20

Numbers 2, 4, 5, and 6 are the correct responses. The worker, in order to become involved with the consumer and help him face reality, must be a responsible person, able to reject requests for sympathy, but sufficiently involved to show empathy and acceptance of the consumer as he is. Return now to Frame 12.

ANSWER 21

Although, for purposes of explanation, reality therapy may be separated into three phases or procedures, in practice these procedures are blended into an integrated whole. Return to Frame 10 for a review, then answer Frame 14 correctly.

ANSWER 22

Excellent. The therapy is near completion when the consumer begins to express his behavior in responsible ways consistently; since this is the goal of reality therapy, when it is reached, therapy ends.

Go on to Frame 14 and tackle the problem presented there.

ANSWER 23

This is a good response but there is a better one in Frame 12. If you have trouble locating it, review Frame 10.

ANSWER 24

Although this is one aspect of reality therapy, it is one of the early forward steps in the process, and does not signify the closing of the process. Return for a review of Frame 10 before attempting another response to Frame 13.

ANSWER 25

Precisely. Although, for purposes of explanation, reality therapy may be separated into three procedures or phases, in practice this process is integrated into a whole, with overlap of all three procedures.

We mentioned earlier that reality therapy is being used increasingly with groups. In groups, the therapist may become less involved with each member of the group, while group members become more involved with each other. Since there is more opportunity for involvement in a group, such therapy tends to move more quickly than does individual therapy. Consumers confront each other with the reality of each other's behavior and, when the group strays, the therapist intervenes and suggests better ways to cope with reality.

Continue with Frame 15.

ANSWER 26

This is correct. Well done. The therapist must reject the unrealistic (irresponsible) behavior of the consumer and yet maintain his involvement with him. The therapist does this by helping the consumer face the fact that he is responsible for his own behavior by giving praise for responsible actions and disapproval for irresponsible actions. Return to Frame 13.

ANSWER 27

No. Reality therapy, in practice, is not used exclusively as a group process, although it is often used with groups since it has more advantages when used this way. Review Frame 10, and then answer Frame 14 correctly.

ANSWER 28

This answer includes one incorrect response. The reality therapist, as you should by now be well aware, is *not* concerned with attitudes and feelings, but with *behavior*. Return to Frame 12 and select the correct answer.

ANSWER 29

If you checked this as the correct response, we strongly suggest that you review this lesson from the beginning. None of the rehabilitating techniques work well with "most" human service consumers!

ANSWER 30

Sorry, but you goofed. Reality therapy emphasizes the *present*, not the past. Return to Frame 16 to review the limitation this presents, and then answer Frame 17 correctly.

ANSWER 31

Correct! You have now completed Lesson 2. Hopefully, you have obtained a beginning understanding of the treatment technique of reality therapy and some of its characteristics. If you wish to learn more about this technique, consult the bibliography at the end of this chapter. Go on now to Lesson 3 and learn about another frequently used rehabilitating technique in the human services—behavior modification.

LESSON 3:
THE REHABILITATING
TECHNIQUE OF
BEHAVIOR MODIFICATION

In this lesson you will be introduced to the rehabilitation technique of behavior modification. Like parenting and reality therapy, behavior modification is also a way of structuring a person's environment in order to change or reshape behavior. However, unlike parenting and reality therapy, behavior modification is a more structured approach to changing behavior, since it focuses on establishing a specific reward system to bring about the desired change. The goal of this lesson and the enabling activities that will help you reach this goal are presented below.

GOAL

When you finish this lesson, you will be able to demonstrate your knowledge of behavior modification by stating examples of three procedures used to change behavior and by listing at least three limitations of this technique.

ENABLING ACTIVITIES

After completing this lesson, you will have done five things:

1. Identified the aim and basic assumption of behavior modification
2. Classified the two main kinds of behavior
3. Explained and given an example of one procedure that is used to modify respondent behavior
4. Explained and given an example of two procedures that are used to modify operant behavior
5. Considered at least three limitations of the behavior modification technique

**Proceed to Frame 1 whenever you
are ready to begin this lesson**

FRAME 1

THE AIM OF BEHAVIOR MODIFICATION

Although the word *behavior* is a very common term, its meaning in behavior modification is very specific. Behavior is the observable way people react to their environment.[1] For example, to say that someone is depressed or lazy does not tell us anything about what that person does. In behavior modification, we would need a detailed description of what observable actions that person actually exhibited.

The aim of behavior modification is to analyze and control the way a person is *responding* to certain conditions in his environment so that the behavior necessary for effective functioning can be developed or reinstated. The basic rule that is applied in achieving this aim is that undesirable behavior is weakened by not being rewarded, and desirable behavior is strengthened when followed with a reward.

Behavior modification is used in many human service settings, but it is probably used most frequently with the mentally ill and the mentally retarded. It is also used with children and sometimes with juvenile delinquents.

Go right on to Frame 2 and find out how well you have understood this material

FRAME 2

Which of the following would be appropriate to describe a person's behavior?

A. He was very angry.

Turn to Answer 3

B. His face was contorted in a scowl, and his body went taut.

Turn to Answer 7

C. He seemed depressed.

Turn to Answer 12

D. A and C above.

Turn to Answer 15

FRAME 3

In behavior modification, the ultimate goal is to help the consumer develop new and more effective ways of

A. understanding his thoughts.

Turn to Answer 2

B. coping with his emotions.

Turn to Answer 5

C. behaving.

Turn to Answer 10

[1] Halmuth H. Schaeffer and Patrick L. Martin, *Behavior Therapy* (New York: McGraw-Hill, 1969).

In order to achieve the goal of behavior modification, the practitioner applies which of the following rules? Check those that apply.

— 1. Desirable behavior is weakened when followed by a reward.

— 2. Undesirable behavior is weakened when unrewarded.

— 3. Desirable behavior is strengthened when followed by a reward.

— 4. Undesirable behavior is strengthened when unrewarded.

— 5. Desirable behavior is strengthened when unrewarded.

**Think you have it? Turn to Answer 1.
Confused? Return to Frame 1
and then go on to Answer 1**

MAJOR TYPES OF BEHAVIOR

To understand the basic techniques of behavior modification, you should first become familiar with how behavior is classified when this approach is used. The two main types of behavior are *respondent* and *operant*. The two basic units that are used to measure behavior are *stimulus* and *response*.

A response is an answer to a stimulus. A stimulus is an object or event which causes a response in the behavior of a person. For example, when a child is given a spanking (stimulus), the child might react by crying (response). When an inmate learns that he will be paroled in a week (stimulus), he may try to show his best behavior (response).

Respondent behavior[2] involves involuntary or automatic responses. Such behavior includes, for example, "tearing" (response) when a grain of sand (stimulus) is caught in the eye and being startled (response) at a loud, unexpected noise (stimulus). This kind of behavior also involves uncomfortable emotional responses. For example, with anxiety the respondent behavior may be shaking; with anger it may be a flushed face; and with fear, perspiring. Such behavior is controlled by an eliciting stimulus, which is usually all that is needed for the behavior to occur.

Operant behavior[3] involves voluntary, purposeful responses, and is represented by doing something such as walking, talking, fighting, and playing. All behavior that interacts with and has an effect on the environment of a person is operant behavior. Unlike respondent behavior, operant behavior is usually a function of more than one stimulus.

Behavior modification deals with both kinds of behavior and uses different kinds of procedures for each. You will be learning more about these in this lesson.

**Go on to Frame 6 if you are sure
you understand the meanings of
operant and respondent behavior**

---

[2] W. W. Wenrich, *A Primer of Behavior Modification* (Monterey, Calif.: Brooks/Cole, 1970), pp. 5–6.
[3] Ibid.

FRAME 6

Underline the proper words in the parentheses.

There are two basic units that are used to measure behavior. The (stimulus/response) is an answer to the (stimulus/response).

Turn to Answer 8

FRAME 7

Behavior modification deals with two major types of behavior, respondent and operant. Operant behavior involves which of the following?

A. Voluntary responses

Turn to Answer 4

B. Involuntary responses

Turn to Answer 9

C. Purposeful responses

Turn to Answer 11

D. A and C above

Turn to Answer 14

E. B and C above

Turn to Answer 16

FRAME 8

Which of the following examples represent activities associated with behavior modification programs. Select the correct examples.

___ 1. The good behavior of school children with behavior problems is rewarded with tokens that can be cashed in at a special store.

___ 2. Retarded persons are rewarded with tokens for dressing themselves each morning.

___ 3. A mentally ill person is praised for helping others on the ward.

___ 4. The loud, attention-getting behavior of delinquent youths in a halfway house is consistently ignored until such behavior is replaced with appropriate requests for attention, which are then praised.

___ 5. Children who learn slowly are rewarded with tokens for each small step of progress in order to reduce frustration and a sense of failure.

Turn to Answer 6

FRAME 9

In the paragraph below, locate examples of respondent and operant behaviors. Place the letter R, for respondent, and O, for operant, in the spaces provided after each behavior.

Bill was walking (___) on the beach at dusk and began to feel chilly (___). He heard voices in the distance and looked up as if startled (___). Seeing people playing (___) by a fire, he decided to join (___) them. Upon approaching (___) them, he heard a dog growl (___).

Turn to Answer 13

Procedures Used to Modify Behavior

Now that you have a clearer understanding of the basic principles underlying behavior modification, the next step is to examine the procedures used. These are numerous, and we can cover only a few in giving you an idea of how this treatment works.

Modifying Respondent Behavior. Procedures for respondent behavior are most commonly used with problems such as *excessive fear and anxiety*. Many of these procedures are based on a method called *counterconditioning*. Among respondent emotional reactions, there are certain responses which do not "go together." For example, one cannot experience intense love and hate at the same time, nor can one be anxious and relaxed at the same time. Using this latter concept, *counterconditioning means replacing an existing response*, such as anxiety, *with a response that will not go with it*, such as relaxation. The following is a familiar example which illustrates this concept.

> Most children do not like bad tasting medicine, and their parents have a very difficult time getting them to take it. But when a parent accompanies the medicine with something like candy or verbal praise, the anxiety is reduced or overcome and the child takes the bad tasting medicine. When a parent does this, he is using basic principles of counterconditioning.

Got it? Okay, then go on to Frame 11

Ralph G. was a patient in a mental institution. One of his major problems was an intense fear of enclosed spaces (claustrophobia). Ralph loved to read novels. If you were assisting the behavior modification therapist in applying counterconditioning to moderate Ralph's fear of closed spaces, which approach would you expect the therapist to use?

A. Make it difficult for Ralph to read except in enclosed spaces.

Turn to Answer 17

B. Each time Ralph reads, reduce the amount of space surrounding him.

Turn to Answer 19

C. Find out what stimulus is sustaining Ralph's fear of enclosed space and remove that stimulus.

Turn to Answer 22

Modifying Operant Behavior. Operant behavior, such as making a bed, self-feeding, or throwing a temper tantrum, can also be modified with certain procedures. Most procedures for operant behavior apply the basic rule in which undesirable behavior is weakened by not being rewarded and desirable behavior is strengthened by being followed with a reward. Two such procedures that are used in human service settings are *reinforcement* and *extinction*.

   Reinforcement. Reinforcement may be defined as the introduction or removal of any event following the occurrence of a behavior in order to maintain or increase the frequency of that behavior. There are two basic types of reinforcement—*positive*
(Frame 12 continued)

and *negative*. Positive reinforcement is the use of any event which, when it follows a response, will increase the strength or maintain the occurrence of that response. Examples of positive reinforcers are food, money, and attention (or anything else that the consumer views as valuable). Positive reinforcers must be identified for each individual consumer. Thus, when this technique is used, a treatment plan is developed that will strengthen or maintain specified desirable behavior by presenting a positive reinforcer immediately following the occurrence of the desired behavior.

> Example: Approval (positive reinforcer) was repeatedly shown to a mental patient who had just made his bed (desired behavior) with the result that in the future he made his bed without the need for reinforcement.

Negative reinforcement is the attempt to maintain or strengthen desired behavior (response) by the use of a stimulus (negative reinforcer) which a person wishes to avoid and which may cause pain or discomfort to that person. When this technique is used, a treatment plan is developed where specified desirable responses will be strengthened by removing the negative reinforcers.

> Example: Self-feeding was increased in mental patients who were previously unwilling to feed themselves, but who did not like to have nurses spill food on them (negative reinforcer) in the course of feeding. When the aide discontinued spilling food on the patients (removed negative reinforcer), patient self-feeding was strengthened and maintained.

Extinction. A second technique for operant behavior is called extinction. When a reinforcement for maintaining certain behavior is removed, the behavior will slowly disappear. When the behavior no longer occurs, or occurs at a very low rate, it is said to be extinguished. This procedure is used to weaken or to eliminate a response.

> Example: If it has been determined that a child's tantrum behavior is sustained by parental attention, this behavior may be reduced or eliminated by withholding parental attention (ignoring child) during tantrum behavior.

**When you find you have
some understanding of the
above, turn to Frame 13**

FRAME 13

Reinforcement refers to the introduction or removal of any event which, when it occurs following a desirable behavior, will help

A. maintain the desired behavior.

Turn to Answer 18

B. strengthen (increase) the probability of reoccurrence of the desired behavior.

Turn to Answer 20

C. weaken (decrease) the probability of reoccurrence of the desired behavior

Turn to Answer 23

D. A and B above.

Turn to Answer 26

E. A and C above.

Turn to Answer 29

FRAME 14

Jerry G. is mentally retarded. His parents have had trouble disciplining him and have requested help from a behavior modification therapist. The therapist has discovered that Jerry's parents give him ice cream or candy to try to stop him from acting up. Jerry likes both ice cream and candy. What might the therapist recommend?

A. Spank Jerry for acting up rather than giving him treats.

Turn to Answer 21

B. Withdraw the treats when Jerry acts up.

Turn to Answer 24

C. Give Jerry loving attention when acting up.

Turn to Answer 27

FRAME 15

In the case presented in Frame 14, the therapist would be applying which of the following modification procedures?

A. Extinction

Turn to Answer 25

B. Positive reinforcement

Turn to Answer 30

C. Negative reinforcement

Turn to Answer 33

FRAME 16

You now should have some understanding of a few of the many procedures used to modify or change undesirable behavior through behavior modification. Can you recall the major procedure used to modify respondent behavior such as fear or anger? How about procedures used to modify operant behavior? Can you define the extinction procedure? If so, go to Frame 17 and find out about the major limitations encountered when employing behavior modification. If not, you need a review of this lesson, so return to Frame 1 and briefly review that and subsequent frames before going on to Frame 17.

FRAME 17

LIMITATIONS OF BEHAVIOR MODIFICATION

The major limitations of behavior modification include the following:[4]

1. *It is mechanistic.* Many people object to behavior modification because it focuses on observable behavior and does not try to deal with the person's

(Frame 17 continued)

[4] For additional discussion of some of the disadvantages of behavior modification see, William R. Morrow and Harvey L. Gochros, "Misconceptions Regarding Behavior Modification," *Social Service Review* 44 (September 1970): 293–307; Halmuth H. Schaeffer and Patrick L. Martin, *Behavioral Therapy* (New York: McGraw-Hill, 1969); and W. W. Wenrich, *A Primer of Behavior Modification* (Monterey, Calif.: Brooks/Cole, 1970).

thoughts and feelings. These people would also say that changing a person's behavior tells us nothing about whether his deeper problems have been solved.

2. *It is manipulative.* Behavior modification is a way of controlling behavior. While this is not a disadvantage by itself, it frightens many people. They see it as being threatening and unnatural for someone to be able to control another's behavior.

3. *It is limited.* Behavior modification is a very difficult treatment to use in settings such as welfare or health, since these are open settings and consumers are usually free to come and go at will. It has been most successful with consumers who are institutionalized and are not free to come and go at will.

These limitations are noted as a reminder that behavior modification does not always work and is usually most successful with people who have very special and identifiable kinds of problems. For example, behavior modification has been very successful with groups such as the mentally retarded, some mentally ill, and some juvenile delinquents. Behavior modification represents just one approach to modifying behavior. We need to understand clearly the consumer's problem in order to be certain that behavior modification techniques will help the person change his behavior in a positive direction so that he can function more effectively.

Forge ahead to Frame 18

FRAME 18

Some persons object to behavior modification because it is too mechanistic. What is meant by this?

A. Behavior modification controls peoples' behavior too much.

Turn to Answer 28

B. Behavior modification can only be used with people who are not free to come and go at will.

Turn to Answer 31

C. Behavior modification focuses on behavior, not feelings and thoughts.

Turn to Answer 34

FRAME 19

Since behavior modification is not the only technique for changing undesirable behavior, and since it does not always work, the therapist, before using this or any other behavior changing technique, should always be sure to find out at least two things. In the space below, state these two important things that should be done before selecting a technique to use with a consumer.

1.

2.

Turn to Answer 32

FRAME 20

Congratulations, you have just completed the last lesson of this chapter. If you believe you have a good conception of the material that has been covered, turn to the summary and review questions at the end of the chapter and find out how well you have learned this material. If not, quickly brush up on the material before completing the review questions.

ANSWERS TO LESSON 3

ANSWER 1

The basic rule of behavior modification involves numbers 2 and 3. When desirable behavior is rewarded, it is usually strengthened, and when undesirable behavior is ignored, it is usually weakened. This is the major theory underlying behavior modification and all its techniques. The converse of this rule may also apply—desirable behavior may be weakened if unrewarded and undesirable behavior strengthened if rewarded.

Go right on now to Frame 5.

ANSWER 2

If you chose this answer, you are confusing behavior modification with other forms of rehabilitating. Behavior is the key here, not thoughts, feelings, or attitudes. We can deal more effectively with behavior than with unseen thoughts and emotions, according to behavior modification theorists. Return to Frame 3 and select the proper answer.

ANSWER 3

Describing behavior in this manner does not explain what the person actually did, only your interpretations of his actions. You may need a review of Frame 1 before selecting the best answer in Frame 2.

ANSWER 4

Yes, operant behavior involves voluntary responses; but there is also another adjective which helps describe these responses. Return to Frame 7 and identify this other adjective, then turn to the proper answer.

ANSWER 5

You are confusing this method with others. Behavior modification theorists believe that dealing with something we can see is more effective than interpreting thoughts, feelings, and attitudes. Return to Frame 3 and identify the correct answer.

ANSWER 6

You should have chosen all of the examples since they all represent activities which could be part of a program in behavior modification treatment. If you did not select one or more of the examples, review them again before proceeding to Frame 9.

ANSWER 7

Exactly. In behavior modification, we describe what a person actually did, and not our interpretations of the person's mental state as depicted by his behavior. Well done, return to Frame 3.

ANSWER 8

In behavior modification there are two basic units for measuring behavior. The response is an answer to the stimulus. Did you underline first the term *response* and then the term *stimulus?* If so, good, go right on to Frame 7. If not, review Frame 5, and then go on to Frame 7.

ANSWER 9

You have operant behavior confused with respondent behavior. Return to Frame 5 for a review, and then you should be able to answer the question in Frame 7 correctly.

ANSWER 10

Yes, you have chosen the proper response. Behavior is the key in behavior modification. According to the theory behind behavior modification, we can be more effective if we deal with that which is visible (behavior) rather than that which is invisible (thoughts, feelings, and attitudes). Some theorists believe that if you change the behavior you change attitudes, and not vice versa. Do you agree? A good topic for debate. Return now to Frame 4.

ANSWER 11

Yes, both operant and respondent behavior involve purposeful responses but one is voluntary. Return to Frame 5 for a review and then choose the more complete response to the question in Frame 7.

ANSWER 12

While this is a better answer than A, it is not the best answer. It does not describe exactly what the person did, only an explanation of another person's interpretation of the meaning of his actions. You may need a review of Frame 1 before answering Frame 2 correctly.

ANSWER 13

Bill was walking (O) on the beach at dusk and began to feel chilly (R). He heard voices in the distance and looked up as if startled (R). Seeing people playing (O) by a fire, he decided to join them (O). Upon approaching (O) them, he heard a dog growl (R).

How well did you do? If you missed more than two of them, you need a review of Frame 5 before going on to Frame 10. If you had two or less wrong, you have a good grasp of these two types of behavior. Move right along with Frame 10.

ANSWER 14

Precisely—well done! Operant behavior involves voluntary purposeful responses and may be represented by the doing something voluntarily. What type of responses are involved in respondent behavior? Think about it, and return to Frame 8.

ANSWER 15

Both of these answers are incorrect since neither describes what the person is doing. In each case the person describing the behavior and the person to whom the description is made are making their own interpretations of the person's actions. Return to Frame 1 for a review, then turn to Answer 7.

ANSWER 16

Although all behavior can be viewed as purposeful, operant behavior is not involuntary. Return to Frame 5 for a brief review then choose the correct response to Frame 7.

ANSWER 17

This procedure would be an example of negative reinforcement, which will be discussed in the next section. Therefore, return to Frame 10 for a review of counterconditioning, and then select the correct response in Frame 11.

ANSWER 18

Right, this is correct; but reinforcement attempts to do more than just maintain desirable behavior. Return to Frame 13 and identify the other correct answer.

ANSWER 19

Yes, very good. Each time Ralph is doing something he enjoys, he is also relaxed. Therefore, if he is relaxed, he cannot be fearful at the same time, and he may slowly lose his fear of enclosed space.

Good work. Go on now to Frame 12 for a lesson in the procedures used to modify operant behaviors.

ANSWER 20

This is the major goal of reinforcement, namely, strengthen the probability of the occurrence or reoccurrence of a desired behavior; but there is also another, lesser, goal in Frame 13. Return there now and locate the more complete response.

ANSWER 21

Spanking Jerry may act as a positive reinforcer for acting up, since Jerry may need parental attention and spanking is one form of attention. If so, the undesirable behavior will be maintained.

Return to Frame 14 and select another response.

ANSWER 22

This would be an example of the use of the procedure of extinction, which will be discussed in the next section. Although extinction can be used to modify both operant and respondent behavior, especially fear, it is mainly used when operant behavior is involved. Return to Frame 10 for a review and then answer Frame 11 correctly.

ANSWER 23

Incorrect. The aim of reinforcement is to strengthen or maintain a desired behavior, never to weaken it.

Return to Frame 12 for a review, and then pick the proper response in Frame 13.

ANSWER 24

Definitely. According to behavior modification theory, the treats (ice cream, etc.) are viewed as positive reinforcers of the undesired behavior (acting up). If they are withdrawn and his undesirable behavior is ignored, Jerry will soon stop acting up. Giving no attention to Jerry at all for his undesirable behavior is the key here.

Go on to Frame 15.

ANSWER 25

You have applied your knowledge well. The procedure of extinction was used by the therapist to reduce the occurrence of Jerry's undesirable behavior. The positive reinforcers (ice cream, candy) were withdrawn, thereby reducing the occurrence of the undesirable behavior (acting up). Go right on to Frame 16.

ANSWER 26

Exactly! Reinforcement is an attempt to maintain or strengthen the occurrence or reoccurrence of a desired behavior by making sure a positive reinforcer is presented after a desirable response or by removing a negative reinforcer which is reducing the probability of a desired response.

Forge ahead to Frame 14.

ANSWER 27

According to behavior modification theory, this would just be substituting one positive reinforcer for another (love for treats); positive reinforcers only strengthen behavior, and weakening it is the goal here.

Return to Frame 12 if you need a review, and then select the correct response to Frame 14.

ANSWER 28

This is the objection of those who feel that behavior modification is too manipulative, not too mechanistic.

If you need a review, turn to Frame 17. If not, select another response to Frame 18, but make sure it's the correct one.

ANSWER 29

Only half of this response is correct. Reinforcement is not used to weaken a desirable response since no therapist would have a reason for such an objective.

Return to Frame 12 if you need a review, and then answer Frame 13 correctly.

ANSWER 30

Positive reinforcement was not applied in this case since the goal was to reduce the occurrence of undesirable behavior. Jerry's parents were misusing positive reinforcement by rewarding undesirable behavior. Such behavior, according to behavior modification theory, should be ignored as much as possible, and it will then be reduced. Return to Frame 12 for a review and then answer Frame 15 correctly.

ANSWER 31

This would describe what some people mean when they say behavior modification is too limited, not too mechanistic.

Return to Frame 17 and review the material presented there before attempting to answer Frame 18 correctly.

ANSWER 32

The therapist, no matter what treatment he decides to use first, should always be sure to understand the consumer's problem and then should choose the best available treatment that will help the consumer change his behavior in the desired direction so as to function more effectively.

Flip back to Frame 20 and complete the lesson.

ANSWER 33

The goal, in this case, was to reduce or eliminate undesirable behavior. As you should know by now, the goal of reinforcement, both positive and negative, is to strengthen desirable behavior.

Return to Frame 15 and select the only answer remaining.

ANSWER 34

Exactly. Mechanistic objectives to behavior modification are based on the fact that behavior modification focuses on observable behavior and does not attempt to deal with feelings and thoughts. Continue now with Frame 19.

SUMMARY

This chapter on rehabilitating is only an introduction to three of the many different techniques used in the human services to help consumers modify their behavior in order to cope more effectively with the demands and challenges of everyday life. In the first lesson we described the reasonably simple but very important technique of parenting. This technique involves the planned development of a caring and structured relationship between the human service worker and the consumer. The parenting technique is based upon an understanding of such basic human needs as security, a structured environment, the ability to cope with frustration, and self-direction. With such an understanding, workers need to be able to show acceptance, provide sound physical care, and help the consumer understand his present situation. The caring component of parenting must be balanced with the component of discipline as training. We described good discipline as that which sets limits and is firm and fair, consistent, and flexible enough to allow the consumer to express feelings of resentment and anger. In addition to describing the kind of behavior needed to be effective using the parenting technique, we concluded the lesson with a discussion of common problems in using this technique, including its simplicity, the difficulty in giving it up, its attractiveness to people enjoying power, and its lack of standards.

In the second lesson, special attention was given to the technique of reality therapy. In addition to describing the aims of reality therapy, the major principles underlying this therapy were discussed. Reality therapy includes procedures for involvement, for rejecting unrealistic behavior while maintaining supportiveness, and for teaching the consumer more realistic ways to fulfill basic needs. The four steps followed in therapy sessions usually include helping the consumer: identify his behavior, make a value judgment of the behavior and/or identify the consequences of the behavior, and formulate a plan for changing the behavior. The lesson concluded with some of the limitations of reality therapy, including the considerable emphasis on using the present situation of the consumer, the worker's involvement with the control of consumers, and the consumer's ability to fake behavioral change.

The final lesson in the chapter described the technique of behavior modification.

The major types of behavior, respondent and operant, were defined. The procedure of counterconditioning was discussed as a technique for modifying respondent behavior. For operant behavior the techniques of reinforcement and extinction were described. Special emphasis was given to the difference between positive and negative reinforcement, since these techniques tend to be the most frequent approaches used in behavior modification programs. We concluded the lesson with a discussion of some of the problems related to behavior modification and the observations that it can be mechanistic, manipulative, and limited.

SUGGESTIONS FOR FURTHER STUDY

As with the previous chapter on counseling, we have merely provided an introduction to the techniques of rehabilitating. In addition to learning more about the vast body of knowledge related to psychoanalysis, further attention should be given to the process of shaping behavior and to the specialized work of Premack. Your knowledge of reality therapy can be expanded by reading the works of Glasser. Further study might include more attention to the procedures of extinction, which are applicable in working with the bothersome behavior of young children or the self-destructive behavior of alcoholics. Further interest in rehabilitating techniques might result from the study of modeling techniques, where the consumer learns how to model his behavior after appropriate role models. Other approaches to rehabilitating include psychoanalysis, psychodrama, Gestalt therapy, bibliotherapy, relaxation therapy, transactional analysis, chemotherapy, and densensitizing. The following list of references should help you get started in acquainting yourself with the complexities of rehabilitation.

SUGGESTIONS FOR FURTHER READING

Beedell, Christopher. *Residential Life with Children*. New York: Humanities Press, 1970.

Berelson, Bernard, and Steiner, Gary A. *Human Behavior: An Inventory of Scientific Findings*. New York: Harcourt Brace Jovanovich, 1964, pp. 287–289.

Bird, Joseph, and Bird, Lois. *Power to the Parents*. Garden City, N.Y.: Doubleday, 1972.

Bixby, F. Lovell, and McCorkle, Lloyd B. "Guided Group Interaction in Correctional Work." *American Sociological Review* 16, no. 4 (August 1951): 455–461.

Glasser, William. *Reality Therapy: A New Approach to Psychiatry*. New York: Harper & Row, 1965.

———. *Schools Without Failure*. New York: Harper & Row, 1969.

Holler, Ronald F., and DeLong, George M. *Human Services Technology*. St. Louis: Mosby, 1973.

Jehu, Derek. *Behavior Modification in Social Work*. London: Wiley Interscience, 1972.

Keane, Sister Mary Charles. *The Housemother: A Member of the Institutional Team*. Washington, D.C.: National Conference of Catholic Charities, 1954.

Keith-Lucas, Alan. *Giving and Taking Help*. University of North Carolina Press, 1972.

Kisker, George W. *The Disorganized Personality*. New York: McGraw-Hill, 1964.

Leibrock, John B. *Manual of Skilled Houseparentry*. Philadelphia: Whitmore Publishing Company, 1967.

Moreno, J. *Psychodrama*. Beacon, N.Y.: Beacon House, 1969.

Morrow, William R., and Gochros, Harvey L. "Misconceptions Regarding Behavior Modification." *Social Service Review* 44 (September 1970): 293–307.

Perls, F. *Gestalt Therapy*. New York: Julian Press, 1951.

Phillips, E. Lakin, and Wiener, Daniel. *Discipline, Achievement, and Mental Health*. Englewood Cliffs, N.J.: Prentice Hall, 1972.

Premack, D. "Toward Empirical Behavior Laws: Positive Reinforcement." *Psychological Review* 66 (1959): 219–233.

Schaffer, Halmuth H., and Martin, Patrick L. *Behavioral Therapy*. New York: McGraw-Hill, 1969.

Sherman, A. Robert. *Behavior Modification: Theory and Practice*. Monterey, Calif.: Brooks/Cole, 1973.

Silverman, Mitchell, Fosselman, John, and Thomas, Gerald B. *Guided Group Interaction as an Instrument of Correctional Treatment: Evaluation of the Functional Roles of Group Leaders*. University of South Florida Criminal Justice Program, 1971.

Tharp, Roland G., and Wetzel, Ralph J. *Behavior Modification in the Natural Environment*. New York: Academic Press, 1969.

Thomas, Edwin J. "Social Casework and Social Group Work: The Behavioral Approach." In *Encyclopedia of Social Work*, vol. II. New York: National Association of Social Workers, 1971, pp. 1226–1237.

———— "The Behavior Modification Model and Social Casework." In Herbert F. Strean, *Social Casework: Theories in Action*. Metuchon, N.J.: Scarecrow Press, 1971, pp. 267–296.

Wenrich, W. W. *A Primer of Behavior Modification*. Monterey, Calif.: Brooks/Cole, 1970.

REVIEW QUESTIONS—CHAPTER VII

Circle the letter corresponding to the answer of your choice.

1. Rehabilitating refers to which of the following?
    A. Structured activities directed toward changing or modifying a consumer's attitudes, feelings, or thoughts
    B. Structured activities directed toward modifying or changing a consumer's behavior, using specialized treatment techniques
    C. Unstructured activities directed toward modifying or changing a consumer's attitudes, feelings, or thoughts
    D. Unstructured activities directed toward modifying or changing a consumer's behavior, using counseling techniques

2. Objections to the use of reality therapy as a technique include which of the following observations?
    A. It is most successful where there is limited control over the consumer.
    B. It is sometimes easy for the consumer to fake a true behavioral change.
    C. It is focused too much on past behavior.

3. Which of the following groups of persons are sometimes unable to respond to the counseling process, and may, therefore, be helped by some form of behavior changing?
    A. The retarded.
    B. The senile.

C. Criminals.

D. All of the above.

E. None of the above; they all respond well to traditional counseling.

4. Which rehabilitating technique is used mainly with consumers who have missed the experience of being loved and taught how to control their behavior?

    A. Behavior modification

    B. Reality therapy

    C. Parenting

    D. Psychotherapy

5. The technique of parenting attempts to fulfill which of the following needs?

    A. The need for knowing one's limits and how to behave within these limits

    B. The need for security

    C. The need to be able to learn to lead one's own life

    D. B and C

    E. All of the above

6. Which of the following methods are used in the technique of parenting?

    A. Loving and self-analysis

    B. Training through discipline and caring

    C. Rejecting unrealistic behavior

    D. Showing interest and giving punishment

7. Disciplining, as used in the parenting technique, means which of the following?

    A. A plan of training to learn direction and control

    B. Punishment

    C. Ignoring the consumer

    D. Overinvolvement

8. The technique of parenting is criticized by some because of which of the following reasons?

    A. It may attract those who enjoy having power over others.

    B. It is an easy relationship to enter but very difficult to end.

    C. It is difficult to decide who is in need of parenting.

    D. All of the above are reasons.

9. The aim of the reality therapy technique is to help the consumer fulfill his essential emotional needs and behave more responsibly.

    A. False

    B. True

10. According to reality therapy, an individual acts irresponsibly and needs treatment mainly because he is

    A. suffering from severe psychiatric problems.

    B. acting irresponsibly.

    C. unable to fulfill his essential emotional needs.

11. The human service worker focuses on behavior, and not on feelings, when applying which of the following treatment techniques?

    A. Psychoanalysis

    B. Reality therapy

    C. Behavior modification

D. B and C

E. All of the above

12. Reality therapy uses which of the following procedures to change a consumer's behavior?

A. Involvement

B. Showing acceptance and giving punishment

C. Rejecting the unrealistic behavior of the consumer

D. Teaching responsible ways of behaving to fulfill needs

E. A, C, and D

13. Which of the following guidelines should be followed in using reality therapy?

A. The focus should be on the consumer's past behavior.

B. The consumer should be asked to evaluate his own behavior.

C. The therapist should be warm and personal with the consumer.

D. A, B, and C should be followed.

E. B and C should be followed.

14. In order to be able to achieve the aim of behavior modification, namely to modify or change specific behavior, the therapist applies which of the following as the basic rule.

A. Desirable or undesirable behavior is weakened when followed by a reward.

B. Rewarding a desirable behavior strengthens it, and not rewarding undesirable behavior weakens it.

C. Desirable behavior is strengthened by ignoring it, and undesirable behavior is weakened by rewarding it.

D. Undesirable behavior is weakened by punishment, and desirable behavior is weakened by not rewarding it.

15. The behavior modification therapist deals with two major types of behavior—respondent and operant. Respondent behavior is which of the following?

A. Involuntary

B. Voluntary

C. Usually a function of more than one environmental stimulus

D. A and C

E. B and C

16. Which of the following is an example of operant behavior?

A. Anxiety

B. A temper tantrum

C. Fear

D. A and C

E. A and B

17. When a behavior modification therapist arranges for a consumer to feel comfortable as he is near something he fears, the therapist is applying which of the following procedures?

A. Negative reinforcement

B. Positive reinforcement

C. Extinction

D. Counterconditioning

18. When behavior modification programs are criticized for being manipulative, this means they are excessive in which of the following way?
    A. Too flexible
    B. Too controlling of people's behavior
    C. Too creative
    D. Too innovative
    E. A and C

19. What do we call the technique or procedure used in behavior modification to reduce or eliminate a behavior by removing the factor that is maintaining the behavior?
    A. Negative reinforcement
    B. Counterconditioning
    C. Extinction
    D. Positive reinforcement

20. Assume that you are working in an institution for the mentally retarded. Margaret is one of the residents and you notice that she really enjoys being hugged and having a chance to sit in your lap. Suppose one of your goals with Margaret is to teach her to stay in a chair for a certain period of time. One day Margaret stays still in a chair for a few seconds and you immediately hug her and say "That's fine Margaret." Which of the following procedures for modifying operant behavior are you using?
    A. Negative reinforcement
    B. Positive reinforcement
    C. Extinction

21. Objections to the use of behavior modification include observations that it is excessive in which of the following ways?
    A. Too manipulative
    B. Too easy to begin and too hard to give up
    C. Too limited
    D. A and C above
    E. All of the above

22. Which of the following are part of reality therapy?
    A. The therapist identifies the problem behavior.
    B. The consumer identifies the consequences of his problem behavior.
    C. The consumer and the therapist plan ways of changing the behavior.
    D. Both B and C are part of reality therapy.
    E. All of the above are part of reality therapy.

**Now check your answers with the
Answer key at the end of the book**

CHAPTER VIII:
CONSULTING

INTRODUCTION

Workers sometimes confront difficult situations when they are trying to help consumers. You have probably had trouble helping certain consumers solve their problems and found that nothing you try seems to help. You may be able to resolve such difficult situations by getting some outside advice. In consulting, a worker asks for help from someone who tries to understand the nature of the problem and tries to provide some useful suggestions. The problem may relate to consumer resistance to your counseling efforts or to a problem the consumer has mentioned which is beyond your area of expertise. Thus, when you seek advice from another worker regarding some problem you are having in helping a consumer, that worker serves as a consultant.

It is also important to recognize that there are situations in which you may act as a consultant. A prime example would be when you find it necessary, in order to help the consumer, to consult with the consumer's parents or other relatives to try to understand the problem better and to come up with useful ideas. In this case, your objective would be to gain from the parents or relatives information and ideas that would be helpful in improving your relationship with the consumer and/or in helping the consumer deal with his problem.

This chapter helps you identify beginning case consultation skills. The overall objective is to assist you in learning how to give help to, and ask for help from, other workers or individuals about consumer-related problems.

**Go on to the next page
and begin the first lesson**

LESSON 1:
THE MEANING
AND COMPONENTS
OF CONSULTING

Before you learn how to give and receive help from other workers, it is important to understand the meaning of consulting. In this lesson you will be learning the purposes of consulting and the main elements of the consulting process. The goal of this lesson and the enabling activities that will help you reach this goal are presented below.

GOAL

You will be able to define consulting and explain the three elements of the consulting process.

ENABLING ACTIVITIES

After completing this lesson, you will have accomplished three things:

1. Reviewed the meaning of consulting
2. Identified the three elements of the consulting process
3. Examined the three common features of all consulting activities.

Turn to Frame 1

FRAME 1

CONSULTING—ITS MEANING AND MAJOR PURPOSES

Consulting is the process of obtaining and providing advice or information to help solve a problem. In the human services, consulting refers to the process of requesting and obtaining help, advice, or information from other workers. Consulting also involves providing help in the form of advice and information to other workers upon request, with the objective of solving some problem, usually related to a consumer.

294

Generally, the major purposes of consulting are as follows:

1. To help others carry out an activity or solve a problem
2. To help others in developing a relationship with consumers
3. To help others set up a plan and consider various alternatives in working with their consumers.

Proceed to Frame 2

FRAME 2

Which of the following would be considered consulting in the human services?

A. Obtaining information from a consumer about his or her background and experience.

Turn to Answer 3

B. Obtaining advice from a friend regarding a decision you must make.

Turn to Answer 7

C. Obtaining information related to a new procedure for helping a consumer.

Turn to Answer 10

FRAME 3

If you discuss a consumer's problem upon the request of his family in an effort to help work with the consumer, you would be consulting.

A. True

Turn to Answer 4

B. False

Turn to Answer 8

FRAME 4

COMPONENTS OF THE CONSULTING PROCESS

There are three components of consulting—the consultant, the consultee, and the process or activity of consulting. Although you will learn more about each of these later in this chapter, you should be familiar with each component.

1. **The consultant.** Consulting will always be an activity that involves two or more persons. One person is called the consultant. He or she has knowledge in the area of the consumer-related problem and helps in solving this problem by *giving advice or information* that leads to greater understanding of the problem, by suggesting other sources of help, or by helping in deciding on a treatment plan.

2. **The consultee.** The other person or persons in consulting are called the consultees. The consultee is *asking for help* regarding a problem and believes the consultant can help. As a worker in the human services, it is important that you know how to be both a consultant and a consultee. You will learn more about each of these activities in the next two lessons.

3. **The consulting process.** The process of consulting is usually carried out within a specific time frame (one week, one day, one hour), or it may take place

(Frame 4 continued)

throughout the year whenever the need arises. The process has three major steps involving the consultant and the consultee:

    a. **The request for help.** The person who will be the consultee becomes aware of a problem and goes to a person who knows about the problem area and can help in solving the problem.

    b. **The working stage.** The consultant and the consultee get to know each other if they have not met before. They work together to understand what the problem is and how they might solve it.

    c. **The closing.** Consulting may end when the consultee has received the help he needs in solving his problem. However, if he needs more help he knows he can go back to the consultant for more advice.

Proceed to Frame 5

FRAME 5

Which of the following activities might be found in consultation processes? Check the activities and turn to Answer 2.

____ A. Talking regularly with a psychiatrist about the behavior of a consumer on your ward.

____ B. Helping a teacher understand a child's behavior problems by sharing information about the child's home life.

____ C. Involving consumers of public welfare services in evaluating the impact of a new agency policy.

____ D. Talking with a nurse about the behavior of an elderly nursing home patient in order to advise family members.

____ E. Responding to a request for assistance regarding the problems experienced by a co-worker in a halfway house for delinquent youths.

FRAME 6

Mitch has a consumer-related problem on which he needs advice. In what way can Mitch initiate the consultation process?

A. By reading several books on the problem area.

Turn to Answer 9

B. By seeking as consultee the best available opinion.

Turn to Answer 11

C. By offering his services to another worker with a similar problem.

Turn to Answer 6

FRAME 7

When does the closing stage of the consultation process occur?

A. When the consultee receives the help he needs in solving the problem.

Turn to Answer 1

B. When the consumer has accepted the advice of the worker.

Turn to Answer 5

C. When the consultant has received a progress report and has reviewed the case thoroughly.

Turn to Answer 13

FRAME 8

COMMON FEATURES OF ALL CONSULTING ACTIVITIES

There are three common features of all consulting activities which are important to remember when you give and ask for help from other workers. Whether you are a consultant or a consultee, it is important to remember the following:

1. Consulting is a voluntary activity. This means that a worker is free to ask or not to ask for help from another worker. It also means that the worker who is being asked to help may say that he is unable to help, especially if he is unfamiliar with the problem area.
2. After receiving advice or information from a consultant, it is up to the consultee to decide how and if the consultant's advice will be used.
3. Consulting is a two-way process—the consultant and the consultee work together, both giving and receiving assistance in order to solve a problem.

Consultation is not requested enough in the human services. Most workers think they can handle the problems they confront, and it is true that many can. However, requesting help is a sign of strength and requires recognizing that there will be some situations in which you would benefit from some assistance. Being too proud to ask for help only serves to limit your potential success with a consumer.

Proceed to Frame 9

FRAME 9

When asked for assistance, the potential consultant is bound by professional ethics to give what help he or she can.

A. True
B. False

Turn to Answer 15

FRAME 10

After a consultation relationship has been established, the consultee should

A. follow the consultant's advice to the letter.

Turn to Answer 16

B. give the consultant all relevant information regarding circumstances surrounding the case.

Turn to Answer 14

C. evaluate the consultant's advice, modifying subsequent actions in the light of his or her own experience with the consumer.

Turn to Answer 12

D. do both B and C above.

Turn to Answer 17

ANSWERS TO LESSON 1

ANSWER 1

Right on target! This concludes the contract of consultation. Go on to Frame 8.

ANSWER 2

All these activities represent events which could take place in the process of giving or receiving consultation. If you missed one or more, review Frame 5 before going on to Frame 6.

ANSWER 3

This would not be considered consulting although it is a task of a human service worker. Return to Frame 1 for a review of the meaning of consulting before answering the question in Frame 2 correctly.

ANSWER 4

Right again! Because you are working out a means of solving the consumer's problem by helping others help him, you are performing as a consultant. Now work on Frame 4.

ANSWER 5

This is indeed an ultimate aim of consultation, but the end of the process of consulting is something else. Review Frame 4 again, and then select a more specific answer in Frame 7.

ANSWER 6

While talking with another co-worker in a similar situation might be beneficial, there is another choice which would more likely bring better results. After reflecting on Frame 4, you will probably see it more clearly. Then you will be able to answer the question in Frame 6 correctly.

ANSWER 7

Although this could be viewed as a form of consulting, it is unrelated to the human services. Return to Frame 2 and answer the question presented there correctly.

ANSWER 8

Sorry, but you would still be acting as a consultant although this might be a form of consultation that is new to you. Return to Frame 3 and select the other answer.

ANSWER 9

This *might* help Mitch, but chances are that books will not give an exact parallel. Mitch also misses the in-depth exchange that may occur between workers. Another answer is better; see if you can identify it in Frame 6.

ANSWER 10

Exactly—this would be considered consulting in the human services. Anytime one worker needs, requests, and obtains advice or information from another worker who has more knowledge or skill in the problem area, a consulting relationship is frequently formed. Return now to Frame 3.

ANSWER 11

You have the right idea. Very good. Continue with Frame 7.

ANSWER 12

A good thing to remember. But so is another of the choices listed in Frame 10. Review them again and select the additional answer you need.

ANSWER 13

Although this is good as far as keeping doors open for further help and communication, it is not a necessary element of the consulting process. Return to Frame 7 and select the correct answer.

ANSWER 14

This is a good answer. But did you look at all the choices? There may be others which are also valid. Review Frame 10 to see if you might choose another answer.

ANSWER 15

False. Did you get it? Good. Good consultants will not accept a job they cannot perform well. They will know when to say no. Proceed to Frame 10.

ANSWER 16

The consultee should always remember that the consultant merely offers suggestions based on his or her knowledge of the specific situation and experience in the problem area. The consultee is obligated to use the information in a manner which seems best for his or her particular consumer. Review Frame 8 and select a more appropriate answer in Frame 10.

ANSWER 17

Correct. You have discriminated carefully and no doubt you will keep this in mind when actually in a consultee's position. You have now completed Lesson 1. Continue with Lesson 2.

LESSON 2: RECEIVING HELP FROM A CONSULTANT

In this lesson you will learn about the process of asking another worker for help with your consumer-related problems. The goal of this lesson and the enabling activities that will help you reach this goal are presented below.

GOAL

Given a description of a worker with a consumer-related problem, you will be able to explain how this worker would decide if he needed help from another worker and also be able to name four steps he should take if he decided to request help.

ENABLING ACTIVITIES

After completing this lesson, you will have done three things:

1. Considered seven questions that will help you in determining when you need to consult with another worker
2. Examined five ways you can help the consultant help you
3. Identified the steps you should take after receiving help from another worker

Now begin work in Frame 1

FRAME 1

You will not need help from another worker every time you have a problem in working with a consumer. Seeking help through consulting is only an aid to your work and planning; it does not take the place of it. But how will you know when to ask for help? While you should not rely on a consultant to help you solve all your problems, you should be able to recognize those problems with which you do require help. Before you seek the help of another worker, you should ask yourself:[1]

1. What am I trying to do?
2. What are the best ways I know to do it?
3. What skills and resources do I need to do this job?

(Frame 1 continued)

[1] Nell McKeever, "How to Use a Consultant," *Adult Leadership* (April 1955): 14–16.

4. What problems are blocking my progress?

5. Have I taken every opportunity to use my own knowledge and skills?

6. In addition to what I can do, what additional knowledge and skills seem to be needed?

7. What people could help me most in this situation?

As you answer these questions, if you find that you have tried every way you know to help the consumer, or are not sure about the true nature of the consumer's problem, you would then seek the help of another worker. In many agencies, your supervisor would be the first person you would contact. Together, you would discuss the problem and then decide which persons could help the most.

Go on to Frame 2

FRAME 2

Place a check beside those statements below which describe the actions you should take before seeking help from a consultant.

___ 1. Explain your objective in writing.

___ 2. List the skills and resources needed to reach the objective.

___ 3. Describe the best ways you know of reaching the objective.

___ 4. Go to the library for information.

___ 5. Describe the problems blocking your progress.

___ 6. Improve your own attitudes.

___ 7. Identify any additional skills and/or knowledge needed that you do not have.

___ 8. Identify the people who could help you most in meeting your objective.

Turn to Answer 7

FRAME 3

Match questions asked prior to seeking consultation on the left with the appropriate aspect of the sample situation on the right. Then turn to answer 14 to check yourself.

1. What am I trying to do?

2. What are the best ways I know to do it?

3. What skills and resources do I need to do this job?

4. What problems are blocking my progress?

5. Have I used my own knowledge and skills to the fullest?

6. What additional knowledge and skills are needed besides what I can provide?

7. Who are the people who could help me most?

___A. The consumer's brother keeps interfering with the consumer's progress.

___B. The goal of working with the consumer is to get her out of the institution and functioning at home.

___C. I have worked with the consumer in a group since she responds well to others.

___D. The consumer's minister seems to reflect a keen interest in the family.

___E. My ability to deal with family members and get needed information is not sufficient.

___F. I must use the group situation and find strong support in the group to help this consumer.

___G. Although I feel confident in my group work skills, I have not been supportive enough of the consumer in the group.

Meeting with a Consultant

Once you have decided that you need help and have made your choice of a consultant, meetings should be set up in which certain things are accomplished in a logical sequence.

1. **Present the problem.** In your first meeting with the consultant, outline the problem. This will mean telling the consultant about the background of the consumer, what you think the problem is, how you have tried to help the consumer, and what you have been having trouble with.

2. **Make your needs known.** After you have stated the problem, tell the consultant what you want him or her to do. Here you should be very specific and should make sure that both you and the consultant are very clear on what the problem is and how you will both work to solve it. You should be willing to accept the questioning and probing of the consultant as the person attempts to understand the problem.

3. **Wait for the consultant to accept or decline.** Give the consultant a chance to decide whether he or she can handle the job you have outlined.

4. **Work together.** If the consultant decides that he or she can help you, work together to seek solutions to the problems. This means answering questions and being willing to expose all the difficulties you are encountering in working with the consumer.

5. **Listen to suggestions.** Don't expect pampering from the consultant and don't expect to be told what to do. The consultant will work with you and suggest possible ways of solving the problem, but it is not the consultant's role to tell you that you must use one particular way of solving the problem. That decision is up to you and your supervisor.

Proceed to Frame 5

Before a consultant can determine whether he or she can be of help, he should have

A. a clear idea of the problem.

Turn to Answer 11

B. knowledge of what the consultee wants him to do.

Turn to Answer 2

C. direct exposure to the consumer.

Turn to Answer 4

D. both A and B above.

Turn to Answer 9

E. all of the above.

Turn to Answer 3

FRAME 6

What should the consultee do after the consultant agrees to work on a problem?

A. Forget about it until called by the consultant.

Turn to Answer 10

B. Tell the consumer not to worry about it again, as the problem will be solved soon.

Turn to Answer 1

C. Work with the consultant by probing the problem, answering questions, and keeping the consultant abreast of new developments and ideas.

Turn to Answer 5

D. Expect the consultant to present a formula to solve this and all similar problems.

Turn to Answer 8

FRAME 7

Below are four steps for a successful consultation. Place them in the order in which they should be accomplished for maximum results by numbering them 1 through 4.

___ A. Give the consultant an opportunity to assess his ability to help.

___ B. Outline the problem to the potential consultant.

___ C. Work with the consultant on possible solutions.

___ D. Specify what you are asking of the consultant.

Turn to Answer 6

FRAME 8

What to Do after Receiving Help from a Consultant[2]

After you have received help from a consultant, it is important to remember that you do not have to follow the suggestions to the letter. You are free to use any or all of the suggestions in the way that you and your supervisor think will help solve the problem.

The way to decide how to use the help from a consultant is to review the help you have received. How much help did you get? What are the best ways to use this information? What can you do to use this help effectively?

Move forward after you have received the help. Go back to the consumer and take a new look at how you can help solve the problem.

As a worker in the human services, it is also important to remember that you should take the initiative in maintaining communication with others who deliver human services. If you are familiar with other workers, in both your own and other agencies, you will have a better idea of who can help you. You may also be able to help these workers, a process which will be discussed in the next lesson.

Continue with Frame 9

---

[2] See Ibid. and also William W. Savage "Making the Most of the Consultant," *Administrators Notebook* I, no. 3 (October 1952); and Edward C. Norman, "Role of the Mental Health Consultee," *Mental Hygiene* 52, no. 2 (April 1968).

FRAME 9

What should you do once you have received help from a consultant and shared the experience with your supervisor?

A. You should follow the consultant's advice.

Turn to Answer 12

B. You should decide whether to use any, all, or none of the consultant's suggestions.

Turn to Answer 15

C. You should disregard the consultant's advice.

Turn to Answer 18

FRAME 10

What will help you decide how to use the suggestions received from a consultant?

A. Answering questions such as "What can I do to use this help?"

Turn to Answer 13

B. Finding out the easiest way to use the help.

Turn to Answer 16

C. Asking the consumer.

Turn to Answer 17

FRAME 11

You have identified the two steps you should take after receiving help as follows: (1) Decide whether to use any, all, or none of the consultant's suggestions in ways that will help you solve the problem or move toward your objective. (2) Review the help you have received by answering questions such as "What are the best ways to use the new information?" and "What can I do to use this help effectively?"

In the space below state another step you should take after receiving consultation.

If you can think of another possible action, state it below and then turn to answer 19.

ANSWERS TO LESSON 2

ANSWER 1

In most cases it is not necessary to inform the consumer of the consultation or problem-solving efforts. Can you spot the better answer in Frame 6? If not, review Frame 4 before making another choice.

ANSWER 2

An important facet, to be sure. But the consultant will need more than just this. Make another selection in Frame 5 and check your answer. Work on it until you have it right.

ANSWER 3

Have you been a little careless in your enthusiasm? One of the choices precludes another. Read them carefully before checking off another answer to Frame 5.

ANSWER 4

Although this might be helpful, it is usually not necessary in order for the consultant to determine if he has the resources to help solve the problem. Return to Frame 4 for a review and then select the correct answer to Frame 5.

ANSWER 5

Precisely! Keep up the good work in Frame 7.

ANSWER 6

Did you number A, B, C, and D as 3, 1, 4 and 2? Good. If you misplaced some, check back to Frame 4 and then work out the logic behind the answer before continuing with Frame 8.

ANSWER 7

Did you check numbers 1, 2, 3, 5, 7, and 8? If so, well done. These are six of the seven major actions you should take before asking for consultant help. There is one more action. Can you recall it? If so, state it below, and then return to Frame 3. If not, return to Frame 1 for a review and find this action.

ANSWER 8

It would not be possible for even the best consultant to have the knowledge and experience needed to produce a foolproof formula for solving problems, even with the help of the consultee. Review Frame 4, and make another selection in Frame 6.

ANSWER 9

Your careful reading and discrimination have paid off in another correct answer. Continue your good work in Frame 6.

ANSWER 10

A review of earlier frames will remind you of the ways in which consultation is a two-way operation. After your review, select a better answer to Frame 6.

ANSWER 11

That's right—but you need to consider the entire field of answers before settling on this one. Read the list of choices in Frame 5 again, then make an additional selection. Be sure to check your answer.

ANSWER 12

This is not necessarily true. Although you should consider the consultant's advice and suggestions, you are not obliged to use it if you believe it will not be helpful. The final decision is yours. Return to Frame 9 and select the correct answer.

ANSWER 13

Right you are—well done! It is possible to decide how to use the ideas and suggestions received from the consultant by reviewing these ideas and answering questions such as "How much help did I get?" What are the best ways to use this new knowledge?" "What can I do to use this help?" Proceed now to Frame 11.

ANSWER 14

Your answers should read as follows:

4 A   7 D
1 B   6 E
2 C   3 F
       5 G

If you missed any of these, review Frame 1 before proceeding to Frame 4.

ANSWER 15

Definitely. You are free to use any, all, or none of the advice or suggestions received from a consultant. Your only obligation is to consider the advice carefully and then decide if it will be helpful or not before using it. Well done. Return to Frame 10 and continue the lesson.

ANSWER 16

The easiest ways are rarely the best ways. One of your tasks after receiving help is to find the *best* ways to use it, if possible. If you cannot find very good ways to apply the suggestions, don't use them!

Return to Frame 8 for a review of actions to take after receiving help, and then answer Frame 10 correctly.

ANSWER 17

This would probably be of little help. Although in some cases the consumer is able to give indirect hints as to how to proceed, coming right out and asking the consumer is generally not recommended. Return to Frame 10 and select a better answer.

ANSWER 18

Of course not! Why did you request the help in the first place if you were going to disregard it? You definitely need a review. Return to Frame 8 and reread the material presented there before attempting another answer in Frame 9.

ANSWER 19

Other than using the consultant's ideas as you see fit and answering relevant questions about the help received, you should move forward toward helping the consumer solve his or her problem and take the initiative in maintaining communication with others who deliver human services. You may now be able to draw upon the help of others as a result of your experience. Did you write down one of these activities, or something else equally appropriate?

You have completed Lesson 2 on receiving help from a consultant. Now go on to Lesson 3 and learn how to provide effective consultation.

LESSON 3:
YOU AS THE CONSULTANT

In this lesson you will be introduced to some ways *you* can give help to other human service workers with consumer-related problems. The goal of this lesson and the enabling activities that will help you reach this goal are presented below.

GOAL

Given a situation where another worker has asked you for help with a consumer-related problem, you will be able to explain how you would know if you could help this worker and you will be able to list the steps you would follow if you decided to give your help.

ENABLING ACTIVITIES

After completing this lesson, you will have done four things:

1. Examined three questions that will assist you in determining when you can help another worker with a consumer-related problem
2. Identified three ways to view your consulting relationship with another worker
3. Reviewed four skills you can use in establishing and maintaining a good consulting relationship with another worker
4. Considered six guidelines to follow in consulting with another worker

Begin this lesson by turning to Frame 1

FRAME 1

WHEN TO ACCEPT A REQUEST FOR CONSULTING

When another worker asks for your help, how do you know if you can provide assistance? Since you recognize that you will be unable to help other workers with consumer-related problems every time you are asked, what factors can aid you in making your decision? Good consultants will listen to the problem and will then ask themselves three questions:[1]

1. What seems to be the difficulty?
2. What are my resources for giving the kind of help that is needed now or that may be needed later?
3. Am I expert enough in the area in which help is sought?

If you have trouble in answering any of these questions, you need to develop the ability to say *no*. You may not be the one to help with this particular problem, and if this is the case, a very good contribution would be to suggest someone else who is able to help.

Turn to Frame 2

FRAME 2

When asked for help, human service workers need to assess the situation in which of the following ways? Check those that apply.

—— 1. Do I have all the possible solutions to the problems presented?

—— 2. Am I expert in this area?

—— 3. What is the problem?

—— 4. Do I like this person requesting help enough to help him or her?

—— 5. Are my resources adequate for this problem?

—— 6. What will I get out of this?

Turn to Answer 5

FRAME 3

Kerry has been asked to consult with another worker about a consumer-related problem. Kerry does not feel he has the experience necessary to do the job well. What should Kerry do?

A. Agree to help

Turn to Answer 21

B. Suggest someone else who has the knowledge needed

Turn to Answer 3

C. Share his doubts about his ability to contribute

Turn to Answer 8

D. B and C above

Turn to Answer 14

E. All the above

Turn to Answer 18

---

[1] See Ronald Lippitt, "Dimensions of the Consultant's Job," *Journal of Social Issues* 25, no. 2 (1959); and Rose Green, "The Consultant and the Consultation Process," *Child Welfare* (October 1965).

FRAME 4

THE CONSULTANT'S RELATIONSHIP WITH THE CONSULTEE

Before you help another worker, you need to remember that you will both be involved in the activity of consulting and that *you* are the consultant. When you are helping another worker with a consumer-related problem, your approach will be important in the following ways:

1. You should take the position that this worker knows more about the problem than he or she thinks. You will need to help bring forth this knowledge.
2. You should always remember that responsibility for the consumer remains with the worker. You will not be evaluating or judging the worker, but helping the worker solve the problem.
3. You must always accept the worker's right to use your help in ways that seem appropriate to him or her.

Is this clear? Yes? Good, then go on to Frame 5. No? In that case you better re-read the above more carefully.

FRAME 5

Suppose you have spent a great deal of time as consultant to a fellow worker. He has been polite and cooperative, but now he has used your advice in a way you did not recommend. Which attitude is appropriate?

A. It is the co-worker's right to use your help in the way he thinks will be most beneficial.

Turn to Answer 2

B. Your help was not appreciated, and you will be more careful about how you help him in the future.

Turn to Answer 7

FRAME 6

As a consultant, you must have all the information possible in order to be of help. What is the best way to obtain this information?

A. Read the case record.

Turn to Answer 11

B. Ask the consultee to write a detailed report.

Turn to Answer 16

C. Talk with the worker several times, questioning him or her and taking notes.

Turn to Answer 20

FRAME 7

As a consultant, you must remember that the final responsibility for dealing with the consumer's problem is

A. yours.

Turn to Answer 17

B. the consultee's.

Turn to Answer 13

Establishing a Positive Relationship. As a consultant, you will be most successful in helping another worker if you try to establish and maintain a good relationship with the worker in four areas:[2]

1. **Sensitive listening.** You should start the relationship where the worker is thinking and feeling. You need to accept and support the worker and to listen to how he or she views the problem.
2. **Understanding.** You need to understand what the problem is and what the worker needs to know.
3. **Communicating.** Show that you think the problem is important and show that you have a desire to maintain communication with the worker by remembering what he or she says, by answering questions about yourself, and by showing continued interest in the worker and the problem.
4. **Doing.** The worker needs to sense that you are both making progress in solving the problem. Since most problems cannot be solved quickly, you can help the worker feel that progress is being made by becoming actively involved. Do not tell the worker what to do, but work together in clarifying the situation and making decisions.

Proceed to Frame 9

FRAME 9

In problem-solving it is important for the consultant to establish and maintain an open channel of communication with the consultee. List below at least three ways by which this may be accomplished.

1.

2.

3.

Turn to Answer 6

FRAME 10

There are several ways for the consultant to assure the consultee that progress is being made. Check those that apply.

__ 1. Listening and talking

__ 2. Reviewing and suggesting solutions

__ 3. Requesting and sending reports

__ 4. Telling the worker what should be done

Turn to Answer 10

---

[2] See Lorene A. Stringer, "Consultation: Some Expectations, Principles, and Skills," *Social Work* (July 1961); Family Service Association of America, *Administration, Consultation, and Supervision* (New York, 1955); and Jacob S. Kounin, "The Personal Touch," *Adult Leadership* (April 1955).

In this chapter, you noted a number of ways in which consultants can make good use of each other's knowledge and experience. In the blanks below, place C next to those statements which demonstrate ways by which the consultant may facilitate consultation, W next to those which are best facilitated by the worker or consultee, and B next to those which describe ways both consultant and consultee may assist in making consultation profitable.

___ 1. Listen carefully to explanations of problems.

___ 2. Carefully select the best available help.

___ 3. Clearly outline the situation and problem.

___ 4. Carefully probe and ask questions.

___ 5. Establish good communications between consultant and consultee.

___ 6. Modify and try out suggestions.

___ 7. Keep up with the outcome of all efforts.

Turn to Answer 4

SIX GUIDELINES FOR EFFECTIVE CONSULTING

You will remember from Lesson 1 that the three steps in consulting include the request for help, the working stage, and the closing. As you move through these steps in helping another worker with a consumer-related problem, you should try to use the skills of establishing a good relationship with the worker. Six guidelines are suggested for establishing an effective working relationship.[3]

1. Adopt a "mind set" toward helping the worker. Ask yourself how you can help this worker solve his or her problem.
2. Establish the rules of the game immediately. You and the worker should work together in determining what the problem is and how you will try to solve it.
3. Communicate a sense of concern about the problem. Speak with the worker in language which is related to the situation and to the style of the worker.
4. While helping the worker see what the problem is, also explore areas where change is needed. For example, you might ask, "From the way you have described the problem, do you think it might be more advantageous to work with the father than the mother?"
5. Offer your own ideas on how to solve the problem and help the worker react to and think about these ideas.
6. When the worker thinks he or she has received the help needed, or when you think you have offered all the help you can, the consulting will end. As it ends, you may help the worker make some choices about subsequent steps. You may both decide that the worker needs to think about the problem some more and

---

[3] See William H. Koch, "A Stance Toward Helping: Reflections on the Role of a Consultant," *Adult Leadership* (December 1967); and Rose Green, "The Consultant and the Consultation Process," *Child Welfare* (October, 1965).

then discuss it with his or her supervisor. Even though your consulting relationship may end, you can still show the worker you are interested in the problem by maintaining communication and finding out how things are going without necessarily appearing nosy.

Go on to Frame 13

FRAME 13

One important aspect of developing a good working relationship with a consultee is to adopt a positive "mind set." To help accomplish this, which of the following actions would you take?

A. Focus your attention on an analysis of the consultee.

Turn to Answer 23

B. Focus your attention on an analysis of the problem and ways of solving it.

Turn to Answer 25

C. Focus your attention on an analysis of the consumer with whom the consultee is working.

Turn to Answer 29

FRAME 14

Suppose you have been serving as a consultant to a human service worker with a unique problem. The problem is now clearly defined and you have made several suggestions for possible solutions. Now is the time for you to do which of the following?

A. End the consultation.

Turn to Answer 1

B. Write out a step-by-step plan for the worker to follow.

Turn to Answer 12

C. Encourage the consultee's reactions by posing questions about hypothetical results and by projecting the possible outcomes of your suggested solutions.

Turn to Answer 19

FRAME 15

When consulting with a worker in a different area of the human services, you should make sure that

A. the worker learns your jargon.

Turn to Answer 9

B. you learn the worker's jargon.

Turn to Answer 15

C. you are aware of and responsive to the worker's style, situation, and language.

Turn to Answer 22

FRAME 16

When is the best time for the consultation to end?

A. When you, as the consultant, believe you have offered all you can.

Turn to Answer 24

B. When the problem has been clearly defined and all possible solutions described.

Turn to Answer 26

C. When the consultee thinks he or she has received the necessary help.

Turn to Answer 28

D. A or C above.

Turn to Answer 30

FRAME 17

After the consulting relationship ends, what should the consultant do to show continuing interest in the problem? Explain your answer below, and then turn to Answer 27.

FRAME 18

Well done, you have just completed this chapter. Before you go on, however, you should turn to the summary and the review questions at the end of the chapter to find out how much you have learned.

ANSWERS TO LESSON 3

ANSWER 1

This is incorrect because you may not have given all the possible help you could have. Review Frame 12, and select another answer to the question in Frame 14.

ANSWER 2

Your choice definitely shows a mature attitude toward your projected role as a consultant. Now try your skills on Frame 6.

ANSWER 3

While this is a good solution to Kerry's problem and to the co-worker's as well, what if Kerry does not know of another consultant he can suggest? Review Frame 1 before choosing another answer to Frame 3.

ANSWER 4

The answers we think are best are C, W, W, C, B, W, and C. You may have used B for several items in addition to number 5, and that is all right. But if your C's and W's were mixed up, maybe you need a review of this chapter to help clarify the respective roles of consultant and consultee. If you feel you need no review, go on to Frame 12.

ANSWER 5

Did you check numbers 2, 3 and 5? Good. If not, which did you leave out? Why? Which did you add? Why? Item 6, ("what will I get out of this") is a particularly important issue for human service workers since many of their rewards come primarily from the satisfaction of helping another worker or consumer. A quick perusal of Frame 1 should clarify this for you. Return there now if necessary. If not, go to Frame 3 and continue the good work.

ANSWER 6

Did you list such things as sensitive (or careful) listening, questioning, showing interest, seeking and giving feedback? Can you think of others? Make a note of them for later reference. Proceed to Frame 10.

ANSWER 7

This may be a natural feeling, especially for the novice consultant. However, you need to remember that the worker should not be locked into a particular method. The worker must have the necessary freedom to move as best as he or she can toward a particular solution. Choose the correct answer in Frame 5.

ANSWER 8

Sharing his doubts is a good thing for both Kerry and the co-worker. But another answer might also apply in some situations. Can you spot it? Look for another possible answer in Frame 3.

ANSWER 9

The consultant has a responsibility to be sure the lines of communication are open and clear. The worker must be able to use his or her own reference points in relation to the problem to be solved. Review Frame 12 again, before selecting the correct response in Frame 15.

ANSWER 10

Did you mark 1 and 2? Very good. You probably knew that 3 was not a good method of involving your consultee, and that 4 was something a consultant should not be expected to do. If you got confused, review Frame 8 before trying Frame 11.

ANSWER 11

This solution might give you a number of facts, but it is not likely to display the subtle nuances which make one particular problem unique. Do you see a better way in Frame 6? Check your answer.

ANSWER 12

This is incorrect. As a consultant, you will not be offering the consultee a step-by-step plan to follow in solving the problem. It is up to the consultee to adapt the consultant's suggestions to fit a consumer's particular needs. Review Frame 12 carefully before answering Frame 14 correctly.

ANSWER 13

Correct again! Now read Frame 8 for ideas on maintaining the good relationship you will want to have with your consultee.

ANSWER 14

You are correct. You indicated that Kerry might do two things—share his doubts about his ability to contribute, and suggest someone else who might be able to help if he knew such a person. Return now to Frame 4.

ANSWER 15

It is always helpful to understand the terms of a particular profession, but just knowing the jargon will not be sufficient to assure sensitive communication. Review Frame 12, and then select the proper response to Frame 15.

ANSWER 16

This choice has the same inadequacies as choice A. Review Answer 11, then check Answer 20. If you have doubts, consult Frame 4 for a more detailed explanation.

ANSWER 17

Taking your consultation seriously is important, but the ultimate responsibility must remain with its point of origin, namely, with the worker or consultee. Check Answer 13 before proceeding to Frame 8.

ANSWER 18

Have you read the Frame correctly? Please review the question in Frame 3 and make the proper choice.

ANSWER 19

Exactly! You are comprehending very well. Continue now with Frame 15.

ANSWER 20

Yes! This is by far the best way to explore all the factors surrounding a problem and to get feedback on suggested courses of action. Now tackle Frame 7.

ANSWER 21

If Kerry feels he cannot meet his co-worker's need, he should not feel obligated to help; such assistance could, in fact, be detrimental and time consuming. Think about the emphasis of this lesson before you make another selection in Frame 3.

ANSWER 22

Definitely the proper attitude to take. This will be reflected in a clearer grasp of the problem and its possible solutions. Return to Frame 16.

ANSWER 23

This would not be advisable. The consultee should never be viewed as a consumer, but as a fellow worker.

Return to Frame 12 for a review of *mind set* and then select the proper answer in Frame 13.

ANSWER 24

While this is true, it is but one possible answer. Look more closely at the choices in Frame 16.

ANSWER 25

We think this would be the wisest choice since the objective of the consulting process is to solve problems. You, as the consultant, would do best to focus on the problem and possible solutions to help you establish a *mind set* for effective consulting. Go right on to Frame 14.

ANSWER 26

Not necessarily. After the problem has been clearly defined and all possible solutions described, the consultee may have questions regarding the best solution, or the one to try first. The consultant may also have other information to impart.

Return to Frame 12 for a review of the last paragraph and then answer Frame 16 correctly.

ANSWER 27

Once the consulting relationship ends, the consultant should show continued interest by maintaining communication with the consultee and finding out if the consultee has been successful in solving the problem and reaching his or her objective. If you had any trouble with this answer, reread Frame 12 and then turn to Frame 18. If you had no trouble, go right to Frame 18.

ANSWER 28

Yes, this is certainly one of the proper answers, but there is another time when the consultation process might end. Reread Frame 16 and select the complete answer.

ANSWER 29

This would probably be both unnecessary and impossible for you to accomplish. The consumer is the consultee's responsibility, not yours. The consultee can supply you with any information about the consumer you may need. You should focus on something else in adopting a *mind set*. Review Frame 12 and then select the proper answer in Frame 13.

ANSWER 30

That's using brain power! The consulting relationships might end when consultants feel they have offered all the help they can or when the consultees feel they have obtained all the help they need. Go right on to Frame 17.

SUMMARY

Most texts concerned with delivering human services neglect the important skills required to request and provide consultation. Yet we know that informal consultation is taking place all the time whether in the lunch room, at coffee breaks, at the nurse's station, in the halls, at case conferences or at community meetings. This chapter provides a preliminary introduction to the complex process of consultation and emphasizes the formal case consultation that takes place between two human service workers or between a human service worker and a family relative or friend.

In the first lesson emphasis was placed on the definition of consultation and the importance of helping others. The consulting relationship includes the consultant, the consultee, and the consulting process which consists of the request for help, the working stage, and the closing or termination stage. It was noted that all consulting relationships are voluntary, based on the consultee making the consumer-related decisions, and that consulting is a two-way process.

In the second lesson special attention was given to the skills needed by the consultee in receiving help from a consultant. Several steps were identified in preparing for receiving consultation, including determining what you are trying to do in helping the consumer, what skills and resources are needed, and what problem is blocking your progress. Several practical steps to take once a decision has been made to request consultation were noted, including outlining the problem, telling the consultant all relevant information, and giving the consultant an opportunity to decline to give assistance. The lesson discussed things to consider after receiving consultation, including the manner in which suggestions are used, reviewing the help provided, the relationship of the help to new approaches to the consumer, and communication with others who may be useful in meeting the needs of the consumer.

The last lesson suggested specific guidelines to follow when considering a request for consultation, and also discussed the consultant's view of the consultee, the recognition that consultees know more about the problem than they think, the consultee's responsibility for the consumer, and the right of the consultee to use or reject the consultant's advice. It was noted that the effective consulting relationship requires that the consultant be a sensitive listener, have an ability to understand and converse about the immediate problem, and share involvement in seeking solutions. The lesson concluded with a discussion of the need for adopting a certain mind set, setting a contract of understanding, and presenting one's own ideas.

SUGGESTIONS FOR FURTHER STUDY

This chapter has concentrated primarily on the process of case consultation, and has provided only a beginning introduction to this complex process. Further study should be undertaken regarding the dynamics of this process as reflected in the considerable works of Gerald Caplan. Further study of the consultation process is also suggested to understand the concept of program consultation, which is based upon specialized knowledge of a certain field, such as how to set up a day-care center. In addition, the work of Edgar Schein should be reviewed in connection with process consultation, where assistance is given to the staff of an agency in order to improve the functioning of the agency. Finally community consultation, an area closely related to the roles of advocating and mobilizing, might be studied in an effort to see how the give and take of consulting services can be effected between the human service worker and community representatives. The following references should provide a beginning for your further study.

SUGGESTIONS FOR FURTHER READING

Caplan, Gerald. *The Theory and Practice of Mental Health Consultation.* New York: Basic Books, 1970.

Delougherty, Grace W., Gebbie, Kristine M., and Neumann, Betty M. *Consultation and Community Organization in Community Mental Health Nursing.* Baltimore: Williams & Wilkins, 1971.

Family Service Association of America. *Administration, Consultation and Supervision.* New York, 1955.

Green, Rose. "The Consultant and the Consultation Process." *Child Welfare* (October 1965): 425–462.

Koch, William H. "A Stance Toward Helping: Reflections on the Role of a Consultant." *Adult Leadership* (December 1967): 202–239.

Kounin, Jacob S. "The Personal Touch." *Adult Leadership* (April 1955): 23–24.

Lippitt, Ronald. "Dimensions of the Consultant's Job." *Journal of Social Issues* XXV, no. 2 (1959): 5–12.

Mackey, Richard A., and Hassler, Ferdinand R. "Group Consultation with School Personnel." *Mental Hygiene* 5 (1966).

Mannino, Fortune V., MacLennan, Beryce W., and Shore, Milton F. *The Practice of Mental Health Consultation.* Washington, D.C.: U.S. Government Printing Office, 1975.

May, Carmilla R. "Community Mental Health Consultation in a Public Agency." *Public Welfare* 28, no. 2 (1970).

McKeever, Nell. "How to Use a Consultant." *Adult Leadership* (April 1955): 14–16.

Musante, Gerard, and Gallemore, Johnnie L. "Utilization of a Staff Development Group in Prison Consultation." *Community Mental Health Journal* 9, no .3 (Fall 1973).

Norman, Edward C. "Role of the Mental Health Consultee." *Mental Hygiene* 52, no. 2 (April 1968).

Rapoport, Lydia. *Consultation in Social Work Practice.* New York: National Association of Social Workers, 1963.

Reding, Georges R., and Goldsmith, Ethel F. "The Non-Professional Hospital Volunteer as a Member of the Psychiatric Consultation Team." *Community Mental Health Journal* 3, no. 3 (Fall 1967).

Savage, William W. "Making the Most of the Consultant." *Administrators Notebook* 1, no. 3 (October 1952).

Schein, Edgar. *Process Consultation.* Reading, Mass.: Addison-Wesley, 1969.

Stringer, Lorene A. "Consultation: Some Expectations, Principles, and Skills." *Social Work* (July 1961): 85–90.

Thomas, Addie G. "Consultation: A Professional Process in Social Work Practice." Paper presented at the National Association of Social Workers Professional Symposium, May 21–23, 1965. (Available from Addie G. Thomas, Johns Hopkins Hospital, Department of Social Work, Baltimore 21205.)

Zwick, Paul A. "Special Problems in the Consultation Function of Child Guidance Clinics." *American Journal of Orthopsychiatry* 28, no. 1 (1958).

REVIEW QUESTIONS—CHAPTER VIII

Circle the letter corresponding to the answer of your choice.

1. In the human services, the consulting process involves which of the following?
   A. Requesting help in the form of advice or information from other workers to solve personal problems
   B. Requesting help from other workers to solve consumer-related problems
   C. Requesting, obtaining, and providing help to solve personal problems
   D. Requesting, obtaining, and providing help to solve consumer-related problems with other workers

2. The major purposes of consulting in the human services include which of the following?
   A. Helping others in developing effective relationships with consumers
   B. Helping others to set up plans to solve their consumer's problems
   C. Helping others to carry out a consumer-related activity
   D. A and B
   E. All the above

3. The three major steps in the process of consulting are the request for help, the working stage, and the closing.
   A. True
   B. False

4. Consulting in the human services is which of the following?
   A. A two way process in which the consultant and the consultee work together
   B. A one way process in which the consultant provides solutions and the consultee applies them
   C. A voluntary activity
   D. A and C
   E. B and C

5. As the consultee, how should you view consulting?
   A. As a way to replace your need to plan your work
   B. As an aid to your work and planning

    C. As an effective way of solving all of your personal problems

    D. As a way to reduce your workload

6. Before you seek the help of a consultant, which of the following should you do?

    A. Make sure you have tried every way you know to help the consumer.

    B. Make sure the consumer has become upset with you.

    C. Identify the problems that seem to be blocking your progress.

    D. A and C.

    E. All of the above.

7. How can you, as the consultee, best help the consultant help you?

    A. Outline your problem.

    B. Be specific in stating what you need from the consultant.

    C. Expect to receive useful solutions and specific methods for applying them.

    D. Assume that the consultant will help you.

    E. A and B.

8. What should you, as the consultee, be willing to do in order to obtain the most help from a consultant?

    A. Expose all the difficulties you have had with the consumer.

    B. Accept probing questions from the consultant.

    C. Follow the consultant's suggestions to the letter.

    D. A and B.

    E. All of the above.

9. After receiving help from a consultant, what should you do?

    A. Review the information and suggestions you have received.

    B. Remember you can use any, all, or none of the consultant's suggestions.

    C. Take a new look at how you can help the consumer.

    D. A and C.

    E. All of the above.

10. When you are acting as the consultant, what should you do?

    A. Accept all requests you receive for assistance.

    B. Be expert enough in all fields in order to handle most requests for assistance.

    C. Be able to say "no" to a request for assistance if you are for any reason unable to competently handle the request.

    D. None of the above.

11. Which of the following should a good consultant be able to do?

    A. Listen carefully to the problem as described by the worker before accepting the consultant role.

    B. Be sure to have sufficient knowledge and experience in the area in which help is sought.

    C. Identify his/her resources for giving the necessary help.

    D. A and C.

    E. All the above.

12. If you are unable to accept a worker's request for your help as a consultant, what should you do?

    A. Be able to say "no" politely.

    B. Remember it is your obligation to handle all requests.

    C. Suggest, if you can, someone else who may have the knowledge needed.

     D. A and B above.
     E. A and C above.

13. As a consultant, which of the following may you assume?
     A. The consultee knows very little about the consumer-related problem.
     B. The consultee knows more about the problem than he realizes.
     C. You will not have to question the consultee about the problem.
     D. You know more about the problem than the consultee.

14. As the consultant, which of the following is it important to remember?
     A. You will be expected to evaluate and judge the consultee.
     B. The responsibility for the consumer is primarily yours.
     C. The responsibility for the consumer remains with the consultee.

15. In order to facilitate the establishment of a positive working relationship with the consultee, what should you do as the consultant?
     A. Accept and support the consultee.
     B. Avoid becoming actively involved with the consultee.
     C. Show interest and concern in the consultee and the problem.
     D. A and C.
     E. All of the above.

16. Which of the following are skills the consultant should use when consulting with another worker?
     A. Communicate a sense of concern about the problem.
     B. Work together with the consultee in determining the problem and identifying possible solutions.
     C. Build the consultee's confidence in you by providing detailed solutions to the problem.
     D. A and B.
     E. A and C.

17. As the consulting relationship ends, what should the consultant do?
     A. Make sure the consultee follows his suggestions to the letter.
     B. Help the consultee make some choices about his next steps.
     C. Show desire to maintain communication with the consultee.
     D. A and B.
     E. B and C.

**Now check your answers with the
Answer key at the end of the book**

UNIT FOUR:
THE MANAGEMENT OF WORK TO DELIVER EFFECTIVE AND EFFICIENT SERVICES

INTRODUCTION

If you asked someone to tell you what human service agencies do, they would probably talk about the human needs that are met by different services and the different ways services are delivered to the consumer. It is unlikely that they would tell you about all the other things that go on in a human service agency in order to deliver services smoothly and efficiently. For example, think for a minute about the large volume of consumer information that a human service agency collects in just one day. All agencies must keep records of such information so that administrators and other workers will know what is happening and will be able to make decisions about the needs of consumers, services, and workers. In this unit you will be learning about the planning and management that is necessary for an agency to deliver services effectively and efficiently.

Communication is a basic need in keeping an agency operating smoothly and efficiently. You are participating in the communication process when you collect information about consumers and keep records of their progress for supervisors and other workers to use in delivering services that will meet consumer needs. When you are giving and receiving supervision, you are making sure that work gets done and that workers have everything they need to perform their jobs. Such communication, whether it involves consumers or other workers, is one of the ways in which human services are managed.

In this unit, you will be developing your skills in collecting information, managing information, and supervising. The goal of this unit is to assist you in developing your knowledge of and skills in these work activities so you will be more effective at managing the services delivered to consumers. As you move through the chapters in this unit, remember that staff communication is the key to effective work in all these activities.

CHAPTER IX:
COLLECTING INFORMATION

INTRODUCTION

All human service workers have at least one main goal in their work with consumers —they want to gain an understanding of the consumer's problem and find out how they can best help the consumer. In their efforts to reach this goal, workers must collect information about the consumer. Information collecting occurs when a worker meets a consumer for the first time and learns about the problem, the factors that contributed to the problem, and the consumer's feelings about the problem. For example, if you are an intake worker in a welfare agency, you might be interested in finding out about the consumer's home life, family situation, and personal background. If you work on a hospital ward, you might be trying to find out what is bothering one of the patients or residents. If you work in a prison, you might be trying to determine if an inmate is eligible for a work-release program. No matter where you work in the human services, you will be collecting consumer information.

Information collecting also involves following up on consumers to see how they are doing, and finding out if their situations have changed. Information would be collected on questions such as the following: Is the consumer making any progress, or are things worse? Is the person functioning more comfortably, or is he or she giving out clues which say "Things aren't working—can't we try something else?" If the consumer needed employment, has the person found a job? If the person needed medical care, has he or she been to a doctor?

In this chapter you will be learning how you collect consumer information. In Lesson 1 you will learn about the interview, which is one of the basic tools used to collect consumer information. In Lesson 2 you will learn about the skills of observing and describing, and how to use them in updating consumer information. The overall objective of this chapter is to assist you in learning how to collect and update consumer information by interviewing, observing, and describing.

Turn to Lesson 1

LESSON 1: COLLECTING CONSUMER INFORMATION: AN INTRODUCTION TO INTERVIEWING

In this lesson you will learn about interviewing, which is one of the major tools we use in collecting preliminary consumer information. The goal of this lesson and the enabling activities that will help you reach this goal are presented below.

GOAL

Given a situation where you are meeting a consumer for the first time, you will be able to obtain specific information about the person and his or her problem by conducting an interview.

ENABLING ACTIVITIES

After completing this lesson, you will have done as follows:

1. Reviewed the definition of interviewing
2. Examined the main types of interviews
3. Identified the two main tasks of the interviewer
4. Examined the two parts of an interview with their definitions
5. Considered three rules to remember when starting an interview
6. Identified the four techniques used in interviewing and given a description of an interviewing situation
7. Identified six guidelines that are helpful for most interviews

**Turn to Frame 1
to begin this lesson**

WHAT IS INTERVIEWING?

All of us have either conducted an interview or have been interviewed. For example, when you go to a hospital, the admissions clerk interviews you to find out who you are and how you are going to pay your bill. When you apply for a job, someone interviews you to determine your qualifications. Similarly, when you meet a human service consumer for the first time, you may interview him to collect the information which will be needed to help him. While information collecting may simply mean filling out forms with the consumer or asking the same questions over and over again, in any human service setting, consumer information is very important. This means that human service workers have to develop their interviewing skills so that they can collect reliable information from the person seeking help.

Interviewing is more than just friendly, casual talking between two people. Interviewing is a *conversation* where the purpose is *to give and receive information* and where *one person takes responsibility for guiding and planning the content and direction.*

As the interviewer, your main tasks are guiding the interview and having a plan for conducting the interview. To keep the interview moving productively in a purposeful direction, you need to work with the consumer in establishing an understanding of the reason for the interview. In so doing, you help the consumer provide the information that is needed. To keep the interview moving, you also need to establish and maintain a good relationship with the consumer and motivate him or her to participate. In the rest of this lesson, you will be learning how you, as the interviewer, can accomplish these two tasks.

Go on to Frame 2

Check which of the following correctly completes the statement.

Interviewing is a special kind of conversation between two people where

___ 1. the purpose is giving and receiving information.
___ 2. the conversation is just friendly casual talking.
___ 3. one person is responsible for guiding and planning the interview.

Turn to Answer 1 to see how well you did

See if you can fill in the two main tasks of the interviewer in the sentence below.
When you are interviewing a consumer, your two main tasks are to _____ the interviewer and to have a _____ for conducting the interview.

Turn to Answer 3

Types of Interviews

Since the method of conducting an interview is influenced to a considerable extent by the type of interview, it is important to recognize the main types of interviews conducted in the human services. Generally speaking, there are two main types of
(Frame 4 Continued)

interviews: (1) the assessment or information-collecting interview, and (2) the therapeutic or feeling-centered interview.[1] The assessment interview is centered around the worker taking responsibility for seeking information from the consumer in order to meet the consumer's specific need as quickly as possible. In the therapeutic interview, however, the worker tries to help the consumer to acknowledge, explore, and deal with his feelings. The therapeutic interview is also characterized by the sharing of responsibility for the interview with the consumer. Most interviews involve a combination of these two types, but the primary emphasis of any given interview will usually be determined by the purpose. In other words, when the interview is directed primarily to obtaining information, it is an assessment interview; when it is directed primarily to the exploration of feelings, it is a therapeutic interview. As we have already indicated, this lesson will present methods and suggestions which are predominantly related to assessment interviews or the collection of information.

Continue with Frame 5

FRAME 5

Check the correct response.

The worker takes responsibility for directing the interview and meeting the client's specific needs in which type of interview?

A. Therapeutic
B. Assessment or information collecting
C. Research
D. Exploration

Turn to Answer 19

FRAME 6

The Two Parts of an Interview

Interviews generally have two main parts or stages, the *preparation* and the *contact* with the consumer. Even though these parts are not always easy to see in any particular interview, they are very important in understanding how an interview is structured. In the preparation stage, which takes place before the interview actually starts, you would prepare in a general way for all the interviewees you are going to see. This involves making sure you have all the information you need before you begin, such as any special forms or records. It also means making all the arrangements for setting up the interview, including writing appointment letters and making phone calls.

The second part of an interview, the contact, is when "the interviewer and the interviewee meet face to face and the flow of communication begins."[2] Once you and the consumer are face to face, there are three separate parts or stages of the actual interview, (1) beginning, (2) middle, and (3) ending.

In the beginning of the interview, you introduce yourself to the consumer; state the purpose of the interview; try to put the consumer at ease; and try to make sure the consumer understands the purpose of the interview so that he can give you the information you need with a minimum of difficulties.

---

[1] This distinction is taken from Robert W. North, Cathy E. Bennett, and Betsy S. Davis, *Freedom to Choose: A Training Manual for Human Service Personnel* (Gainesville, Fla.: Santa Fe Community College, June 1973).

[2] Alfred Kadushin, *The Social Work Interview* (New York: Columbia University Press, 1972), p. 130.

The second part of the contact phase, the middle or body of the interview, is where you are getting the information you need from the consumer and giving any information that is requested or needed. In the middle of the interview you are also helping the consumer stick to the purpose of the interview, and getting him back on track if he begins to wander.

The third part of the contact phase is the ending. As the interview draws to a close, you will be reviewing what has been discussed, repeating your understanding of the purpose, and summarizing what you both have accomplished.[3] You will also be explaining what will happen next. Will you interview the consumer again? Is there anything he needs to do?

Although the main parts of an interview (preparation and contact) and the three stages of contact (beginning, middle, and ending) are not always clearly apparent in an interview, they do help in understanding how an interview is structured. In addition, being aware of the parts and stages can help you determine how your interview progressed. For example, if in one interview you spent most of your time putting a consumer at ease and explaining your purpose, you would know that this interview had only reached the beginning stage. You would need to see the consumer again in order to move the interview to its middle and ending stages.

Go on to Frame 7

FRAME 7

Is the statement below true or false?

Preparation for an interview means making the necessary arrangements to set up the interview and introducing yourself to the consumer.

___ True

___ False

Turn to Answer 4

FRAME 8

Place a check mark beside each of the activities that are part of the beginning of an interview.

___ 1. Introducing yourself to the consumer

___ 2. Making an appointment to set up the interview

___ 3. Stating the purpose of the interview

___ 4. Trying to put the consumer at ease

Turn to Answer 2

FRAME 9

Match the three parts of the contact phase of an interview on the left with their definitions on the right.

A. Beginning

B. Middle

___ 1. Getting and giving information

___ 2. Getting acquainted with the consumer and stating the purpose of the interview

(Frame 9 continued)

[3] Rose C. Thomas, *Public Service Careers Program: Training Manual for Case Aide Trainees* (New York City Department of Social Services, March 1968), pp. 40–41.

C. Ending   __ 3. Reviewing what has been discussed and deciding what will be done next

Choose your answer from those listed below.

B, A, C

Turn to Answer 6

A, B, C

Turn to Answer 9

B, C, A

Turn to Answer 7

FRAME 10

TECHNIQUES OF INTERVIEWING

How to Begin an Interview

One of the first questions anyone asks when learning how to interview is "How do I begin?" Beginning an interview can be a very difficult situation, especially to someone with limited experience. Since the beginning is always crucial, particularly in a new situation, it is important to have some idea of the basic principles involved. There are three basic principles which experienced interviewers have found helpful when starting an interview.[4]

1. Give the consumer your full attention. If consumers are going to tell you what you need to know, they must be put at ease. If your thoughts and actions indicate that you are thinking about something else, you will not be able to give them your full attention and they may have a hard time telling you what you need to know.
2. Do not jump to any conclusions. Remember that people are individuals—they react differently to the same situations. Make sure you understand what the facts are.
3. When you do not understand something, ask for clarification. Do not hesitate to ask questions. You need to collect information, and it is important that both you and the consumer agree upon the facts. So when consumers say something which you do not understand, ask them about it.

Go on to Frame 11

FRAME 11

Check the three things that are helpful when you are starting an interview.

__ 1. Get the information you need as quickly as possible.

__ 2. Give the consumer your full attention.

__ 3. Be careful not to ask questions.

__ 4. Be careful not to jump to conclusions.

__ 5. Ask for clarification when something is not clear.

Turn to Answer 8

---

[4] Margaret Schubert, *Interviewing in Social Work Practice: An Introduction* (New York: Council on Social Work Education, 1971), p. 4.

We expect that some of you are probably thinking: "These principles are all very nice, but they still do not tell me how I begin an interview. What do I say? What if the consumer has difficulty getting started?" There are no absolute answers to these questions, so you should consider the following as suggestions. When you meet consumers for the first time, it is helpful if you can greet them by name and tell them your name. This shows you recognize them as individuals and symbolizes the giving of your full attention. You should also make sure consumers are comfortable by taking their coat, offering them a chair, and giving them a chance to get settled, thus showing your concern for their comfort. At the beginning of any interview you can also make general conversation such as "How are you?" and "How is it going?"—which says to the consumer "I see you, I greet you, I acknowledge you, I am friendly."[5]

What if consumers still have trouble getting started and do not seem to be responding to your efforts to make them feel at ease? This happens in any human service setting, and overcoming it means an extra effort on your part. For example, if you work in an institution such as a prison or a mental hospital, inmates or residents may show some resistance to being interviewed. If the interview makes them late for a meal, they may approach the interview in an irritated frame of mind. Or they may be unwilling to talk because they are afraid of what other residents or inmates will think of them. In these situations you need to help the consumers with whatever is bothering them by asking questions such as, "Can you tell me about it?" "What's on your mind?" or "How can I help you?" Since you really do not have the information you need, you should ask neutral questions to help the consumer get started.

Go on to Frame 13

Read the following passage from an interview and think about the worker's technique before answering the question below.[6]

Mr. Long: I don't know where to begin.
  Worker: Where do you want to begin?
Mr. Long: I don't know . . . Where shall I hang my coat?
  Worker: Where do you want to hang it?
Mr. Long: (Hangs coat over chair) Well, where should I sit?
  Worker: Does it make a difference to you?
Mr. Long: No.
  Worker: All right . . . now, why don't you tell me what's on your mind?
Mr. Long: Well, I just don't know where to begin . . .

Based on your understanding of the interview process, what would you say about this worker's approach to interviewing Mr. Long?

—— 1. The worker did a good job of making Mr. Long comfortable and helping him get started talking.

Turn to Answer 10

—— 2. The worker forgot to make sure Mr. Long was comfortable and at ease before trying to collect the information he needed.

Turn to Answer 11

---

[5] Alfred Kadushin, *The Social Work Interview* (New York: Columbia University Press, 1972), p. 130.

[6] Ibid. The passage is an adaptation.

Collecting the Needed Information

Once you have started your interview, and made sure the purpose of the interview is clear to the consumer so that there is agreement and understanding, you are ready to collect the needed information. But how do you do this?

Listening. A number of different techniques are used in the fact-finding interview, and one that is important in all interviews involves listening. Careful listening requires skill, and to do it well presents a challenge to any interviewer. What differentiates a person who is a good listener from one who isn't? "One who frequently interrupts to say what he would have done under similar circumstances is not a good listener, but neither is he who sits like a bump on a log."[7] Effective listening involves three specific skills—hearing, observing, and remembering:[8]

1. **Hearing accurately.** This means concentrating your attention on the consumer and what he or she is saying. It also means keeping alert throughout the interview and letting the consumer know that you have heard and understood what was said.

2. **Observing the consumer accurately.** There is more to effective listening than just "hearing" what the consumer is saying. You have to use your eyes and your ears; you have to listen to the consumer's tone of voice and observe his or her posture, where he or she looks, and what he or she is doing. Since observing is a critical skill in the collection of information, it is a major topic of study and is discussed separately in the second lesson of this chapter.

3. **Remembering what the consumer has said.** Skill in remembering the information you have received is very important in listening. The consumer must be shown by your responses that you are following what is being said and that you are not forgetting the information he or she is giving you.

Proceed to Frame 15

Read the following passage from an interview, then answer the question below.[9]

Mrs. Jones: My neighbors, the Smiths, have been very helpful these past few days.
 Worker: It's fortunate the Smiths live so close to you.
         (Ten minutes later)
Mrs. Jones: So I found out from the Smiths that Jim was being expelled from school for taking drugs.
 Worker: The Smiths?
Mrs. Jones: Yes, the Smiths, my neighbors . . . I just finished telling you about them.

Do you think the worker in this interview was listening effectively to Mrs. Jones?

Yes

Turn to Answer 12

No

Turn to Answer 14

[7] Annette Garrett, *Interviewing: Its Principles and Methods* (New York: Family Service Association of America, 1942).

[8] Raymond L. Gordon, *Interviewing: Strategy, Techniques, and Tactics* (Homewood, Ill.: Dorsey Press, 1969), p. 310.

[9] Passage adapted from Alfred Kadushin *The Social Work Interview* (New York: Columbia University Press, 1972).

FRAME 16

Questioning. A second technique in interviewing involves questioning in order to obtain and help the consumer give the needed information. If you are asking the consumer questions for reasons other than these, you should make sure you really need to be asking the questions. Questioning is a skill that is very often abused by interviewers. This is because interviewers sometimes find it difficult to ask clear and understandable questions, and to be quiet long enough to let the consumer answer. Four principles are important and should be remembered when you are asking questions in an interview:[10]

1. Questions need to be understandable and short enough so the consumer can remember what is being asked. Any question of more than two sentences is usually too long.
2. In general, questions that cannot be answered by a brief "yes" or "no" are to be preferred. Questions should be phrased in such a way that the consumer is stimulated to answer freely.
3. Ask one question at a time! Many times interviewers ask a question, and then before the consumer answers, they ask another question. This only confuses the consumer.
4. Try to emphasize "what" questions instead of "why" questions. Most people find it much easier to respond to a question asking "what," since it does not require them to analyze why they did something.

Turn to Frame 17

FRAME 17

Circle the important principles to remember when you are asking questions in an interview.

1. A good question should be understandable and short.
2. A good question should require the consumer to answer just "yes" or "no."
3. A good question will usually ask "what" not "why."
4. Good questions are asked one at a time.

Turn to Answer 15

FRAME 18

Let's see if you understand the technique of questioning. After each question below, circle "yes" if you think the question is a good one and "no" if you think it is a poor one.

1. "Are you managing better with your crutches, and how about your glasses, do they fit?"   Yes   No
2. "Why do you feel that way?"   Yes   No
3. "What scares you about the medical examination?"   Yes   No
4. "Do you have to miss work a lot?"   Yes   No
5. "Are you worried about applying for food stamps at the welfare department?"   Yes   No

Turn to Answer 13

[10] Ibid., pp. 147, 157–165.

FRAME 19

Guiding. A third technique used in interviewing is guiding the discussion. Throughout the interview, the discussion must be channeled in such a way that the consumer gives you the information you need. You may have to remind the consumer of the purpose of the interview if the discussion starts to ramble. It is a good idea to let consumers first tell you their story before you try to guide them toward giving specific information. You can guide the discussion in an interview by questioning, by making short comments that restate the purpose of the interview, and by following the printed intake or follow-up forms that are used in many agencies.

Go on to Frame 20

FRAME 20

Circle the statements that reflect the interviewer's ability to guide the discussion.

1. "We have almost completed the intake process—with just a few more questions . . ."
2. "Your comments are most helpful, but I need to ask you a few more questions . . ."
3. "Would you care for some coffee before we finish this part of your discharge process?"

Turn to Answer 5

FRAME 21

Keeping silent. A fourth technique used in interviewing involves knowing when to maintain silence. This might seem to be an odd technique in interviewing since interviewing is talking with a purpose. But it is important to understand the use of silence in an interview, and not to become alarmed or embarrassed by periods of silence. As the interviewer, you should be careful not to talk too much or you will overpower consumers and make them feel ill at ease. If consumers are silent at some time during the interview, they may be deep in thought, or they may be considering what to say next. If they do not break the silence themselves after a reasonable period of time, you might ask a pertinent question, for example: "You were telling me about your daughter. What did the school nurse say was the trouble?"

Go on to Frame 22

FRAME 22

Choose the answer that correctly completes the following sentence.

As the interviewer, you should use the technique of _____ to give the consumer a chance to compose his or her thoughts.

___ 1. talking

Turn to Answer 16

___ 2. guiding the discussion

Turn to Answer 17

___ 3. silence

Turn to Answer 18

FRAME 23

General Guidelines to Help You in Interviewing

It should be emphasized that no two interviews are exactly alike and that the way you conduct an interview depends on the particular consumer you are interviewing. Although there are no hard and fast rules you can follow in interviewing, it will be helpful if you remember the main points of this lesson and bear in mind some general guidelines for interviews in which you will be collecting information.

1. Avoid any show of haste or hurry. The atmosphere should be relaxed with no pressure.
2. Make sure you and the consumer both understand the purpose of the interview.
3. Be an effective listener.
4. Do not be embarrassed or anxious about periods of silence.
5. Ask questions that are clear and understandable.
6. Make sure you and the consumer both clearly understand and agree on the next steps that will be taken.

As a worker in the human services, your ability to interview, ask questions, listen to answers, and collect the information that is needed to deliver services will be your most useful and necessary skills.

Turn to Frame 24

FRAME 24

Circle the guidelines that are helpful to follow in most interviews.

1. Be an effective listener.
2. Try to avoid any periods of silence.
3. Ask questions that are clear and understandable.
4. Use as little time as possible.
5. Make sure the consumer understands your purpose.
6. Make sure you and the consumer are clear on what the next steps are.

Turn to Answer 20

ANSWERS TO LESSON 1

ANSWER 1

You should have checked 1 and 3. Interviewing is a special kind of conversation between two people where the purpose is giving and receiving information, and one person is responsible for guiding and planning the interview.

If you missed either answer, you should reread Frame 1 before you go on to Frame 3.

ANSWER 2

You should have checked 1, 3, and 4. The interview begins when you introduce yourself to the consumer, state the purpose of the interview, and try to put the consumer at ease. These distinctions should not be viewed as fixed in a certain order in actual practice. Each interview is a unique situation, and, therefore, different activities occur at different stages. The only way to understand interviewing fully is practical experience. With this caution in mind, proceed to Frame 9.

ANSWER 3

When you are interviewing a consumer, your two main tasks are guiding the interview and having a plan in carrying on the conversation.

Go on to Frame 4.

ANSWER 4

You should have checked *false*, because preparation takes place before you actually meet the consumer. Preparation means making sure you have all the information you need before you begin and making any necessary arrangements to set up the interview. This may appear to be an insignificant point; however, if you want to understand the process of the interview, it is important to begin with a basic understanding of these distinctions. Continue now with Frame 8.

ANSWER 5

You should have circled all three of the statements as reflecting the interviewer's ability to guide the discussion. If you did not circle all of them, you may want to review Frame 19 before proceeding to Frame 21. If you answered correctly, proceed directly to Frame 21.

ANSWER 6

Right! You've done a good job of defining the three parts of the contact phase of an interview.

Middle: getting and giving information
Beginning: getting acquainted with the consumer and stating the purpose of the interview
Ending: reviewing what has been discussed and deciding what will be done next

Go on to Frame 10.

ANSWER 7

No, you've confused the middle of the interview with the ending of the interview. Go back to Frame 9 and try it again.

ANSWER 8

If you checked 2, 4, and 5, you are 100 percent correct. If you missed any, you should review Frame 10 before you continue. Before you continue with Frame 12, see if you can think of some additional principles you may have found helpful in beginning an interview. Or perhaps you disagree with the rules just mentioned. This might be a good topic to discuss with other workers or students.

ANSWER 9

Sorry, but you have confused the beginning of the interview with the middle of the interview. Go back to Frame 9 and try it again.

ANSWER 10

Sorry, but in our opinion this worker has *not* done a very good job of making Mr. Long comfortable and getting the interview started. Mr. Long should not have to ask where he should hang his coat. Mr. Long feels very ill at ease and is having a hard time getting started because the worker has not made an effort to help him feel at ease.
Go on to Frame 14 to learn some techniques to use in interviewing.

ANSWER 11

We agree. This worker has forgotten to make sure Mr. Long is comfortable and relaxed before he tries to get the information he needs.
Go on to Frame 14 to examine some techniques to use in interviewing.

ANSWER 12

Sorry, but this worker was *not* listening effectively to Mrs. Jones. You may want to review Frame 14 before you continue to Frame 16.

ANSWER 13

You should have answered as follows:

1. No. ("Are you managing better with your crutches, and how about your glasses, do they fit?")

    Reason: This is asking two questions at one time.

2. No. ("Why do you feel that way?")

Reason: We usually try to avoid "why" questions in information collecting interviews.

3. Yes. ("What scares you about the medical examination?")

Reason: Questions asking "what" are usually easier for most consumers to answer.

4. No. ("Do you have to miss work a lot?")

Reason: Most consumers would just answer "yes" or "no" to this question. Something like, "Tell me about how often you have to stay home from work" would be better.

5. Yes. ("Are you worried about applying for food stamps at the Welfare Department?")

Reason: This question is clear and understandable, and most consumers would have no trouble answering it.

If you got at least four answers right, you are doing very well. Go on to Frame 19. If you missed two or more, review Frame 16 before you go on to Frame 19.

ANSWER 14

Good choice. This worker was *not* listening effectively to Mrs. Jones.
Go right on to Frame 16.

ANSWER 15

You should have circled the following:

1: A good question should be understandable and short.
3: A good question will usually ask "what" not "why."
4: Good questions are asked one at a time.

Go on to Frame 18.

ANSWER 16

No, talking is not the right answer here. Return to Frame 22 and try it again.

ANSWER 17

Sorry, but guiding the discussion is not the technique we're looking for here. Return to Frame 22 and try it again.

ANSWER 18

Right! Silence is the interviewing technique to use to give the consumer a chance to think.
Go on to Frame 23.

ANSWER 19

The correct answer is B, the interview for assessment or information collecting. If you are interested in learning more about various kinds of interviews, you should consult some of the sources listed at the end of this chapter. Interviewing may appear to be simple when it is described and divided into parts; however, the skills required for effective interviewing are actually difficult to master. Extensive practice, coupled with knowledge of the principles of interviewing, is critical to success.

Turn to Frame 6.

ANSWER 20

You should have circled the following:

1: Be an effective listener.
3: Ask questions that are clear and understandable.
5: Make sure the consumer understands your purpose.
6: Make sure you and the consumer are clear on what the next steps are.

If you missed any answers, you need to review Frame 23.

You have now completed Lesson 1. Go on to Lesson 2, and keep up the good work!

LESSON 2:
UPDATING CONSUMER INFORMATION THROUGH OBSERVATION AND DESCRIPTION

Once you have completed an assessment interview, it is extremely important to follow up and determine how the consumer is progressing and if the situation has changed. In this lesson you will learn about some additional skills used in the process of collecting and updating consumer information. The goal of this lesson and the enabling activities that will help you reach this goal are presented below.

GOAL

Given a situation requiring the updating or evaluating of a consumer's situation, you will be able to select appropriate observation methods and describe the clues you should mentally catalogue.

ENABLING ACTIVITIES

After completing this lesson, you will have done the following:

1. Reviewed three questions regarding all observations
2. Examined several factors which influence accurate observations
3. Identified four observation procedures
4. Distinguished between verbal and nonverbal communications
5. Considered the four items needed in the description process
6. Examined some guidelines to remember in updating consumer information

Turn to Frame 1

FRAME 1

OBSERVING[1]

The primary goal of collecting and updating consumer information is to determine additional unmet needs of consumers. In the human services observation and description are two important skills necessary to achieve this goal, and they require an ability to watch, listen, and objectively utilize the information you are collecting and updating.

(Frame 1 continued)

[1] Eveline D. Schulman, *Intervention in Human Services* (St. Louis: Mosby, 1974), pp. 12–37. The discussion of observation in this and following frames is adapted, unless otherwise noted.

In human service work, a large amount of information passes between consumers and workers. Observation can be defined as the act of obtaining or collecting information through one's senses. (The five senses are seeing, hearing, touching, tasting, and smelling.) As you refine your observation skills, it is important to be able to answer three questions with regard to the information you are collecting:

1. What is it for? In order to answer this question, it is necessary to determine the purpose of your observation and the objectives you are seeking to accomplish.
2. How will you get it? Depending on the purpose of the observation, the observer must decide on the procedures and techniques to be used in gathering the facts.
3. What can I find out? The basic ingredient of the observation process is a detective-like observer who will search to make sure the necessary clues and facts are obtained and reported accuratey and objectively.

The factors that influence the accuracy of observations generally are physical and psychoecological. Physical factors relate to the sharpness of one's senses. For example, changes in voice tones may be lost if the observer has a slight hearing loss. Psychoecological factors relate to all the people, things, and physical surroundings affecting an individual's behavior. For example, the situation and location of the observation, the cultural background of the individual being observed, and the individual characteristics of the observer all may affect the thoroughness and objectivity of observations.

Proceed to Frame 2

FRAME 2

Check the best answer to the following question.

In carrying out the process of observation, what must the observer determine?

___ A. Purpose, procedures, facts, and clues

Turn to Answer 1

___ B. Procedures, techniques, and facts

Turn to Answer 2

___ C. Goals, facts, clues, and interpretations

Turn to Answer 3

___ D. Goals, techniques, and purpose

Turn to Answer 4

FRAME 3

Which of the following factors can interfere with accurate observation? Check all the appropriate responses.

___ A. The way the observer feels physically

___ B. The weather

___ C. The ethnic background of the observer or the observed

___ D. How well a person can see, hear, and attend to what is happening

___ E. Prejudice or bias against certain religious groups

Turn to Answer 5

General Observational Procedures

There are at least four general observational procedures which are commonly used in the human services to gather and update consumer information.

1. **Using secondary sources.** Secondary sources include records and reports about the consumer, and comments made by others who have been in contact with the consumer. Using secondary sources is a way of observing the consumer indirectly. This procedure can provide information such as an identification of the consumer's problem as presented and described when he first came to your agency's attention; an indication of the original service plans that were made by your agency; and a summary of the actions taken to date to assist the consumer.

2. **Spectator observation.** As a spectator, the observer tries to position himself outside the focus of attention of the observed person, for example, by sitting beyond the immediate visual range of the observed person or by talking with someone else out of the immediate hearing range of the observed person. In spectator observation, the observer usually attempts to minimize the effect of his presence on the observed person.

3. **Participant observation.** In this procedure, the observer actively participates in the treatment or rehabilitation of the observed person, while mentally noting what the observed persons says and does and his interaction with other people and things in the setting.

4. **Interviews.** In Lesson 1, we discussed the interview as a means of collecting consumer information. Obviously, observation is a critical element in any interview. In fact, Kadushin has suggested that "one can observe without interviewing, but one cannot interview without observing."[2] Thus the interview may be used both to collect and to update consumer information.

When you are engaged in the process of observation to update consumer information using any of these general procedures, it is important to determine (1) whether there is any new information which your agency needs to know in order to help the consumer more effectively and (2) whether the consumer is functioning better or worse than noted earlier.

Turn to Frame 5

Match the observational procedures on the left with the appropriate examples on the right.

___1. Using secondary sources
___2. Interviewing
___3. Spectator observation
___4. Participant observation

A. The observer reads a story to the observed person, noting what the observed person is doing.
B. The observer consults records and reports about the observed person to obtain background information.
C. The observer tries to place himself outside the immediate focus of attention of the observed person.
D. The observer conducts and directs a purposeful conversation with the observed person.

Turn to Answer 6

[2] Alfred Kadushin, *The Social Work Interview* (New York: Columbia University Press, 1972), p. 45.

Verbal and Nonverbal Clues

Since observation is the act of collecting consumer information through one's senses, it follows that the effective observer must attend to the many communication channels. Communications are received through the eyes (visual), ears (auditory), nose (olfactory), and through observing body movements (arms and legs). Messages that are sent through communication channels are usually divided into categories of verbal and nonverbal clues.

Verbal clues can tell the observer a great deal about the observed person. The *choice of words* may suggest a person's ethnic group, religious background and affiliations, geographical origins, and feelings about oneself and others. In addition, other vocal sounds uttered at the same time as the words serve to modify and emphasize the message. For example, *pronunciation* may be clear or slurred; *rate of speech* may be slow, rapid, or jerky; *voice tone* may be clear or accompanied by breaks, trembles, or chokes; and *breathing* may be deep, rapid, or even. Sighs, laughs and all other vocal characteristics send messages you should note when you are observing.

In human service work, a great deal of information which passes between consumers and workers is never put into words. It is this information, which we call *nonverbal* clues, that gives you another indication of how a consumer is progressing. The way consumers stand, use their hands, move their eyes, and make facial expressions, are all nonverbal clues which suggest additional responses to a situation. While the meaning of any nonverbal clue is dependent on the time, the place, and the person, it is still important to be familiar with the way such information is communicated.

Observing what people look like, what they do and how they do it will uncover nonverbal clues that tell you about the person. Visual signals include *body language* (posture, body movement, position of arms and legs, gestures, and the distance a person keeps between himself and someone else); *facial language* (frowning, smiling, blinking, staring, and similar expressions of ideas and feelings); and *material things* (clothing, hairstyles, makeup, home furnishings, etc.).

In addition to picking up clues about the consumer, you will also be sending out your own nonverbal signals. It is important to be aware of your own nonverbal signals in order to be sure you are communicating the message you intend and also so that you can note how the consumer reacts to these signals. Your *clothing* may be a nonverbal clue. If it is very different from the clothing of other workers, for example, it may be confusing to the consumer. Maintaining *eye contact* with the consumer is important if you are to communicate your interest. If you look away or never smile, you may be communicating coldness. And yet in some cultures, the absence of consumer eye contact with the worker may be a sign of respect. Head nodding, smiles, and body movements toward rather than away from the individual offer encouragement and support and emphasize verbal messages such as "go on" and "yes, I understand." Finally, you send nonverbal messages through the *setting*—the seating arrangement, for example. The removal of barriers, such as a desk between you and the individual, will usually encourage open interaction and will also allow you to observe all the nonverbal clues.

Go on to Frame 7

Read the following conversation between a worker and a consumer, and then answer the question below.

Worker: Would you tell me what you can about any difficulties you have had in finding a job since you were released?

John: Well, I followed your suggestion and went to the state employment office. They were pretty nice, and I expect to be hearing from them soon.

Worker: Good—that's encouraging. (Nods head in a "yes" motion while smiling.)

This worker is using which type of nonverbal signal?

1. Eye contact

Turn to Answer 7

3. Facial language

Turn to Answer 8

3. Material things

Turn to Answer 9

DESCRIBING

How does one organize nonverbal clues and other information gained from observing a consumer? Information such as clues about a person's level of functioning need to be transferred from your memory to a written description. The process of describing involves a mental summing up of all that has been learned about a consumer through direct contact.[3] In the human services, describing is the step that is taken before further decisions are made regarding consumer problems and how they can be resolved. To be skillful in describing, you have to (1) make an effort to review mentally each bit of information you have received from or about the individual, (2) match these clues against previous information, and (3) sum up the problems. The key to the skill of describing is to detect clues during your observation that can be written down at a later time. This is a mental and not a verbal process. You will be making mental notes. You will not be telling the consumer, for example, "I see you are frowning, and that is a nonverbal clue that tells me you are angry."

There are four considerations which are basic to mentally noting clues or pieces of information about consumers.

1. **Individuality.** Make sure you understand what the consumer is saying both verbally and nonverbally. It is very difficult to make definitive rules that will tell you in advance what different verbal and nonverbal signals mean. This is because consumers are individuals. People may use words and gestures differently in communicating. Before you mentally catalogue any clues, make sure you understand what they mean to that individual consumer. In addition, if consumers are from a culture that is different from yours, you should remember that they may intend a different message from the one you think their actions are communicating.

(Frame 8 continued)

[3] Alice H. Collins, *The Human Services: An Introduction* (New York: Odyssey Press, 1973).

2. **Frequency.** You need to consider how often the clue occurs. If people are rigid and tense for only a single fleeting instant, you can not automatically assume that they are anxious or nervous. However, if they send this signal repeatedly throughout your contact with them, you would probably then have a basis for making a mental note of this as a clue to understanding the consumer's behavior.

3. **Quality and context.** You should consider the way in which you got the clue. Was it done in a hesitant manner or was it done in a deliberate and open manner? Was the consumer in a crisis situation? Was he or she at home? Was he or she on a ward?

4. **Past behavior.** You need to have some understanding of the way the consumer acted in the first contact with you or your agency. If you do not know how the consumers talked and acted during the first contact, you may have a hard time figuring out what clues the person is sending you. For example, suppose an individual spoke loudly and quickly when first coming to your agency and was, therefore, thought to be very angry. Knowing this, you now observe this individual and note that while the person is still talking loudly and quickly, he or she is also smiling and sitting in a very relaxed position. At this point you might mentally make a note that although this individual is someone who has a tendency to talk loudly and quickly, this does not necessarily indicate anger.

Go on to Frame 9

FRAME 9

Two guidelines you need to consider before you describe or make a mental note of a clue are written below. Can you name two or more guidelines which you should remember? If you have any trouble doing this, review Frame 8 and then try this frame again.

1. Make sure you understand what the consumer is saying both verbally and non-verbally.
2. Consider how often the clue occurs.
3.
4.

Turn to Answer 10

FRAME 10

Read the following passage, and then answer the question below.

Margaret was a psychiatric technician in a state mental hospital. One day, Allen, a patient who had made remarkable progress and who was about to be released, became involved in a noisy and violent fight with one of the attendants on the ward. Margaret and several other technicians heard what was happening and stepped in to break it up. Afterwards, the other technicians wanted to fill out a report on Allen's behavior and felt the report should state that Allen might not really be ready to be released. Margaret, having had considerable contact with Allen during his stay at the hospital, was sure that there was some reason for his unusual behavior. She persuaded the other technicians to help her explore the reasons for Allen's behavior before they filled out any reports.

Check which of the following things Margaret considered before she decided to take the step of describing Allen's behavior.

___ 1. She wanted to consider what Allen was saying both verbally and nonverbally.

Turn to Answer 11

___ 2. She considered how often this clue had occurred.

Turn to Answer 12

___ 3. She considered the way in which she had received the clue.

Turn to Answer 13

___ 4. She considered her prior knowledge of Allen during his stay at the hospital.

Turn to Answer 14

___ 5. She considered all of the above.

Turn to Answer 15

FRAME 11

GUIDELINES TO REMEMBER IN UPDATING CONSUMER INFORMATION

You have learned that the two primary skills in updating consumer information are observing and describing and that time and effort are needed to review what you have seen and heard in order to compare new information and past information. In other words, once you have gathered information through direct observation and interaction with a consumer, and also indirectly from other sources, you begin the process of describing the observed person's behavior.[4]

In general, you should remember four important guidelines in updating consumer information:

1. Try to observe a broad range of verbal and nonverbal activity, look for behavior that differs from earlier behavior, and watch for situations where the consumer may be saying one thing verbally and something else nonverbally.
2. Be alert for changes in the consumer's own behavior and nonverbal activity, rather than only being aware of how his behavior is different from someone else's.
3. Always describe your clues in the context of the whole situation—what the consumer says, how he says it, what nonverbal clues were observed, and the situation in which you are contacting the consumer.
4. Finally, make sure you gather sufficient facts to support your observations.

Continue to Frame 12

FRAME 12

Circle whichever guidelines would be useful in updating consumer information.

1. Look for verbal and nonverbal behavior that do not go together.
2. Try to observe a limited range of verbal and nonverbal activity.
3. Focus your observations on comparing how the consumer differs from someone else.
4. Always interpret your clues in the context of the whole situation.
5. Observe a broad range of verbal and nonverbal activity, and be alert for any changes.

Turn to Answer 16

---

[4] Eveline D. Schulman, *Intervention in Human Services* (St. Louis: Mosby, 1974), p. 19.

ANSWERS TO LESSON 2

ANSWER 1

This is the best response. Proceed to Frame 3.

ANSWER 2

No, there is a more complete answer contained in Frame 2. If you feel you need a review, return to Frame 1 before you return to Frame 2.

ANSWER 3

Sorry, but you have overlooked an important aspect of the observation process. Review Frame 1 before you answer Frame 2 correctly.

ANSWER 4

No, you've overlooked the complete answer. Return to Frame 2 and try again.

ANSWER 5

All the factors listed in Frame 3 (A, B, C, D, and E) can interfere with accurate and objective observations. Continue to Frame 4.

ANSWER 6

The correct answers for 1, 2, 3, 4 are B, D, C, A.
    If you missed any, review Frame 4. Otherwise, proceed to Frame 6.

ANSWER 7

No, there is a better answer to this question. Return to Frame 7 and try again.

ANSWER 8

Right you are! By nodding his head in a yes motion and smiling while at the same time saying "Good—that's encouraging," this worker is using facial language to make sure his nonverbal signals correspond with his verbal message.
    You're doing a great job! Turn to Frame 8.

ANSWER 9

Sorry, but this response is incorrect. A review of Frame 6 is in order before continuing.

ANSWER 10

Two additional guidelines are to consider the quality of the clue and the way in which you got it, and to have some understanding of the way the consumer acted when he first came in contact with you or your agency.

Turn to Frame 10.

ANSWER 11

This is partially correct, but Margaret considered more than just what Allen was saying both verbally and nonverbally.

Return to Frame 10 and check the best answer.

ANSWER 12

Yes, you are partially correct in saying that Margaret was considering how often Allen has behaved this way. But don't you think Margaret was also considering other things in making her decision to explore the reasons for Allen's behavior?

Return to Frame 10, and try it again.

ANSWER 13

While you are correct in stating that Margaret was carefully considering the way in which she received the clue, you are overlooking some other things that helped Margaret decide to explore Allen's behavior further before drawing any conclusions.

Return to Frame 10, and try it again.

ANSWER 14

Yes, Margaret was using her prior knowledge of Allen's behavior to decide that in this instance the reasons for his outburst needed to be explored. But was this the *only* thing Margaret was considering? We don't think so. Return to Frame 10, and try it again.

ANSWER 15

We think this is the best response here. Margaret considered all these factors in deciding that the reasons for Allen's behavior should be explored before any conclusions were drawn.

Proceed to Frame 11 to learn about four guidelines to remember in updating consumer information.

ANSWER 16

You should have circled 1, 4, and 5 as the guidelines which are helpful to remember in updating consumer information.

If you had any trouble recognizing these guidelines, return to Frame 11 for a review.

You have now reached the end of Lesson 2, which is also the end of chapter IX. If you think you are ready, turn to the summary and review questions at the end of this chapter to see how well you have learned the skills required for information collecting.

SUMMARY

In this chapter, special attention was given to the process of collecting consumer information. Lesson 1 presented some of the important issues and skills related to interviewing and focused on the assessment interview, which is characterized by the worker taking responsibility for seeking information from the consumer in order to meet the consumer's needs as quickly as possible. The interview process was described in two main parts, the preparation and the actual contact. The contact phase of the interview was further defined as having a beginning, middle, and ending. Four general techniques utilized in the assessment interview were also discussed—listening, questioning, guiding the discussion, and silence. Finally, it was suggested that in any interviewing situation, it is important to give the consumer your full attention, to ask for clarification when things are not clear, and to make sure both you and the consumer have a clear understanding of the purpose of the interview.

The second phase of the information collection process was discussed in Lesson 2 in terms of updating consumer information. Observation and description were presented as the two major skills utilized in this process. Observation, which is the act of obtaining information through one's senses, is most effective when you are able to identify the purpose, procedures, facts, and clues for each situation. Physical and psychoecological factors influence the accuracy of these observations, so it is important to recognize when these factors are interfering with an acurate observation. Emphasis was also given to some general observational procedures—using secondary sources (such as records and reports), spectator observation, participant observation and interviewing.

Since the information collection process is basically a communication system, special attention was also directed to recognizing the differences between verbal and nonverbal communications. In addition to noting the verbal and nonverbal clues being transmitted, we also indicated the importance of determining whether *what* consumers say agrees with *how* they say it. Finally, the skill of describing was presented as a process that involves mentally summing up all that has been learned about a given consumer. Thus, the process of collecting consumer information entails gathering information through observation and interaction, and also updating information to develop a comprehensive description of the consumer's situation.

SUGGESTIONS FOR FURTHER STUDY

This chapter has served only as a brief introduction to the information collection process in the human services. With regard to interviewing, there are a number of additional areas which will require further study if the worker is to achieve a comprehensive understanding. First, your efforts should include an investigation of the different types of interviews—we discussed two major types, but there are others. Second, further study of the various techniques utilized in interviewing (e.g., probing and using special kinds of questions) is essential to effective interviewing. Third, you should be concerned with expanding your knowledge and skills in the areas of verbal and nonverbal communication. There is a growing body of literature relating to body language, body motion, and developing appropriate kinds of communication skills, which should be useful in this process.

Expanding your knowledge of information collecting should also include attention to the processes of observation and description. The next step after collecting and updating information involves testing your conclusions in order to determine whether or not there are enough observational facts to support them. This testing procedure was not discussed in this chapter, but it is important for you to become familiar with it. In this regard, the text by Eveline D. Schulman, listed in the bibliography, should be useful. Finally, attention to expanding your knowledge of cultures other than your own will improve your effectiveness in communicating with consumers.

SUGGESTIONS FOR FURTHER READING

Birdwhistell, R. L. *Kinesics and Context: Essays on Body Motion.* University of Philadelphia Press, 1970.

Benjamin, Alfred. *The Helping Interview.* Boston: Houghton Mifflin, 1969.

Collins, Alice H. *The Human Services: An Introduction.* New York: Odyssey Press, 1973.

Fenlason, Anne F. *Essentials In Interviewing.* New York: Harper & Row, 1952.

Garrett, Annette. *Interviewing: Its Principles and Methods.* New York: Family Service Association of America, 1942.

Gordon, Raymond L. *Interviewing: Strategy, Techniques, and Tactics.* Homewood, Ill.: Dorsey Press, 1969.

Hinde, R. A. *Nonverbal Communication.* London: Cambridge University Press, 1972.

Kadushin, Alfred. *The Social Work Interview.* New York: Columbia University Press, 1972.

Kahn, Robert L., and Cannell, Charles F. *The Dynamics of Interviewing.* New York: Wiley, 1957.

North, Robert W., Bennett, Cathy E., and Davis, Betsy S. *Freedom to Choose: A Training Manual for Human Service Personnel.* Gainesville, Fla.: Sante Fe Community College, June, 1973.

Richardson, Stephen. *Interviewing: Its Form and Function.* New York: Basic Books, 1965.

Rosenberg, Janet. *Breakfast: Two Jars of Paste.* Cleveland: Case Western Reserve University Press, 1972.

Schubert, Margaret. *Interviewing in Social Work Practice: An Introduction.* New York: Council on Social Work Education, 1971.

Schulman, Eveline D. *Intervention for Human Services.* St. Louis: Mosby, 1974.

Spiegel, John P., and Machotka, Pavel. *Messages of the Body.* New York: Free Press, 1974.

Thomas, Rose C. *Public Service Careers Program: Training Manual for Case Aide Trainees.* City of New York Department of Social Services, March, 1968.

Wicks, Robert J., and Josephs, Ernest H., Jr. *Techniques in Interviewing for Law Enforcement and Corrections Personnel: A Programmed Text.* Springfield, Ill.: Thomas, 1972.

REVIEW QUESTIONS—CHAPTER IX

Circle the letter corresponding to the answer of your choice.

1. Which of the following is a definition of interviewing?
    A. A way of collecting consumer information
    B. Friendly casual talking between two or more people
    C. Purposeful conversation between two or more people, with one person taking responsibility for guiding and planning
    D. A short interaction between two people

2. The two main tasks of the interviewer are _____ the interview and having a _____ for carrying on the conversation.
   Choose one of the following to fill in the blanks in the above statement.
   A. preparing, greeting
   B. guiding, plan
   C. arranging, technique

3. Once you and the consumer meet face to face, the actual interview begins. Which of the following would be important to do in the beginning phase of any interview?
   A. Introduce yourself to the consumer.
   B. Try to put the consumer at ease.
   C. State the purpose of the interview.
   D. A and B.
   E. A, B, and C.

4. Which activity is important at the end of an interview?
   A. Making general conversation to put the consumer at ease
   B. Mentioning the consumer's name
   C. Reviewing what has been discussed and explaining what will happen next
   D. Exploring the consumer's problem more fully

5. Suppose you are a worker in a community mental health center and you are interviewing Fred, who is making his first visit to the center. During the interview, Fred says, "My wife left me last week (pause). . . . She said she didn't like the climate here." If Fred then lapses into a period of silence, what should you do?
   A. Immediately ask him, "Where did your wife go?"
   B. Maintain silence for awhile, hoping to give Fred a chance to think about what he wants to say.
   C. Say, "Listen Fred, I've got another interview scheduled in five minutes, so it would be helpful if you could tell me exactly why you've come here."

6. Which of the following questions would be good to ask in information-collecting interviews?
   A. "Could you tell me the results of your interview and how you handled it?"
   B. "I don't know much about you—why do you feel so depressed?"
   C. "Could you tell me something about what kinds of activities you are interested in?"
   D. A, B, and C above.

7. A good interviewer makes a conscious effort to *guide* the interview so that he or she will be able to collect the information needed. Which of the following would be considered guiding the discussion in an interview?
   A. "Your comments have been very helpful, but what else can you add about your daughter's difficulties in school?"
   B. "Now that we have identified your weekly expenses, would you tell me something about your family's medical expenses?"
   C. "We have almost completed your social history, except for two more questions related to your work experience."
   D. A, B, and C.
   E. None of the above.

8. Which of the following are important skills to use in updating consumer information?
    A. Writing and questioning
    B. Referral and follow-up
    C. Observing and describing
    D. Planning and advocating

9. Clothing, facial expressions, posture, and seating arrangements are all examples of _____ which can be observed or utilized in updating consumer information.
    A. Secondary sources
    B. Feelings
    C. Nonverbal signals
    D. Verbal signals

10. Which of the following would be helpful in most information collecting interviews?
    A. Avoid any period of silence.
    B. Give the consumer your full attention.
    C. Make sure you and the consumer agree on what the next steps are.
    D. Ask as many questions as possible.
    E. B and C.

11. _____ involves a mental summing up of all that has been learned about a consumer from direct contact.
    A. Describing
    B. Observing
    C. Communicating
    D. Interviewing

12. Before you take the step of describing in updating consumer information, what must you do?
    A. Make sure you understand what the consumer is saying both verbally and nonverbally.
    B. Consider how often the nonverbal clues have occurred.
    C. Consider the way you got the clue.
    D. Use your knowledge of the consumer's past history.
    E. All of the above.

13. Which of the following would be important when you are updating consumer information?
    A. Try to observe a limited range of verbal and nonverbal activity.
    B. Always interpret clues in the context of the consumer's whole situation.
    C. Focus your observations on how an individual consumer differs from other consumers.
    D. Describe a consumer's situation as quickly as possible.

14. Which of the following factors influence the accuracy of observations?
    A. Physical factors and psychoecological factors
    B. The cultural background of the observer
    C. The setting in which the observation takes place
    D. A and C
    E. A, B, and C

15. Which of the following best describes the observational procedure in which the observer minimizes the effect of his presence on the observed person?
    A. Participant observation
    B. Spectator observation
    C. Interviewing
    D. Counseling

16. Which of the following are appropriate observational procedures?
    A. Using reports, records, and interviews
    B. Talking with someone else while observing a consumer
    C. Organizing a self-help group
    D. A and B
    E. A, B, and C

17. Which of the following is *not* correct?
    A. Verbal clues include facial expressions, rate of speech, and choice of words.
    B. Nonverbal clues include body language, objects, and the setting.
    C. The meaning of a nonverbal clue is almost entirely dependent upon the person sending it.
    D. Verbal clues include voice tone, breathing, and pronunciation.

18. When using the skill of observing in updating consumer information, it is important to strive for harmony between your own nonverbal and verbal clues.
    A. True
    B. False

Now check your answers with the Answer key at the end of the book

CHAPTER X:
MANAGING INFORMATION

INTRODUCTION

Collecting and updating consumer information is one part of the information process in the human services. However, if this information is not documented and shared with other workers, the chances of providing adequate services are substantially decreased. Managing information is the activity which provides the means for organizing, handling, and sharing consumer and other agency-related information.

In this chapter you will learn about managing information through the skills of recording and reporting. Since all human service agencies require that some kind of record be maintained on each consumer, the first lesson will address methods of efficient recording. The second lesson will discuss how oral and written reports are prepared for other workers and for administrators to assist them in making decisions about consumers, services, and worker needs. The third lesson is concerned with the case conference, which is a special kind of meeting where workers use recording and reporting skills to share information on consumer-related problems. The overall objective of this chapter is to assist you in learning how to manage information using the skills of recording and reporting.

Turn to Lesson 1

LESSON 1: RECORDING SKILLS

All human service agencies require that some kind of written records be kept on each consumer. In this lesson you will learn why records are kept and you will be given some guidelines to follow in writing information in these records. The major goal of this lesson and its enabling activities are as follows.

GOAL

Using information you have collected or been given about a human service consumer, you will be able to demonstrate your recording skills by writing the relevant and necessary information in the record.

ENABLING ACTIVITIES

After completing this lesson, you will have done as follows:

1. Identified four reasons for keeping agency records
2. Reviewed seven items that are included in the records of most human service agencies
3. Examined five important items to include in your log regarding a consumer
4. Considered guidelines for keeping your own notes on a consumer
5. Identified six helpful hints for good recording
6. Considered what is meant by "being honest" in recording

Turn to Frame 1

FRAME 1

WHY KEEP AGENCY RECORDS?

There is a certain amount of variation among agencies regarding the kinds of records and the amount of detail required. Nevertheless, the same general reasons for keeping records apply to all human service agencies.

1. The record provides agency management with a *permanent, documented account of services* that have been given to an individual consumer. It shows what happened from the time the individual first came to the attention of the agency up to the present time.
2. The record tells other workers who may be involved with the consumer *what has already been done* to date and what is in progress.
3. The information in the record is needed to *plan what will happen next.* Since supervisors and other workers do not always meet with the same individual consumers, they use records to learn about the consumer and to plan services and treatment.
4. The record helps workers *organize their thinking* about a consumer, decide if they need any additional information, and evaluate their consumer-related activities.

Go on to Frame 2

FRAME 2

For what reason do human service agencies usually require records to be kept on all consumers?

A. To inform workers in other agencies about services being provided to a consumer by the agency

Turn to Answer 3

B. To help workers evaluate their progress with consumers

Turn to Answer 8

C. To provide data on which to base budget requests

Turn to Answer 1

D. For reasons given in A, B, and C above

Turn to Answer 10

FRAME 3

Agency records are permanent documented accounts of services provided to consumers. They are used by agency personnel to identify and provide the most helpful services to each consumer. How do records fulfill this function? Check those that apply.

___ A. By helping workers to evaluate the progress made by a consumer

___ B. By identifying areas which need additional information

___ C. By helping workers to develop service and treatment plans

___ D. By reaching out to consumers who need help

Turn to Answer 5

FRAME 4

If you can think of any reasons for *not* keeping agency records, list them in the space below, and then turn to Answer 6.

FRAME 5

WHAT ARE THE COMPONENTS OF MOST AGENCY RECORDS?

The records you would keep on a ward if you were working in a mental hospital would obviously be a little different from the records you would keep if you were working in a prison or a welfare department. However, in both situations your records would include some of the same basic items.

Since you have probably had some experience with agency or other types of records, mention below two components of all such records, and then turn to Answer 2.

1.

2.

FRAME 6

Seven major items are included in most agency records.

1. The date of the activity
2. The identifying information about the consumer, such as name, age, address, sex
3. The purpose of the activity (e.g., reason for interview) and a short statement of the major problem as identified by the consumer and clarified by the worker
4. Important facts surrounding the problem
5. How the problem was handled and why it was handled that way
6. What follow-up activities, if any, are being planned
7. Comments and questions to discuss with a supervisor or another worker

**After studying these seven
items, go on to Frame 7**

FRAME 7

Suppose you saw a consumer for the first time and entered the following information in the case record: the *date* you saw this person, his *name*, and an explanation of *why you saw him*; a brief *statement of the problem* you discussed with him; a description of *how you handled the problem*; and some *questions* you had concerning the case.

Besides the elements underlined, can you think of any others that should also have been included? If so, state what they are in the space provided, and then turn to Answer 11.

Return to Frame 6 and review once again the seven components of an agency record. Then see if you can think of any other important elements you might include in a case record. When you have completed this exercise, turn to Answer 14.

NOTE TAKING: AN AID IN EFFECTIVE RECORDING

Since you are probably in contact with many individual consumers during your daily activities, it is very important that you remember what happened with each consumer. With all the activities you are involved in everyday, how can you improve your ability to remember specific information about an individual you have observed or talked with? One method is to keep your own personal log or notebook for jotting down important information about an individual.[1] You can then refer to this when you start to write in the record.

While you should try to complete agency records as quickly as you can after you have seen an individual, many times you just will not have the time to do this right away. This is why many workers keep their own logs or notebooks and jot down the important information they need to remember about each individual. The most important items to include in a log are (1) the date of activity, (2) the name of the individual, (3) a description of your involvement, (4) what happened, and (5) your observations and impressions.

You can see how the log can be a short simple account of your activity. In keeping a personal log, it is important that the time between your contact with the individual and your note taking be as short as possible. The longer you wait to write down important information, the more likely it is that you will forget or change it. It should be pointed out, however, that although it is a good idea to write down facts such as name, address, and age during an interview, it can be very distracting to the consumer if you spend a lot of time writing. The best thing to do is to set aside a few minutes immediately after each contact to jot down your notes—and try to make them as brief as you can. Remember you only need the most important information in a log.

Go on to Frame 10

What is the best way of making notes to keep track of the important aspects of each observation or interview and to aid in writing case records?

A. Take notes throughout every interview.

Turn to Answer 12

B. Jot down most of your notes immediately following each interview.

Turn to Answer 9

C. Jot down your notes at a preset time during each day.

Turn to Answer 4

[1] See Rose C. Thomas, *Public Service Careers Program, Training Manual for Case Aide Trainees* (City of New York Department of Social Services, March, 1968), pp. 46–47.

FRAME 11

When taking notes or keeping a personal log of interviews, it is important to try to keep the length of time between your contact with each consumer and your note taking as _____ as possible.

Fill in the blank, and turn to Answer 15

FRAME 12

Although there are seven major items which most agencies include in case records, in note taking it is not necessary to cover all of them, since notes are used primarily to refresh your memory. The notes you take for each case will vary according to such things as your ability to remember related facts and the intricacies of the interview. However, five types of information have been found helpful by most workers when included in a log as an aid in recording. Check which types are most important, and then turn to Answer 7.

____ 1. Date of the interview or activity

____ 2. Person's name

____ 3. Description of the problem

____ 4. Questions you wish to ask your supervisor

____ 5. Brief description of your actions

____ 6. Brief explanation of significant things that happened during the activity

____ 7. Brief description of some impressions and observations concerning the consumer

---

FRAME 13

GUIDELINES FOR EFFECTIVE RECORDING

Now that you understand why records are necessary and how notes may aid in writing records, it is helpful to examine some tips on how to write effective records.[2]

1. Use clear, simple sentences and watch your spelling and punctuation. If you are not sure of the spelling or meaning of a word, borrow a dictionary.
2. Write clearly and legibly so other people can read what you have written. Remember that one reason forms and records are kept by agencies is to make sure that services can be offered in a continuous fashion, regardless of whether the same worker is always available to see the consumer. If others can not read your writing, this goal will be difficult to achieve.
3. Select pertinent information to record. Some records will require simple facts, while others will require that you summarize or give a brief description of what happened. You can not record everything that happened, but if you write enough, another worker will not repeat what you have already done.
4. Do not try to use big words or technical language unless you are very sure of what you are saying.
5. Avoid making entries which tell only how hard you are working. This fools no

(Frame 13 continued)

[2] Ibid. and also see Gertrude S. Goldberg et al., *New Careers: The Social Service Aide: A Manual for Trainees* (Washington, D.C.: University Rescarch Corporation, October, 1968).

one, is annoying, and is not particularly helpful to other workers who use the records.

6. From time to time look at your old records, see how you are doing, and decide whether there are any areas that need improvement (e.g., incomplete descriptions of consumer's behavior, missing dates, missing notes on consumer successes, etc.)

Go on to Frame 14

FRAME 14

In the space below, explain why it is important to write your records in a clear and concise manner using simple sentences and proper spelling and punctuation.

Go on to Answer 17

FRAME 15

Records can contribute to providing effective services to consumers and achieving smooth agency operations if you

A. record only what is important.

Turn to Answer 13

B. record everything that happened.

Turn to Answer 18

C. record only simple facts.

Turn to Answer 21

FRAME 16

In keeping records, it is helpful to write clearly and legibly using simple sentences and proper spelling and punctuation, and to write only what is important. What other things can be helpful when writing records?

___ 1. Try to tell how well you are doing with each consumer.

___ 2. Use technical language whenever possible so that other professionals will know precisely what you have accomplished.

___ 3. Check your old records occasionally to identify areas needing improvement.

___ 4. Use technical language only when you know precisely what you are saying.

Turn to Answer 19

FRAME 17

Being "Honest" in Recording

What do you say to an individual if he wants to see his record? And what do you say when he wants to know if anyone else is going to look at his record? Most individuals who are using human services take it for granted that some sort of record will be made of their activities and requests. Although you usually do not need to explain your agency's recording procedures to every consumer, when they do ask about it, you should be able to explain how your agency uses the record and what goes into it. This is what we mean by being honest in recording. We also mean that the individual should know that his record will be shared with other workers, such as supervisors, but only because they need this information to give help to the individual. A safe rule to follow is to write the record in terms that you would be willing to have the consumer read it if the occasion arose.[3]

Honesty also means not making promises you cannot keep and not changing the information you have collected just to make it look better. If someone says "If I tell you what happened, do you promise not to tell?" you should be very cautious before you say "Yes, I promise." It is better to say something like, "I can not promise without knowing, but I do promise that if you tell me about it, I will not do anything without first letting you know what it is and discussing it with you."

Go right on to Frame 18

FRAME 18

Which of the following statements are true regarding honesty in recording?

___ 1. You should explain your agency's recording procedures to every consumer.

___ 2. You should be able to explain how your agency uses records and what goes into them if the consumer asks about it.

___ 3. You should record with the possibility that the consumer might read what you have written.

___ 4. You should realize that the consumer will never be allowed to read the record so your recording should not be tempered by this possibility.

___ 5. You should avoid making promises to consumers regarding who will see their records.

___ 6. You should avoid making the record look good by changing information.

___ 7. You should know that records are shared with other workers when necessary.

Turn to Answer 16

FRAME 19

Explain below how you would handle a situation where a consumer requests that his or her records be kept secret.

Turn to Answer 20

FRAME 20

You have now completed the lesson on managing information. When you are writing consumer records, you should try to apply the rules and suggestions presented in this lesson. Proceed now to Lesson 2, in which you will be presented with methods for developing or improving your reporting skills.

---

[3] See Alfred Kadushin, *The Social Work Interview* (New York: Columbia University Press, 1972).

ANSWERS TO LESSON 1

ANSWER 1

Although agency records could be used as a basis for budget requests, this is only part of a correct answer. Return to Frame 2.

ANSWER 2

Two components of all records that would quickly come to mind are the date of the entry or activity and the identifying information about the consumer, such as name, address, age, sex. If you mentioned these, congratulations. If you listed others, perhaps they are included in the complete listing of components which you will find in Frame 6.

ANSWER 3

Yes, the record does inform workers in other agencies who are involved with the consumer about what has already been done and about the results and thus aids them in providing help. However, this is only part of the answer. Return to Frame 2 and select the more complete answer.

ANSWER 4

This may be the best strategy for you, but most people will forget a lot of important information or become confused after interviewing many consumers, and it is better for them not to wait too long before taking notes. Return to Frame 10 and select the answer that applies to the majority of workers.

ANSWER 5

You should have checked A, B, and C as some of the ways in which records fulfill the function of providing permanent documented accounts of consumer services.
   Turn to Frame 4.

ANSWER 6

Some possible reasons for not keeping records are the additional work for human service workers and clerical help, the additional cost, and space problems. When you compare these with the reasons for keeping records (as stated in A, B, and C of Frame 3), do you feel that such records are necessary? Perhaps you could discuss this with fellow workers or classmates; but before you do, go on to Frame 5 to find out what is included in most agency records.

ANSWER 7

The types of information which are helpful to include when taking notes are numbers 1, 2, 5, 6, and 7. In addition to the name of the consumer, a description of what happened, what you had to do (your action), and the impressions and observations which might give insight into what may be most helpful in future sessions with the consumer, you may think of other items depending on the situation and conditions surrounding each case. Return now to Frame 13.

ANSWER 8

Although this is correct, it is only part of the proper answer. There is another correct response. Records help workers evaluate their activities with each consumer by facilitating the organization of their thinking about the consumer and by identifying additional information needed. Return to Frame 2.

ANSWER 9

Yes, this is the most helpful method of note taking for most workers since their memory is fresh immediately after each interview and since the consumer is not necessarily distracted during the interview.
Now flip back to Frame 11 and continue the lesson.

ANSWER 10

Exactly—the agency record informs other workers who are involved in helping a consumer about what has been done and about the results, thereby facilitating the provision of proper services to the consumer. The record also helps workers evaluate their progress with each consumer by organizing their thinking and helping them identify any missing information. Go on now to Frame 3.

ANSWER 11

Other components that could have been included in the case record are identifying information, such as address, age, sex, and any past services he has had. This information was needed since this was the first interview. Records of subsequent interviews will not require inclusion of this data. Other information could also have been given concerning the important facts surrounding the problem, why you handled the problem the way you did, and what follow up activities you planned. Turn to Frame 8.

ANSWER 12

Although this method may be most useful to you, the worker, it is usually very distracting to consumers and may interfere with their progress during the interview. Very little if any information should be written down during an interview.
Return to Frame 9 for a review, and then answer Frame 10 again.

ANSWER 13

Exactly! An important rule to try to apply when recording is to write only what is important. In some cases, this will mean recording merely simple facts while, in others, it may mean summarizing, or presenting a brief description of what happened during an interview or activity. Record, in other words, enough so that another worker handling your case won't repeat things already accomplished or tried by you. Return to Frame 16.

ANSWER 14

In addition to the seven components of data—identifying information, purpose, problem, facts surrounding problem, how you handled it and why, follow-up activities planned, and comments and questions to discuss with other professionals—you may have added such items as your own observations of the consumer during the interview and his reactions to your suggestions of how to handle the problem. Return now to Frame 9.

ANSWER 15

You should, of course, have written the word *short* or *brief*, since the longer you wait to jot down important information the greater the probability becomes that you will forget or become confused about this information.

Return to Frame 12 and continue the good work.

ANSWER 16

Answers 2, 3, 5, 6, and 7 are correct. Honesty in recording may be very difficult to apply in practice, but it can mean the difference between a positive working relationship and one that fails to progress because of a lack of trust. Return to Frame 19.

ANSWER 17

It is especially important to write your records clearly and concisely so that services can be provided to agency consumers in a continuous fashion. If others cannot read your records and you are not available, the consumer's progress may suffer, since other workers may simply cover the same ground you did. Did you think of other reasons? There are many, but this one is most important when it comes to agency records. Return now to Frame 15.

ANSWER 18

No, you should avoid recording too much. Only the events, observations, impressions, and facts that are essential to the case need be recorded.

Return to Frame 13 for a review before answering Frame 15 correctly.

ANSWER 19

You should have checked numbers 3 and 4. The six helpful guidelines for record writing are writing clearly and legibly; using simple sentences and proper spelling and punctuation; recording only what is important; avoiding technical language unless you know exactly what you are saying; avoiding self praise; and checking your old records to see how you can improve your recording skills. Return to Frame 17.

ANSWER 20

In such a situation, it would be best to let consumers know that their records are kept secret from everyone unless the need arises to reveal their contents to a colleague or to someone who can help improve the services they receive. Consumers should be told that all use of records will be discussed with them and have their approval. It is then your responsibility to follow through on the agreement. Return now to Frame 20.

ANSWER 21

Although recording simple facts may be enough for some records, it is not sufficient for others. Return to Frame 13 for a review, and then answer Frame 15 correctly.

LESSON 2: REPORTING SKILLS

In this lesson you will learn about the activity of reporting, which is another skill for managing consumer services. You will be using your reporting skills whenever you are called upon to summarize your observations and contacts with consumers. For example, you may need to summarize all important information about a consumer by reading his files; or you may be asked to complete a consumer service report summarizing the services that have been delivered to a number of consumers. The goal of this lesson and the enabling activities that will help you reach this goal are presented below.

GOAL

You will be able to prepare an oral or written report on information which you have submitted or gathered regarding an agency consumer or service.

ENABLING ACTIVITIES

After completing this lesson, you will have done the following:

1. Identified three reasons for preparing reports
2. Reviewed the four basic steps of report preparation
3. Considered four guidelines that will help you in organizing and presenting an oral report
4. Examined the purpose of a memo and four principles that will help you in writing effective memos
5. Reviewed the three steps that are followed in summarizing information
6. Considered three guidelines useful in writing reports

Turn to Frame 1

FRAME 1

WHY PREPARE REPORTS?

A report should communicate information to someone who wants or needs it in the most convenient and usable form. This is true whether it is a student's book report, the news report of the day on TV, or a mother's report on her child's behavior. In the human services, oral reports are used, for example, to convey information about consumers to supervisors or to other workers in case conferences. Written reports, such as letters and memos, may be used to inform administrators about consumer services and about your needs as a human service worker. There are three main reasons for preparing agency reports.

1. To identify and explain worker and consumer needs
2. To communicate information about consumer progress to supervisors and administrators
3. To share problems, impressions, and information with workers in your own and other agencies

Go on to Frame 2

FRAME 2

Which of the following could be considered a report?

A. A memo to a fellow worker concerning your impressions of one of your consumers

Turn to Answer 5

B. An oral presentation at a case conference

Turn to Answer 8

C. An explanation of consumer progress to the director of your agency

Turn to Answer 2

D. A, B, and C above

Turn to Answer 12

FRAME 3

Place a check beside each item that is a reason for preparing an agency report.

___ 1. To tell a friend about your job

___ 2. To explain to the director that you are in need of more clerical support

___ 3. To relate to your supervisor the problems you have been working on with a consumer

___ 4. To explain your feelings to a fellow worker

___ 5. To confirm a meeting with a worker in another agency

___ 6. To describe problems you are having to fellow workers at an agency conference

___ 7. To outline consumer needs not being fulfilled by the community at a local conference

Turn to Answer 1

FRAME 4

Would an agency budget be considered a report?

___ Yes

___ No

**Explain your answer below
and then go on to Answer 6**

FRAME 5

STEPS IN PREPARING REPORTS

Whether you are using an oral or a written report, there are certain steps you can follow that will help you in preparing your report so that it is easily understood.

1. Be *clear* about the purpose of the report.
2. *Identify* the consumer, the problem, and/or the information you will be reporting on.
3. *Collect* current information that is relevant to the purpose of your report.
4. *Organize* your information so that you can present the report in a clear manner.

Turn to Frame 6

FRAME 6

Assume that you are having a difficult time trying to help a consumer make progress toward a more effective method of handling his or her problems. You decide to seek help from your supervisor, who asks you to make a report concerning this case. Explain below the first step you would take before presenting your report to your supervisor.

Turn to Answer 4

FRAME 7

Once you have identified the consumer, the problem, and the relevant information that will be included in your report, your next task is to

A. gather all up-to-date information relevant to the purpose of the report.

Turn to Answer 7

B. clarify the purpose of the report.

Turn to Answer 11

C. organize your information.

Turn to Answer 14

FRAME 8

After collecting up-to-date information which is relevant to the purpose of your report, what should you do to prepare your report in a clear and concise manner? Explain below.

Go on to Answer 3

FRAME 9

PRESENTING REPORTS

Oral Reports

There will be many occasions in your work in the human services where you will orally report information to other workers. For example, you may share your information regarding a consumer with your supervisor, or you may share your observations and problems about one or more consumers with other workers in staff meetings or in case conferences. No matter where you are reporting orally, the following guidelines should help you in presenting your report.

1. Remember that you give an oral report primarily to share useful information with others. Be careful not to ramble on and on. You need to be well organized and keep to the point.
2. Know what you are going to say and how you are going to say it. If you follow the basic steps of preparing reports, this should be easy.
3. Jot down some short notes of your main points so you will be able to keep on track, and remember your main purpose.
4. Stand up and speak up. Stand or sit straight, be friendly, and do not start out by apologizing ("I don't know if I can say what I mean"). Listen carefully to any comments or suggestions you receive, and concentrate on the issues and information—not on personalities.

Turn to Frame 10

FRAME 10

Oral reports are used in agencies mainly to share information with supervisors and other workers in the agency regarding one or more consumers. Check the items below that you should try to accomplish when presenting a report and then turn to Answer 9.

___ 1. Avoid using notes since this will detract from your presentation.

___ 2. Use impressive words and statements that will show your hard work in preparing the report.

___ 3. Be sure you know what you are going to say and how you are going to say it.

___ 4. Stick to the purpose of your report.

___ 5. Prepare a few notes to help you remember the major points you want to cover.

___ 6. Concentrate on personalities not issues.

___ 7. Avoid making any apologies especially at the beginning of your presentation.

FRAME 11

Written Reports

The Memo. A common type of written report is the memorandum, or the memo, which is usually used to announce information or to remind someone about a service that is needed or about an important event. You will probably be using memos to report to administrators in your agency, and you may sometimes use a memo to

(Frame 11 continued)

communicate with other service workers, especially in a large agency. Each agency usually has a set form for memos, and you should be familiar with yours. To make your memos effective you should try to do the following:[1]

1. *Keep them brief.* Give all the necessary information by answering the questions who, what, when, where, how, and why. If you have several thoughts on a single subject, put each thought into a separate paragraph. Above all, keep it short—a short memo is much more likely to be read than a long one.
2. Send the memo out *early enough* so that there is time to comply with what you are requesting. Generally, you should allow at least a week so that people have time to plan their response and their work accordingly.
3. Use words that everyone will understand. Be as specific as possible in your wording—*be clear.*
4. State the general *purpose* of the memo very near the beginning, so the receiver will be very clear about what he is expected to do.

If you think you understand the purpose of memos and the methods for effective memo writing, go right on to Frame 12. If not, reread this frame first, and then proceed to Frame 12.

FRAME 12

Place a check beside the situations in which it would be best to send a memo.

— 1. To report to your supervisor on a difficult problem you are having with a consumer

— 2. To make an announcement to co-workers about an article that you found useful

— 3. To remind fellow workers of a staff conference

— 4. To describe your impressions of a consumer to a fellow worker

— 5. To advise your agency director about a needed resource

— 6. To report the services already received by a consumer to a worker in another agency

— 7. To submit a request for additional services to your administrator

Turn to Answer 15

FRAME 13

Read the following memo, and then answer the questions presented below.

11–15–73

Memo
To: Joan Wright, Director
From: Phyllis Bright, Service Worker
    Please excuse my delay in fulfilling your request. I was unable to understand some of the tasks you expected me to accomplish as stated in your memo. Since you had stated a completion date of November 20th for all tasks, I would appreciate it if we could meet sometime during the next two days to discuss these tasks.
PB/pm

---

[1] See Thora Kron, *Communication in Nursing* (Philadelphia: Saunders, 1972).

1. Check which of the following are true.

   __ A. Mrs. Wright, it can be assumed, is not an effective memo writer.

   __ B. Mrs. Bright, the service worker, is a very effective memo writer.

   __ C. Both Mrs. Wright and Mrs. Bright could benefit from a lesson on effective memo writing.

   __ D. There is a strong possibility that the tasks requested of Mrs. Bright will be completed on time.

   __ E. Mrs. Bright's request for a meeting within two days is reasonable.

Turn to Answer 17

2. Which of the following helpful hints for effective memo writing did Mrs. Bright apply in her memo?

   A. She used easily understood terms.

Turn to Answer 10

   B. She allowed sufficient time for a reply.

Turn to Answer 18

   C. She provided sufficient information to allow Mrs. Wright to prepare for the meeting.

Turn to Answer 22

3. Explain below what Mrs. Bright could have written at the beginning of her memo to help identify its purpose immediately.

Turn to Answer 13

FRAME 14

In the space below, rewrite Mrs. Bright's memo as if it were from you. Use the ways identified above to make it more effective.

11–15–73

Memo
To: Mrs. Wright
From:

Go on to Answer 24

FRAME 15

The summary. Another kind of written report involves writing a summary of information and observations from one or more sources. For example, you may be asked to read agency reports concerning consumers' needs and progress and to submit your observations in writing; or the personnel office of your agency may ask you to write a short summary of the kind of training you would like. In all such situations, you need to be able to write a short report that summarizes the important facts that are being requested.

Writing is putting thoughts on paper and speaking is saying thoughts out loud. However, many people find it much harder to write than to speak. How many times do you say or hear others say "I know what I want to say, but I can't put it down on paper." The problem is that many of us are unable to write the way we talk. We talk easily, but when we have to write, we do not know where to begin. Nevertheless, writing a summary report is not too difficult. Just remember that the key to writing a report is *planning* what you are going to say. If you follow three basic steps when you are summarizing information, you should not have any trouble.

1. **Get your facts together.** If you need to read agency files or other agency papers involving consumers and/or services, read them with the purpose of your report in mind. Look for ideas and main activities instead of concentrating on single words. Also try to see the difference between someone's personal opinion and the facts.
2. **Organize your facts.** In organizing ideas and facts, many workers find that listing all the facts on a single sheet of paper helps in deciding what needs to be reported. After they have chosen the main facts, they expand the list into an outline by going back and filling in additional information they will need under each fact. It is also important to organize ideas by placing them in a logical order or progression.
3. **Remember the purpose.** Once you have gathered and organized your facts and ideas, you are ready to summarize. When you are writing your summary always keep asking yourself, "What is my purpose in writing this report?" and "Who am I writing it for?" Asking these questions will serve as a constant reminder to you to include only the most important information in your report.

Proceed to Frame 16

FRAME 16

Underline the correct response.

The key to summarizing a written report is (planning/researching).

Turn to Answer 20

FRAME 17

The first step in planning a summary report is to gather the relevant facts and ideas. Which of the following would be helpful to follow when performing this task?

A. Look for descriptions of all activities.

Turn to Answer 16

B. Keep in mind the purpose of your report.

Turn to Answer 19

C. Search for key words.

Turn to Answer 23

FRAME 18

Suppose a service worker from another agency has requested information on a consumer who had previously obtained services from your agency, and your supervisor has requested that you write a report and send it to the service worker. After you have obtained the relevant facts on the consumer, what would your next step be?

A. Organize your facts.

Turn to Answer 26

B. Summarize the relevant facts.

Turn to Answer 21

FRAME 19

Guidelines for writing. When writing your summary report, you should expand upon the main ideas and facts you have put in your outline. Some people have a personal organizing method which works best for them. Whatever method you use, once you have planned your summary by gathering and organizing your facts and ideas, you are ready to write your summary report. You may find the following guidelines helpful to you in writing your reports:

1. **Purpose.** At the beginning of your report, explain why you are writing the report.
2. **Clarity.** Use specific, concrete, familiar words and write short sentences, which are easier for you to write and easier for the reader to understand.
3. **Brevity.** Most of your reports should be short—usually no more than one page. Remember to stop writing once your message is finished.

Go on to Frame 20

FRAME 20

We return now to the report mentioned in Frame 18 concerning the consumer who had previously obtained services from your agency and is now requesting services from another agency. The following report, in letter form, concerns a similar situation.

July 1, 1970

Mr. Arthur Davis
Regional Rehabilitation

Dear Mr. Davis:

Rebecca Holmes has been in our program for two years.
She appeared to be the most deprived child in the class
according to our first report. She was often absent and
sometimes upset when arriving for school.

In 1968, Rebecca had a speech screening test at age
3 years. At that time she was functioning verbally at an

(Frame 20 continued)

age level of 2.1. years. During the first year in our
program both her parents were in the home. Her attention
span was short, but she seemed to be well adjusted and
happy during the second year.

In 1970, Rebecca had a second speech screening test
and she had only increased to 2 years 3 months. During the
second school year, Rebecca's mother was out of the home.
Because of her father's difficulty in running the household,
Rebecca was bathed and dressed at school and her clothing
was provided and cleaned by volunteers and staff. She
was picked up daily by the director. Rebecca's father was
always waiting for her at the end of the day, and the two
expressed much affection for each other.

At the beginning of this year, Rebecca left school for
three months, and when she returned she was passive and
much more aggressive than the previous year. This behavior
was still continuing when school closed this year.

Sincerely,

Arnold Armstead
Jones Elementary School

**Answer the questions based on
this report in the next three
frames. Begin with Frame 21**

FRAME 21

Was this an effective report?

Yes.

Turn to Answer 25

No.

Turn to Answer 29

FRAME 22

What did Mr. Armstead fail to do when writing this report?

A. Make it brief.

Turn to Answer 27

B. Organize the facts.

Turn to Answer 30

C. Obtain the facts.

Turn to Answer 33

FRAME 23

In order to organize the facts better, Mr. Armstead could have used an outline, writing down the major facts and then filling them in with additional relevant information. In addition to not organizing the report, what else did Mr. Armstead fail to do?

A. Write clearly.

Turn to Answer 28

B. Stop writing once the message was finished.

Turn to Answer 31

C. State the purpose and keep it in mind when writing the report.

Turn to Answer 32

FRAME 24

You should now be prepared to rewrite the report presented in Frame 20. Remember to outline the facts first and then fill them in with additional information as you write the report.

**After completing this report
go right on to Frame 25**

FRAME 25

Did you include the following in your report?

1. A statement of the purpose at the beginning of the report
2. Each of the major facts in chronological order by the year of occurrence
3. Detailed facts and statements based on the major facts
4. A summary of what you believe to be the needs of Rebecca and her family that regional rehabilitation can help fulfill
5. Clear sentences and specific concrete words
6. A concisely written page, with no excessive statements after the purpose of the message was fulfilled

If you are able to answer yes to five of the above you have successfully completed this lesson. Go right on to Lesson 3. However, if you failed to include more than one of the above, rewrite the report, and make sure to include them, before you proceed to Lesson 3.

ANSWERS TO LESSON 2

ANSWER 1

The numbers you should have checked are 2, 3, 5, 6, and 7. Number 4 is not an agency report since it does not include a reference to a consumer or agency activities. Return to Frame 4.

ANSWER 2

Such an explanation, whether oral or written, would indeed be considered a report. However, this is only one type of report given in the question, so return to Frame 2 and select the correct answer.

ANSWER 3

The last step you should take before preparing your report is to organize the information you have obtained so as to help you prepare and effectively deliver the report in a clear and concise manner whether orally or in written form. Go on now to Frame 9 and get some hints on how to organize and present an oral report.

ANSWER 4

Your first step would be to clarify the purpose of the report in your mind and, if necessary, to write it down in terms that will be readily understandable to the receiver, in this case your supervisor.

Return to Frame 7.

ANSWER 5

Although such a memo would be considered a report, it is not the only one mentioned. Return to Frame 2 and select the correct answer.

ANSWER 6

Yes, an agency budget would be considered a report, since it is one of the major ways the agency has of reporting its needs and the needs of workers to funding sources. As is evident, most important information is communicated in and between agencies by use of reports. Return now to Frame 5.

ANSWER 7

Right you are. After identifying the consumer, the problem, and the relevant information to be included in your report, it is important to gather the up-to-date information relevant to the purpose of the report. Return now to Frame 8 and continue the good work.

ANSWER 8

Yes, this is indeed a report, but there are others mentioned, so return to Frame 2 and select the proper answer.

ANSWER 9

Numbers 3, 4, 5, and 7 are the correct responses. When preparing a report one should be organized and use short helpful notes pertaining to the main topics; then one should present the report without rambling, stick to the purpose, speak up, stand or sit erect, and concentrate on issues and information, not personalities. Return now to Frame 11.

ANSWER 10

Yes, this and brevity were the two positive aspects of Mrs. Bright's memo. However, she did not allow Mrs. Wright sufficient time to schedule a meeting and she failed to identify the tasks that she could not understand. In addition, the purpose of the memo could have been made clearer. Return now to Frame 13, question 3.

ANSWER 11

No, this is the first step of reporting. Return to Frame 5 for a review before answering Frame 7 correctly.

ANSWER 12

Exactly, all three would be considered a report within the definition cited in Frame 1; a report is the communication of information to someone who wants or needs it, in the most convenient and usable form. Return to Frame 3.

ANSWER 13

In order to clarify the reason or purpose of any memo so that the receiver knows immediately what the sender is talking about, it is advisable to insert, just below the line telling who the memo is from, the word "Re," which means regarding. Or else one should simply write "Subject"; and then state the purpose, for example, "Re your memo of Sept. 1, 1973, pertaining to the tasks expected of me." Return now to Frame 14.

ANSWER 14

No, this is the last step you should take before actually writing your report. Return to Frame 5 for a review before answering the question in Frame 7 correctly.

ANSWER 15

Numbers 2, 3, 5, and 7 are situations where memos would probably be used, although 2 and 3 could also be oral communications in a small agency, unless you wanted it in writing for future reference. Memos are most frequently used in agencies to communicate with administrators or when you want something in writing in order to keep a record of the communication. Can you think of situations in which our answers would not be the preferred choices? You should be able to disagree with us! Return to Frame 13.

ANSWER 16

Although you may skim through reports on all activities, your task is to gather ideas and facts that are relevant; therefore, you should be looking only for major activities related to your purpose in writing your report.

Return to Frame 15 for a brief review, and then answer the question in Frame 17 correctly.

ANSWER 17

Those statements which are true are A and C. It can be assumed that Mrs. Wright's memo was unclear, since Mrs. Bright had trouble understanding what was expected of her. The memo by Mrs. Bright is also ineffective for many reasons which you will be asked to identify shortly. There is insufficient time to complete the tasks expected of Mrs. Bright, and her request for a meeting on such short notice is unreasonable, especially since the request was made of a busy administrator.

Return to Frame 13, question 2.

ANSWER 18

Sorry, but two days is not sufficient time for Mrs. Wright to receive the memo, schedule a meeting time, and send a reply. In addition, there is little time to prepare for the meeting. A week is usually considered minimum time for expecting feedback, unless a phone call is requested. Return now to Frame 13, question 2, and answer the question correctly.

ANSWER 19

Exactly—when gathering ideas and facts for your summary, you must keep the purpose of your report in mind and select only those ideas, facts, and activities that are relevant to the purpose.

Return now to Frame 18.

ANSWER 20

If you said that the key to summarizing in a report is *planning* what you are going to write in the report (gathering and organizing relevant facts and ideas), you were absolutely correct.

Return now to Frame 17.

ANSWER 21

Sorry, but this would not be your next step. You have overlooked an important process, so return to Frame 18 and choose the correct response.

ANSWER 22

No, Mrs. Wright could not prepare for a meeting with Mrs. Bright since the tasks to be discussed were not identified in the memo. Other pieces of information, such as, when Mrs. Wright was free for a meeting, the specific memo that Mrs. Bright was referring to, and possible other topics of discussion at the meeting, were missing from the memo. Return to Frame 13 and answer question 2 correctly.

ANSWER 23

When gathering relevant ideas and facts, it is better to look for main ideas, activities, and facts rather than concentrating on key words. Return to Frame 15 for a brief review and then answer the question in Frame 17 correctly.

11–15–73

Memo
To: Mrs. Wright, Director
From: Service worker's name
Re: Your memo dated September 1, 1973 regarding tasks to be
    accomplished by November 20
    I have been unable to complete two of the tasks that you requested
since I am unable to understand what you expected. These tasks include
numbers 4 and 6 in your September 1st memo as follows:
    4. (Explain task 4 here.)
    6. (Explain task 6 here.)
    Since the deadline for completion is November 20th, perhaps you could
clarify these tasks by phone as soon as possible or postpone the completion
date.
    I have enclosed reports on the completed tasks for your review and
approval.
SW/pm
Enclosures

Although the form and terms used in your memo may be different from those
above, you should have included the following items:

1. A brief statement that includes the necessary information.
2. An allowance for time to respond or comply with requests. In this case, a deadline was eminent so alternative possibilities were presented to allow sufficient
time for Mrs. Wright to respond.
3. Clear easily understood words.
4. Immediate statement of purpose using "Re," and add further clarification in
contents of memo.

Did your memo contain these elements? Good—go on to Frame 15.

If you turned to this answer you had better return to Frame 15 and carefully review
the lesson from that point on. There is very little that is positive about this report.

Right! Your second step would probably be to organize the information you have
obtained from agency records concerning this consumer. Have you considered what
method you would use to help you organize this information? Think about your
answer and then return to Frame 19.

This is one of the few things that is positive about this report! It is brief enough—
probably too brief. Return to Frame 22 and select the correct answer.

Clarity was not a major problem with this report. The sentences were short and the
words were familiar and specific. Return to Frame 23 and select a better answer.

ANSWER 29

Right! There is little if anything that could be said about this report to commend it. Mr. Davis would be justified in thinking that Mr. Armstead is an ineffective report writer.

Return now to Frame 22.

ANSWER 30

Exactly. Mr. Armstead has failed to organize his facts in a way that would make them clear and understandable. What method would you suggest to help Mr. Armstead organize his facts? Think of a method and then return to Frame 23.

ANSWER 31

It would appear that Mr. Armstead did stop when the message was completed. There was no excess writing, although more facts could have been presented and clarified. Return to Frame 23 and select the correct answer.

ANSWER 32

This is probably one of the major problems with this report. The writer not only neglected to state the purpose at the beginning of the report so that the receiver would immediately know what it was about, but it would seem that he also failed to have any specific purpose in mind when writing it, except to finish quickly and be done with it. Well done, return now to Frame 24.

ANSWER 33

This could be one of his omissions, since he was stating personal opinions and left out other facts that may be important for Mr. Davis to know in order to work more effectively with Rebecca and her family. However, he has gathered some relevant facts, and, therefore, this is not the major failure of the report. Return to Frame 22 and select his failure.

LESSON 3:
THE CASE CONFERENCE

As a worker in the human services, you are probably familiar with the activity of meeting with other workers and with your supervisor to discuss problems and/or service plans regarding consumers. This kind of meeting, called a case conference, is one situation where workers use their recording and reporting skills to share and manage information. The goal of this lesson and the enabling activities that will help you reach this goal are presented below.

GOAL

You will be able to demonstrate your knowledge of information management by explaining what you would include in presenting a problem case at a case conference, and by identifying the steps that are followed in this kind of meeting.

ENABLING ACTIVITIES

After completing this lesson, you will have done four things:

1. Identified major purposes of the case conference
2. Reviewed two main types of case conferences
3. Reviewed five topics that are important to include in your summary of a problem case
4. Considered four steps usually followed in a case conference

Turn to Frame 1

FRAME 1

MAJOR PURPOSES OF CASE CONFERENCES

A case conference is a meeting of workers, either within an agency or between different agencies, that provides an opportunity for working together and sharing information on consumer-related problems. A case conference can serve one or more of the following purposes:

1. It may help clarify the diagnosis of a consumer's problem.
2. It may help in understanding the behavior of a given consumer.
3. It may help in setting up new plans for treatment or services and in supporting those that are already proving effective with consumers.

A case conference is called when a worker and/or a supervisor who are working to clarify and evaluate a consumer's problem see the need to share information related to the diagnosis, the treatment goal, and/or the service plan. The case conference in human service agencies is usually a regular activity for workers to meet and share information with each other regarding consumers. For example, if a young boy has been in trouble with the law and is not doing well in school, a case conference could be called between the probation office, school social worker, and the teacher to clarify the boy's problem and seek to understand his behavior.

Go on to Frame 2

FRAME 2

Whose personal problems are the major focus of a case conference?

A. Service workers

Turn to Answer 5

B. Consumers

Turn to Answer 12

C. Supervisors

Turn to Answer 16

FRAME 3

What is one of the major purposes of a case conference?

A. To clarify an agency policy

Turn to Answer 2

B. To clarify a worker's role

Turn to Answer 7

C. To clarify the diagnosis of a consumer problem

Turn to Answer 11

FRAME 4

If a service worker wished to understand more clearly the reasons for a consumer's actions and how to relate to these actions in a positive manner, what type of a meeting should be requested?

A. Case conference.

Turn to Answer 8

B. Conference with the consumer.

Turn to Answer 4

C. Conference with supervisors and agency administrators.

Turn to Answer 17

FRAME 5

When should case conferences be called?

A. Only when a supervisor decides it is necessary.

Turn to Answer 3

B. Only when a worker sees a need for one.

Turn to Answer 10

C. Whenever any worker or supervisor believes it is necessary.

Turn to Answer 15

FRAME 6

MAJOR TYPES OF CASE CONFERENCES

You may participate in two types of case conferences. One is the case conference that includes workers in your own agency or in a unit of your agency. For example, if you work on a ward in a psychiatric hospital, a case conference might include a nurse, a psychiatrist, the director of the unit, you, and a member of the consumer's family. A second kind of case conference is the kind that will include workers from other settings. For example, if you work in youth services, a case conference might also include the offender's school counselor or school teacher.

Turn to Frame 7

FRAME 7

Case conferences may include which of the following people?

A. Workers within the agency.

Turn to Answer 1

B. Workers from outside agencies.

Turn to Answer 6

C. Relatives of consumers.

Turn to Answer 9

D. A and B above.

Turn to Answer 13

E. A, B, and C above.

Turn to Answer 18

FRAME 8

If you were a service worker in a mental health clinic, which type of case conference might you set up?

A. One that includes workers in your own agency.

Turn to Answer 14

B. One that includes workers from other agencies.

Turn to Answer 19

C. Both A and B above.

Turn to Answer 23

FRAME 9

CONTENTS OF THE SUMMARY FOR PRESENTATION AT A CASE CONFERENCE

At a case conference, you will have to (1) keep a record of the discussion and (2) share information orally and in writing with other workers. If you are working on a case that has been selected for discussion at a case conference, you will have to prepare your presentation. Whether you are asked to present your case orally and/or in writing, you will have to *review* the case, *summarize* the background of the consumer, and *explain* the problem. Your summary should include the following items:

1. A statement of the consumer's problem
2. Your observations of the consumer
3. How you have been working with the consumer—the service plan to date
4. A summary of the results of any treatment used or service delivered
5. The reasons this particular information is being shared with other workers and specific questions highlighting the problem areas that other workers can help you in answering

In preparing your case summary you should try to include only the information that is important and necessary to understanding the situation. However, do not be afraid to admit the problem areas! Other workers need to understand these problems so that the group can work together on possible solutions.

Go on to Frame 10

FRAME 10

In addition to an explanation of the consumer's problem and the service plan to date, which of the following components should be included in your case summary for presentation at a case conference?

A. A brief explanation of the results of treatments employed so far.

Turn to Answer 20

B. An explanation of all your impressions of the consumer.

Turn to Answer 22

C. An explanation of why you are sharing this information, including the major problem areas.

Turn to Answer 26

D. A and C above.

Turn to Answer 30

E. A, B, and C above.

Turn to Answer 33

Read the case summary presented below, and then answer the questions in the following five frames.

Name of worker: Miss Anne Harper

Date of report: 4-5-74

1. Mrs. Harold is totally disabled due to several mild strokes and an extremely disoriented mental condition. She is gentle and well meaning, but the least little thing puts her in a panic. At the present time, her condition seems to have worsened, and her train of thought wanders so rapidly that she cannot even complete one sentence without changing the subject. She continues to live alone and while she keeps her house very neat and orderly, she continuously needs help in managing her affairs.

2. Mrs. Harold needs adult protective services, health services, home-management services, and, sometimes, housing improvement services.

3. At the present time, Mrs. Harold has been in a dither because her glasses have broken and she can hardly see to walk across the room without them. It is only the frames that are broken; however, she feels she needs her lenses changed since they haven't been done in many years and the lenses are inadequate. Since Mrs. Harold has only her assistance grant to live on and has no friends or relatives able or willing to help her, it is very difficult for her to pay for glasses, especially since the optometrist requires at least half the payment in advance. Mrs. Harold also needs help getting her food stamps and her marketing done.

4. I cannot see any possibility of Mrs. Harold being completely able to function on her own. Mainly, we need to enlist the help of volunteers and various aides and assistants to help her to continue to function on a basic level.

5. We have been working toward getting her glasses, and at the present time have made an appointment for July 10th with Dr. Jarrod Williams. Mrs. Harold preferred to wait for this appointment, rather than go to a different eye doctor. We were able to get a $10 donation from the United Methodist Church toward the purchase of the glasses, and also, we have been promised $10 from our own emergency fund. I will also see if I can get another $10 from somewhere when the time comes for her to go to the doctor.

Turn to Frame 12

Which of the following components of an effective case summary are included in the one presented in Frame 11?

A. The worker's observations of the consumer.

Turn to Answer 36

B. A clear statement of the consumer's problem.

Turn to Answer 40

C. An explanation of the reasons for sharing this information with other workers.

Turn to Answer 43

FRAME 13

Does the case summary presented in Frame 11 include a summary of the results of any treatment used or service provided by the worker?
    Review Frame 11 if necessary.

A. Yes, in paragraph 2.

Turn to Answer 35

B. Yes, in paragraph 3.

Turn to Answer 42

C. Yes, in paragraph 4.

Turn to Answer 45

D. Yes, in paragraph 5.

Turn to Answer 47

E. No.

Turn to Answer 37

FRAME 14

Is there a tentative service plan (that is, one not fully worked out) included in the case summary presented in Frame 11? Review Frame 11 if necessary.

Yes.

Turn to Answer 41

No.

Turn to Answer 48

FRAME 15

Assuming that Mrs. Harold's major problem is her inability to manage her affairs so as to be able to function effectively, state below at least one question that the worker could use to gain help from other workers.

Proceed to Answer 44

FRAME 16

You should now have some ideas for rewriting this case summary to make it more effective for presentation at a case conference. In the space below, try to rewrite it, making sure to include the five major components (see Frame 9), and also to invent some identifying information about Mrs. Harold, for example, her address, age, race, and marital status. Such information is usually included in a written summary and

(Frame 16 continued)

is also appropriate in an oral summary report. Use additional paper if you need more room.

When you finish this exercise, turn to Answer 46, and then go on to Frame 17

FRAME 17

STEPS TO FOLLOW FOR EFFECTIVE CASE CONFERENCES

In a case conference, the focus is on what the workers need to know in order to improve services to consumers. The meeting usually proceeds in the following steps:

1. The worker presents a summary of the case and the problem and raises specific questions.
2. The group discusses the case, asks questions, and makes observations and suggestions.
3. A member of the group sums up the discussion. The case presenter is asked whether the discussion provided any help for solving the problem or for thinking of new ways to help the consumer.
4. The meeting either ends or goes on to discuss another case. Usually, the worker who presented the case writes a short report of the session and enters it in the case record.

Remember that the case conference is really a formal way of managing and sharing information with other workers. Information is managed informally when you share it with other workers over the phone or just talk to other workers during the course of the day. It is your responsibility to make sure that you share the information you collect with other human service workers at the appropriate times in order to gain new perspectives and, thereby, to guarantee consumers the best services possible.

Continue to Frame 18

FRAME 18

If you were a service worker setting up a case conference, it would be your responsibility to do which of the following?

A. Share the information you have collected with other workers.

Turn to Answer 21

B. Sum up the discussion.

Turn to Answer 25

C. Demonstrate your ability to solve consumer problems by yourself.

Turn to Answer 29

FRAME 19

Which of the following should be part of a well-managed case conference after the service worker has presented his case summary and raised appropriate questions related to the problems he is having with the case?

A. Summary of the discussion by another worker at the conference

Turn to Answer 27

B. Discussion of the case by the group in attendance at the conference

Turn to Answer 31

C. Presentation of another case summary, if more than one case is to be discussed at the conference

Turn to Answer 34

FRAME 20

Once the service worker presents his or her case summary, and conference attendees have discussed the case, asked questions, and made observations and suggestions, which of the following usually occurs?

A. The meeting ends.

Turn to Answer 24

B. The worker presenting the case writes a short report of the conference and enters it in the agency case record.

Turn to Answer 28

C. A member of the group attending the conference sums up the discussion.

Turn to Answer 32

D. Another case is discussed.

Turn to Answer 39

FRAME 21

Other than putting the results of the conference to use in working with the consumer, the worker presenting the case usually has one further responsibility after the conference is over. Explain this responsibility below.

Turn to Answer 38

FRAME 22

You have now completed the chapter on information managing. Go on now to the summary and review questions for Chapter X. If you think you need a review before tackling these questions, return to Lesson 1, review the material on recording skills, and skim through the rest of the chapter. Then flip to the review questions.

ANSWERS TO LESSON 3

ANSWER 1

This is only partially correct. All case conferences include workers from the agency setting up the conference, but other persons may also be included.
   Return to Frame 6 for a review before answering Frame 7 again.

ANSWER 2

The case conference is usually not the setting for clarifying agency policy although the subject may arise. Return to Frame 1 for a review, and then choose the best answer in Frame 3.

ANSWER 3

Case conferences are called frequently in a human service agency. They are called by workers or supervisors whenever they see the need to share information about a consumer. This is not a function of the supervisor only.
   Return to Frame 5 and select the correct answer.

ANSWER 4

While this may be an appropriate action in some instances, it is generally more profitable to seek advice from your fellow workers or supervisors. Knowing this, return to Frame 4 and select the best answer.

ANSWER 5

The major focus of a case conference is on the personal problems of a consumer. Although attempting to solve these may lead to other problems, the focus at a case conference should be on solving the problems of a consumer, not the personal problems of a service worker.
   Return to Frame 2 and select the better answer.

ANSWER 6

Although workers from outside agencies (youth services, schools, etc.) may be included in case conferences, there are other groups that can also be included.

397

Return to Frame 6 for a review before answering the question in Frame 7 correctly.

ANSWER 7

Although this topic may arise at a case conference, it is usually not the main focus of such a conference. The staff meeting is more often the proper place to clarify worker roles.

Return to Frame 1 for a review before answering the question in Frame 3 correctly.

ANSWER 8

Exactly—this is a consumer-related problem and, therefore, it would be most appropriately discussed at a case conference.

Return to Frame 5 and continue the good work.

ANSWER 9

Yes, members of a consumer's family are sometimes included in case conferences to give and receive relevant information aimed at helping the consumer; but they are, of course, not the only persons in the conference.

Return to Frame 6 for a review, and then answer the question in Frame 7 correctly.

ANSWER 10

A case conference can be called whenever a worker finds it necessary to discuss a consumer-related problem, but the worker is not the only person who can call such a conference.

Return to Frame 5 and select the correct answer.

ANSWER 11

Well done—one of the major purposes for having a case conference may be to clarify a worker's diagnosis of a consumer's problem.

Return now to Frame 4.

ANSWER 12

Precisely—helping solve the problems of the consumer is usually the major focus of any case conference. Personal problems of the worker, supervisor, etc., should be discussed in other situations, not at the case conference.

Return now to Frame 3.

ANSWER 13

This is almost correct. Workers both within the agency setting up a case conference and those from outside agencies may be included; but in some cases, others are also included.

Return to Frame 7 and select the correct answer.

ANSWER 14

This is only partially correct. Both types of case conferences could be held in any type of agency, depending upon the purpose of the conference and the information to be shared and discussed.

Return to Frame 8 and select the correct answer.

ANSWER 15

This is correct. In most agencies case conferences are called frequently when either a worker or a supervisor sees a need to share and discuss any information, ideas, feelings, etc., related to clarifying a diagnosis of a consumer's problem, understanding the behavior of a given consumer, establishing a treatment goal, and/or selecting a service plan.

Go on to Frame 6.

ANSWER 16

We can think of few, if any, situations where the personal problems of a supervisor should ever be brought up in a case conference. The case conference is used as a method for discussing ways to improve services to a consumer, and its major focus is, therefore, the personal problems of the consumer.

Return to Frame 2 and select the correct answer.

ANSWER 17

It would not be appropriate to discuss such a problem at this type of conference. Supervisor's problems and administrative problems, rather than consumers' problems, are the focus of such a meeting.

Return to Frame 4 and select the correct answer.

ANSWER 18

Right you are—well done! Workers from within the agency setting up the conference are always included in the conference, but in some cases, workers from other agencies are also included (e.g., youth service workers, school social workers) as well as members of a consumer's family if they have relevant information to share and can help in facilitating the consumer's progress.

Return now to Frame 8.

ANSWER 19

You are only partially correct. All agencies use both types of case conferences. The type depends upon the purpose of the conference and the information to be shared and discussed.

Return to Frame 8 and select the proper answer.

ANSWER 20

This is partially correct; but there are also other components, one or more of which are given in the responses to this question. Return to Frame 9 for a review, and then answer the question in Frame 10 correctly.

ANSWER 21

Right you are—well done! Your major responsibility as the service worker in a case conference is to share the information you have collected and summarized with other workers and participants at the conference. The focus is, therefore, on sharing information that other workers need to know in order to improve services to consumers. Return now to Frame 19.

ANSWER 22

This would not be required, although you should include in your summary observations of the consumer that relate directly to the problems you wish to discuss in the case conference.

Return to Frame 9 for a brief review and then answer the question in Frame 10 correctly.

ANSWER 23

Absolutely. All types of human service agencies use both types of case conferences. The type used depends mainly on the purpose of the conference and the type of information to be shared and discussed.

Return now to Frame 9 and continue the lesson.

ANSWER 24

The conference should not end at this time. One additional activity usually takes place before the meeting ends or before a new case is presented.

Return to Frame 17 for a review before answering the question in Frame 20 again.

ANSWER 25

In most cases (although not always), summing up the discussion that has occurred at a case conference is the responsibility of another member of the group, not the service worker whose case is being discussed.

Return to Frame 17 for a brief review and then choose a better response to the question in Frame 18.

ANSWER 26

This is partially correct, but not complete enough. There are other components that should be included in a case summary for presentation at a case conference. If you need a review, return to Frame 9, and then answer the question in Frame 10 correctly.

ANSWER 27

A summary of the discussion by a member of the group attending the conference would not occur until the case summary had been discussed and the group at the conference had asked questions regarding the case and made observations and suggestions.

Return to Frame 17 for a review of the proper steps in a case conference, and then answer the question in Frame 19.

ANSWER 28

This is usually done after the end of the meeting. One important activity usually occurs before the conference ends and a report is written.

Return to Frame 17 for a review, and then answer the question in Frame 20 correctly.

ANSWER 29

The major reasons for holding a case conference are to obtain help in solving consumer-related problems and to improve services offered to the consumer. It is unwise to think you must solve all consumer problems on your own. Such a feat is close to impossible, even for a very competent service worker.

Return to Frame 17 for a review before correctly answering the question in Frame 18.

ANSWER 30

Precisely correct. In addition to a statement of the consumer's problem and the service plan you have used up to the present time, your case summary should include an explanation of treatment results and reasons for sharing the information, with highlights of the major problems you are experiencing. You should not include all your impressions of the consumer, but merely those that are directly related to the problem areas.

Return now to Frame 11 and continue the lesson.

ANSWER 31

We agree with this choice. The second step in a well-managed case conference would include a discussion of the case summary by those in attendance. Group members would also ask questions about the case and make suggestions and observations during this second phase of the conference.

Return now to Frame 20.

ANSWER 32

Yes. Once a discussion regarding the case has ended, one of the members usually summarizes the discussion. This person should also be sure to ask the worker who presented the case whether the discussion, suggestions, and observations of the group were helpful to him or her for solving the problem or for thinking of new ways to help the consumer. If not, then further discussion could ensue. If so, and there is no other case to be presented, the conference can end. Now return to Frame 21.

ANSWER 33

This answer is partially incorrect. You have correctly identified two components, but one is incorrect.

Return to Frame 9 for a review before answering the question in Frame 10 correctly.

ANSWER 34

In our opinion, and in the opinion of a number of practitioners, this would be unwise. When more than one case is presented at a conference, one case should be thoroughly discussed and summarized by conference members before another case is presented. Based on your own experiences, you may disagree with this point of view. If so, discussions with other workers and students may prove helpful.

Return to Frame 17 for a review before selecting the correct answer in Frame 19.

ANSWER 35

Paragraph 2 explains Mrs. Harold's service needs, not a summary of the results of any treatment used.

Return to Frame 13 and answer the question again.

ANSWER 36

This answer is absolutely correct. The worker's observations of the consumer are included in the summary. There are many different problems presented, but the major problem is not clear, and there are no reasons stated for sharing the information with the group. Return now to Frame 13.

ANSWER 37

This is an incorrect response. The writer has explained the results of a service provided to help Mrs. Harold solve a pressing problem.

Return to Frame 13 and select another answer to the question.

ANSWER 38

Once the conference ends, the worker presenting the case should write a report of what was covered in its major phases—presentation of the case, group discussion, summary of the discussion, and ending—and file it in the case record for future reference. Turn now to Frame 22.

ANSWER 39

If there is to be another case presented at the conference, this would not be the time to present it. Another activity should occur before the conference ends or a new case is presented. What is this activity? Return to Frame 20 and find the answer.

ANSWER 40

There is no clear statement of the consumer's problem, although there are allusions to many different problems that Mrs. Harold is having.

Return to Frame 11, reread the summary, then answer the question in Frame 12 correctly.

ANSWER 41

Right you are, a tentative service plan is outlined in paragraph 4. Return to Frame 15.

ANSWER 42

Paragraph 3 gives an explanation of Mrs. Harold's immediate problems not a summary of the results of treatment used.

Return to Frame 13 and answer the question correctly.

ANSWER 43

There is no reference whatsoever in the summary regarding the worker's reasons for sharing this information with the other workers, nor are any specific questions stated that the worker wishes to discuss.

Return to Frame 11 for a review of the summary before answering the question in Frame 12 correctly.

ANSWER 44

Some of the possible questions that the worker could obtain help in answering are as follows:

What suggestions do the workers have for providing Mrs. Harold with continuous services to help meet her needs?
Is the suggested plan a possible solution?
How can I provide other than crisis services?

Did you mention one or another of these?
Return now to Frame 16.

ANSWER 45

There is no information in paragraph 4 regarding the results of any treatments used.
Return to Frame 13 and select the correct answer to the question.

ANSWER 46

Your summary is probably better than anything we could have written. It should have included the following components:

1. Identification information
2. A clear statement of Mrs. Harold's major problem
3. The service plan
4. A summary of the results of treatments used or services provided
5. Reasons for sharing this information and specific questions you need answered about problem areas

Turn now to Frame 17.

ANSWER 47

You have selected the correct paragraph. Well done. The results of the services that were provided to help Mrs. Harold solve her most immediate problem are presented in paragraph 5.
Return now to Frame 14.

ANSWER 48

You need to return to Frame 11 and review it carefully. There is a tentative service plan outlined in this case summary, so see if you can find it now.

**Now check your answers with the
Answer key at the end of the book**

SUMMARY

This chapter focused on some of the skills and activities used in managing information in the human services. Attention was first directed to developing recording skills. Records are required in any human service agency for four general reasons: (1) to provide a permanent documented account of services that have been received by a consumer; (2) to help workers in planning what will happen next; (3) to tell others about what has been accomplished and how things are working out; and (4) to help workers organize their thinking, see if they need additional information, and evaluate their activities with a consumer. Most agency records include date of the activity, identifying consumer information, purpose of the activity, facts of the case, how the problem was handled and why, follow-up activities, and comments and questions to discuss with other workers. It was also suggested that keeping your own personal log regarding consumers may assist you in effective recording, especially if the time between your contact with the individual and your note taking is kept at a minimum. General guidelines for effective recording were identified, including the importance of being honest in recording.

Another major skill discussed in this chapter was reporting. As a means of summarizing observations, impressions, and facts, reports communicate information in the most convenient and useful form to someone who wants or needs it. In the human services, both oral and written reports are prepared (1) to identify and explain worker and consumer needs, (2) to communicate consumer progress to human service administrators, and (3) to share problems, impressions, and information with other workers.

Four basic steps to remember in preparing any kind of report are (1) identify the purpose of the report, (2) identify the consumer, the problem and/or the information you will be reporting on, (3) collect the relevant information, and (4) organize the information. With regard to oral reports, we stressed the importance of planning what you are going to say and how you will say it and delivering the report in a confident, straightforward manner. Two major kinds of written reports were discussed, the memo and the summary. The memo is used to communicate with other service workers, and suggestions were presented for its preparation. The summary involves a combination of facts, information, and observations from one or more sources. The key to effective summarizing is planning, that is, getting your facts together and organizing them, perhaps using an outline, before summarizing the material. In preparing any report, it is always helpful to identify the purpose and to be as clear, concise, and brief as possible.

The last lesson in this chapter reviewed the case conference, which is a formal meeting among workers to discuss problems and service plans relating to consumers. Case conferences may include workers from your own agency and/or workers from other settings. The lesson discussed the use of recording and reporting skills at case conferences. When presenting a case or a problem at a case conference, it is important to include (1) a statement of the problem, (2) your observations, (3) a summary of the service plan to date, (4) a summary of the results of any treatment that has been used or services provided, and (5) your questions regarding the problem areas. The following steps in the case conference process were described: (1) a worker presents a case and the problems, (2) the group discusses the case, (3) a member of the group sums up the discussion, and (4) the meeting ends, after any other cases are discussed, and a report of the session is entered in the appropriate case record.

SUGGESTIONS FOR FURTHER STUDY

Although the basic components of information management have been presented in this chapter, further study will be necessary for a comprehensive understanding of this process. Most of the discussion and examples in this chapter were drawn from assessment or information-collecting situations. Further study should include attention to recording and reporting therapeutic information, with particular emphasis on becoming more familiar with diagnostic labels and agency terminology. For example, particular terminologies are used in medical settings, mental health settings, retardation settings, correctional settings, and welfare settings. The special skills and knowledge needed for effective recording and reporting of therapeutic information may differ somewhat from those described in this chapter. Since communicating important facts and observations is so essential in the information-management process, it may also be useful to locate additional sources for studying the techniques of organizing, summarizing, and presenting information effectively.

Further investigation regarding the case conference should be directed toward the skills required for managing and planning case conferences, effectively organizing consumer data from a wide variety of sources, and coordinating and managing worker input regarding consumer problems. It may also be profitable to pursue the basic communication skills needed for managing effective groups and for managing conferences between workers and between workers and consumers.

SUGGESTIONS FOR FURTHER READING

Benjamin, Alfred. *The Helping Interview*. Boston: Houghton Mifflin, 1969.
Cooper, Joseph D. *How to Get More Done in Less Time*. Garden City, N.Y.: Doubleday, 1962.
Davison, Evelyn. *Social Casework*. London: Bailliere, Tindall and Cox, 1965.

Ehlers, Walter H., Krishef, Curtis H., and Prothero, Jon C. *An Introduction to Mental Retardation: A Programmed Text.* Columbus, Ohio: Merrill, 1974.

Favanna, A. R. et al. *Guide to Mental Health Workers.* University of Michigan Press, 1970.

Garrett, Annette. *Interviewing: Its Principles and Methods.* New York: Family Service Association of America, 1942.

Goldberg, Gertrude S.; Kogut, Alvin B.; Lesh, Seymour; and Yates, Dorothy E. *New Careers: The Social Service Aide: A Manual for Trainees.* Washington, D.C.: University Research Corporation, 1968.

Hamilton, Gordon. *Theory and Practice of Social Casework.* New York: Columbia University Press, 1951.

Kadushin, Alfred. *The Social Work Interview.* New York: Columbia University Press, 1972.

Kron, Thora. *Communication in Nursing.* Philadelphia: Saunders, 1972.

Nicholds, Elizabeth. *In-Service Casework Training.* New York: Columbia University Press, 1966.

Schubert, Margaret. *Interviewing in Social Work Practice: An Introduction.* New York: Council on Social Work Education, 1971.

Schulman, Eveline D. *Intervention in Human Services.* St. Louis: Mosby, 1974.

Thomas, Rose C. *Public Service Careers Program, Training Manual for Case Aide Trainees.* City of New York Department of Social Services, March, 1968.

Waldo, Willis H. *Better Report Writing.* New York: Van Nostrand Reinhold, 1965.

Winicki, Sidney. "The Case Conference as a Consultation Strategy." *Psychology in the Schools* IX, no. 1 (January 1972).

REVIEW QUESTIONS—CHAPTER X

Circle the letter corresponding to the answer of your choice.

1. Agencies require that records are kept on all consumers for which of the following reasons?
    A. To provide a permanent account of services that have been given to the consumer.
    B. To help reduce the supervisor's workload
    C. To help increase the workload of all agency personnel
    D. To help workers organize their thinking about a consumer
    E. For reasons in A and D

2. How are agency records useful to the supervisor?
    A. For learning about the consumer and what has been done for him or her
    B. For planning services and/or treatments to help the consumer
    C. For reducing the supervisor's workload with individual consumers
    D. For reasons in A and B above
    E. For reasons in A, B, and C above

3. Which of the following should be included in an agency record?
    1. The identifying information about the consumer
    2. Information regarding your supervisor's evaluation of your job performance
    3. The date of each activity
    4. A short statement of the consumer's problem
    5. The amount of time you spent with the consumer

6. How you handled the consumer's major problems and why you handled them that way
7. A description of follow-up activities, if any
8. Comments and questions you would like to discuss with your supervisor

Select your answer from the following:
   A. 2, 3, 4, 5, 6, 8
   B. 1, 4, 5, 7, 8
   C. 1, 3, 4, 6, 7, 8

4. One of the best ways to help you remember important information regarding a consumer for later inclusion in the case record is by taking notes. Which of the following should be observed in taking notes?
   A. The longer you wait after the session to take notes, the clearer your memory will be of the information to be included in the record.
   B. Take detailed notes during an interview with a consumer.
   C. Take notes as soon as possible after an interview with a consumer.
   D. Include in your notes all the information you can remember.

5. If you were given the following advice related to writing effective records, which one would you *dis*regard?
   A. Record simple facts only.
   B. Write clearly, using simple sentences.
   C. Avoid emphasizing how hard you are working.
   D. Occasionally review your records to identify weak areas of information.

6. In which of the situations below is the service worker being honest with consumers regarding case records?
   A. By letting consumers know that their records will be read by no one else
   B. By telling consumers that they will never be allowed to see their records
   C. By promising consumers that their records are shared with other workers only to provide help to consumers

7. Why do agencies prepare reports?
   A. To communicate consumer progress to human service administrators
   B. To identify and explain worker and consumer needs
   C. To share problems and information
   D. For reasons in A and B
   E. For reasons in A, B, and C

8. Which of the following would you consider to be a report?
   A. A consumer's case record
   B. A memo to a fellow worker
   C. An oral presentation at a case conference
   D. B and C
   E. A and C

9. Of the following activities, which would be helpful when preparing both oral and written reports?
   A. Identifying the consumer, the problem, and the information you will be discussing
   B. Clarifying your purpose
   C. Jotting down important facts and observations

D. A and B above

E. A, B, and C above

10. When preparing to write or present a report, which task should you accomplish *last?*

    A. Collect your information.

    B. Identify the consumer.

    C. Organize your information.

    D. Be clear about your purpose.

11. Which of the following would be important when presenting an oral report?

    A. Avoid rambling.

    B. Jot down some notes of your main points.

    C. Stand up and speak up.

    D. A and C above.

    E. A, B, and C above.

12. Which of the following suggestions is useful for writing both memos and summary reports?

    A. Be as brief as possible.

    B. Be clear and specific.

    C. State your purpose at the end.

    D. A and B above.

    E. A, B, and C above.

13. When writing a report, what is the key to summarizing?

    A. Reading agency files

    B. Planning what to say

    C. Length

    D. Discussions with other workers

14. Which of the following questions should be kept in mind when writing a summary report?

    A. What is my purpose?

    B. Have I included all the important facts?

    C. Who am I writing this report for?

    D. A and C

    E. A, B, and C

15. A case conference should serve which of the following purposes?

    A. Help clarify the diagnosis of the personal problems of a service worker

    B. Support ways of helping a consumer that are already proving effective

    C. Identify the training needs of agency supervisors

    D. Help in solving a supervisor's personal problems

16. Which of the following skills would you have to use if you were a worker requesting help with a problem at a case conference?

    A. Interviewing skills

    B. Reporting skills

    C. Recording skills

    D. A and B

    E. B and C

17. If you are to present a case orally at a case conference rather than submit it in writing, what should you remember when preparing your summary?
    A. Include aspects of the case that you would normally omit in a written summary.
    B. Include the same aspects of the case that you would include in a written summary.
    C. Be briefer than you would be if it were written.
    D. None of the above.

18. Which of the following should be included in both oral and written case summaries for presentation at case conferences?
    A. Your observations of the consumer
    B. A summary of the supervision you have received
    C. The reasons you are sharing this information
    D. A and C above
    E. A, B, and C above

19. What is the major objective of a case conference?
    A. To share information on consumer related problems
    B. To help improve services to consumers
    C. To discuss supervisor and/or management problems
    D. To demonstrate reporting capabilities
    E. A and B

20. Which of the following activities should occur at a case conference after the worker has presented his case summary and raised pertinent questions and the group has discussed the case and made observations and suggestions?
    A. The meeting will end.
    B. A summary of the discussion is made by a member of the group attending the case conference.
    C. Another case is presented.

Now check your answers with the Answer key at the end of the book

CHAPTER XI:
SUPERVISING

INTRODUCTION

Have you ever thought about all the things that have to be done in order for a family to get food stamps or a mental patient to get treatment? To help us perform our jobs and deliver services to consumers, money, equipment, and supplies are needed, special training is required, and interaction among workers is necessary. Someone needs to be "in charge," someone who will see to it that the work gets done and make sure we have everything we need to do our jobs.

In the human services, we get our work done by communicating with consumers, with other workers, with supervisors, and with agency administrators. These people also have to keep in touch with us, to keep the agency operating and to make sure the work is getting done. Unless workers communicate with each other, services to consumers cannot be delivered effectively and efficiently.

In this chapter, you will learn about communicating with other workers, about some approaches to the use of supervision, and about what your supervisor can offer you. In addition, you will learn how you can supervise—how you can carry out your responsibilities when you are in charge of other workers. The overall objective is to assist you in learning how human service personnel work together to manage services by communicating with each other and by giving and receiving supervision.

Go on to Lesson 1

LESSON 1:
USING SUPERVISION

How do you use supervision? What does your supervisor do? In this lesson you will learn about your relationship with your supervisor, the purpose of supervision, and how it can help you in your work. The goal of this lesson and the enabling activities that will help you reach this goal are presented below.

GOAL

You will be able to demonstrate your skill in identifying how a worker might better use supervision.

ENABLING ACTIVITIES

After completing this lesson, you will have accomplished the following:

1. Examined the meaning of supervision
2. Reviewed four primary tasks of the supervisor
3. Identified six expectations of supervisors
4. Examined the primary elements of the communication process
5. Reviewed the basic methods of communication
6 Identified and explained five common blocks to effective communication
7. Identified and explained five bridges to understanding and improving communications

Turn to Frame 1

FRAME 1

WHAT IS SUPERVISION?

Not long ago, the supervisor was often viewed with suspicion and fear and was seen as someone who told workers what to do. Even today, many workers do not trust their supervisors or believe what they say. However, effective supervision is not something to be feared. It is a function that is necessary if we are going to deliver services to people who need them.

Supervision is the art of getting work done through the efforts and abilities of other people. It is making sure that the work gets done and that the workers know what they are doing and how they should do it. Supervision helps workers to do a better job. It also serves as a means of communicating throughout the agency, and keeps the work moving toward accomplishing the objectives of the agency.

Continue with Frame 2

FRAME 2

Supervisors are an agency's communication links between administrators and workers. Check those answers below which indicate methods by which a supervisor may facilitate intra-agency communication.

___ A. By handling complaints too insignificant to be passed on to administrative heads
___ B. By passing along policy information from the administration to the field workers
___ C. By seeking out problem areas and communicating the problems and the solutions suggested by the workers to the administration
___ D. By sharing with other supervisors and departments information about the programs and activities in one's own area of supervision

Turn to Answer 8

FRAME 3

Supervisory Responsibilities

If you want to be able to use supervision, you need to know what a supervisor does. The responsibilities of supervisors include the following:

1. **Planning and organizing the work.** Supervisors are leaders. They plan the work which must be done and how it should be done. Then they assign workers specific tasks and make sure the tasks are completed.
2. **Instructing workers.** Supervisors must also make sure that workers know how to do their jobs. They do not always do this training themselves, but they make sure that workers have the knowledge and skills needed to perform their job.
3. **Communicating with workers.** Supervisors see that the word gets through. They make sure communications are clear from administrators to workers, from workers to administrators, and from workers to other workers. They also make assignments, hold interviews, make phone calls, and talk with workers.
4. **Making improvements.** Supervisors find out if things need to be done differently. They look for problems that need attention, and they let a worker know how he or she is doing.

Try your hand at Frame 4

FRAME 4

Supervisors have four major areas of responsibility in managing workers. They (1) plan and organize the work, (2) instruct, (3) communicate, and (4) make improvements. Place the appropriate number beside each of the supervisory functions below.

___ A. Set up worker training

___ B. Pass along information from the administration

___ C. Hold interviews with workers

___ D. Assign specific tasks

___ E. Act as troubleshooter

___ F. Map out complete schedules

___ G. Determine needs based on an evaluation of each worker's output

Turn to Answer 10

FRAME 5

What Your Supervisor Expects from You

Now that you know what a supervisor does, we can talk about what your supervisor expects from you:[4]

1. **Cooperation.** You will be expected to be cooperative with all your co-workers and to demonstrate a willingness to work and learn alongside them.
2. **Initiative.** Your supervisor will expect you to complete whatever duties you are given and then, if you haven't been told what to do next, to look around, see what needs to be done, and do it if you can.
3. **Willingness to learn.** Your supervisor expects you to learn about your job and your agency and the way things are done in your agency. You should not be ashamed to say "I don't know" and to seek your supervisor's help when you need it.
4. **Willingness to follow directions.** Your supervisor will expect you to be able to follow directions and, after you have been working a while, to be able to work on well-established routines without direction.
5. **Being knowledgeable and liking your work.** Your supervisor expects you to know your job, to like your work, and to show that you like your work. You are also expected to be familiar with your agency's procedures and to be able to apply them in your daily activities.
6. **Acceptance of criticism.** Criticism is necessary since it is the way your supervisor lets you know how he or she expects the job to be done. You should accept it with a smile and try to improve when it is justified and constructive.

Advance to Frame 6

[1] See Gladys Kimbrell and Ben S. Vineyard, *Succeeding in the World of Work* (Bloomington, Ill.; McKnight and McKnight Publishing Company, 1970), p. 69.

FRAME 6

Underline the correct word or words in the parentheses.

Don had recently started work at a youth services agency. His former job had been with a similar agency in another state. Although his supervisor gave him explicit instructions in accordance with the regulations and policies of this agency, Don continued to handle his cases as he had in his former job. Don exhibited (willingness/unwillingness) to learn his new job. He also demonstrated a (desire/lack of desire) to follow the instructions of his supervisor.

Turn to Answer 7

FRAME 7

Your supervisor tells you that your field work is excellent but that you need to keep your records more up to date. What should your reaction be?

___ A. Inform your supervisor that people are more important than paper and you will eventually get around to the forms.

Turn to Answer 9

___ B. Thank your supervisor for the compliment, accept the necessity for the paperwork, and make an effort to update your files.

Turn to Answer 5

FRAME 8

Miraculously, you have finished a long project. It is 4:00 P.M. on Friday afternoon, too late to make those visits you've been planning. What would be a good thing to do?

___ A. Carefully clean your desk until 5:00 P.M.

Turn to Answer 14

___ B. Assist your co-worker, who is trying to meet a 5:00 P.M. deadline.

Turn to Answer 6

FRAME 9

What You Can Expect from Your Supervisor

Now that you know what your supervisor does and what he or she expects from you, it will be useful to think about what you can expect from your supervisor and how you can use supervision to help you do a better job. Your supervisor will or should provide the following:

1. **Training.** Your supervisor should see to it that you receive whatever on-the-job training is necessary for you to do your job. If you are not sure how to do something and you tell your supervisor, you can expect him or her to teach you or make sure someone else shows you how to do it.
2. **Explanations.** You can expect your supervisor to explain what he or she expects from you and also to explain any important policies, rules, and regulations of your agency that you should know.
3. **Changes.** You can expect your supervisor to tell you about any changes in your duties and responsibilities, and about anything else which affects you and your work.

(Frame 9 continued)

4. **Evaluations.** Your supervisor will be evaluating your performance on the job by assessing your work and making suggestions on how you can improve.

5. **Discipline.** If you don't follow rules and regulations, or if you don't live up to what is expected of you, you may be disciplined by your supervisor.

6. **Support.** You can expect your supervisor to give you the opportunity to demonstrate your ability, to understand your viewpoints, to encourage you to improve your performance, and to try to help you when you request assistance with a problem.

Proceed to Frame 10

FRAME 10

You have probably noticed in working through the last several pages that a supervisor's actions and duties to a subordinate are often a result of the attitudes and actions of the subordinate. If a new employee exhibits a lack of knowledge about his or her duties and methods of performing them but has an eagerness to learn, a supervisor must

A. make changes.

Turn to Answer 13

B. give discipline.

Turn to Answer 2

C. set up a training session.

Turn to Answer 11

FRAME 11

After an employee has been given training and is ready to begin a project, the supervisor should

A. evaluate the employee's work.

Turn to Answer 1

B. give clear explanations of the methods by which the project goals may be achieved.

Turn to Answer 3

C. offer support as the project gets underway.

Turn to Answer 17

D. do both B and C above.

Turn to Answer 20

FRAME 12

Albert had received good training and repeated instructions, but would not follow directions. The supervisor was then forced to

A. reprimand Albert.

Turn to Answer 18

B. change the instructions.

Turn to Answer 15

C. retrain Albert.

Turn to Answer 4

Greer has discovered a way of completing a routine job more effectively. When presenting this idea to her supervisor, she may reasonably expect

A. an evaluation of the idea.

Turn to Answer 16

B. support for her initiative.

Turn to Answer 19

C. the supervisor to facilitate changes to bring about the new routine if the evaluation is good.

Turn to Answer 21

D. all of the above.

Turn to Answer 12

THE COMMUNICATION PROCESS

Once again, we return to the important process of communication, only this time we are emphasizing communication with your supervisor. Communication is a two way street; it is the creation of understanding. When you communicate with your supervisor, you are sending and receiving messages, and the reason you are sending and receiving these messages is that you want to be understood.

Human service agencies are complex organizations that utilize large numbers of people with different skills and responsibilities to do certain tasks. If we did not communicate constantly and effectively with each other, it would be impossible to perform our jobs effectively. There are guidelines and procedures that everyone in the organization needs to understand so that new and old policies can be communicated to everyone concerned. The administrators of the agency must know what is happening at all levels, and the communication processes that provide this information are vital. If communication in either direction fails, the continued life of the organization is in danger.

It is deceptively simple and easy to define communication as the transferring of information from one person to another. This definition is basically correct, however, it leaves unstated some important characteristics of the communication process. Without going into great detail, we shall now take a closer look at some of the major aspects of successful communication.

The sequence of events that begins the communication process starts with someone who wants to share information with someone else. This person, the *sender*, must decide exactly what he or she wants to communicate and assemble it in the form of a written or spoken *message*. The message must be prepared with the overall purpose of the communication in mind, and with an appreciation for the language generally used by the person receiving the message. The entire message must be carefully constructed to be as clear and concise as possible. The message goes to the *receiver*, the person or group for whom the message is intended. Unless the receiver gets the message, understands it as it was meant, and takes the intended action, the communication has failed.

The final stage of the communication process is concerned with determining whether the receiver has understood the message and was offered opportunities for

(Frame 14 continued)

clarification. The sender needs to be alert to *feedback* from the receiver so that he or she can make sure the receiver gets the correct message. By noting the effect of communications, the sender should be able to continually improve the quality and effectiveness of future communications. A diagram of the communication process generally looks like this:

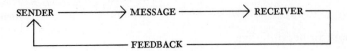

Turn to Frame 15

FRAME 15

Select the phrase that best defines communication.

A. a sequence of events
B. deceptively simple
C. the transfer of information
D. dependent on the sender

Turn to Answer 40

FRAME 16

Which of the following most clearly describes communication?

A. Passing information along

Turn to Answer 23

B. Creating a situation whereby each person involved has a clear understanding of the message and its import to him or her

Turn to Answer 27

C. Regular conferences with co-workers and associates

Turn to Answer 30

FRAME 17

In order to make certain he or she understands the communication, the receiver should

A. repeat the information as presented.

Turn to Answer 22

B. write it down for future reference.

Turn to Answer 26

C. begin a discussion with the sender by asking questions or summarizing prior discussions.

Turn to Answer 24

FRAME 18

Methods of Communicating

At this point, you are well aware of the three basic methods of communication—oral, written, and nonverbal. If you feel you have a clear understanding of each of these methods, you may choose to skip to Frame 20. If, however, you are interested in a refresher, the following discussion may be helpful.

Oral communication. The most common form of communication between people is through the spoken word, although it is customary to put complicated and/or important communications in writing. Oral communication takes place in different situations such as when workers talk to a consumer or a group of consumers or to a supervisor or a group of supervisors. Oral communication is especially useful when relating an urgent message such as a command. A spoken communication offers the advantage of giving people a chance to "talk it over" and arrive at an understanding or decision. Another advantage is the opportunity for the sender and receiver to be sure they have the same exact understanding of the message because clarification can be given on the spot. Most of the time we are listeners (receivers) not speakers (senders); the total burden of communicating is not carried by the speaker but is shared between speaker and listener.

Written communication. Communication is usually written when a particular action is expected from the receiver. Written communications should spell out exactly the intended message. The original and any copies can serve as a record and as a reminder. Written messages are more formal and are typically used for matters that are important. Some typical forms of written communications are letters, memos, manuals of policy and procedure, and newsletters. The most effective form to use depends on the subject matter and the situation.

In preparing a written communication, the writer should keep in mind that the message must be perfectly clear so that the receiver will be able to understand readily. A misunderstood message can sometimes be much worse than no message at all. Perhaps the biggest pitfall in preparing a written communication is not taking enough time to get the message across. The sender should be aware that the receiver will not hear a voice or see a face and should, therefore, clearly define all potentially confusing aspects of the message. The greatest limitation of written communications is that the receiver usually does not have an immediate opportunity to ask clarifying questions and is thus tempted to make interpretations. This reason itself is enough to prompt us to exercise great care and state clearly what we mean when preparing written communications.

Nonverbal communication. Communication by gestures is a method of limited use because there is not a universal language of gestures. A certain gesture or facial expression may mean something to one person or group and something else to another. Although we are alert to gestures, understanding them usually requires that they be part of a more direct verbal communication. If you encounter someone you have not seen for some time in a store and the person says how nice it is to see you while slowly edging toward the exit, you may reasonably wonder exactly how "glad" the person was to see you. Gestures affect the meaning of oral communications and may even change the meaning of the message.

Common gestures and body cues include signs of nervousness, physical discomfort, anger, fear, and helplessness. By noticing these cues, we can better control our own actions and reactions to alleviate the discomfort of the other person. The conscious use of gestures is a little more difficult because gestures are largely habits of long standing that are difficult to change or modify. We can begin by trying to be more aware of ourselves as others see us and noting the kind of nonverbal communications we use. If you are discussing a stressful situation with your supervisor, do your facial expressions, tone of voice, and posture reflect support? Do they communicate disinterest or boredom? Watch your own gestures the next time you talk to someone.

Proceed to Frame 19

FRAME 19

Indicate what form of communication (oral, written, nonverbal) would probably be used in each of the following situations by writing your choice in the blanks beside each statement.

_____ 1. The building is on fire and everyone is in danger.

_____ 2. You are at a boring staff meeting.

_____ 3. Your office mate wants to know the time.

_____ 4. You have to set up a complex procedure for handling case records.

_____ 5. An attractive new staff member smiles at you in the coffee room.

Turn to Answer 41

FRAME 20

Blocks to Effective Communication with Your Supervisor

One of the main reasons you should learn about communications is so that you will understand how communications break down or are blocked. This happens because people don't always say what they mean and because they sometimes get the wrong idea about what is being said to them.

In most communications, the sender of a message hopes to get feedback from the receiver. But often, while the message is being sent, there are blocks or barriers that prevent the receiver from understanding the message. These blocks may be created by the sender, the receiver, or the message. Experts in communications have identified many such blocks to communication, and we have chosen five of the more important blocks to discuss:[2]

1. **Listening blocks.** It is entirely possible for a person to hear every word that someone else says but to have none of it register. Senders or receivers may nod their heads and look as though they understand what is being said, but one cannot be sure.
2. **Word blocks.** Words mean different things to different people. If the message is confusing or uses very technical words, it may not be understood and the communication will be blocked.
3. **Self-interest blocks.** We listen to what we want to hear and shut out what we do not want to hear. When our personal interests and emotions become most important, understanding is nearly impossible.
4. **Blocks due to lack of planning.** When the sender does not spend time planning the message with a specific purpose in mind, the communication is almost sure to be blocked.
5. **Blocks to seeing needs.** This is when we just don't see the need to communicate with other workers at all. "I don't think it was necessary to tell them" is a common response of people creating such a block to communication.

Go on to Frame 21

[2] Bradford B. Boyd, *Management-Minded Supervision* (New York: McGraw-Hill, 1968), p. 49.

FRAME 21

Some of the five blocks to communication listed in Frame 20 are caused by the sender, some by the receiver, and some through the faults of either party. For each barrier to communication listed below, indicate who would be at fault by writing S for sender, R for receiver, and E for either.

___ 1. Self interest

___ 2. Failure to plan the message

___ 3. Differences in word interpretation

___ 4. Careless listening

___ 5. Failure to see the need for communicating a message

Turn to Answer 33

FRAME 22

A self interest block may result when which of the following subjects are discussed?

A. Emotional subjects (e.g., religion, politics)

Turn to Answer 31

B. Behavior of co-workers

Turn to Answer 36

C. Interesting case studies

Turn to Answer 25

D. Items in A and B above

Turn to Answer 29

E. All of the above

Turn to Answer 37

FRAME 23

Jack was assigned to take over three cases from Bill. When Jack went for the initial interviews with the three families, he realized that Bill had wasted his time by blocking communication through:

A. poor planning of the message

Turn to Answer 35

B. failure to see the need to inform Jack

Turn to Answer 32

C. allowing self interest to stand in his way

Turn to Answer 28

FRAME 24

Bridges to Understanding Communication

Now that you know some of the ways communications are blocked, we need to talk about ways to remove these blocks in order to improve your communications. Let's look at each block to communication and talk about a bridge you can use to make sure you are being understood.[3]

(Frame 24 continued)

[3] Ibid., p. 50.

Removing listening blocks. In any communication, it is up to the sender to make sure the receiver understands the message by using the feedback bridge. In face-to-face communications, the receiver is constantly sending back reactions to what is being said and sending out signals that tell whether he or she is listening. These signals may be seen in a person's posture and the look on his or her face or heard in the person's voice. The sender can check to see if the message is getting across by saying, for example, "Let me see if I can put it another way," or by asking questions to see if the message has been understood. In this manner the sender gets feedback to see if the receiver is listening.

Removing word blocks. How do you remove the problem of having your words misunderstood? You bridge the gap by gearing your message to the receiver. You have to consider the vocabulary of the receiver. If you are using words he or she doesn't understand, you'll have to put the message another way. As a receiver of a message, you have to swallow your pride and admit it when you aren't sure of a word's meaning. Asking what a word or term means shows your interest in understanding the message and tells the sender that he or she needs to make the message clearer.

Removing self-interest blocks. How do you keep your personal interests and emotions from becoming all important? You use the empathy bridge. This means putting yourself in the other person's shoes and seeing things from his point of view. It means asking yourself, "Why is he saying that? Why does he feel that way? What would make him ask that?" It means trying to understand the message that the other person is sending.

Removing planning blocks. How can you plan your communications better? You can bridge the planning gap by trying to pinpoint the answers to the following six questions before you send the message: (1) What am I trying to get across? (2) Who will receive my communication? (3) When is the best time to communicate? (4) Where is the best place to communicate? (5) How should I communicate? and (6) Why am I communicating?

Removing blocks to seeing the need. How do you prevent yourself from not communicating at all? You can use the awareness bridge. As a worker in the human services, you should be aware of your responsibility to communicate with other workers. You can do this by always striving for understanding, by working at listening to others, and by making sure they have the information they need. You can put communication on a positive basis when problems arise by finding ways to keep them from happening again instead of blaming someone else. Accept your responsibility to communicate with your co-workers, and do everything you can to keep your agency operating smoothly as you help consumers. Develop an awareness of the importance of communication in performing your job.

Go on to Frame 25

FRAME 25

Both the sender and the receiver must make an effort to avoid word blocks in the communication process. Below are some solutions. Write S if the solution is more appropriate for the sender to use, R if the receiver would be the one to initiate the solution, and E if either party can effectively use the aid.

____ 1. Ask for clarification of terms.

____ 2. Select words, jargon, and technical terms which are clearest and most appropriate to the situation.

____ 3. Restate the message using different words.

Turn to Answer 38

FRAME 26

Every newspaper reporter has learned the cardinal rule of the communications media, namely, the use of the five W's—the secret to planning the communication of information quickly and effectively. The underlined words below are the what, why, when, where and who of the message. In the blanks following the underlined words, indicate which W is being used.

We want <u>you</u> (_____) to know the <u>principles of communication</u> (_____) as <u>soon as possible</u> (_____) so that you can <u>effectively serve</u> (_____) your client group in the <u>community</u> (_____).

Turn to Answer 34

FRAME 27

Joe received a memo from his supervisor saying that the new program Joe had planned for his clients would not be initiated because of budget considerations. Joe immediately became angry and called the supervisor's office, whereupon he was told to put his complaints in writing. In the space below, state at least two ways in which the sender and two ways in which the receiver could have avoided the unpleasantness surrounding this communication problem.

What the sender could have done:

1.

2.

What the receiver could have done:

1.

2.

Turn to Answer 39

FRAME 28

You have now successfully completed this lesson, and Lesson 2 should be a snap. If you are satisfied with your accomplishments, move right on; if not, briefly review this lesson before going on to Lesson 2.

ANSWERS TO LESSON 1

ANSWER 1

An evaluation of work in progress or work completed is not possible before the project actually begins. Reread the question in Frame 11 carefully before making another selection.

ANSWER 2

Discipline cannot correct a lack of knowledge. Look over Frame 9 once more, then make a better choice in Frame 10.

ANSWER 3

This is a very important task for the supervisor; but another answer is also important for good interpersonal relationships. You will see it too, after rereading Frame 11 completely.

ANSWER 4

Since Albert's training for this job has been *good*, retraining is not likely to remedy the situation. Make a better selection to answer the problem expressed in Frame 12.

ANSWER 5

Your supervisor will appreciate your good use of empathy to accept this criticism and will also expect you to keep your word. Now continue to Frame 8 to check your understanding of further expectations.

ANSWER 6

Marvelous! Your willingness to cooperate and to take the initiative in helping is what a supervisor will value, as will your co-workers. Now turn to Frame 9.

ANSWER 7

You marked "unwillingness" and "lack of desire," didn't you? Good. It's now clear that you are beginning to understand two of the six things supervisors must expect from their staff. Advance to Frame 7 and continue the good work.

ANSWER 8

Answers A, B, C, and D are ways a supervisor can handle a flow of information. If you had any trouble with this, review Frame 1 and then proceed to Frame 3. If you had no trouble, go right on to Frame 3.

ANSWER 9

This reaction may be the natural one for you, but your supervisor expects you to accept constructive criticism with good grace. Try to place yourself in your supervisor's shoes before you express your reaction. Return to Frame 7 and select the correct answer.

ANSWER 10

A: The answer is 2. Remember that supervisors must make sure workers know how to do the job.

B: The answer is 3. Passing on information is one of the important elements in seeing that the work outcome is what is desired.

C: The answer is 3. Interviews are a form of communication that determine whether the work is being done properly and whether others have access to information needed to carry out their tasks.

D: The answer is 1. Assignments reduce both duplication of effort and under-achievement.

E: The answer is 4. If supervisors are aware of problems and potential delays, they can then take steps to make necessary improvement.

F: The answer is 1. Scheduling assures that a project will be completed with minimal waste in time, materials, and personnel.

G: The answer is 4. By evaluating, supervisors can make recommendations to improve the worker's efficiency.

Did you answer all these correctly? If so, very good; go on to Frame 5. If two or more gave you trouble, review Frame 3, then check your logic in Frame 4 once more.

ANSWER 11

We think this is the best solution in the situation described. This will probably be most efficient, least complicated and produce the best results. Should this not work, changes may then be in order. Continue with Frame 11.

ANSWER 12

That's it. Greer may reasonably expect each of these steps from her supervisor as he considers her new plan. Hopefully she will appreciate the time and attention he accords her. Return to Frame 14.

ANSWER 13

The phrase "but an eagerness to learn" is the key that tells a supervisor that there is probably an answer which will remedy the situation more readily than switching jobs. Glance at Frame 9 before selecting another response to Frame 10.

ANSWER 14

While there is nothing basically wrong with this choice, it demonstrates neither cooperation nor initiative. Check over Frame 5 again to be familiar with what your supervisor expects of you and then answer the question in Frame 8 correctly.

ANSWER 15

This will probably not solve the problem nor accomplish the project goals. Albert has evidently had an opportunity to express any sound reasons for disregarding instructions in the past. The key words are "repeated instructions." Try another answer to Frame 12.

ANSWER 16

This is, of course, a reasonable expectation. But the best supervisors will go further than that—even with a seemingly bad idea. Consider the choices once more and then answer Frame 13 correctly.

ANSWER 17

This is an important task for this supervisor and will help to build strong employee relationships. But before work can begin, more information is needed by the subordinate. Consider all parts of Frame 11 again and then select the correct answer.

ANSWER 18

This appears to be the best choice since Albert seems to have no excuses as the situation is described. To make certain, the supervisor should talk with Albert first to ascertain if there might be an unknown reason for the violation. Discovering such a reason might then suggest an approach other than reprimand. See if you are as astute in handling the problem in Frame 13.

ANSWER 19

Initiative on the part of an employee should always be supported, if it is reasonable. A conscientious supervisor will not just hand out pats on the back, however. After reconsidering the alternatives, make a more complete choice to the question in Frame 13.

ANSWER 20

Agreed. A supervisor will be building excellent worker-supervisor relations by giving clear explanations and offering support during the project work. Frame 12 should now be a breeze.

ANSWER 21

Certainly any employee has a right to expect assistance with a good idea. But the supervisor must arrive at that point through other considerations. Flip back to Frame 13 and select another route.

ANSWER 22

A verbatim repeat of the information does not assure that the message is understood, especially if the message contains highly technical terms or words which have a variety of connotations. Check Frame 14 for a refresher, before answering the questions in Frame 17 correctly.

ANSWER 23

This is the end result of effective communication. Review Frame 14 and select a better answer to the question in Frame 16.

ANSWER 24

The best choice. This allows both sender and receiver to be sure the message is properly received. It may clarify any misunderstandings caused by vague language, technical terms or complex problems. Now move on to Frame 18 and continue the good work.

ANSWER 25

It is unlikely that interesting case studies would arouse enough personal feeling to cause a self-interest block. Review Frame 20 and then choose another answer to the question in Frame 22.

ANSWER 26

Writing out the message may help you remember it, but if the message is not understood, a written copy does not clarify it later. Review Frame 14 and make a better selection to the question in Frame 17.

ANSWER 27

You have chosen the best answer. Your communication skills are already showing improvement. Turn to Frame 17.

ANSWER 28

While Bill may have personal reasons for failing to talk with Jack about the new cases, the paragraph does not mention them. Your choice should be based upon the information given, try another answer to the question in Frame 23.

ANSWER 29

This answer shows good comprehension. You can probably list several other self-interest blocks as well which might occur within a communications effort. Continue on to Frame 23.

ANSWER 30

This may be one way to open the door to better communication in your organization, but it is not the best description of communication. Return to Frame 16 and try again.

ANSWER 31

This is true. But there are other similar situations which you must have overlooked. Review Frame 20 and select another alternative to the question in Frame 22.

ANSWER 32

A good choice. Everyone's time would have been better spent if Bill had realized Jack's need to know what to expect. Advance to Frame 24.

ANSWER 33

Number 1 is a shortcoming on the part of the receiver, although a sender can also be blocked by self interest. The sender must accept responsibility for numbers 2 and 5. Numbers 3 and 4 may result on the part of either party. In number 3, the sender should take special care to choose words which will be clearly understood by the receiver. In number 4, the receiver must listen carefully, but so must the sender in order to check out the feedback information from the receiver.

How well did you do? If you had any trouble, review Frame 20. If you wrote all the correct answers, congratulations! Go on to Frame 22.

ANSWER 34

You would be the person *who* is to get the message. Principles of communications are *what* must be learned. As soon as possible is *when* they should be learned. To serve effectively is *why* these methods should be learned. The community is *where* these principles will be put to use. Advance to Frame 27.

ANSWER 35

Poor planning cannot be at fault unless a message is sent. Careful consideration will no doubt lead you to the proper choice—so try another answer to the question in Frame 23.

ANSWER 36

Because of close working relationships, a discussion of this sort might lead to communication blocking on the self-interest level. However, there are other ways in which this blocking may also occur. After reviewing Frame 20, make another choice to the question in Frame 22.

ANSWER 37

Please read carefully and with greater attention to detail. Review Frame 20 before making another choice to the question in Frame 22.

ANSWER 38

The receiver (R) should seek clarification or definition of the terms or words. The sender (S) should choose the language appropriate to the receiver and the message topic. The chances of establishing effective communication are enhanced if either (E) party restates the message by paraphrasing it. Can you think of situations where both the sender and the receiver would be responsible for clarifying, selecting words or restating the message? Now you may continue with Frame 26.

ANSWER 39

Sender: (1) Could have chosen a better method of communicating—perhaps a one-to-one conference. (2) Could have chosen language more carefully, giving explicit reasons for the cancellation and using specific terms. (3) Might have anticipated the disappointment and reaction of the receiver and thereby planned the tone and impact to elicit the best possible response. (4) Should have been aware of the need to communicate with Joe personally after the message was received.

Receiver: (1) Could have tried to overcome the self-interest block by placing himself in his supervisor's position of having to balance the budget. (2) Before reacting so strongly, could have sought clarification of the memo to ascertain its true import and the possibilities for compromise, revision, or rescheduling of his project.

Do you need more review? Try making up your own communication problem and then solving it. Return to Frame 28.

ANSWER 40

Every answer given is correct, but C is more correct than the others:

A. Communication is a sequence of events but this doesn't say much about what those events accomplish.
B. This is a very shallow answer and is probably the poorest choice.
C. The essence of communication is the transfer of information. This is the best answer.
D. Communication is dependent on the sender but it also depends on the receiver. This response is not complete enough to be a really good answer.

Go on to Frame 16.

ANSWER 41

The most appropriate methods are as follows:

1. Oral
2. Non-verbal
3. Oral
4. Written
5. This situation is a matter of personal preference, and you'd be on your own. Good luck!

Return to Frame 20.

LESSON 2:
AN INTRODUCTION
TO SUPERVISION

Suppose you are placed in charge of a number of other workers. What will your actions be toward them? You will remember from Lesson 1 that supervision means getting work done through the efforts of other people. Therefore, in this lesson you will be learning some of the skills you need to be an effective supervisor. The goal of this lesson and the enabling activities that will help you reach this goal are presented below.

GOAL

You will be able to describe each of the four supervisory duties and explain how the supervisor carries them out.

ENABLING ACTIVITIES

After completing this lesson, you will have accomplished four things:

1. Identified the four purposes of supervision
2. Described a method the supervisor can use to carry out each of his four duties
3. Explained what is meant by a supervisor "bringing out the best in people"
4. Reviewed five guidelines that are helpful in fulfilling supervisory responsibilities

Turn to Frame 1

FRAME 1

If you are in charge of other workers, you have moved into a whole new territory. You have moved from doing the job to supervising others who do the job; thus, you are now responsible for seeing that the work gets done. As a first step in understanding supervision, you should be familiar with the purposes of supervision or why it is needed in a human service agency.

(Frame 1 continued)

1. Supervision helps workers do a better job. The supervisor is their leader who makes sure that the work gets done.
2. Supervision promotes each worker's individual growth and capacity. The supervisor is there to help his or her workers and to see that they learn about their job and their agency.
3. Supervision is a means of communicating throughout the agency. The supervisor is the link between the top administrators of the agency and individual workers. He or she passes on messages from higher administrators to individual workers. The supervisor also reports back individual worker's responses to top administrators and other supervisors.
4. Supervision keeps work moving toward the objectives of the agency. By keeping the work moving and making sure the work gets done, supervision makes sure that agency objectives are carried out.

Move on to Frame 2

FRAME 2

Which of the following is false?

A. Supervision is a leadership role.

Turn to Answer 3

B. Supervisors are a major communications link in an agency.

Turn to Answer 6

C. A supervisor is the final arbiter in all disputes in the agency.

Turn to Answer 2

D. Supervisors promote individual growth in each worker.

Turn to Answer 8

FRAME 3

How does the supervisor help make sure the objectives of an agency are carried out?

A. Keeps the work moving

Turn to Answer 1

B. Makes sure the work gets accomplished

Turn to Answer 4

C. Attends state and national conferences

Turn to Answer 7

D. A and B above

Turn to Answer 10

E. A, B, and C above

Turn to Answer 13

FRAME 4

You will remember that the four duties of the supervisor are planning and organizing the work, instructing workers, communicating with workers, and making improvements. How does a supervisor fulfill these duties? A basic rule about supervision is that a supervisor must be effective at getting results through the efforts of other people. If you are going to be effective at getting results through the effects of other workers, where do you begin? The first thing a supervisor must know is what job has to be done and how to do it. Supervisors must also be secure in their own abilities and must be able to recognize talent in others.

But in order to be effective, a supervisor must also demonstrate certain skills. He or she must be able to carry out each of the four duties or tasks we talked about earlier. Chances are you already know how, but in case you do not, we shall review some of the ways a supervisor performs each of these duties.

1. **Planning and organizing the work.**[1] If you are going to achieve results through employing people, you must be able to plan and organize the work and lead your workers so that the work will get done. Planning and organizing are the *thinking* you do before you get any action at all. You need answers to the following questions when you are planning.

> **What.** Is your goal clearly in mind? What work do you have to do to reach your goal?
> **When.** How long will it take to do the job and each part of the job? When is the best time to start?
> **Where.** Do you need to meet with your workers, and if so, where? Where will the work get done?
> **Who.** Who will do the work? Who is best qualified?
> **How.** How will the work get done? What methods will you use?

2. **Instructing workers.**[2] There are many methods a supervisor uses to make sure workers know how to do their jobs. Staff meetings serve the double purpose of giving information and helping workers understand various problem areas. For instructing individual workers, a supervisor may ask another worker or an agency trainer to teach a certain subject or skill area, or the supervisor may personally demonstrate specific skills and techniques. When doing this, the supervisor should be patient, prepare what will be said, avoid giving too many details at one time, and try to demonstrate as well as inform about the skills and techniques that are needed on the job.

3. **Communicating with workers.** We talked about communicating with other workers in Lesson 1 of this chapter. The supervisor has a special responsibility to communicate with each of his or her workers. As a supervisor you should let workers know how they are getting along, make sure all workers understand what you are saying, listen to workers when they have problems, and tell workers in advance about changes which will affect them.

4. **Making improvements.** It is up to the supervisor to observe the work that is being done and to find the problems that need attention. Supervisors should make sure their workers feel free to come up with ideas about how things could be done better. This can be done by asking questions such as "Why is this done?" "How is it done?" "How could it be done better?" Supervisors also involve their workers in efforts at making improvements.

The supervisor is responsible for evaluating how workers are performing. Ratings tell the supervisor when workers need additional training, if they are misplaced in their job due to lack of some special abilities, and whether they are eligible for any promotions and/or pay increases.

Review by turning to Frame 5

---

[1] See Bradford B. Boyd, *Management-Minded Supervision* (New York: McGraw-Hill, 1968), pp. 223–225.
[2] Ibid., p. 142.

FRAME 5

Which of the following is *not* the aim of worker evaluation?

A. To uncover a need for special training.

Turn to Answer 5

B. To demonstrate the superior authority of the supervisor.

Turn to Answer 9

C. To find out if the employee is misplaced in the job due to lack of special skills.

Turn to Answer 14

FRAME 6

Bringing Out the Best in Workers

Just being the supervisor does not always mean workers are going to follow your instructions. Nor does it mean you are never going to have any complaints or discipline problems. What can you do when things like this happen? Bringing out the best in people means helping them use their enthusiastic, ambitious, and creative desires on the job.[3] To do this, supervisors must treat workers fairly, encourage them, and create a climate of teamwork.

When a worker complains about something or disobeys a rule or does something wrong, what should you do? As a supervisor, you must show regard for people's feelings. You must be able to discipline people, even crack down if necessary, without hurting their feelings. You have to point out errors tactfully. Two ways of bringing out the best in people when these things happen are (1) giving clear instructions and making sure everyone understands the instructions and (2) disciplining people in private.

Fortunately, few workers ever need to be disciplined. But when something happens that makes this necessary, here are some guidelines you can follow: Control your temper, be sure of your facts, talk to the offender in private, get the other side of the story, be firm but fair, and express confidence in the person's ability to improve.[4]

**Frame 7 gives you a chance to test
your understanding of these skills**

FRAME 7

For the past month Eliott has been late. Three times in the last week he has come to the office an hour late, twice he has returned from lunch at an unreasonable time —all without informing his secretary, co-workers, or supervisor. Eliott is an excellent worker, often making up the time (and more) at night and on weekends. However, he misses many calls and visitors and his co-workers are beginning to take offense. Although the supervisor, Hugh, has spoken to Eliott twice before, it is obvious that something must be done. Below are some possible ways Hugh might try to remedy the situation. Check those you think would be beneficial.

—— 1. Call Eliott on the intercom and begin reading the "riot act."

—— 2. Set up a meeting with Eliott and Hugh's immediate superior.

---

[3] See Raymond J. Burby, *An Introduction to Basic Supervision of People* (Reading, Mass.: Addison- Wesley, 1966).

[4] Bradford B. Boyd, *Management-Minded Supervision* (New York: McGraw-Hill, 1968), pp. 170–173.

__ 3. Mention the matter at the next staff meeting.

__ 4. Ask Eliott if there is a special reason for his chronic lateness—get his side of the story.

__ 5. Avoid being goaded into an argument.

__ 6. Compliment Eliott on the quality of the work done, but present the difficulties of his irregular hours; seek his empathy.

__ 7. Circulate and attach to the bulletin board a new list of stricter rules warning offenders of severe punishment for all tardiness.

__ 8. In a private meeting, explain this is the last warning and suggest that Eliott take the day off to consider whether or not he can accommodate the agency's policies.

Turn to Answer 11

FRAME 8

To help you in fulfilling your responsibilities as a supervisor, here are some suggested overall guidelines:

1. Earn the worker's respect; be fair and show genuine concern.
2. Build the worker's confidence by helping him master his responsibilities.
3. Do not talk down to him; avoid a pitying approach.
4. Show the worker the part he plays in the agency and the importance of his work to the agency.
5. Set a good example; show what you expect of others by what you do.
6. Discuss new procedures, terms, and instructions very carefully and slowly. Find ways to get feedback from the worker that shows he understands, without giving the impression you think he is stupid.
7. Be friendly; have an interest in your workers as individuals.

**Try an application of these
guidelines in Frames 9 and 10**

FRAME 9

Eric spoke to his supervisor, David, about what he thought were the beginnings of racial discrimination in his section. David told Eric he understood Eric's sensitivity to racial overtones, commented on the problems Eric must have overcome in spite of his race, and suggested that those in Eric's section were really nice people and surely meant no harm. As a supervisor, David expressed (friendliness/pity) in his conversation with Eric.

**Underline the correct word
and then turn to Answer 16**

FRAME 10

Sam was delighted with his new job as supervisor. It marked a large step toward his long-range goal, and he felt it to be only a matter of time before he was one of the agency's top administrators. With frequent overtime demanded of a supervisor, Sam allowed himself the luxury of arriving at his office after the morning traffic rush had subsided. When it became evident that his subordinates were also arriving later, what should Sam have done?

(Frame 10 continued)

A. Taken decisive action to reduce tardiness by reducing leave time

Turn to Answer 12

B. Realized he had not set a good example and corrected his own habit before reprimanding others

Turn to Answer 17

C. Explained to his staff that he was due the time because of his heavy responsibilities, but tell the others to be on time

Turn to Answer 15

ANSWERS TO LESSON 2

ANSWER 1

Yes, this is one way the supervisor helps see to it that the objectives of the agency are met, but there are other ways. Return to Frame 3 and identify the other ways.

ANSWER 2

You caught it! A supervisor should certainly attempt to settle minor difficulties, to smooth ruffled feathers. However, supervisors must recognize the need to involve others in solving agency problems. Proceed to Frame 3.

ANSWER 3

Did you read the question properly? Reread it, then make the proper choice to the question in Frame 2.

ANSWER 4

This is one of the major ways in which the supervisor makes sure agency objectives are met. However, there are others. Return to Frame 3 and identify the other way.

ANSWER 5

This is one of the most valuable outcomes of worker evaluation. As you are seeking the *false* answer, please weigh all choices critically before making another selection in Frame 5.

ANSWER 6

Supervisors certainly are a major communications link in an agency. You are looking for the *false* alternative. Now you can make the proper choice for Frame 2.

ANSWER 7

This is the only incorrect answer of the three stated in the question. Although attending state and national conferences may assist the supervisor in his or her professional competence, it is not considered a major method for accomplishing agency objectives. Return to Frame 1 for a review and then select the correct answer to the question in Frame 3.

ANSWER 8

Since individual growth of workers adds to the agency's aggregate good, supervisors would be remiss if they did not do their best to promote such growth. Remember, you are seeking the *false* answer to the question in Frame 2, so return there now and try it again.

ANSWER 9

Correct. Both A and C are valid reasons for evaluation. B is not an aim because its only purpose is to irritate staff members. Proceed to Frame 6.

ANSWER 10

Well done—the supervisor helps assure that agency objectives are reached by keeping the work in the agency moving and by making sure the work gets done.

Return to Frame 4 and examine all the major functions of a supervisor identified there.

ANSWER 11

You should have checked numbers 2, 4, 5, 6, and 8. If you checked any of the other choices, review Frame 6. If there are correct ones you left unchecked, try to imagine circumstances in which they would be acceptable, and then proceed to Frame 8.

ANSWER 12

If Sam does this, he (1) fails to reason from the particular to the general and (2) stands to lose the respect of his subordinates. Review Frame 8 before accepting the second choice in Frame 10.

ANSWER 13

This answer is but two-thirds correct. Attending state and national conferences is not a major method by which the supervisor helps make sure the objectives of an agency are fulfilled. Return to Frame 3 and select the correct answer.

ANSWER 14

Perhaps a glance at Frame 4 will clarify any misconception of the purposes of evaluation. Which choice in Frame 5 is *not* a positive reinforcement for the worker?

ANSWER 15

While Sam's excuse may be true, it is unlikely to encourage his subordinates to exert any special effort. Check point 6 in Frame 8 for a better solution to Sam's problem, and then select a more appropriate response to the question in Frame 10.

ANSWER 16

While David's answer may have been aimed at friendliness, we think the choice of language indicates pity or talking down to Eric. For additional hints on supervising minority group members see James H. Morrison's *Human Factors in Supervising Minority Group Employees* (see the bibliography).

Proceed to Frame 10.

ANSWER 17

Right again! This option allows both Sam and his subordinates to retain respect for his integrity and wisdom.

You have reached the end of the chapter on supervising, which is also the end of

Unit Four. We're sure you are now ready to tackle the short review of Chapter XI at the end of this lesson. If you are, go there now. If you have any doubts, return to the beginning of this chapter for a review before you begin the review questions.

SUMMARY

In this chapter special attention was given to supervision as one of the major processes necessary in managing human services. Lesson 1 was concerned with two important concepts: how to use supervision and how to improve your skills in communicating both with your own supervisor and with other workers. Supervision was defined (1) as the art of getting work done through the efforts and abilities of other people and (2) as a means of facilitating communication throughout the agency. You learned about using supervision effectively. The major tasks of the supervisor are planning and organizing the work, instructing workers, communicating with workers, and making improvements. In performing these tasks, a supervisor expects you to be cooperative, to show initiative, to demonstrate a willingness to learn and follow directions, to know and like your work, and to accept constructive criticisms. You, on the other hand, can expect your supervisor to provide you with training, explanations of his or her expectations for you, communications regarding your work, evaluations of your performance, discipline, and support.

Communication was discussed as one of the basic processes involved in both using and giving supervision. The elements important in any communication were identified as the sender, the receiver, the message, and feedback. A short review of the three basic methods of communication was presented. Five common blocks which prevent communications from being understood were discussed—the listening block, the word block, the self-interest block, the planning block, and the block of failing to see the need to communicate. The bridges which can remove these communication blocks and bring about effective communication are the feedback bridge, gearing your message to the receiver, the empathy bridge, the planning bridge, and the awareness bridge.

Lesson 2 was concerned with the purposes of supervision and with providing an introduction to the basic skills necessary in supervising other workers. Supervision (1) helps workers do a better job, (2) promotes each worker's individual growth and capacity, (3) is a means of communicating throughout the agency, and (4) keeps the work moving toward the objectives of the agency. Methods of performing each of the supervisor's major tasks (discussed in Lesson 1) were also presented. We emphasized the supervisor's responsibility for bringing out the best in workers by helping them use their own creative desires on the job, to their own and the agency's advantage. Finally, some general guidelines to follow in fulfilling the responsibilities of a supervisor were presented.

SUGGESTIONS FOR FURTHER STUDY

This chapter should be viewed as a very basic introduction to the process of supervision, and therefore, further study will be most important for those interested in achieving an in-depth understanding of this important function. Supervisors need to have a comprehensive understanding of all of the work performed in the agency. Thus, one area of further study should be directed toward reviewing the roles and functions performed by direct service workers, supervisors, and administrators, and toward identifying ways in which the supervisor should relate to all of these workers. Additional study will also be needed to understand fully each of the major tasks of the supervisor. For example, in planning, it is important to be able to define objectives and to coordinate the efforts of several people or agencies. In training, supervisors need to be able to assess training needs, provide training, and evaluate the results of training. The reference listed in the bibliography by John Ingalls may be useful to review in this area. In providing leadership, supervisors have to be able to delegate responsibilities, motivate staff, resolve differences among staff, and introduce and manage changes in services and in the work. The references by Lassey and Boyd provide some information regarding these responsibilities.

The ability to analyze work is also an important skill needed by a supervisor. Functional job analysis is one method used, and a review of the reference by Sidney Fine and Wretha Wiley provides a general introduction to this technique. Additional study should also address the skills needed for using management information systems, using performance standards, and taking corrective action. In this regard, the references by Calhoon, Mee, and Batson provide some information that may be helpful.

By now it should be clear that supervision includes a vast amount of skills and knowledge which need to be mastered for effective performance. Hopefully, this chapter has made you curious to learn more about this function and locate some of the suggested references. We hope the suggestions for further study will be useful in your efforts.

SUGGESTIONS FOR FURTHER READING

Batson, Robert J. *Employee Evaluation: A Review of Current Methods and a Suggested New Approach*. Chicago, Ill.: Public Personnel Association, 1963.

Boyd, Bradford B. *Management-Minded Supervision*. New York: McGraw-Hill, 1968.

Brieland, Donald, Briggs, Thomas, and Leuenberger, Paul. *The Team Model of Social Work Practice*. Manpower Monograph, no. 5. Syracuse University School of Social Work, 1973.

Burby, Raymond J. *An Introduction to Basic Supervision of People*. Reading, Mass.: Addison-Wesley, 1966.

Calhoon, Richard P. *Managing Personnel*. New York: Harper & Row, 1963.

Denova, Charles C. "Supervisory Guides." *Supervision* XXXIII, no. 9 (September 1971).

Ehlers, Walter, Austin, Michael J., and Prothero, Jon. *Administration for the Human Services*. New York: Harper & Row, 1976.

Fine, Sidney A., and Wiley, Wretha W. *An Introduction to Functional Job Analysis: A Scaling of Selected Tasks from the Social Welfare Field*. Kalamazoo, Mich.: W. E. Upjohn Institute for Employment Research, 1971.

Ingalls, John D. *A Trainer's Guide to Andragogy*. Washington, D.C.: U.S. Government Printing Office, May, 1973.

Kimbrell, Grady, and Vineyard, Ben S. *Succeeding in the World of Work*. Bloomington, Ill.: McKnight and McKnight Publishing Company, 1970.

Lassey, William R., ed. *Leadership and Social Change*. Iowa City, Iowa: University Associates Press, 1971.

Lateiner, Alfred. *The Techniques of Supervision*. Connecticut: National Foreman's Institute, Inc., 1954.

Mee, John F., ed. *Personnel Handbook*. New York: Ronald Press, 1952.

Morrison, James H. *Human Factors in Supervising Minority Group Employees*. Chicago, Ill.: Public Personnel Association, 1970.

Shout, Howard F. *Start Supervising*. Washington, D.C.: Bureau of National Affairs, 1972.

Spriegel, William R., Schulz, Edward, and Spriegel, William B. *Elements of Supervision*. New York: Wiley, 1957.

Weissman, Harold H. *Overcoming Mismanagement in the Human Service Professions*. San Francisco: Jossey-Bass, 1973.

REVIEW QUESTIONS—CHAPTER XI

Circle the letter corresponding to the answer of your choice.

1. Select the best phrase to complete the following statement. Communication is
   A. passing along information.
   B. creating understanding among two or more people.
   C. talking to people.
   D. all of the above.

2. What are the major components of the communication process?
   A. Beginning, middle, afterthought
   B. Verbal, nonverbal, written
   C. Sender, message, receiver, feedback
   D. Worker, consumer, neighbor

3. The common blocks to communication are the listening block and the block of failing to see the need to communicate. Which of the following are other common blocks to communication?
   A. Mumbling block, planning block, self-interest block
   B. Handwriting block, self-interest block, mumbling block
   C. Self-interest block, word block, planning block

4. What is the best definition of a word block?
   A. Lack of understanding because the speaker does not pronounce his or her words clearly
   B. The listener does not concentrate on what the speaker is saying
   C. A misunderstanding which occurs because the message contains words or terms which are vague, unknown, or too technical

5. One way to overcome the word block is by
   A. gearing the message to the receiver.
   B. speaking clearly.
   C. putting all messages in writing.

6. The feedback bridge is used to overcome which of the following communication blocks?
   A. Planning block
   B. Self-interest block
   C. Failure to see the need to communicate block
   D. Listening block

7. Check the statement below which is false regarding supervision.
   A. Supervision is the art of getting work done through the efforts of others.
   B. Supervision is the main link of communication in an agency.

    C. Supervision is most effectively used to cause fear in workers.

    D. Supervision helps workers do a better job.

8. One of the supervisor's responsibilities is instructing workers. Which of the following would also be supervisory responsibilities?
    1. Planning and organizing the work
    2. Making improvements
    3. Serving as the agency's informer
    4. Organizing the agency's social functions
    5. Communicating with workers

   Select your answer from the following.
   A. 1, 2, 4
   B. 2, 4, 5
   C. 1, 2, 3
   D. 1, 2, 5
   E. 2, 3, 5

9. Which of the following would be part of a supervisor's communication duties?
   A. Passing on information from agency administrators to workers
   B. Talking individually with each worker
   C. Passing along suggestions from workers to administrators
   D. Listening carefully to any problems workers want to discuss
   E. All of the above

10. A supervisor should expect certain things from his or her workers. Which of the following items should your supervisor expect from you?
    1. Acceptance of criticism
    2. Frequent overtime
    3. Willingness to follow directions
    4. Cooperation
    5. Initiative
    6. Agreement with all new ideas
    7. Cooperation on team projects

    Select your answer from the following.
    A. 1, 2, 3, 4, 6
    B. 1, 3, 4, 5, 7
    C. 2, 3, 4, 5, 6

11. A supervisor should expect you to like your work.
    A. True
    B. False

12. A worker may expect which of the following from his supervisor?
    1. Evaluations
    2. Explanations
    3. Support
    4. Favoritism
    5. Discipline
    6. Action on all complaints
    7. Training

Select your answer from the following.
A. 1, 2, 3, 4, 5
B. 2, 3, 5, 6, 7
C. 3, 4, 5, 6, 7
D. 1, 2, 3, 5, 7

13. Which of the following items would be a purpose of supervision?
A. To keep work moving toward accomplishing agency objectives.
B. To promote competition among agency workers.
C. To serve as a communication link throughout the entire agency.
D. To promote growth and increase capacity of each worker.
E. A, C, and D.
F. B, C, and D.

14. The purpose of worker evaluation is
A. to determine any needs for special training.
B. to promote competition among co-workers.
C. to find reasons for denying salary raises.

15. A supervisor can help to bring out the best in people by
1. creating a climate of team work.
2. seeking workers' ideas for improvements.
3. pitting one worker against another.
4. giving clear instructions.
5. publicly disciplining a worker.

Select your answer from those given below.
A. 1, 2, 3
B. 1, 2, 4
C. 1, 2, 5
D. 1, 3, 4, 5
E. 1, 2, 4, 5

16. When disciplining a worker, the supervisor should
A. do so privately.
B. seek reasons for the wrongdoing.
C. express doubt in the worker's ability to improve.
D. do A and B above.
E. do A, B, and C above.

17. One of the best ways a supervisor can gain cooperation is by
A. keeping a close watch on routine work.
B. setting a good example.
C. remaining aloof from the other workers.

18. A supervisor should
A. praise only in private.
B. commend a worker infrequently.
C. give recognition whenever possible.

19. A worker should understand the contribution he or she makes to the agency's total program.
A. True
B. False

20. A supervisor should build worker confidence by
    A. never reprimanding the worker.
    B. telling the worker how other people have performed in the same job.
    C. helping the worker master his or her tasks and responsibilities.

21. The process of communication is important when a worker is trying to reach
    A. a consumer.
    B. a co-worker.
    C. a supervisor.
    D. all of the above.
    E. none of the above.

22. Nonverbal communication does *not* include the use of
    A. eyes.
    B. arms.
    C. microphones.
    D. shoulders.
    E. face.

23. Effective written communication includes
    A. preplanning to clarify in your mind what you want to say.
    B. writing with the sender in mind.
    C. reviewing your written message prior to sending it.
    D. ignoring receiver feedback.
    E. only A and C.

**Now check your answers with the
Answer key at the end of the book**

ANSWER KEY
TO REVIEW QUESTIONS

CHAPTER I

Question	Answer	Question	Answer
1.	D	6.	D
2.	C	7.	B
3.	D	8.	A
4.	E	9.	B
5.	C	10.	E

CHAPTER II

Question	Answer	Question	Answer
1.	A	9.	A
2.	E	10.	A
3.	D	11.	C
4.	A	12.	E
5.	C	13.	A
6.	D	14.	B
7.	B	15.	D
8.	E		

CHAPTER III

Question	Answer	Question	Answer
1.	A	10.	E
2.	E	11.	E
3.	C	12.	B
4.	B	13.	E
5.	A	14.	A
6.	C	15.	E
7.	D	16.	C
8.	B	17.	B
9.	E	18.	B

CHAPTER IV

Question	Answer	Question	Answer
1.	E	11.	B
2.	B	12.	A
3.	B	13.	B
4.	D	14.	C
5.	C	15.	D
6.	B	16.	A
7.	A	17.	B
8.	D	18.	D
9.	C	19.	B
10.	D	20.	E

CHAPTER V

Question	Question	Answer	Answer
1.	D	9.	E
2.	E	10.	B
3.	D	11.	D
4.	D	12.	D
5.	B	13.	A
6.	C	14.	E
7.	B	15.	D
8.	C	16.	E

CHAPTER VI

Question	Answer	Question	Answer
1.	A	13.	D
2.	B	14.	A
3.	E	15.	C
4.	B	16.	E
5.	E	17.	B
6.	D	18.	C
7.	B	19.	E
8.	C	20.	A
9.	B	21.	D
10.	C	22.	A
11.	B	23.	C
12.	E	24.	D

CHAPTER VII

Question	Answer	Question	Answer
1.	B	12.	E
2.	B	13.	E
3.	D	14.	B
4.	C	15.	A
5.	E	16.	B
6.	B	17.	D
7.	A	18.	B
8.	D	19.	C
9.	B	20.	B
10.	C	21.	D
11.	D	22.	D